£30.00

.inguistics

The Complete Guide To IELTS

Bruce Rogers
Nick Kenny

CONTENTS

INTRODUCTION TO THE IELTS TEST

Background

If you're preparing to take the IELTS test, you're not alone. Over two million people all over the world take the test each year. A knowledge of English is increasingly important for people who want to enter higher education, or work in countries where English is the first language, and IELTS is widely recognised by universities and colleges, professional bodies, employers, immigration authorities and other government agencies. You can find a list of over 9,000 organisations which recognise the test on the IELTS website at www.ielts.org.

Academic and General Training tests

There are two versions of IELTS, Academic and General Training (or GT). When you enrol, you can choose which version you want to take.

You should take IELTS Academic if you want to study in higher education, for example on an undergraduate or postgraduate course at a university where the teaching is in English. You should take the General Training version if you intend to live and work in an English-speaking country and need to show the migration authorities that you have the required level of English. Your teacher can advise you on the version which is appropriate for you, or you can contact the organisation you intend to apply to and find out which one they require.

The Test

There are four parts to the test: Listening, Reading, Writing and Speaking, and you must take them all. The total test time is two hours and 45 minutes. The tests of Listening and Speaking are the same for all candidates, but the tests of Reading and Writing are different depending on whether you chose the Academic or General Training versions. You do the Listening, Reading and Writing tests on the same day, and usually the Speaking test is done a few days before or after the other components.

The test is available very frequently, typically once or twice each month, and you can find your local centre and information about how to register for the test on the IELTS website at www.ielts.org.

Scoring

IELTS assesses your language knowledge and skills and gives you a Band Score from 1 to 9 in each of the four parts of the test, and also an overall Band Score from 1 to 9 for the whole exam, which is an average of the scores for each part. There is no pass or fail in IELTS because the college, university or organisation you're applying to will tell you the Band Score you need to achieve.

IELTS BAND SCORES

Band 9: Expert user

Has fully operational command of the language: appropriate, accurate and fluent with complete understanding.

Band 8: Very good user

Has fully operational command of the language with only occasional unsystematic inaccuracies and inappropriacies. Misunderstandings may occur in unfamiliar situations. Handles complex detailed argumentation well.

Band 7: Good user

Has operational command of the language, though with occasional inaccuracies, inappropriacies and misunderstandings in some situations. Generally handles complex language well and understands detailed reasoning.

Band 6: Competent user

Has generally effective command of the language despite some inaccuracies, inappropriacies and misunderstandings. Can use and understand fairly complex language, particularly in familiar situations.

Band 5: Modest user

Has partial command of the language, coping with overall meaning in most situations, though is likely to make many mistakes. Should be able to handle basic communication in own field.

Band 4: Limited user

Basic competence is limited to familiar situations. Has frequent problems in understanding and expression. Is not able to use complex language.

Band 3: Extremely limited user

Conveys and understands only general meaning in very familiar situations. Frequent breakdowns in communication occur.

Band 2: Intermittent user

No real communication is possible except for the most basic information using isolated words or short formulae in familiar situations and to meet immediate needs. Has great difficulty understanding spoken and written English.

Band 1: Non-user

Essentially has no ability to use the language beyond possibly a few isolated words.

Band 0: Did not attempt the test

No assessable information provided.

INTRODUCTION TO *THE COMPLETE GUIDE TO IELTS*

The Complete Guide To IELTS offers a step-by-step programme that gives you lots of practice in the various tasks you will have to do in the IELTS exam. The aim of the book is to help you get the best possible score in each part of the IELTS exam by showing you what skills are being tested and how you can develop them. The practice materials in this book are designed to help you get a high score in IELTS Academic. Band Score 6 to 9 is the sort of score usually required for university entrance. Specific material for the General Training version is found on the DVD-ROM.

The main body of the book is divided into four modules, reflecting the four test papers in the exam. For each of the skills (Listening, Reading, Writing and Speaking) there is:

1 **An 'About' Section:** This gives information about the test and some general advice about how to do your best on the day of the test.

2 **Preview Test:** This allows you to see how the test is organised and gives you the chance to see how well you're doing in each of the tasks.

3 **Task-specific lessons:** This provides separate lessons on each of the task types which you may have to do in the test, with specific advice on how to approach the questions. Each lesson is divided into four sections:

    A **About the task:** explains how the task works and what you have to do

    B **Sample question:** an example of the task for you to try

    C **Tips and tactics:** advice on how to approach the task

    D **Skills-building exercises:** exercises to help you develop the skills you need, and a full-length IELTS practice task for you to do

4 **Review Test:** This allows you to see how much progress you have made and if you need to do more work on some tasks.

For each of the tasks, there is further practice on the DVD-ROM. There is also a complete IELTS Practice Test at the end of the book.

It's good to work through each lesson from start to finish, but you can approach the lessons in any order you like. Working through the lessons in the book will help you to:

- increase your general knowledge of English
- know what the exam tasks are testing and how to do your best in them
- be familiar with the format and instructions
- make the most of your preparation time
- use time wisely during the test
- know how to complete the answer sheet
- analyse your strengths and weaknesses
- feel confident on the day of the test

Vocabulary

There are seven separate Vocabulary lessons which deal with common vocabulary areas and lexical features of the IELTS reading passages and listening sections, for example, wordbuilding, collocations, synonyms and anotonyms, prefixes and affixes. These lessons also cover common IELTS topics such as the natural world, academic life, business and industry and technology.

National Geographic Video lessons

There are six National Geographic videos which cover a range of topics. The videos have been selected to provide engaging and motivating video lessons which increase familiarity with the Listening task types, as well as providing you with opportunities to speak about the topics on the videos.

Resource and Reference section

The Resource and Reference section includes a **Grammar Resource Bank** and additional **Speaking test video worksheets** and scripts. There is no grammar syllabus for IELTS as it is a skills-based exam. However, grammatical accuracy and range are part of the marking criteria in the Writing and Speaking tests. The Grammar Resource Bank provides a comprehensive grammar reference and practice exercises covering key grammar needed for the test.

There are two Speaking test video worksheets which correspond to the two model IELTS Speaking test videos on the DVD-ROM. You can use these to analyse the Speaking test videos in more depth. Full scripts for the IELTS Speaking test videos are also provided.

DVD-ROM

The DVD-ROM contains:
- six National Geographic videos
- two model IELTS Speaking test videos
- downloadable PDFs
- the audio for the Student's Book and for the additional practice activities on the DVD-ROM

IELTS Speaking test videos

The aim of the model Speaking test videos is to show you real students completing a full Speaking test interview. There are two interviews, with two different candidates. As you watch the interviews, you can see what the Speaking test is like and you can also analyse the students' strengths and weaknesses. This will help you to improve your own performance in the Speaking test.

Downloadable PDFs

Extensive additional practice exercises for all the task types covered in the Student's Book (Listening, Academic Reading, Academic Writing, Speaking) is provided on the DVD-ROM. There is also practice material for the General Training Reading and Writing test, as well as General Training Reading and Writing test papers.

The DVD-ROM also provides complete audioscripts and answer keys as downloadable PDFs. There are full instructions on the DVD-ROM for how to download these materials.

Intensive Revision Guide

The Intensive Revision Guide covers common errors made by candidates taking IELTS, and provides targeted practice and support to help you gain the best possible score. You should use this in the weeks leading up to the exam and it will help you avoid losing marks. The common errors that are dealt with are:

- Listening: Spelling mistakes; Numbers, dates and times; Singular or plural?; Not following instructions; Problems with maps; Background knowledge is dangerous!; Jumping to conclusions; Not using the time effectively
- Reading: Spelling mistakes; Not following instructions; Jumping to conclusions; Using the wrong strategies; Careless reading; Incomplete reading; Missing clues in questions; Grammar mistakes
- Writing: Including too much detail: Not identifying the main idea; Using the wrong tenses; Not answering the question; Not giving supporting examples; Using the wrong register; Repeating words from the question; Lack of cohesion
- Speaking: Feeling nervous; Not answering the question; Not using planning time; Using the wrong tenses; Overcomplicating your answer; Not extending your answer; Repeating yourself; Grammar mistakes

On the inside front cover of this book you will find login details and instructions for how to access the Intensive Revision Guide.

ABOUT THE LISTENING TEST

A The Test

Listening	Description	Interaction pattern	Setting
Section 1	10 questions	dialogue	Work and social situations
Section 2	10 questions	monologue	Work and social situations
Section 3	10 questions	two or three speakers	Academic or educational situations
Section 4	10 questions	monologue	Academic situations

The IELTS Listening Test tests your ability to understand spoken English in different situations. The test lasts for approximately 30 minutes and has four sections.

In each section, you listen to a recording and answer ten questions. Before each section, you hear information about who is speaking, the situation and the topic. The voice on the recording then tells you which questions to look at and you read the instructions for the task on the question paper.

The recordings in each section are divided into parts and there is a generally a pause between each part so that you can read the questions before you listen. After the pause, you hear a continuation of the same recording. You should use the pause to read the task so that you're ready to answer the questions.

You hear each section of the recording ONCE only. You should answer the questions as you listen, and write your answers directly onto the question paper. You have ten minutes at the end of the test to copy your answers on to the separate answer sheet.

Section 1

In this part of the test, you hear a conversation between two people. The conversation is generally about living, studying or working in an English-speaking country. For example, you may hear a conversation between an employer and an employee, or one between a student and a college administrator or two friends talking about how to spend their free time.

The conversation has a purpose, such as giving instructions, asking for information, making a booking or making plans. Most of the questions test your ability to understand the detailed information that is exchanged between the speakers and the conclusions they reach. You often have to complete the missing information in a form, a table or a set of notes. Sometimes, you may have to choose the correct answer from a list of alternatives (A, B, C, etc.).

Section 2

In this part of the test, you hear one speaker giving a talk to a group of people. The talk is generally about living, studying or working in an English-speaking country, for example an employer talking to a group of employees or someone making an announcement.

The talk or announcement has an aim, such as giving instructions. Most of the questions, therefore, test your ability to understand detailed information.

The questions usually ask you to choose the correct answer from a list of alternatives (A, B, C, etc.). You may have to answer multiple-choice questions, for example, or match the information you hear to one answer in a longer list of options. Sometimes the questions in Section 2 are based on visual material and you may, for example, have to choose the correct labels to go on a map. Sometimes you may have to complete missing information in a set of sentences.

Section 3

In this part of the test, you hear a conversation between two or three people in an academic setting. The conversation is generally about an academic topic and the two main speakers are exchanging both information and ideas. For example, the conversation may involve two people who are working together on a research project, or a meeting between a tutor and two students reporting on their progress.

The speakers may agree or disagree on certain points before coming to a conclusion. Most of the questions test your ability to follow the ideas being discussed, to identify each speaker's point of view and to understand the outcome of their discussions. You need to listen to what the speakers say about each issue to be sure of the answer.

The questions usually ask you to choose the correct answer from a list of options (A, B, C, etc.). You may have to answer multiple-choice questions, for example, or match the information you hear to one answer in a longer list of options. Sometimes the questions in Section 3 are based on visual material and you have to choose the correct labels to go on a diagram or flow-chart.

Section 4

In this part of the test, you hear one speaker giving a lecture or presentation. The talk is about an academic topic and the speaker is discussing the topic in depth. You could, for example, hear about some research that the speaker has been involved in, or the speaker may be discussing different people's ideas and opinions on a subject.

The lecture or presentation has a purpose, such as updating the audience on developments in a field of research or providing students with an overview of an area of study. Most of the questions test your ability to understand and make a note of the detailed information the speaker presents, as well as following the arguments.

Most of the questions ask you to write a word or short phrase to show that you've understood the information and arguments that you hear. You often have to complete the missing information in a set of sentences or notes that summarise the main ideas discussed in the talk. Sometimes, you may have to choose the correct answer from a list of alternatives (A, B, C, etc.).

B Marking

Each numbered question in the Listening test is worth one mark. If you write the correct answer, then you get the mark. No marks are taken off for wrong answers, so it's always a good idea to write an answer, even if you're not sure whether it's correct or not.

The instructions tell you how many words you can write. If the instructions say 'WRITE ONE WORD for each answer', then you must only write one word. If you write two words, you don't get the mark, even if the information is correct.

The words you write must be spelled correctly. Most of the words you have to write are familiar words that most students know how to spell. Both UK and US spellings are accepted as correct. The answers aren't technical words or words that have difficult spellings. Sometimes the names of people and places are spelled out for you on the recording. This tests your knowledge of the alphabet.

Remember to write clearly. If your handwriting is unclear, or if individual letters are not clearly written, you don't get the mark.

Remember that the words you need to write are the words you hear on the recording. Don't try to use your own words. For example, if the word you hear on the recording is 'incredible' and you write 'unbelievable' as your answer, you don't get the mark. This is why it's important to write the words as you listen. If you try to remember afterwards, you may have understood what you heard, but not remember the actual words the speaker used.

You can write your answers in either UPPER CASE or lower case – both are marked correct, and you don't need to worry about punctuation. For example, if the answer to the question is 'online' and you write 'on-line', you still get the mark. In questions where the answer is a letter, you only write the correct letter next to the number on the answer sheet.

C Strategies

Before the test

- Familiarise yourself with the format of the Listening test. Make sure you know exactly what you have to do in each part – then you can feel confident and prepared on the day of the test.

- For example, listen to whole tests to know what you have to do in each part, what information is given on the recording and what information is given on the question paper.

- The information you hear about the speaker, the situation and the topic can help you to be ready to understand what you hear.

- Predict the type of vocabulary and information that you're going to hear.

- Practise using the time during the pauses between the sections and parts to read the task on the question paper.

- Practise predicting the type of words and information that is missing in tasks where you have to write the answer.

- Remember that reading the task also helps you to know about the type of information you're going to hear and the order the information is going to come in.

- Try to make the most of every opportunity to practise your listening. For example, listen to broadcasts and podcasts in English as often as you can.

- Use the Internet to keep up with the latest news and current affairs in English. While you're listening, think about the type of language the speakers use to make their points.

During the test

- The voice on the recording gives you all the instructions during the test and guides you through the four parts.

- Remember that you hear each recording ONCE only.

- Remember that the questions follow the order of information in the recording.

- Remember that you hear words and information from the question paper as you listen to the recording – these will help you to keep your place.

- Remember there are pauses between each part and halfway through each part so you can read the tasks and get ready to answer.

- Always write an answer while you're listening, even if you're not sure whether it's right or not.

- Don't worry about spelling while you're listening – you have time to check that later – but write clearly so that you can read your own answers later.

- Don't stop to think if you're not sure of an answer. You need to be ready to answer the next one.

- Don't panic. You have plenty of time.

At the end of the test

- When the recording has finished, you have ten minutes to copy your answers on to the separate answer sheet.

- You have time to check your answers, especially the spelling of the words you wrote while you were listening.

- Try not to change your answers at this stage. What you wrote while you were listening is probably correct.

- Remember you have to write one answer. If you're not sure, don't put two answers. If you do that, you don't get the mark.

- Check very carefully that you put your answers next to the correct number on the answer sheet, and keep checking that you haven't made a mistake in the numbering.

- If you don't know the right answer to a question, always write something. You may have understood more than you think.

- Only write in the column to the right of the numbers – don't write anything in the columns marked /x.

- If you finish before the ten minutes is up, double check that your answers are in the correct boxes.

- At the end of the test the question paper and the answer sheet are both collected in.

- Only the answers on the answer sheet count; the question paper is destroyed.

01 **SECTION 1** *Questions 1–10*

Questions 1–10

Complete the form below.

Write **NO MORE THAN TWO WORDS AND/OR A NUMBER** *for each answer.*

**NATIONAL UNIVERSITY
ACCOMMODATION REQUEST FORM**

Surname: *Blake*

First name: **1** ....

ID number: **2** ....

Gender: *male*

Email address: *d.blake@internet.com*

Telephone number: **3** ....

Course attending: **4** ....

Start date: **5** ....

Accommodation type: **6** ....

Room type: **7** ....

Type of bathroom: **8** ....

Vehicle: **9** ....

Amount of deposit: **10** £ ....

02 **SECTION 2** *Questions 11–20*

Questions 11–16

Where can you find each of the following items?

*Choose **FIVE** answers from the box and write the correct letter,
A–H, next to questions 11–16.*

Places

A   immediately inside the kitchen
B   in the manager's office
C   near the back door
D   beside the entrance
E   behind the bar
F   underneath the cash desk
G   outside the staffroom
H   in the food preparation area

Useful items

11 cutlery   ....

12 clean tablecloths   ....

13 spare menus   ....

14 fresh flowers   ....

15 paper towels   ....

16 first-aid kit   ....

Questions 17–20

Who should each type of complaint be referred to in the first instance?

*Write the correct letter, **A**, **B** or **C**, next to questions 17–20.*

A   the manager
B   the head chef
C   the head waiter

17 complaints received before the meal   ....

18 complaints about a particular dish   ....

19 complaints about a whole meal   ....

20 complaints after payment has been made   ....

03 SECTION 3 *Questions 21–30*

Questions 21 and 22

*Choose **TWO** letters, **A–E**.*

Which **TWO** sources of data will Mark look at next?

A local history collection
B newspaper reports
C planning applications
D contracts
E geological survey

Questions 23 and 24

*Choose **TWO** letters, **A–E**.*

Which **TWO** tasks will Kirsty do next?

A approach individual gardeners
B design a questionnaire
C draw a plan of the site
D look at previous research studies
E get permission from the management

Questions 25–27

*Choose the correct letter, **A**, **B** or **C**.*

25 What will their research focus on?
    A the productivity of the land
    B the attitude of the gardeners
    C the problems facing the gardeners

26 They agree to consult their tutor
    A before going any further.
    B when a detailed plan is in place.
    C once they have set up some interviews.

27 They agree that their main difficulty will be
    A writing an adequate proposal.
    B constructing a valid questionnaire.
    C deciding how many interviews to conduct.

Questions 28–30

Label the diagram below.

*Write the correct letter, **A–G**, next to questions 28–30.*

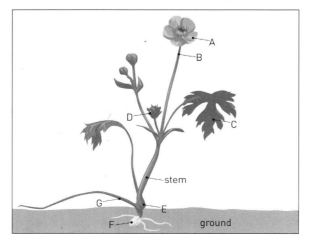

CREEPING BUTTERCUP

28 no sepals ....
29 polygonal shape ....
30 stolon ....

04 **SECTION 4** *Questions 31–40*

Questions 31–36

Complete the sentences below.

*Write **NO MORE THAN TWO WORDS** for each answer.*

Problems affecting small areas of rainforest

31 A process called .... has a negative effect in these areas.
32 There is less food, especially .... , for animals to eat.
33 Larger animals may see a fall in .... because of lack of contact with other populations.
34 The 'edge effect' can change both the .... and the amount of light at the forest edges.
35 There is probably more .... activity in forest areas close to farmland.
36 Small animals which have a particular .... may be most at risk.

Questions 37–40

Complete the notes below.

*Write **ONE WORD ONLY** for each answer.*

ASSESSING BIODIVERSITY

Basic method:

- Walk through the forest

- Some animals make a lot of noise, for example **37** ....

- Some birds have easily identified nests

- Some animals always hide in certain places, for example **38** ....

Trapping methods:

- Simple traps using a sheet of plastic and **39** .... for small animals

- Mist nets can trap birds

- Camera traps for other species

- A **40** .... can be used to identify animals trapped more than once

---

TASK TYPE 1 Sentence Completion

Your job is to listen and complete the gaps.

Gentoo penguins heading to sea, Falkland Islands

A About the task

1 **Read the information about the task type. Then look at and correct the notes a student made about the task. The student has made four mistakes.**

The Sentence Completion task tests your ability to locate and record specific information from a recording. It's often used to test your understanding of a lecture or talk about a specific subject. You usually hear facts about a subject, and you may be asked to write words or numbers. Some of the information you hear is already written on the question paper, your job is to listen and complete the gaps. On the question paper, you see a set of sentences that report the information you hear on the recording. In each sentence, some key words are missing. You listen and write the missing words in the gap.

Here are the basic rules for the Sentence Completion task:

- The spoken instructions tell you about the speaker(s) and the topic.
- The written instructions tell you how many words to write in each gap.
- The sentences come in the same order as the information in the recording.
- You don't hear the same sentences that you read on the question paper, but you do hear the same information.
- When you listen, you hear the words that you need to write.
- You write the words in the same form as you hear them on the recording (e.g. singular/plural) – you don't need to change them in any way.
- Spelling counts! The words you write must be spelled correctly.
- You hear the recording ONCE only.

It's especially important to read through the sentences before you listen, and think about the type of information you're listening for. You hear different words that could fit logically into each gap. You have to listen carefully to choose the correct information, so that the sentence reports the meaning of the recording exactly.

Sometimes you see the set of sentences presented as a summary (a piece of continuous text) but the rules of the task are the same. (See IELTS Practice Task Questions 5–10 on page 15.)

Notes
1   You always hear one speaker.
2   You are listening for facts and figures.
3   You always have to write three words.
4   The questions are in the same order as the information on the recording.
5   You hear the sentences read out on the recording.
6   You have to spell the words correctly.
7   You can listen again if you don't understand the first time.

B Sample questions

2 05 Listen and complete the sentences. Use the rules about the task from Section A to help you. Then check your answers. Which questions did you find difficult?

IELTS PRACTICE TASK

Questions 1–5

Complete the sentences below.

*Write **NO MORE THAN TWO WORDS AND/OR A NUMBER** for each answer.*

THE SPORT OF SQUASH

1 The name of the country where squash was first played is ....
2 The name 'squash' was first used to describe the .... which is used in the game.
3 The material used to make the first squash racquets was ....
4 The colour used to indicate an advanced level ball is ....
5 In an advanced squash match, the ball generally travels at .... kilometres per hour.

C Tips and tactics

3 **Work in pairs. Read the tips and tactics and discuss these questions.**

a **Which tips and tactics do you think are the most useful?**
b **Did you use any of these tips and tactics when you answered the sample questions in Section B?**
c **Which tips will you use in the future?**

1 Before you listen, you have time to read the heading and the sentences and think about what you're going to hear.
2 Think about the type of information that's missing in each sentence. For example, are you listening for a name, a number, a specific term or something else?
3 Look for clues in the sentence that tell you what to listen for, e.g. 'a total of' and 'what's called a'.
4 Sometimes the sentence tells you what to listen for, e.g. 'A beaver is ... in colour'. But you may hear a number of colours in the recording. Listen carefully to know which one is correct.
5 Most of the missing information is facts about the topic, so the words you need to write are mostly either numbers or nouns. If they are nouns, think about whether your answer needs to be singular or plural. The sentence may help you to decide.
6 The word or words you need to write are on the recording. Don't try to put the information you hear into your own words.
7 The instructions tell you how many words to write – if you write more, your answer will be marked wrong. Most answers are single nouns, e.g. 'water', or compound nouns that include two words, e.g. 'water quality'.
8 There's no need to write words that are already in the sentence.
9 Write numbers as figures, e.g. '104' – <u>not</u> as words, e.g. 'one hundred and four'.
10 The sentences follow the order of information in the recording.
11 When you listen to the recording, you hear some words or ideas from the sentence. These tell you that the words you need to write are coming.
12 You won't hear exactly the same sentences that you read on the question paper. This task isn't a dictation. Think about the meaning and listen for the information.
13 Don't just write down the first word you hear that fits the gap – keep listening and keep thinking about the meaning.
14 You should think about your spelling. If you spell a word incorrectly, your answer will be marked wrong. But the words you need to write are words which you know, and which are easy to spell.
15 If you aren't sure, always write something. No marks are taken off for wrong answers.
16 Remember, you hear the recording ONCE only.

Q **FOCUS**

Identifying the
target information

D Skills-building exercises

4 Read the sentences (1–4). What type of information is missing in each of the gaps?

1 You could see a total of .... motorcycles at the museum when it first opened.
2 There was a .... at the museum in the year 2003.
3 The speaker mentions the up-to-date .... facilities in the conference centre.
4 The museum's oldest two-wheeled bike was built in the year ....

5 ⚪ **06 Listen to a short talk about about a motorcycle museum and make a note of this information:**

1 You hear information about the number of motorcycles in the museum at different times. Write down the numbers you hear.
2 You hear three dates when things happened at the museum. Write down the things that happened.
3 You hear about different facilities for visitors at the museum. Which three facilities do you hear about?
4 You hear about old motorcycles in the museum and when they were built. Write down three years you hear.

6 ⚪ **06 Look at the sentences (1–4). Listen again and complete the sentences. Use your answers from Exercise 5 to help you. Write _NO MORE THAN TWO WORDS AND/ OR A NUMBER_ for each answer.**

1 You could see a total of .... motorcycles at the museum when it first opened.
2 There was a .... at the museum in the year 2003.
3 The speaker mentions the up-to-date .... facilities in the conference centre.
4 The museum's oldest two-wheeled bike was built in the year ....

7 ⚪ **06 Listen again and look at the audioscript on the DVD-ROM. Think about why the answers to the questions in Exercise 6 are correct, and why other words and numbers you hear are not the correct answers.**

8 Work in pairs. Look at the sentences and photo below. What type of information is missing in each of the gaps?

The Brough Superior

1 The Brough Superior on show in the museum dates from the year ....
2 In his first race, Brough established a new .... at the Brooklands track.
3 Brough won a total of .... races on the Brough Superior.
4 Approximately .... of the Brough Superiors ever built still survive.
5 Each Brough Superior was designed to match the .... , height and riding style of its owner.
6 In its pre-delivery test drive, the SS100 model reached at least .... kilometres per hour.

9 ● 07 **Listen to a tour guide talking about the motorcycle museum and complete the sentences in Exercise 8. Write** *NO MORE THAN TWO WORDS AND/OR A NUMBER* **for each answer.**

10 ● 07 **Listen again and look at the audioscript on the DVD-ROM. Discuss these questions.**

1 How did the sentences on the question paper help you to find the correct information?
2 Why do some words you hear fit the gaps and others do not?

11 **Work in pairs. Look at this student's answers. Why were they marked wrong?**

1 nineteen thirty eight
2 52
3 a new record
4 around a third
5 wait
6 130

IELTS PRACTICE TASK

● 08 *Questions 1–10*

Questions 1–4

Complete the sentences below.

Write **NO MORE THAN TWO WORDS AND/OR A NUMBER** *for each answer.*

SCOTTISH BEAVER TRIAL

1 There have been no beavers in the UK since the .... century.

2 Because they make .... better, beavers are regarded as a 'keynote' species.

3 A total of .... families of beavers are now living in Knapdale Forest.

4 What's called a .... will tell scientists how the beavers affect the local environment.

Questions 5–10

Complete the summary below.

Write **NO MORE THAN TWO WORDS** *for each answer.*

Eileen is spending a short period at the Scottish Beaver Trial on what is called an **5** .... She is actually a post-graduate student and her particular area of research is **6** .... , which is why she finds the beaver project so interesting. On the project, Eileen has the job of studying the **7** .... behaviours of the beavers. Eileen was fortunate enough to see some beavers when she went out on a **8** .... on her first evening in Knapdale. Eileen's particular task is to **9** .... the dams and other things that the beavers make, and she has set up what's called a **10** .... so that she can observe them more closely.

Which statement best describes how you feel about Sentence Completion tasks?

☐ I feel confident about doing Sentence Completion tasks.
☐ I did OK, but I still need to do more work on Sentence Completion tasks.
☐ I need more practice with Sentence Completion tasks. I need to focus on …

▶▶ **For further practice, see the DVD-ROM.**

VIDEO 1 Mega Green Museum

Skylights on the roof of the California Academy of Sciences Natural History Museum

Before you watch

1 You will watch a video about the California Academy of Sciences Natural History Museum, which has been described as 'a green building that breathes'. Brainstorm answers to the following questions:

1 What kind of exhibits might you see in this kind of museum?
2 What things give a building the label 'green'?

While you watch

2 Watch the video. Check your ideas from Exercise 1.

3 Read the sentences about the museum's green credentials. Then watch the video (from 01.50–03.16) and complete the sentences. Write *NO MORE THAN TWO WORDS AND/OR A NUMBER* for each answer.

1 The museum's roof is covered with flowers and plant life and allows .... from inside the building to escape.
2 The building is constructed entirely from .... materials.
3 The domes which contain the planetarium and the rainforest are .... high.
4 The museum's roof also contains .... solar panels.

4 Watch the whole video and complete the summary of the architect Renzo Piano's design process. Write *NO MORE THAN TWO WORDS* for each answer.

The first stage of an architect's job is to visit the site and understand the topography of the **1** .... For Renzo Piano, the next stage is to make a simple **2** .... sketch of the building. The simplicity of this sketched design does not reveal how **3** .... the building actually is. In fact, in this case, it's one of the largest **4** .... buildings in the world. The **5** .... of the museum is one of the most innovative design features and once Renzo Piano has approved this, work can start on the next phase.

After you watch

5 Work in small groups. Think about a building which has inspired you. Which of these terms you heard in the video apply to this building?

elegance   innovative   like a flying carpet   living architecture
low environmental impact   simplicity   state-of-the-art   stunning visual impact
sustainable   unique   visionary

6 Tell your group about your chosen building. Say where it is, what your experience of it was and how it made or makes you feel.

7 Work in pairs. Look at the list of modern building developments. Can you add any more to the list? Choose one development and discuss the questions (1–4) with your partner. Together decide if the overall impact of the development is a positive one or a negative one.

1 What is the impact on the local environment?
2 What is the impact on the local community?
3 How sustainable is the development?
4 What benefits does the development bring?

Modern building developments

- La Défense Business District, Paris
- Olympic Park, Rio de Janeiro
- Shipping Container Student Housing, Amsterdam

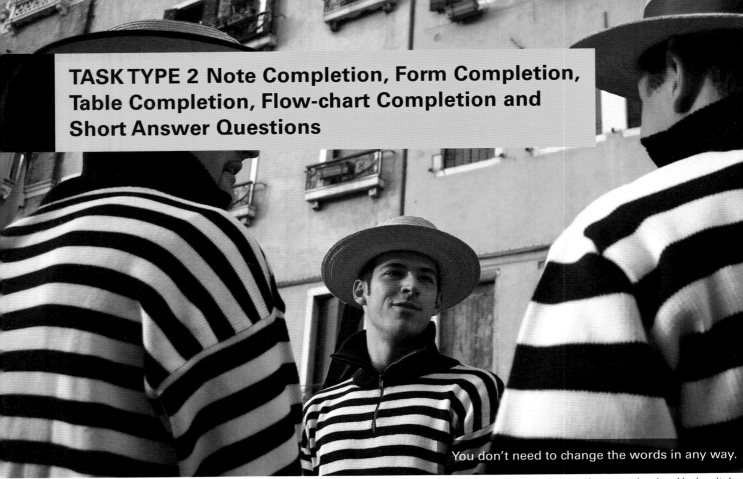

TASK TYPE 2 Note Completion, Form Completion, Table Completion, Flow-chart Completion and Short Answer Questions

You don't need to change the words in any way.

Gondoliers chat to each other, Venice, Italy

A About the task

1 **Read the information about the task type. A friend who missed the lesson has emailed you some questions. Look at your friend's questions on page 19 and answer them.**

The Note Completion, Form Completion, Table Completion, Flow-chart Completion and Short Answer Questions tasks in IELTS test your ability to locate and record specific information from a recording. You sometimes listen to a conversation where one person is giving factual information to another, and sometimes you listen to a lecture or presentation about a specific subject. In both cases, some of the information you hear is already written on the question paper. You see a set of notes that includes the information you hear on the recording. In each set of notes, some key words or numbers are missing. Your job is to listen and fill in the gaps.

Here are the basic rules for these tasks:

■ The spoken instructions tell you about the speaker(s) and the topic.
■ The written instructions tell you how many words to write in each gap.
■ When you listen, you hear the words that you need to write.
■ You won't hear exactly the same words that you read on the question paper, but you will hear the same information in the same order.
■ You write the words in the same form as you hear them on the recording (e.g. singular/plural) – you don't need to change them in any way.
■ Spelling counts! The words you write must be spelled correctly.
■ You hear the recording ONCE only.

It's very important to read through the notes before you listen, and think about the type of information you're listening for. You'll hear different words that could fit into each gap. You have to listen carefully to choose the correct information, so that the notes match the meaning of the recording exactly.

The set of notes may be presented in different ways. For example, you could see:

■ notes with subheadings and bullet points
■ a table with information under headings
■ a form that somebody has partly filled in
■ a flow-chart with information in stages
■ a set of questions with spaces to write the answers

Hi there
Help! I missed the lesson.
Can you tell me about the Note Completion tasks, please?
1 How many speakers do you hear?
2 Could the answers be numbers?
3 How do you know how many words to write?
4 Do you hear the answers in order?
5 Does it matter if you make a spelling mistake?
6 How many times can you listen to the recording?
Thanks!

B Sample questions

2 ⬤ 09 Listen and complete the notes below. Use the rules from Section A to help you. Then check your answers. Which questions did you find difficult?

IELTS PRACTICE TASK

Questions 1–7

Complete the sentences below.

*Write **NO MORE THAN TWO WORDS** for each answer.*

THE YAVARI: AN INCREDIBLE SHIP

TODAY

Where you can see the ship now: close to a **1** .... at Puno Bay in Peru.

What visitors can do:

- *take a* **2** ....
- *sleep on the ship*

HISTORY

Year when the ship was built: **3** ....

Main material used in building the ship: **4** ....

How it was transported to Peru: *by sea in small sections.*

How it was transported across Peru:

- *by* **5** ....
- *on horseback*

WORKING LIFE

Raw materials carried by the ship:

- *precious metals*
- **6** ....

Type of engine first fitted on the ship: **7** ....

C Tips and tactics

3 **Work in pairs. Read the tips and tactics and discuss these questions.**

  a **Which tips and tactics do you think are the most useful?**
  b **Did you use any of these tips and tactics when you answered the sample questions in Section B?**
  c **Which tips will you use in the future?**

1 Before you listen, you have time to read the notes and think about what you're going to hear.

2 Think about the type of information that's missing in each gap. For example, are you listening for a name, a number or another type of word?

3 Look for clues in the notes that tell you what to listen for, e.g. the information already written under each heading.

4 Sometimes the notes tell you what to listen for, for example, 'type of engine'. But you may hear more than one type of engine mentioned in the recording. Listen carefully to know which is correct.

5 Most of the missing information is facts about the topic, so the words you need to write are mostly either concrete nouns or numbers. If the words are nouns, think about whether your answer needs to be singular or plural. The rest of the notes may help you with this.

6 The word or words you need to write are on the recording. Don't try to put the information you hear into your own words.

7 The instructions tell you how many words to write – if you write more, your answer will be marked wrong. Most answers are single nouns, e.g. 'iron', or compound nouns that include two words, e.g. 'guided tour'.

8 Write numbers as figures, e.g. '104' – not as words, e.g. 'one hundred and four'.

9 The notes follow the order of information in the recording. The question numbering will help you to see how the information is organised, especially in tables.

10 When you listen to the recording, you hear some words or ideas from the notes. These tell you that the words you need to write are coming. There's no need to write the words that are already in the notes.

11 Use the headings in the task to help you. Think about the meaning and listen for the main ideas – headings can help you with this.

12 Don't just write down the first word you hear that fits the gap – keep listening and keep thinking about the meaning.

13 You should think about your spelling. If you spell a word incorrectly, your answer will be marked wrong. But the words you need to write are words which you probably know, and which are easy to spell.

14 Some words, like the names of people and places, may be spelled out for you on the recording.

15 If you aren't sure, always write something. No marks are taken off for wrong answers.

16 Remember, you hear the recording ONCE only.

D Skills-building exercises

Q FOCUS

Identifying the target information (1)

4 Look at this task. Which kind of task is it?

a a set of notes with subheadings and bullet points
b a table with information under headings
c a form that somebody has partly filled in
d a set of questions with spaces to write the answers

APPLICATION TO JOIN THE COLLEGE TENNIS CLUB

TITLE: Mr

FIRST NAME(S): John Paul

SURNAME: **1** ....

HOUSE NAME OR NUMBER: Room 42 **2** .... Hall of Residence

STREET ADDRESS: **3** .... Street

POSTCODE: CD3 7GB

EMAIL: johnpaul24 @SPL.ed.uk

MOBILE NUMBER: 09114 87877

FACULTY: **4** ....

STUDENT ID: JPR440021

DATE OF BIRTH: **5** ....

NATIONALITY: **6** ....

TENNIS LEVEL: **7** ....

ANY DISABILITIES: none

OTHER SPORTS CLUBS JOINED: **8** ....

---

5 Look at the numbered questions in the form in Exercise 4.

1 In what order do you expect to hear the information? What helped you to know this?
2 In which question(s) are you listening for:
a numerical information?
b an adjective describing ability?
c the name of an activity?
d a word which is likely to be spelled for you?

6 🔘 **10 Listen and complete the form in Exercise 4. Write NO MORE THAN THREE WORDS AND/OR A NUMBER for each answer.**

7 🔘 **10 Now check your answers with the answers on the DVD-ROM. Are your answers exactly right? Why?/Why not?**

8 🔘 **10 Listen again. Look at the audioscript on the DVD-ROM and think about the following.**

a How did the words in capitals (TITLE, FIRST NAME(S), etc.) on the set of notes help you to find the correct information?
b Why do some of the words and information you hear fit in the gaps and others do not?

Q FOCUS

Identifying the
target information
(2)

9 Look at this task. Which kind of task is it?

a a set of notes with subheadings and bullet points
b a table with information under headings
c a form that somebody has partly filled in
d a set of questions with spaces to write the answers

CONFERENCE PROGRAMME

Time	Venue	Speaker	Subject
10.30	Main Auditorium Green Room 3	Pedro Novak Grace 2 .... Maria Bruni	1 .... engineering copyright law international banking
13.00	Lunch break		
14.00	Main Auditorium Green Room 6	Alex Lorusso Kathy Lin Declan Boyd	4 .... biology 5 .... astronomy
15.45	Main Auditorium	Professor Makin	7 ....
16.00	Main Auditorium	The Vice Chancellor	8 .... ceremony

10 Look at the numbered questions 1–8 in the notes above.

1 In what order do you expect to hear the information? What helps you to know this?
2 In which question or questions are you listening for:
 a a location?
 b part of a compound noun?
 c a word which is likely to be spelled for you?

11 ◐ 11 Now listen and complete the notes. Write *NO MORE THAN TWO WORDS AND/OR A NUMBER* for each answer.

12 ◐ 11 Check your answers with the answers on the DVD-ROM. Are your answers exactly right? Why?/Why not?

13 Work in pairs. Look at this student's answers. Why were they marked wrong?

1	electrical	5	pronuntiacion
2	ENDYUNA	6	in the red room
3	Yellow Library	7	online courses not work placements
4	Life Sciences	8	closing

Q FOCUS

Identifying the
target information
(3)

14 ◐ 12 Listen to a speaker giving a presentation about the work of the biologist Dr Gray. Make notes.

1 Write the names of animals you hear.
2 Write the numbers you hear.

15 ◐ 12 Listen again and answer the questions.

1 Which animal did the research mostly focus on?
2 Which of the numbers you wrote in Exercise 14 are:
 a distances? b periods of time? c heights?

16 Look at the Practice Task on page 23. What kind of task is it?

a a set of notes with subheadings and bullet points
b a table with information under headings
c a form that somebody has partly filled in
d a set of questions with spaces to write the answers

17 Now listen to the complete presentation and do the Practice Task on page 23.

IELTS PRACTICE TASK 1

🔘 **13**

Questions 1–8

Answer the questions below.

*Write **NO MORE THAN TWO WORDS AND/OR A NUMBER** for each answer.*

PRESENTATION: ARCTIC HARE RESEARCH

1 Which other animals did the researchers study? ....

2 What term is used to categorise Dr Gray's study? ....

3 What was the approximate height above sea level of the area studied? ....

4 Which part of the animal's body makes the clearest marks in the snow? ....

5 What is a good place to look for hare droppings? ....

6 What was put inside traps to attract the hares? ....

7 What is the maximum distance for identifying individual animals with a telescope? ....

8 Which was the best shift for seeing hares in breeding season? ....

IELTS PRACTICE TASK 2

🔘 **14**

Questions 1–5

Complete the flow-chart below.

*Write **NO MORE THAN TWO WORDS** for each answer.*

Five stages in the process of designing a building

Schematic Design Stage:
Architect uses various tools to assess the **1** ....

↓

Design Development Stage:
Design starts to take shape and **2** .... are chosen.

↓

Construction Documents Stage:
A complete set of **3** .... is produced including diagrammatic and written information.

↓

Bidding and Negotiations Stage:
Owner looks for **4** .... from various contractors.

↓

Construction Administration Stage:
Architect is responsible for **5** .... the diagrammatic information and dealing with unforeseen problems.

Which statement best describes how you feel about Note Completion, Form Completion, Table Completion, Flow-chart Completion and Short Answer Questions?

☐ I feel confident about doing these tasks.

☐ I did OK, but I still need to do more work on these tasks.

☐ I need more practice with these tasks. I need to focus on …

▶▶ **For further practice, see the DVD-ROM.**

Performers in Celtic dress, Brittany, France

Before you watch

1 Look at the photo. Do you know which regions of Europe are associated with Celtic music?

2 Work in pairs. Tell your partner about the kind of music you like to listen to and/or play. Explain why you like it and how it affects you. Try to use these adjectives in your discussion.

> acoustic   instrumental   jazzy   light   melancholic   passionate   relaxing   soulful
> upbeat   uplifting

While you watch

3 Watch the first part of the video (00.00 to 00.32) about the singer Iarla Ó Lionáird. How would you describe his music? Do you like it?

4 Watch the video and complete the missing information from the concert promotion. Write *NO MORE THAN THREE WORDS AND/OR A NUMBER* for each answer.

5 Work in pairs. Watch the video again and make notes to answer these questions. Then discuss your answers.

1 How did Iarla's family background influence him?
2 What style of singing is Sean-nós?
3 In what way was Iarla's first teacher, 'Mrs Mac', important in his life?
4 When Iarla grew up there was a crisis in his life. What form did it take and how did his life take a new direction?

WAITES PROMOTIONS
IS PROUD TO PRESENT

IARLA Ó LIONÁIRD

∼ IN CONCERT ∼

The unique voice of the man from
1 ....
on an unmissable tour.

Praise for Iarla:
'Divine sounds. He's been singing since before he was **2** .... ,
and boy, does it show!'
'After **3** .... perfecting his singing, he's a master performer.'
'Through his experience of singing with the Afro-Celt Sound System, Iarla has been inspired by African
4 .... to perform again.'

After you watch

6 Work in small groups. What do these sentences from the video mean?

1 'There were shoes there waiting for me to put my feet into.'
2 'I felt like a museum piece.'
3 'He found himself on a dead-end street.'
4 'There's a genuineness and a largeness of heart in African music.'

7 Make notes on ONE of the following topics. Then talk for a minute or two to your partner about the topic.

1 Your family heritage: what do you know about previous generations of your family and how has this influenced your life?
2 Formative experiences: how have your school days influenced you? Was it a positive or negative experience? In what way?
3 Key people: think about a person – a teacher, friend or family member – who is or has been important to you. Explain their importance.

8 Work in small groups. Discuss the questions.

1 To what extent do people in your country follow in the footsteps of their parents or grandparents?
2 What are the biggest influences these days on young people as they grow up?

VOCABULARY 1

Times, dates and numbers

1 **Read the information about times, dates and numbers in sentence completion tasks.**

In the Listening paper of the IELTS test you frequently have to listen and complete sentences including times, dates or numbers. These can appear in different forms in the listening so it's important to recognise phrases that have a similar meaning.

2 **Match a word or expression from column A (1–9) with one from column B (a–i) that has a similar meaning.**

A		B	
1	instant	a	adding up to
2	meanwhile	b	1980–1990
3	over a twenty-year period	c	at first
4	the early 1900s	d	at least
5	the late 1900s	e	immediate
6	a minimum of	f	1900–1930
7	originally	g	more than twenty
8	a total of	h	at the same time
9	over twenty	i	for twenty years

Which of the words are more formal/academic (column A or column B)?

3 **Complete the sentences below with a word or phrase from Exercise 2.**

1 The new design was a(n) .... success.
2 To pass the exam, you need .... 60%.
3 .... there were a lot of problems, but now it is fine.
4 Harry made the dinner. .... , Susan finished her essay.

Phrasal and prepositional verbs

4 **Read the information about phrasal and prepositional verbs.**

Phrasal and prepositional verbs are usually informal. They are more often used in speech and informal contexts.
*He **gets on with** his brother.* (= He **has a good relationship with** his brother.)

5 **Match the phrasal or prepositional verbs in bold with the verbs in the box.**

appeared unexpectedly   conducted   continued   created   develop   understand

1 George Brough **set up** a workshop in Nottingham.
2 He **went on** to win 51 races.
3 A scientific monitoring trial will be **carried out**.
4 A beaver **popped up** really close.
5 He had to **build up** a database.
6 It was not easy to **figure out** how to do this.

Compound nouns

6 **Read the information about compound nouns.**

Most compound nouns consist of adjective + noun or noun + noun.
- Adjective + noun: *greenhouse*
- Noun + noun: *orange juice*

Compound nouns can have hyphens, spaces or no space. Recognising compound nouns and phrases helps you to understand the whole text more fully.

7 **Match a word from column A with a word from column B to make compound nouns.**

	A		B
1	sea	a	materials
2	guided	b	source
3	train	c	level
4	raw	d	engine
5	precious	e	engine
6	steam	f	journey
7	fuel	g	metal
8	diesel	h	tour

8 **Now complete the following sentences with your own ideas.**

1 Due to global warming, **the sea level** …
2 A **train journey** in my country can take between …
3 Manufacturing in my country needs **raw materials** such as …

Wordbuilding

9 **Read the information about wordbuilding.**

Being aware of the different forms of words can help you to guess the meaning of words if you recognise the root. Awareness of typical suffixes is particularly useful in the IELTS listening and reading papers.

final (adj/noun) + *-ly* = final**ly** (adverb)

10 **Look at the word or phrase in bold in the sentences. What part of speech is it (noun, verb or adjective)?**

1 The **final** lecture is at 3.00 p.m.
2 We have **amended** the schedule.
3 The **structure** of the building is very strong.
4 They will **present** their findings at the conference.
5 In the end, most issues are resolved in the work**place**.
6 This is a major **industry** for work placements.

11 **Look at the suffixes. Match each root word from Exercise 10 with the correct suffix. Then decide what part of speech the new word is (noun, verb or adjective). Make changes to spelling where necessary.**

-ings	-ment	-ation	-al	-ise	-ment	-ial

1	final	finalise	verb
2	amend		
3	structure		
4	present		
5	place		
6	industry		

12 **Complete the following sentences with a word from the table in Exercise 11.**

1 He's going to talk about .... engineering.
2 She wants to get a work .... with an accountancy firm.
3 He's giving a .... on linguistic diversity.
4 We need to .... the accommodation arrangements as soon as possible.
5 Paul is studying the .... process of glass recycling.
6 There are some .... to the programme, so we'll need to print it again.

Research data

13 **Read the information about using research data in note completion tasks.**

In the Listening paper of the IELTS test, you frequently have to listen and complete gaps about research data. These can appear in different forms in the listening so it's important to recognise phrases that have a similar meaning, and forms that have more than one grammatical use.

14 **Complete the sentences with a word or phrase from the box.**

corresponded	frees the hands	live	prime	season	shifts	stretch	tagged

1 The study area was a seven-kilometre .... of the Sverdrup Pass.
2 The research team trapped .... Arctic hares.
3 Once inside the trap, each hare was weighed, measured and ....
4 A tripod .... for note-taking.
5 Researchers work in ....
6 They concentrated on shifts which .... to feeding cycles.
7 More effort was spent on the midnight shift during the breeding ....
8 Late evening and early morning are .... times for breeding activity.

Look at the words in the box and identify the typical grammatical form. Which are used differently in the sentences in IELTS Practice Task 1 on page 23?

Common IELTS topic: The natural world

Phrasal and prepositional verbs

15 **Complete the sentences with the option (A, B, C or D) which best fits each gap.**

1 'You will need to .... an application form before you can take part in the southern petrel research programme.'
A fill up
B write in
C fill in
D write up

2 'The chicks were reared in captivity at the local zoo before being .... to park rangers for eventual release into the wild.'
A handed over
B handed up
C handed in
D handed through

3 'The lake was monitored over a period of six months in order to .... a picture of how the newly introduced fish were interacting with the existing species.'
A weigh up
B make up
C get up
D build up

4 'They gave careful consideration to a number of possible sites for the research project and in the end .... a location in the Southern Alps of New Zealand.'
A put up
B came about
C went for
D gave out

5 'After many years of research the team finally .... why the birds were so vulnerable to disease.'
A worked through
B figured out
C brought about
D came over

6 'The team should be congratulated for .... their research despite the terrible weather conditions.'
A carrying on with
B putting off
C getting over
D getting away with

7 'Your research project on climate change is so detailed and well written that you should consider .... to do a masters degree.'
A going up
B going by
C going in
D going on

8 'The eco-tourism business was .... in 2009 and has built up an international reputation for good practice since then.'
A set by
B set in
C set out
D set up

Wordbuilding

16 **Put the word in brackets in the correct form to complete the sentences.**

1 In order to complete the research, the team will recreate the fish's natural habitat inside the laboratory. However, the exact specifications (specify) have not been decided yet.

2 The increase in bird numbers around the petro-chemical plant is a good .... (illustrate) of the beneficial environmental effect of the conservation programme.

3 There are a number of .... (various) between the species that have been of particular interest to researchers.

4 Peer review discovered so many .... (adequate) in the research design that the programme was cancelled.

5 It was .... (correct) reported that the species was extinct when in fact a small population was still living in a remote corner of the rainforest.

6 There was no .... (indicate) that storms in the region could be so severe, so the weather that night was unexpected.

7 Researchers were astonished to find that birds such as crows and rooks behaved so .... (intelligence); several of the birds were observed using tools to access food.

8 Many local people .... (voluntary) to take part in the research despite the cold and uncomfortable conditions in the forest.

9 The work of Professor Sterling transformed our understanding of the subject and was .... (benefit) to every subsequent researcher in the Antarctic.

10 .... (theory), an earthquake is highly unlikely in that part of the continent, but the researchers decided not to take any chances.

TASK TYPE 3 Map/Plan/Diagram Labelling

The information that you hear comes in the same order as in the questions.

School buses parked in a row, Washington, USA

A About the task

1 Read the information about the task type. Then look at the notes on page 31 made by two of your classmates. For each point, who is right (Classmate A or Classmate B)?

The Map/Plan/Diagram Labelling task tests your ability to use the information in a recording to label a map, a plan or a diagram. It is often used to test your understanding of a conversation or talk in which a place, an event or a piece of equipment is described. On the question paper, you see a map, a plan or a diagram that represents the information you hear on the recording. Your job is to listen and label the map, plan or diagram by choosing the correct letter. There are two different types of map/plan/diagram labelling task. They look slightly different, but they both test the same listening skills in the same way.

Here are the basic rules for the Map/Plan/Diagram Labelling task:

- The spoken instructions tell you about the speaker(s) and the topic.
- On the question paper you see a map, plan or diagram with information in the form of labels.
- The labels are sometimes written directly on the map, plan or diagram, or sometimes they are arranged around it – with arrows pointing to the relevant place.
- Some or all of the labels contain a letter or number instead of written information.
- There are five to eight numbered questions.
- When you listen, you hear information about the map, plan or diagram.
- You may hear one person or two people talking.
- The questions follow the order of information in the recording.
- You listen and decide what information each label should contain.
- There are more letters than questions and you can use each letter only once.
- Write only the correct letter on the answer sheet.

Type 1 On the question paper, you see the numbered questions on the map, plan or diagram and a set of labels (e.g. **A–E**) in a box. You listen to the recording and decide which label from the box fits in each numbered gap. (See the diagram in the IELTS Practice Task on page 33 for an example.)

Type 2 On the question paper, you see the numbered questions separate from the map, plan or diagram. The labels on the map, plan or diagram have letters to show where information is missing. You listen to the recording and choose the label (e.g. **A–E**) for each question. (See the map in the IELTS Practice Task on page 31 for an example.)

<u>Notes</u>

1	Classmate A	You hear only one person speaking.
	Classmate B	You sometimes hear two people talking.
2	Classmate A	The questions usually follow the order of information in the recording.
	Classmate B	The questions always follow the order of information in the recording.
3	Classmate A	There are more letters than numbered questions.
	Classmate B	There are the same number of letters and numbered questions.
4	Classmate A	You can use the letters only once.
	Classmate B	You can use each letter as many times as you like.
5	Classmate A	You have to write the correct words on the answer sheet.
	Classmate B	You have to write the correct letter on the answer sheet.

B Sample questions

2 ◯ 15 **Listen and label the map. Use the rules about the task from Section A to help you. Then check your answers. Which questions did you find difficult?**

IELTS PRACTICE TASK

Questions 1–6

Label the map below.

*Write the correct letter, **A–I**, next to questions 1–6.*

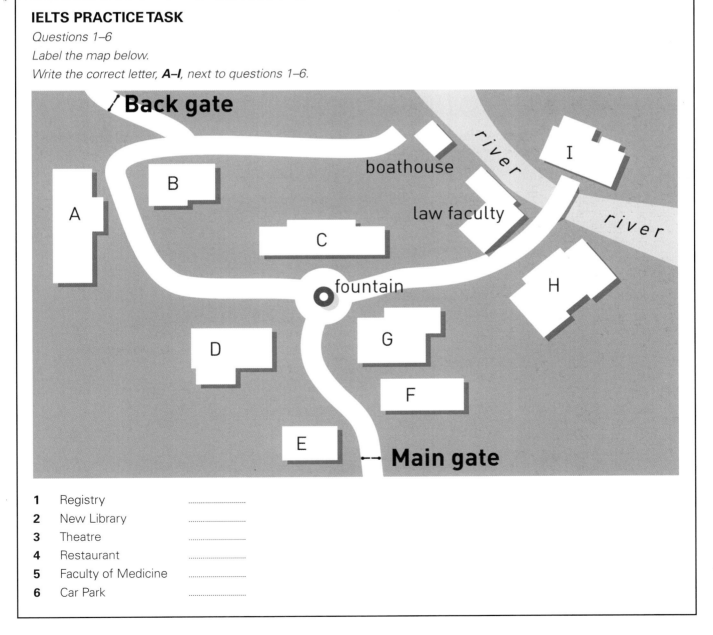

1	Registry	....
2	New Library	....
3	Theatre	....
4	Restaurant	....
5	Faculty of Medicine	....
6	Car Park	....

C Tips and tactics

3 Work in pairs. Read the tips and tactics and discuss these questions.

    a Which tips and tactics do you think are the most useful?
    b Did you use any of these tips and tactics when you answered the sample questions in Section B?
    c Which tips will you use in the future?

    1 Before you listen, you have time to look at the map, plan or diagram and think about what you're going to hear.
    2 Look at the list of numbered questions or list of labels and think about how the labels relate to the map, plan or diagram.
    3 Remember that the information in the recording comes in the same order as the numbered questions.
    4 At the beginning of the recording, you hear information about where to start looking at the map, plan or diagram.
    5 When you listen to the recording, you hear some words or ideas from the map, plan or diagram. Look at it as you listen and follow the information.
    6 You may also hear some of the words from the labels in the recording. This tells you that the information you need is coming.
    7 Remember, the correct answer reports the meaning of the recording, but doesn't always use exactly the same words and expressions – listen for the meaning.
    8 If you aren't sure, always write something. No marks are taken off for wrong answers.
    9 Remember, you hear the recording ONCE only.

Q FOCUS

Identifying the target information

D Skills-building exercises

4   16 Listen to a museum guide talking about an exhibition. Number the rooms 1–5 in the order you hear them mentioned.

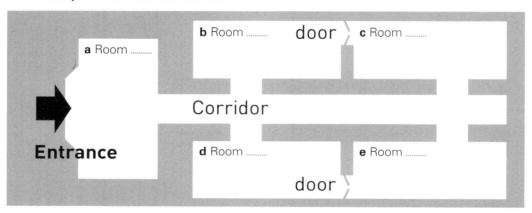

5   16 Listen again and decide which label (A or B) gives the main theme of the exhibits in each room.

Room 1
A rainforest environments
B marine environments

Room 2
A polar environments
B mountain environments

Room 3
A polar environments
B mountain environments

Room 4
A hostile environments
B tropical environments

Room 5
A desert environments
B river environments

6 🔘 **17 Listen to two friends who are visiting the second floor of the museum. Listen and label the plan below.**

*Write the correct letter, **A–G,** next to questions **1–5**.*

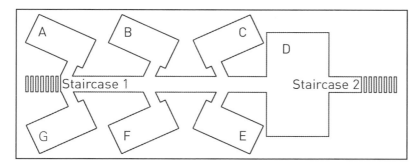

1 General Astronomy ....
2 Big Bang Theory ....
3 Manned Spaceflight ....
4 Space Exploration ....
5 Planet Mars ....

IELTS PRACTICE TASK

🔘 18

Questions 1–5

Label the diagram of the bike below.

*Choose **FIVE** answers from the box and write the correct letter, **A–H**, next to each one.*

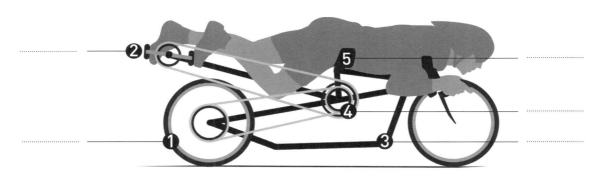

A	soft material gives extra comfort
B	uses a standard design
C	special shape reduces weight
D	made from old kitchen equipment
E	relatively narrow
F	allows rider to change position
G	exceptionally light
H	recycled from old bikes

Which statement best describes how you feel about Map/Plan/Diagram Labelling tasks?

☐ I feel confident about doing Map/Plan/Diagram Labelling tasks.

☐ I did OK, but I still need to do more work on Map/Plan/Diagram Labelling tasks.

☐ I need more practice with Map/Plan/Diagram Labelling tasks. I need to focus on …

▶▶ **For further practice, see the DVD-ROM.**

VIDEO 3 Eco-detectives

▶

Heat loss through the walls of a house with poor insulation, New Haven, Connecticut

Before you watch

1 Where in a house would you expect to find these domestic appliances? Can you add any more to the list?

> coffee machine   dishwasher   DVD player   food mixer   fridge freezer   hair dryer
> kettle   toaster   TV   VCR   washing machine   water heater

2 Which of the things mentioned in Exercise 1 do you consider to be essential in your life?

While you watch

3 Watch a video about energy efficiency in the home. Are the sentences true (T) or false (F)?

1   In the USA, houses and buildings consume almost half of all the energy that is used.
2   Many homes waste more energy than they consume.
3   We can't save energy and keep the conveniences we are used to.
4   Vampire loads don't actually waste electricity.
5   Temperatures in the area where Amory Lovins lives can reach -47°F.
6   Lovins' house can run on about the same power as one light bulb.

4 Watch the video again and pay attention to these expressions. Try to explain what they mean.

1   energy-eating monster
2   eco-detective
3   innocent-looking thing
4   vampire loads
5   good old common sense
6   the climate problem

5 After watching the video, how energy efficient do you think your home is?

After you watch

6 ⬤ 19 Listen to a tour of an eco-house by its new owner. Label the plan below. Choose FIVE answers from the box and write the correct letters, A–I, next to the spaces 1–5.

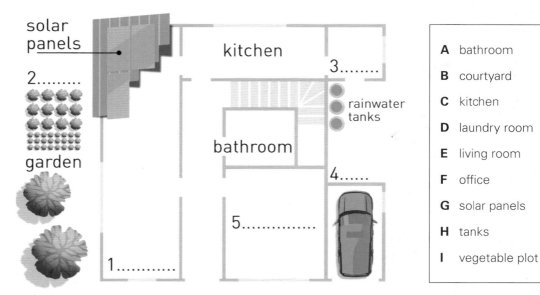

solar panels

2........

garden

kitchen

3.......

rainwater tanks

bathroom

4......

5..............

1...........

A	bathroom
B	courtyard
C	kitchen
D	laundry room
E	living room
F	office
G	solar panels
H	tanks
I	vegetable plot

7 Think about the place where you live at the moment. What do you like or dislike about it? What would you change, if you could? Make notes of your ideas.

8 Work in small groups. Talk for about a minute each, using your notes from Exercise 7. Answer any follow-up questions your classmates have.

TASK TYPE 4 Multiple Choice

Only one option matches the meaning of the recording exactly.

Giraffe and wildebeests roam the landscape, Kenya

A About the task

1 **Read the information about the task type. Then look at an online quiz. Choose the correct options to complete the quiz.**

The Multiple Choice task tests your ability to understand detailed factual information, as well as the speakers' attitude and opinion. It's used to test your understanding of both monologues and dialogues. On the question paper, you see a set of question stems with three possible answers. Your job is to listen to the recording and decide which one of the three options correctly answers the question. There are two types of question:

- A question which has three different answers (A, B or C).
- An incomplete sentence which has three possible endings (A, B or C).

Here are the basic rules for the Multiple Choice task:

- The spoken instructions tell you about the speaker(s) and the topic.
- You may hear one person or two people talking.
- The questions follow the order of the information in the passage.
- The question stem tells you what to listen for.
- When you read the question stems, you see some words and names that you also hear on the recording. These help you to know when relevant information and ideas are coming.
- The wording of the options is not exactly the same as the wording of the recording.
- You hear information relevant to all three options on the recording, but only one option matches the meaning of the recording exactly.
- You write the correct letter on the answer sheet.

Multiple Choice

1   You have to choose *one / two* of the three options in each set.
2   The questions are in *random order / the same order as the information in the passage*.
3   The incorrect options refer to information you *hear / do not hear* in the recording.
4   You are *likely / unlikely* to hear the words used in the options in the recording.
5   You write a *letter / number* on the answer sheet.

B Sample questions

2 ● 20 Listen and answer the questions. Use the rules about the task from Section A to help you. Then check your answers. Which questions did you find difficult?

IELTS PRACTICE TASK

Questions 1–6

*Choose the correct letter, **A**, **B** or **C**.*

1 What research finding surprised the speaker?

   A The majority of phone owners fail to use simple security measures.
   B A large number of lost phones end up in the hands of criminals.
   C Most people who find lost phones look at the data on them.

2 With regard to shopping apps, the speaker suggests that her listeners

   A remove all sensitive information from them.
   B log out of them when they're not in use.
   C choose those which are most secure.

3 The device known as a 'scream' is most useful when

   A a phone has been left in a public place.
   B a phone has been temporarily mislaid.
   C a phone has been stolen.

4 What does the speaker think of the 'complete data-wipe feature' offered by some apps?

   A It may not offer value for money.
   B It shouldn't really be necessary.
   C It's useful as a last resort.

5 What problem with passcodes does the speaker regard as most serious?

   A They make it harder to recover missing phones.
   B People find it difficult to remember them.
   C They can also be lost or stolen.

6 What service does the 'global lost-and-found' service offer?

   A It arranges the return of lost phones to their original owners.
   B It provides financial rewards for people returning lost phones.
   C It enables people who find lost phones to get in touch with owners.

C Tips and tactics

3 Work in pairs. Read the tips and tactics and discuss these questions.

   a Which tips and tactics do you think are the most useful?
   b Did you use any of these tips and tactics when you answered the sample questions in Section B?
   c Which tips will you use in the future?

1 Before you listen, you have time to read the question stems and options and underline the most important words and ideas.
2 Remember that the questions follow the order of the information in the recording.
3 When you listen to the recording, you hear words and ideas from the question stems. These help you to know that the relevant information is coming.
4 Remember, the correct answer reports the meaning of the recording, but doesn't use exactly the same words and expressions – listen for the meaning.
5 Don't use your own knowledge of the subject to help you to choose an option. Remember, you are being tested on your understanding of the recording.
6 Remember to write one letter on the answer sheet.
7 Always answer all the questions, even if you're not entirely sure.
8 Remember, you hear the recording ONCE only.

D Skills-building exercises

Q **FOCUS**

Identifying the
target information

4 Look at the question stems (1–4) and underline the main words and ideas.

1 What main point is the tutor making about proposals?
2 In terms of topic, the tutor suggests beginning with …
3 The tutor says that the best procedure to adopt is one that …
4 What does he say about the outcome of a research project?

5 Look at the excerpts from the recording (A–F). Choose the excerpts which best match the question stems (1–4) in Exercise 4. (There are two extra excerpts.)

A After you have a topic, you'll want to focus on the procedure that you'll follow to do the research.
B In order to complete your idea for research, you need to have a possible outcome for your research in your head.
C The topic you start with should be quite wide, so that you can narrow it down as you get more ideas.
D For space exploration, your outcome might revolve on whether the space programme is moving forward …
E One of the key aspects of the proposal is getting off on the right track.
F Whereas if you're researching an author, you might strive to find out what his motivation was, or what her enduring influence will be …

6 🔘 21 Look at the questions. Listen to the university tutor talking about student research projects. Choose the best answer (A or B) for each question.

1 The tutor's main point about proposals is
 A submit them by the deadline.
 B think them through carefully.
2 He suggests starting with
 A a broad area of research.
 B a specific area you're familiar with.

3 He says the best procedure
 A draws on the experience of other researcher.
 B supports your intended conclusion.
4 The outcome of the research project
 A will become evident once it's underway.
 B should be clear to you from before you begi

Q **FOCUS**

Identifying the focus
of the question

7 Look at the question stems (1–6) and decide what you will listen for in the recording (A, B or C). Then underline the main words or ideas in each stem.

A factual information   B one speaker's point of view   C both speakers' point of view

1 When should the research projects be submitted?
2 How does Graeme organise the notes he takes during background research?
3 What problem does Lisa have with detailed references?
4 Graeme agrees with Lisa that mind maps …
5 Graeme and Lisa agree that when using direct quotes from another writer …
6 What point does Lisa make about oral presentations?

8 🔘 22 Look at the questions. Listen to two students discussing a research project. Choose the correct letter, A, B or C.

1 When should the research projects be submitted?
 A Tuesday   B Wednesday   C Thursday
2 How does Graeme organise the notes he takes during background research?
 A on his reading list   B on his outline plan   C in a separate file he sets up
3 What problem does Lisa have with detailed references?
 A keeping accurate records
 B deciding what information to include
 C finding her notes when she needs them
4 Graeme agrees with Lisa that mind maps
 A aren't as useful as some people suggest.
 B help keep you focussed on the main topic.
 C can create a false impression of what's important.
5 Graeme and Lisa agree that when using another writer's ideas
 A it's always best to reword the information.
 B it's important to keep a clear record in your notes.
 C direct quotes can be an effective way of making a point.
6 What point does Graeme make about oral presentations?
 A You need to make a new set of notes.
 B It's better to work from your written report.
 C Your original notes can be a good source of reference.

IELTS PRACTICE TASK

 23

Questions 1–6

*Choose the correct letter, **A**, **B** or **C**.*

1   The original aim of Fiona and Jack's research was to find out

   A   whether the migration patterns of robins changed over time.
   B   how robins knew which direction to fly in at different times of year.
   C   if the findings of previous studies of robin migration were accurate.

2   They agree that the most surprising aspect of the birds' behaviour was

   A   how much it changed.
   B   how quickly it changed.
   C   how regularly it changed.

3   Fiona's first theory was that the birds had been affected by

   A   something they had eaten.
   B   something they had heard.
   C   something they had breathed in.

4   How did Fiona react initially to Jack's suggestion about radio waves?

   A   She realised that the birds must be sensitive to them.
   B   She thought it was an unlikely explanation.
   C   She refused to take it seriously.

5   How did Jack feel immediately after the experiment with the Faraday Cage?

   A   relieved to be able to get back to his normal task
   B   sure that they had uncovered something significant
   C   doubtful whether they had drawn the correct conclusion

6   What implications have Jack and Fiona drawn from their further research?

   A   Other forms of communication could have the same effect.
   B   It is only a matter of time before all birds are at risk.
   C   Birds in cities are more likely to be affected.

Which statement best describes how you feel about Multiple Choice tasks?

   I feel confident about doing Multiple Choice tasks.

   I did OK, but I still need to do more work on Multiple Choice tasks.

   I need more practice with Multiple Choice tasks. I need to focus on …

▶▶ **For further practice, see the DVD-ROM.**

VIDEO 4 Picture Perfect

Grand Central Station, New York, USA

Before you watch

1 You will watch a video about the photographer Steve McCurry, who has had many of his photos published in *National Geographic* magazine. What kind of photos do you associate with *National Geographic*? Compare with your partner.

2 Work in pairs. Answer the questions about taking photos.

1 What do you take pictures of – special occasions or people (e.g. family and friends), things that speak to you personally or are visually interesting (e.g. landscapes or architecture), or something else?
2 What do you use to take photos? A digital camera, your phone, a tablet, or something else?
3 How often do you take photos? Do you print your photos out or store them digitally?

While you watch

3 Watch the video about Steve McCurry and say which statements are true according to what you hear. Write NOT GIVEN if there is no information about the statement.

1 He studied photography at college.
2 He's retiring after 30 years with National Geographic.
3 He's looking for 36 shots to take on the roll of film.
4 He's decided to shoot all the frames at Grand Central Station.

4 Watch the video again and choose the correct letter, A, B or C.

1 What was Steve McCurry's ambition?
   A to be a professional photographer
   B to take pictures for a newspaper
   C to travel around the world

2 How does he describe loading the last roll of Kodachrome into his camera?
   A It reminded him of the past.
   B It felt unfamiliar to him.
   C He felt the same as he always had.

3 What does he say is fun about photography?
   A being outside
   B looking for the unexpected
   C learning about life

4 What does he think might lead to a good photo at Grand Central Station?
   A the activity in the main hall
   B the interesting light conditions
   C the interactions between the people there

5 What do you think of the shot he takes at Grand Central Station at the end of the video?

After you watch

6 Work in pairs. In the video, the narrator asks, 'What would you take pictures of if you had the last roll of Kodachrome film ever made?' Discuss your answers to this question.

7 Now think about each of the following. Then compare your ideas with your partner. Explain the reasons for your choices. Do you have any items in common?

- two things you always take with you when you leave the house
- three things you would save from your house in a flood or fire
- five items you would put into a time capsule in your town or school

8 Work in small groups. Discuss TWO of these questions.

1 News stories are usually made up of both images and words. Which do you find is more informative? Why?
2 How do changes in technology change the way we live our day-to-day lives? Give examples.
3 Does the list of things which are important to you change at different times of your life? In what way?

VOCABULARY 2

Dependent prepositions

1 Read the information about dependent prepositions.

Prepositions have various functions in English, such as indicating time, direction or place. Additionally, certain verbs, nouns and adjectives are followed by particular prepositions, for example, *depend **on***.

In the Listening paper of the IELTS exam, being aware of which prepositions to use is important. Correct use of prepositions is also valuable in both the Speaking and Writing papers of the IELTS exam.

2 Complete the table. Match the verbs (1–8) with the correct prepositions. Some verbs match with more than one preposition.

1 divide
2 focus
3 deal
4 conduct research
5 look
6 make
7 rest
8 sit

at	into	on	out of/from	with

3 Complete the sentences below with a verb and preposition from the table. Use the correct form of the verbs.

1 The course is .... seven modules.
2 This year we are .... core subjects.
3 Each student conducts his own .... his chosen topic.
4 The department secretary .... any scheduling problems.

Recognising and organising synonyms and antonyms

4 Look at the following words used to describe bikes in the listening on page 33. Find three pairs of antonyms and one pair of synonyms.

hard   high   light   narrow   new   old   ordinary   normal   smooth   soft   wide

5 Match the remaining words from Exercise 4 with their antonyms (a–c).

a low
b heavy
c rough

Formal and informal synonyms

6 **Read the information about synonyms.**

Listening and Reading tasks rely on you recognising synonyms and paraphrases. Build your awareness of synonyms by collecting words into pairs and groups with similar meanings.

7 **Match the words from column A with the words from column B to make pairs of synonyms. Which column has more formal words (column A or column B)?**

A		**B**
1	locate	a	many
2	mislay	b	lose
3	foolish	c	easy
4	significant	d	silly
5	simple	e	safe
6	select	f	choose
7	secure	g	think about
8	a large number (of)	h	find
9	consider	i	important

8 **Use a word from column A to complete the following sentences. Use the correct form of the word as necessary.**

1 The speaker suggested that phone owners should .... secure apps.
2 A .... number of people do not use a password for their phone.
3 Even when a phone has been temporarily .... , you should still report it as lost.

Guessing the meaning from context

9 **Look at the following extracts from the IELTS Practice Task on page 37. What is the meaning of the words and phrases in bold? Match them with the words in the box.**

brief look   annoying   finds   it is obvious   private   take the trouble

1 We generally keep a lot of **sensitive** information on our phones.
2 70% of people never **bother** to lock their phone.
3 Have a **browse** through your apps later.
4 **It goes without saying** that you need to have your data backed up.
5 Passcodes, however, can be **a pain**.
6 How is the kind person who **comes across** the phone by chance able to return it?

10 **Complete the following sentences with your own ideas.**

1 It goes without saying that …
2 … can be a pain.
3 I don't usually bother …

Wordbuilding

11 **Look at the word or phrase in bold in each sentence. What part of speech is it?**

    a noun
    b verb
    c adjective

  1 You should **submit** your proposal in writing.
  2 Your ideas should **relate** to your field of study.
  3 You should do plenty of **background reading**.
  4 You should **cite** references at the end of the paper.
  5 You should keep your reading **relevant** to the main topic.
  6 You should use quotation marks to avoid **plagiarising** another person's work.

12 **Complete the table.**

Verb	Noun	Adjective
submit	**1**	
	2	relevant
relate	**3**	
plagiarise	**4**	
5	quotation	
research	research	
6	citation	

13 **Complete the sentences with a word from the table in Exercise 12.**

  1 It's important .... our references accurately.
  2 The .... between your research question and the outcome should be very clear.
  3 .... is taken very seriously. You can fail a paper or lose a percentage of marks.
  4 You have to .... your paper on time, meeting any deadline set.
  5 Staying on topic is important, so keep your reading ....
  6 Always acknowledge your source if you .... someone in your paper.

14 **Look at the advice in Exercises 11 and 13. Which ideas do you agree with? Write three pieces of advice for developing academic skills, using words from the table.**

Common IELTS topic: Academic life

Formal and informal synonyms

15 Look at the word or phrase in bold in each sentence. Replace it with the word or expressions with a similar meaning (A, B, C or D).

1 If you **lose** your key to the laboratory, you should inform security immediately.
   A unlock   B mislead   C destroy   D mislay
2 The examples on display in the exhibition **show** the students' wide range of backgrounds.
   A illustrate   B argue   C tell   D explain
3 If you are unable to **hand in** your assignment on time it is essential that you apply for an extension.
   A propose   B turn out   C submit   D apply
4 The **idea** behind this particular course is for the students to get real world experience by visiting different factories and working in the production process themselves.
   A opinion   B philosophy   C publication   D practice
5 It is clear from the graph that **most** students at the university have a part-time job.
   A the plural of   B the minority of   C the significance of   D the majority of
6 Students whose assignments are **copied** from another source will be severely penalised.
   A plagiarised   B repeated   C cited   D quoted
7 The researchers then **did** a second study with a much larger group of subjects.
   A composed   B conducted   C collaborated   D corrupted
8 Remember, in order to continue as a member of the sports club, your membership fee must be paid **each year**.
   A monthly   B quarterly   C promptly   D annually
9 In my view, each student should set themselves clear **goals** at the beginning of each academic year.
   A undertakings   B objectives   C supplements   D regulations
10 On the other hand, the figure for public transport use between 2.00 a.m. and 4.00 a.m. was relatively **small**.
   A predictable   B light   C minor   D moderate

Prepositions

16 Complete the sentences by writing in the correct preposition. In some cases there may be no preposition.

1 The course consists .... two lectures each week and a weekly tutorial.
2 We have been forced to restrict .... the number of students who can apply for each course.
3 I am not convinced that this quotation is relevant .... the point you are trying to make.
4 It is essential that we persuade the government to invest .... the university's research and development programme.
5 In particular, your assignments should focus .... research before 2010.
6 The university has decided not to regulate .... the number of additional classes students take this semester.
7 Scientists have now confirmed .... the findings of previous researchers at the University of Edinburgh.
8 Research subjects were divided .... four groups based on their age and each group was then observed for a period of seven weeks.
9 It is essential that candidates respond .... the question that is actually asked, so you should read it carefully.
10 This department doesn't deal .... research of that type.
11 Researchers looked .... six different cities and found that most respondents held similar views.
12 The report concluded that the research had had no significant impact .... the local environment.

TASK TYPE 5 Multiple Choice (with more than one answer)

Only two options match the meaning of the recording exactly.

Pair of bottlenose dolphins, Honduras

A About the task

1 Read the information about the task type. Then look at and correct the notes in the email from your classmate. Your classmate has made three mistakes.

The Multiple Choice (with more than one answer) task tests your ability to understand detailed factual information, as well as the speakers' attitude and opinion. It's used to test your understanding of both monologues and dialogues. On the question paper, you see a question with five possible answers. Your job is to listen to the recording and decide which two of the five options correctly answer the question.

Here are the basic rules for the Multiple Choice task:

- The spoken instructions tell you about the speaker(s) and the topic.
- You may hear one person or two people speaking.
- The question tells you what to listen for.
- When you read the question and the options (A–E), you see some words and names that you also hear on the recording. These help you to know when relevant information and ideas are coming.
- The questions follow the order of information in the recording, but the options (A–E) come in random order.
- You hear information relevant to all five options on the recording, but only two options match the meaning of the recording exactly.
- When there are two speakers, the question often focuses on what they both say about the topic, and whether they agree or not.
- You write the two correct letters on the answer sheet.
- There are two question numbers on the answer sheet. You can put your answers in either order.

Hi there
Are my notes about the Multiple Choice task correct?
1 You always hear two speakers.
2 Three of the answers are correct and two are wrong.
3 The options (A–E) follow the order of the recording.
4 You write the correct letters on the answer sheet.
5 You can write your answers in any order.
Thanks!

B Sample questions

2 ⬤ 24 **Listen and answer the questions. Use the rules about the task from Section A to help you. Then check your answers. Which questions did you find difficult?**

IELTS PRACTICE TASK

Questions 1–6

*Choose **TWO** letters, **A–E**.*

Which **TWO** facilities in the student residence have been upgraded recently?

- **A** the study bedrooms
- **B** the main entrance
- **C** the shared kitchens
- **D** the bathrooms
- **E** the laundry room

1 ....

2 ....

Which **TWO** services are provided free of charge to residents?

- **A** replacement key
- **B** parking place
- **C** weekly room cleaning
- **D** electricity
- **E** extra bedding

3 ....

4 ....

Which **TWO** problems should be reported to the management?

- **A** lost or stolen items
- **B** faulty equipment
- **C** poor internet connection
- **D** problems with other residents
- **E** complaints about staff

5 ....

6 ....

C Tips and tactics

3 **Work in pairs. Read the tips and tactics and discuss these questions.**

    a **Which tips and tactics do you think are the most useful?**

    b **Did you use any of these tips and tactics when you answered the sample questions in Section B?**

    c **Which tips will you use in the future?**

1 Before you listen, you have time to read the numbered questions and options and underline the most important words and ideas.

2 The numbered questions follow the order of the information in the recording.

3 Remember that the five options (A–E) are in random order, and may use the same words as the recording.

4 When you listen to the recording, you hear words and ideas from the questions. These help you to know that the relevant information is coming.

5 Remember, you are often listening for the speakers' ideas and opinions – not just individual words and facts.

6 If there are two speakers, the questions often test your understanding of things they agree and disagree about. Listen to what both speakers say about the ideas.

7 Don't use your own knowledge of the subject to help you choose an option. Remember, you are being tested on your understanding of the recording.

8 Remember to write TWO letters on the answer sheet.

9 Always answer all the questions, even if you're not entirely sure.

10 Remember, you hear the recording ONCE only.

D Skills-building exercises

Q FOCUS

Identifying the
target information

4 Look at the exam task and answer the questions.

a Who is speaking?
b What is the topic?
c What do you have to do?
d Underline the main information in the question and options.

You hear a teacher telling her class about a guest speaker who's coming to their college.

Which **TWO** pieces of information does she give about the event?

    A the venue
    B where to get tickets
    C how to obtain a written copy of the talk
    D the speaker's background
    E the subject matter of the talk

5 Look at these words you will hear on the recording. Match the words (1–5) with the options in Exercise 4 (A–E).

1 transcript   2 to sign up   3 held (in)   4 the topic   5 biography

6   25 **Listen and do the exam task in Exercise 4. When you hear the words above, listen to what follows and decide if the information in the options (A–E) is given or not.**

Q FOCUS

Identifying
agreement and
disagreement

7 Look at these expressions. For each one, decide if they are agreeing or disagreeing with something. Write *A* (agreeing) or *D* (disagreeing).

1 I couldn't agree more.
2 I would dispute that actually.
3 I'd go along with that idea.
4 That's hardly true in this case.
5 I wouldn't be so sure actually.
6 You've got a point there.
7 I can't fault that idea.
8 There's no doubt in my mind that …
9 There's no denying that …
10 I think that's rather debatable.

8 ⬤ **26 Listen to two students discussing the issue of CCTV cameras in public places. Which TWO points do they agree about?**

   A CCTV cameras protect the public.
   B CCTV cameras invade people's privacy.
   C CCTV cameras discourage criminals.
   D CCTV cameras stop people behaving badly.
   E CCTV cameras shouldn't be hidden.

9 ⬤ **26 Listen again. Which of the expressions in Exercise 7 did you hear?**

IELTS PRACTICE TASK

⬤ 27

Questions 1 and 2

*Choose **TWO** letters, **A–E**.*

Which **TWO** advantages of the website are mentioned?

   A It has links to other popular websites.
   B It can be used by non-academics.
   C It saves researchers time.
   D It helps researchers to organise their data.
   E It is specifically designed to help students.

   1 ....
   2 ....

Questions 3 and 4

*Choose **TWO** letters, **A–E**.*

Which **TWO** disadvantages of the website do the two speakers agree about?

   A The database is now getting too large.
   B It doesn't offer complete reliability.
   C The 'suggest' feature is not very effective.
   D Data can only be uploaded in one format.
   E It doesn't provide information free of charge.

   3 ....
   4 ....

Which statement best describes how you feel about Multiple Choice tasks?

☐ I feel confident about doing this type of Multiple Choice tasks.
☐ I did OK; but I still need to do more work on this type of Multiple Choice tasks.
☐ I need more practice with this type of Multiple Choice tasks. I need to focus on …

▶▶ **For further practice, see the DVD-ROM.**

A kiteboarder jumps high over the Pamlico Sound, North Carolina, USA

Before you watch

1 **Look at the photo. Which of these sports is it?**

bodyboarding   jet skiing   kiteboarding   parasailing   water-skiing   windsurfing

2 **Work in pairs. Discuss the other sports in Exercise 1.**

1   How do these sports get their names?
2   What equipment do you think you need to do them?
3   What else do you need – water, waves, surf, wind, sunshine, etc?

3 **How would you feel if you were the person in the photo?**

While you watch

4 **Watch the video about Cory Roeseler as he does two sports in the Columbia River Gorge in the United States. Answer the questions.**

1   How does the narrator describe the weather?
2   What sport is Roeseler doing in the first part of the video?
3   Why is the wind so important in this sport?
4   Does Roeseler's new invention work?

5 **Watch the video again. For each question, choose TWO letters, A–E.**

1   Why does he like the Columbia River Gorge?

A   He enjoys himself there.
B   He went there a lot as a teenager.
C   It's close to his home in Washington State.
D   It's the home of kiteboarding.
E   It's where he experiments with new sports equipment.

2   How is Roeseler's wakeboarding boat different from anyone else's?

A   His invention is the only one that has worked.
B   It has been extensively tested on the water.
C   Its tower gives it more height than other boats.
D   Nobody else has used a tower.
E   The addition of a sail gives it more stability.

After you watch

6 **One of Roeseler's friends says he's nervous because he's 'never seen anything like that before'. Tell your partner about an experience you had that made you feel nervous.**

7 **Complete these sentences with your own ideas. Then talk for a minute or two to your partner about each one.**

1   Personally, I think adventure sports …
2   My best sports experience was …
3   The typical things I enjoy doing with my friends include …
4   Things I have in common with my friends are …

8 **Work in small groups. Discuss the questions.**

1   What kind of things might people learn about themselves doing adventure sports?
2   Do people who enjoy adventure sports have a negative or a positive impact on the environment? How?

TASK TYPE 6 Matching

Match the information and ideas in the questions to the correct options.

Bright yellow car parked in front of matching house, Hawaii

A About the task

1 **Read the information about the task type. Then look at some information you found on two websites, on page 53. For each point, which is right – Website A or Website B?**

The Matching tasks test your ability to listen to a recording and understand the main ideas as well as detailed information and arguments. Matching tasks are used to test your understanding of both monologues and dialogues. There are two different types of Matching task. They look slightly different, but they both test the same listening skills in the same way.

Type 1: On the question paper, you see a focus question and a box containing a set of options (for example, A–G) which answer it. The options can be features of a place or opinions about something, and they are grouped under a heading. There are then five numbered questions, also grouped under a heading. The questions could be a list of places, experiments or any other feature that is found in the recording. Your job is to listen to the recording and match the information or ideas in the questions to the correct options. (See page 53.)

Here are the basic rules for the Matching Type 1 task:

- The spoken instructions tell you about the speaker(s) and the topic.
- The list of numbered questions follows the order of information in the recording.
- The answer to each question is the letter that appears next to the relevant option in the box.
- There are more options than questions.
- Each letter may be used once only.
- You write the correct letter on the answer sheet.

Type 2: On the question paper, you see a focus question and a box containing a set of options (A–C) which answer it. There are fewer options than in Type 1, however, and it may be possible to use them more than once. As in Type 1, your job is to listen to the recording and match the features in the questions to the correct options. (See page 55, Exercise 5.)

Here are the basic rules for the Matching Type 2 task:

- The list of numbered questions follows the order of information in the recording.
- The answer to each question is the letter that appears next to the relevant option in the box.
- There are fewer options than questions.
- Each letter may be used more than once.
- You write the correct letter on the answer sheet.

Website A

1   There is always one speaker.
2   The numbered questions usually follow the order of the recording.
3   There are more letters than numbered questions in Type 1.
4   You can use the letters only once in Type 1.
5   You have to write the correct words on the answer sheet.

Website B

1   There may be one or two speakers.
2   The numbered questions always follow the order of the recording.
3   There are more letters than numbered questions in Type 2.
4   You can use each letter only once in Type 2.
5   You have to write the correct letter on the answer sheet.

B Sample questions

2   28 Listen and answer the questions. Use the rules about the task from Section A to help you. Then check your answers. Which questions did you find difficult?

IELTS PRACTICE TASK

Questions 1–5

What job does each of the following people do in the hotel?

*Choose **FIVE** answers from the box and write the correct letter, **A–H**, next to questions 1–5.*

JOB TITLES
A   Head Receptionist
B   Bookings Manager
C   Events Co-ordinator
D   Catering Manager
E   Head Chef
F   Personnel Manager
G   Head of Accounts
H   Head Waiter

EMPLOYEEES

1   Damian Rose   ....
2   Clara Ford   ....
3   Petra Snell   ....
4   Oliver Ansell   ....
5   Luca Petronelli   ....

C Tips and tactics

3 **Work in pairs. Read the tips and tactics and discuss these questions.**

  a **Which tips and tactics do you think are the most useful?**
  b **Did you use any of these tips and tactics when you answered the sample questions in Section B?**
  c **Which tips will you use in the future?**

1 Before you listen, you have time to read the question, the set of options in the box and the numbered questions. Underline the most important words and ideas.
2 Remember that the numbered questions follow the order of the information in the passage.
3 When you listen to the recording, you hear words and ideas from the numbered questions. These help you to know that the relevant information is coming.
4 Remember, the correct answer reports the meaning of the recording, but doesn't use exactly the same words and expressions – think about the overall question and listen for the meaning.
5 Don't use your own knowledge of the subject to help you choose an option. Remember, you are being tested on your understanding of the recording.
6 Remember to write one letter for each numbered question on the answer sheet.
7 Remember you can use the letters more than once in Type 2 tasks.
8 Always answer all the questions, even if you're not entirely sure.
9 Remember, you hear the recording ONCE only.

Q FOCUS

Identifying the target information (Type 2)

D Skills-building exercises

4 **Look at these words and expressions which can be used to talk about a course of study. Put them into the best group (A, B or C) according to what they are likely to refer to.**

> coverage of topics   workshops   library   lectures   syllabus   seminars   overview
> examination preparation   suitable for beginners   purpose-built
> well-equipped classrooms   location   personal feedback   online support
> individual assignments   presentations

A the venue	**B** the course content	**C** teaching methods

5 🔘 **29 Look at the names of the institutions (1–6). Listen and decide what the speaker recommends about the course at each of the institutions. You may use each of the letters (A–C) more than once.**

> **A** the venue
>
> **B** the course content
>
> **C** teaching methods

1 Pilkington College ....
2 City Study Centre ....
3 Gladstone University ....
4 Roseborough College ....
5 International Learning Centre ....
6 Bevington University ....

IELTS PRACTICE TASK

🔘 **30**

Questions 1–5

What view of interpreting does each academic or group of academics (1–5) hold?

*Choose **FIVE** answers from the box and write the correct letter, **A–H**, next to questions 1–5.*

> **A** An interpreter must know the original language perfectly.
> **B** Client satisfaction is the best way to measure quality.
> **C** Interpreters and their clients often have different aims.
> **D** Clients associate quality with aspects of delivery.
> **E** Successful communication is the main aim of interpreting.
> **F** Interpreters often misinterpret clients' needs.
> **G** Clients sometimes criticise interpreters unfairly.
> **H** An interpreter must speak the target language fluently.

1 Russian School ....
2 Paris School ....
3 Kalina ....
4 Buhler ....
5 Donovan ....

Which statement best describes how you feel about Matching tasks?

☐ I feel confident about doing Matching tasks.

☐ I did OK, but I still need to do more work on Matching tasks.

☐ I need more practice with Matching tasks. I need to focus on …

▶▶ **For further practice, see the DVD-ROM.**

Rooftops, houses and palm trees, Cairo, Egypt

Before you watch

1 Look at the photo of Cairo. In what ways is it similar or different to your own hometown or city?

2 You will watch a video about a community project in Cairo. Look at the list of words. Find five pairs of words with a similar meaning. You will hear all but one on the video.

> homeowners   animals   goldmine   livestock   garbage   reused   trash
> urban dwellers   repurposed   treasure

While you watch

3 Watch the video and make notes to answer the questions. Then compare your answers.

1 What do these Cairo residents traditionally use their rooftops for?
2 What does Thomas Taha Culhane hope to demonstrate with the system you see on the video?
3 What improvements do the water heaters provide?

4 Watch the video again. Which things mentioned in the video match the descriptions? Choose FOUR answers from the box and write the correct letter, A–E, next to the descriptions 1–4.

A rooftop garbage	**1** considered valuable ....
B satellite dishes	**2** funded by grants ....
C a natural resource	**3** plentiful ....
D the hot water system	**4** made by hand ....
E solar heaters	

5 According to the video, anyone can build a water system like this. Can you remember what you need and how it works? Watch the video to check your answer.

After you watch

6 Culhane says 'One man's garbage is another's goldmine'. What does this statement mean to you?

7 Look at these slogans which encourage people to recycle. Do you think they are effective as slogans? Why?

> NEVER REFUSE TO REUSE.
>
> Recycle today for a better tomorrow.
>
> **Recycle your trash or trash your Earth.**
>
> **When there is doubt, don't throw it out.**
>
> Why recycle glass? The answer is clear.

8 Work in pairs. Develop a short survey to find out about your community's experience of recycling. Then work with a new partner. Ask the questions on your survey and note down their answers.

9 Work in your original pair. Report the findings of your survey to each other. Each person should speak for about a minute.

VOCABULARY 3

Informal and academic language

1 Look at the expressions. Match an expression from column A with an expression from column B.

A		B	
1	get on with	a	belongings
2	quite a few	b	pay a small fee
3	allow in	c	several
4	stuff	d	a fee
5	pay extra	e	report
6	a (small) charge	f	continue with
7	tell	g	give access to
8	fall out with	h	have an argument (with)

Which column in (A or B) has formal/academic terms and which has informal terms?

2 Complete the sentences below with an expression from column A in Exercise 1. Make sure it fits grammatically as well as for meaning.

1 The bills for electricity are included in the rent but there is .... for cleaning.
2 This year I .... my roommate and so I had to move out of our shared house.
3 Each student has to submit .... essays each term.
4 Please leave your .... in the hall until your room is ready.

Views and opinions

3 Read the information about views and opinions.

In certain listening tasks, you hear speakers discussing various issues and expressing their views and opinions. The speakers may agree or disagree on certain points before coming to a conclusion. Try to identify the language used to express views and opinions.

4 Look at the expressions in bold in the sentences below. Match them with the expressions in the box.

> I don't recognise it   I don't like it   I don't agree   it's important   locate
> it puts people off   I feel sure

1 You **shouldn't miss this event.**
2 His name **isn't familiar to me.**
3 I'm hoping to **get hold of** the information.
4 **I would dispute that** actually.
5 **It's a deterrent to** crime.
6 **There's no doubt in my mind.**
7 **I'm not keen on** the idea.

5 Complete these sentences with your own ideas.

1 I'm not keen on ...
2 I'd like to get hold of ...
3 Visitors to my country shouldn't miss ...
4 There's no doubt in my mind that ...

Synonyms: academic language

6 **Match a word from column A with its synonym in column B.**

	A		B
1	to catalogue	a	to spot
2	to annotate	b	to organise (alphabetically or otherwise)
3	to flag	c	to add comments to a document
4	to cite	d	to mark for (someone's) attention
5	to network	e	a disadvantage
6	a downside	f	to quote or reference another work
7	to download	g	to make contact socially or professionally
8	to notice	h	to get from the Internet

7 **Use the expressions in Exercise 6 to describe academic processes in your country.**

Expressing responsibility: verb + preposition

8 **Choose the correct preposition to make expressions.**

1 be in charge *for / of / with* ....
2 be responsible *for / of / with* ....
3 deal *for / of / with* ....
4 work *for / of / with* ....
5 liaise *for / of / with* ....
6 have/take responsibility *for / of / with* ....

Which of the expressions take an object (someone or something)?

9 **Look at the sentences from the listening in the Practice Test on page 53. Highlight the verb + preposition phrases.**

1 Now one person you've already had dealings with is Damian Rose. He's in charge of recruitment and staff issues.
2 It's also important to know who's who and who's responsible for what areas.
3 Clara doesn't deal with the details of guest bookings in terms of room allocation and special requests, but she does deal with quotes for events and for invoicing.
4 Luca's in charge of front of house, so if you are working there … you'll certainly be working with him.
5 If you're in the kitchen or the dining room, you'll need to liaise closely with Petra Snell.
6 She'll be taking direct responsibility for those of you on work placements in those areas.

What is the difference between *work with* and *work for*?

10 **Complete the sentences (1–5) with the duties in the box. Add your own ideas.**

> co-ordinates kitchen activities   invoicing guests   salary queries   the cooking
> welcoming guests

1 A chef usually has responsibility for ....
2 A personnel manager usually deals with ....
3 A head of accounts takes responsibility for ....
4 A head chef ....
5 A receptionist is in charge of ....

Recognising and identifying paraphrases

11 **Read the information about recognising and identifying paraphrases.**

In the IELTS exam you frequently have to listen and evaluate speakers' contributions. These can be expressed differently in the listening text and the questions, so it's important to recognise paraphrases – expressions that have a similar meaning.

12 **Look at the words and phrases in bold. Complete each sentence with a word or phrase from the box that acts as a paraphrase.**

> accuracy   comprehensibility   concerns   fluent   hesitations   proficient
> simultaneous

1   .... interpreting is done **at the same time**.
2   .... is important in translation, as the interpreter tries to capture **the exact meaning** of the speaker.
3   Usually you should be more .... in the original language, which is the one **you are better at**.
4   A good interpreter should be **easily understood**. So .... is essential.
5   Interpreters who **speak quickly** are considered .... in the language.
6   Interpreters who **pause a lot** are thought of as weaker because .... are not associated with good quality translation.
7   What the client and the interpreter **are interested** in is not always the same. Their .... are different.

Common IELTS topic: Business

Paraphrase

13 **Look at the pairs of sentences below. For each one, complete the second sentence with the best option, A, B, C or D, so that it has the same meaning as the information in the first sentence.**

1   a   The people who live in the area around the business will be its main customers.
   b   The local .... will be the business's main customers.

   A   tenants
   B   residents
   C   landlords
   D   properties

2   a   The board has decided to make improvements to the factory in order to boost productivity.
   b   The factory will be .... to boost productivity, according to the board.

   A   uplifted
   B   relocated
   C   downsized
   D   upgraded

3   a   We are still trying to make up our minds where to hold the conference.
   b   The .... for the conference hasn't been decided yet.

   A   place
   B   venue
   C   site
   D   neighbourhood

4   a   You should include some facts about yourself and your life experience in your portfolio.
   b   Your portfolio should include .... information.

   A   biographical
   B   historical
   C   experimental
   D   critical

5   a   The amount our customers have to pay to get into the event has not changed for three years.
    b   There has been no change in the entry .... for three years.
    A   money
    B   ticket
    C   fee
    D   cost

6   a   One of the things that our company thinks is really important is protecting the environment.
    b   Protecting the environment is one of our company's ....
    A   products
    B   principles
    C   processes
    D   promises

7   a   You need to look carefully at all of the data before you make your decision.
    b   Only make your decision after you have .... the data.
    A   quoted
    B   compiled
    C   analysed
    D   recorded

8   a   It is against the law to manipulate the share price using confidential information.
    b   Manipulating the share price with confidential information is ....
    A   disloyal
    B   unconfident
    C   immoral
    D   illegal

Informal and academic language

14 **Look at the sentences below. Replace the informal words in bold with a more academic word from the box.**

> accommodation   assist   colleague   distribute   install   investment   liaise
> recruit   refurbish   salary

1   They are going to have to **do up** the hotel if they want to remain in business. The interior design is very old-fashioned.
2   Now that Mr Conway has resigned, we're going to have to **find** a new driver as soon as possible.
3   You will have to **talk** with the operations manager each morning to ensure that you know which orders need to be filled that day.
4   When I first started work my **pay** was barely enough to cover my rent and food, but fortunately I'm making more money.
5   We are going to have to **put in** fire detection equipment before the plant can reopen.
6   Don't forget to **hand out** the rota to every member of the new shift when they start work.
7   Part of your role is to **help** the marketing team to increase our market share in East Asia.
8   It is a large **amount of money** but I am confident that the company will see that it's been worthwhile in the long term.
9   One serious issue for employees moving into the area is finding **a place to live** in the already overcrowded housing market.
10   She has been a **workmate** of mine for twenty years now and over that time she has become a good friend.

31 **SECTION 1** *Questions 1–10*

Questions 1–6

Complete the notes below.

*Write **NO MORE THAN TWO WORDS AND/OR A NUMBER** for each answer.*

Student Health Centre

Appointments:

Phone at **1** .... for same-day appointments

Evening Surgery for **2** .... problems

Standard consultation lasts for **3** ....

Home visits must be requested before **4** ....

To make appointments online you must have: a **5** ....

a **6** ....

Questions 7–10

Complete the form below.

*Write **NO MORE THAN TWO WORDS AND/OR A NUMBER** for each answer.*

Student Health Centre

Name: David **7** ....

Address: **8** .... , TT43 7TY

Student ID: 9 ....

Faculty: **10** ....

---

32 **SECTION 2** *Questions 11–20*

Questions 11–16

Label the map below.

*Write the correct letter, **A–J**, next to questions 11–16.*

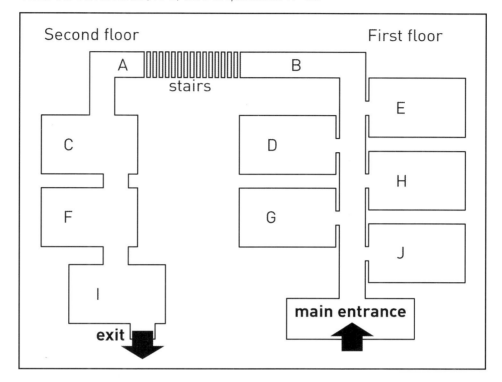

Where can you see each of the following?

11 trophies ....

12 photographs ....

13 items of clothing ....

14 an interactive display ....

15 posters ....

16 films ....

Questions 17–20

*Choose the correct letter, **A**, **B** or **C**.*

17 When will the tour of the stadium finish?
 A 3.15
 B 3.30
 C 4.00

18 What is not allowed during the tour?
 A using a camera
 B talking to the players
 C consuming refreshments

19 In the changing room, visitors
 A should not touch anything.
 B can see where each player usually sits.
 C may be photographed next to their favourite player's shirt.

20 When can visitors ask questions?
 A before leaving each area
 B whenever they think of one
 C at the end of the complete tour

🔘 33 **SECTION 3** *Questions 21–30*

Questions 21 and 22

*Choose two letters, **A–E**.*

Which **TWO** facts reported in the media are true?

A   The amount of domestic rubbish being recycled has fallen.
B   More commercial rubbish is recycled than domestic rubbish.
C   People dislike having two rubbish bins at home.
D   Some rubbish from recycling bins is transported to other countries.
E   The local recycling plant can't cope with the volume of rubbish.

Questions 23 and 24

*Choose **TWO** letters, **A–E**.*

What does the male student agree to do?

A   give a presentation
B   present statistical information graphically
C   produce a flow-chart
D   write the body of a report
E   compile references and appendices

Questions 25–30

Complete the flow-chart below.

*Choose **FIVE** answers from the box and write the correct letter, **A–H**, next to questions 25–30.*

A Beyond Repair Route	E Segregation Area	
B Redistribution Centre	F Testing Area	
C CRT Recycling Unit	G Direct Destruction Area	
D Imaging Consumables Unit	H Dismantling Area	

Recycling Electronic Items

All recyclable items pass though the **25** .... first.

⬇

Items unusable in their current state pass to the **26** ....

⬇

Items are assessed in the **27** ....

⬇

Unrecyclable components are removed in the **28** ....

⬇

Items such as inks and toner are dealt with by the **29** ....

⬇

Monitors and screens go to the **30** ....

⬇

Metals and plastics go to dedicated recycling units.

34 SECTION 4 *Questions 31–40*

Complete the sentences below.

Write **NO MORE THAN TWO WORDS AND/OR A NUMBER** *for each answer.*

Memory

31 William James used the word .... to describe memory in 1890.

32 The speaker says that it's a mistake to think that memory works like a ....

33 Loftus and Palmer's experiment in the year .... used a film of a car accident.

34 Loftus and Palmer found that when they used the word .... in questions, students remembered the car travelling more slowly.

35 Loftus was responsible for what's called the .... technique, which is used by police forces.

36 In Dr Thompson's story, one woman's memory of a crime was affected by a .... she'd just been watching.

37 The speaker says that .... is now regarded as more reliable than eyewitness reports.

38 In another experiment, Loftus used details of a visit to a .... to influence people's memories.

39 Loftus found that as many as .... of people in the experiment thought they remembered the visit.

40 The speaker uses the term .... to describe a situation in which innocent people claim to have committed crimes.

A The Test

Reading	Description	Suggested time	Length
Passage 1	13 questions	20 minutes	about 950 words
Passage 2	13 questions	20 minutes	about 950 words
Passage 3	14 questions	20 minutes	about 950 words

The IELTS Academic Reading Test is designed to test your ability to read and understand passages on academic topics from journals, books, newspapers and magazines. The test lasts for 60 minutes and there are 40 questions to answer on three separate passages. There are two or three different tasks on each passage, and these test a range of different reading skills. As you can see from the lessons in this book, there are 13 main types of reading task in IELTS (e.g. multiple choice, sentence completion, etc.), and you may find any of these tasks in any part of the exam.

Passage 1 tends to include simpler language and ideas than the other two passages, whereas Passage 3 tends to include the most complex language and ideas. The tasks and questions also tend to become more challenging as you work through the test. The tasks and questions mostly follow the order of information in the passages. Some of the tasks require you to look at visual information, such as a diagram or flow-chart, and relate the information in the reading passage to this. The instructions advise you to spend about 20 minutes on each Reading Passage. All your answers have to be copied on to the answer sheet within the 60 minutes of the test. You do not have extra time at the end of the test to transfer your answers.

Passage 1

In this part of the test, you read a passage that contains mostly factual information about a topic. There are two or three tasks and a total of 13 questions for you to answer. In order to answer the questions, you need to use the skills of skimming and scanning to locate specific information and then to answer detailed questions relating to that information. For example, you may be asked to read statements about the passage and decide if they are true, false or if no information is given about them. Alternatively, you may be asked to write the missing information in gaps in a table or a set of notes.

Passage 2

In this part of the test, you read a passage that contains mostly factual information about a topic, but may also contain some opinions and arguments. There are two or three tasks and a total of 13 questions for you to answer. In order to answer the questions, you need to use global reading skills in addition to the skills of skimming and scanning to locate specific information. Tasks in this part of the test often test your ability to match information in the questions with the relevant section or feature of the passage. There are also often tasks where you have to complete the missing information in a set of sentences or notes, for example when the ideas from one section of the passage are summarised.

Passage 3

In this part of the test, you read a passage that contains mostly detailed information and arguments about a topic, where the writer may be expressing an opinion or reporting and commenting on the opinions of others. There are two or three tasks and a total of 14 questions. In order to answer the questions, you need to use a wide range of reading skills including skimming and scanning to locate specific ideas and information, global reading skills and reading to understand detailed arguments. Tasks in this part of the test often ask you to choose the correct answer from a list of alternatives (A, B, C, etc.). You may have to answer multiple-choice questions, for example, or match the ideas and information you read to one answer in a list of options. Often there are questions which require you to read statements and decide whether they agree with the views of the writer or not, or whether there is no information about this in the passage.

There are thirteen Academic Reading lessons, which deal one by one with the different task types in the Reading paper.

B Marking

Each numbered question in the Academic Reading test is worth one mark. If you write the correct answer, then you get the mark. If your answer is wrong for any reason, you don't get the mark. No marks are taken off for wrong answers, however, so it's always a good idea to write an answer, even if you're not sure whether it's correct or not.

In questions where you have to write a word, a number or a short phrase, it's important to read the instructions carefully. The instructions tell you how many words you can write. If the instructions say *Write ONE WORD for each answer*, then you must write only one word. If you write two words, you don't get the mark, even if the information is correct.

The words you write must be spelled correctly. Most of the words you have to write are taken directly from the passage, so you only have to copy the spelling correctly. Both UK and US spellings are accepted as correct. Remember to write clearly so that your answers can be read easily. If your handwriting is unclear, or if individual letters are not clearly written, you don't get the mark.

You can write your answers in either UPPER CASE or lower case – both are marked correct, and you don't need to worry about punctuation. For example, if the answer to the question is 'online' and you write 'on-line', you still get the mark.

In questions where the answer is a letter or a Roman numeral, you only write the correct letter or numeral next to the number on the answer sheet. Never write the words next to the letters in a set of options.

C Strategies

Before the test

- It's a good idea to familiarise yourself with the format of the Reading test. Make sure you know exactly what you have to do in each of the different task types – then you can feel confident and prepared on the day of the test.

- Practise doing the tasks within the time limit. You can see how long it takes you to complete each of the passages and the different task types. Use the practice tests in the book and the tasks on the DVD-ROM to help you with your timing.

- If you're finding one of the task types particularly difficult – if you're taking too long, or getting the answers wrong – go back to the tips and tactics section and check that you're using the right approach.

- Try to make the most of every opportunity to practise your reading. For example, read newspaper and magazine articles in English as often as you can and use the Internet to keep up with the latest news and current affairs in English.

- While you're reading articles, think about the type of language the writers are using to make their points, how the writing is organised into paragraphs, and how the ideas in the passages are developed and linked together.

- Practise skimming and scanning skills. Don't try to understand every word the first time you read something. Read quickly to find out how the writer has organised the information, then decide which sections you need to read in more detail.

During the test

- It's best to read the passages in order. Remember Passage 1 is the least complicated, so don't spend more than 20 minutes on it. If you can finish the questions on Passage 1 in less than 20 minutes, you'll have more time for Passage 3, which is more complex.

- Remember that the tasks follow the order of information in the passage, so it's best to answer the questions in numerical order.

- Most tasks refer to a specific part of a passage. Your first job is to make sure you've located the correct part.

- Remember to use the most appropriate reading skills for the type of task you're doing.

- Most tasks involve different reading skills: skimming and scanning to find the relevant part of the passage, then reading that part carefully to answer the detailed questions.

- It's OK to write on the question paper. In fact, it's a good idea to write question numbers in the margin and mark the text to show which sections are relevant to each task and each question.

- Each part of the passage is usually only tested once, so when you move on to a new task, you usually need to look at the next section of the passage. (Some matching tasks are the exception here.)

- Use the words and information in the questions and the task to help you locate the relevant information.

- Remember you have to write one answer. If you're not sure, don't write two answers. If you do that, you don't get the mark.

- Remember that you have to enter all your answers onto the answer sheet within the 60 minutes. There is no extra time to copy your answers in the Reading test.

- You can write your answers on the question paper, but it's best to copy them on to the answer sheet as you complete each task. If you leave all the copying until the end, you may run out of time or make a mistake if you're under time pressure.

- Check very carefully that you put your answers next to the correct number on the answer sheet, and keep checking that you haven't made a mistake in the numbering.

- If you don't know the right answer to a question, always write something. You never know, you may have understood more than you think.

- Only write in the column to the right of the numbers – don't write anything in the columns marked /x.

- If you finish before the 60 minutes is up, go back and double-check that you have put your answers in the correct boxes.

At the end of the test

- At the end of the test the question paper and the answer sheet are both collected in.

- Only the answers on the answer sheet count; the question paper is destroyed.

READING PASSAGE 1

*You should spend about 20 minutes on **Questions 1–13**, which are based on Reading Passage 1.*

Black Bears and Grizzlies in Canada

Black bears and grizzly bears are both found in North America, and, because they look quite similar to each other, are often confused. Although closely related, however, the two species are in fact quite distinct. Part of the confusion arises out of the fact that both species are characterised by considerable colour variations, and there are also variations in size and weight. So using those criteria alone, it is not easy to make a confident identification. A large black bear, for example, could be either a black bear or a grizzly bear, and so could a smaller, paler individual.

Black bears have a wider geographic range than grizzlies, and can be found in every Canadian province except Prince Edward Island. Today, grizzlies are found only in western and far northern Canada and in small pockets of the western United States. Black bears are primarily adapted to forested areas and their edges and clearings. Although grizzly bears make substantial use of forested areas, they also make much more use of large, non-forested meadows and valleys than black bears do. Black bears have short, curved claws better suited to climbing trees than digging. In contrast, grizzly bears have longer, less curved claws and a larger shoulder muscle mass more suited to digging than climbing. This enables grizzlies to forage efficiently for foods which must be dug from the soil, such as roots, bulbs, corms and tubers, as well as to catch burrowing rodents. The primary difference between the dietary habits of black bears and grizzly bears is the amount of meat, fish and root foods eaten. Grizzly bears tend to be more carnivorous, whereas black bears eat more plant material.

A behavioural difference between black bears and grizzly bears is the length of time cubs are under their mother's care. Black bear cubs are born in the winter hibernation den, spend the summer following birth with their mother, stay with her in her den again in the fall, then separate from her early the next summer as yearlings, whereas grizzly bear cubs can spend up to three and a half years under their mother's care before separation.

Black bears are generally much less aggressive than grizzly bears and rely on their ability to climb trees to allow themselves and their cubs to escape predators such as wolves, grizzly bears or other black bears. Grizzly bears are more likely to rely on their size and aggressiveness to protect themselves and their cubs from predators or other perceived threats.

One behavioural difference between the two varieties of bears is significant if you hike in the backcountry. There are two types of bear attacks, the defensive attack and the predatory attack. The former can occur when hikers are walking into the wind so that bears do not smell them coming.

If you come within three to six metres of a grizzly bear, and it suddenly notices you, he/she may react defensively and even attack out of response to a possible threat. This is especially likely if you disturb a mother grizzly bear and her cubs. According to some experts, in this type of attack, you should play dead. This enforces the impression to the grizzly that you are not a threat and the bear most often walks away once the perceived threat is gone. The predatory attack, on the other hand, is most often launched by black bears; this is its natural method of hunting animals. While it is highly unlikely that people will be stalked by a predatory black bear, if they are, the recommended response is just the opposite to that for a defensive attack. Shout! Wave your arms and try to appear as large as possible. Don't run. If actually attacked, throw rocks at them. All bears prefer not to have to fight for their food, and if you put up a strong enough defence, they will likely leave you alone.

Questions 1–8

Do the following statements agree with the information given in Reading Passage 1?

In boxes 1–8 on your answer sheet, write

TRUE	*if the statement agrees with the information*
FALSE	*if the statement contradicts the information*
NOT GIVEN	*if there is no information on this*

1 It can be difficult to distinguish a black bear from a grizzly bear.

2 Grizzly bears have fewer colour variations than black bears.

3 Black bears are generally heavier than grizzly bears.

4 Both types of bear can be found in forested areas.

5 Generally, black bears are better at digging than grizzly bears.

6 Both types of bear eat fish in preference to other foods.

7 The diet of grizzly bears includes a larger proportion of meat.

8 Both types of bear build a hibernation den.

Questions 9–13

Answer the questions below.

Choose **NO MORE THAN TWO WORDS** *from the passage for each answer.*

Write your answers in boxes 9–13 on your answer sheet.

9 What do black bears do if threatened by predators?

10 What type of attack on humans is more typical of grizzly bears?

11 What are people advised to do if a mother grizzly bear defending cubs attacks them?

12 What shouldn't people do if a predatory black bear threatens them?

13 What weapons should you use to counter a black bear attack?

READING PASSAGE 2

You should spend about 20 minutes on **Questions 14–26**, *which are based on Reading Passage 2.*

Questions 14–20

Reading Passage 2 has seven paragraphs, **A–G**.

Choose the correct heading for paragraphs **A–G** *from the list of headings below.*

Write the correct number, **i–x**, *in boxes 14–20 on your answer sheet.*

i	A possible explanation for why a discovery was made in a particular location
ii	A recent study casts doubt on an accepted interpretation of events
iii	Analysis reveals the origins of objects discovered by chance
iv	Documentary evidence that supports the study's initial findings
v	How the current study is going to be organised
vi	Evidence suggesting that traders once lived on the Wessel Islands
vii	A long-standing suggestion that further discoveries are possible
viii	The significance of a chance discovery goes undetected
ix	The aims of the current study
x	Written and anecdotal evidence of early trade in the region

14 Paragraph **A**

15 Paragraph **B**

16 Paragraph **C**

17 Paragraph **D**

18 Paragraph **E**

19 Paragraph **F**

20 Paragraph **G**

African Coins

A In 1770, the explorer James Cook landed on the east coast of Australia and claimed the territory for Great Britain. It seems that, contrary to popular myth, he may not actually have been the first European to set foot on the continent. A new expedition, led by an Australian anthropologist, is investigating the possibility that ancient exploration may have taken place long before Cook and other Europeans ever journeyed to the continent. The expedition will follow a seventy-year-old treasure map to a sandy beach where a cache of mysterious ancient coins was discovered in the 1940s. The researchers are setting out to discover how the coins ended up in the sand; whether they washed ashore following shipwrecks and whether they can provide more details about ancient trade routes.

B The coins were originally found by an Australian soldier named Maurie Isenberg, who was stationed in a remote area known as the Wessel Islands. The Wessel Islands are part of Arnhem Land, a region in Australia's vast Northern Territory. Isenberg was assigned to a radar station located on the Wessel Islands, and during his off-duty hours, he often went fishing along the idyllic beaches. One day in 1944, he came across a few old coins and put them in a tin. He marked the spot where he'd found the coins with an X on a hand-drawn map, but didn't think that he'd unearthed anything of great note.

C Indeed, it wasn't until 1979 that Isenberg sent the coins to be authenticated and learned that some of them were estimated to be of great age. As it turned out, five of them had been produced in the sultanate of Kilwa in East Africa and are thought to date back to the twelfth century. Kilwa was a prosperous trading centre in those days, located on an island that is part of present-day Tanzania. Australian anthropologist Mike Owen, a heritage consultant in Darwin, is leading the upcoming expedition, and he says that the coins, 'have the capacity to redraft Australian history'. The copper coins, which were seldom used outside of East Africa, probably held very little monetary value in Kilwa: 'Yet, there they were – on a beach ten thousand kilometres to the east.'

D Along with the African coins, there were a number of seventeenth and eighteenth-century Dutch coins in the cache of the type known as *duits*. The first record of European activity in the islands actually dates back to 1623, when sailors aboard a Dutch ship called the *Wesel* gave the islands their current name. However, oral history from the indigenous Yolngu people who inhabit the islands suggests that they played host to many visitors over the centuries. The expedition's main researcher is Australian anthropologist Dr Ian McIntosh, who has spoken in depth with the Yolngu people. 'There was much talk of the Wessel Islands as a place of intense contact history,' he says.

E McIntosh points out that Northern Australia may have drawn early visitors because it lies close to the terminus of the ancient Indian Ocean trade route that linked Africa's east coast with Arabia, Persia, India and the Spice Islands (now part of Indonesia). 'This trade route was already very active, a very long time ago, and this find may be evidence of early exploration by peoples from East Africa or the Middle East.' According to McIntosh, the shape of the Wessel Islands serves as a 'big catching arm' for any ships blown off course, which may point to the coins coming from a shipwreck, or even multiple shipwrecks.

F It is difficult to tell whether there was routine contact with the outside world or whether there is any connection between the Dutch coins and the far older African coins, which may simply have ended up in the same place, but it is hoped that more evidence may come to light. Adding to the sense of anticipation is a persistent rumour that, in one of the many caves in the islands, there are more coins and antique weaponry.

G The expedition is sponsored by the Australian Geographic Society and intends to follow the hand-drawn map given to them by Isenberg. Included in the team is a geomorphologist, whose task is to examine how the coastal landscape has changed over time. If shipwrecks are involved, how the coins washed up may provide clues to the location of a wreck, say the experts. Meanwhile, a heritage specialist has the job of looking after the documentation and ensuring that the site is protected, and anthropologists working with local indigenous people hope to identify likely sites of contact with foreign visitors. 'There is great interest on the part of the Yolngu in this project, and in uncovering aspects of their own past,' says McIntosh.

Questions 21–26

Complete the sentences below.

*Choose **NO MORE THAN THREE WORDS AND/OR A NUMBER** from the passage for each answer.*

Write your answers in boxes 21–26 on your answer sheet.

21 Maurie Isenberg first discovered the coins in the year ....

22 The African coins which Isenberg found were made of ....

23 The African coins are thought to have been made in the .... century.

24 The later coins Isenberg found are called ....

25 The islands where Isenberg found the coins are named after a ....

26 Local people think there may be .... as well as more coins on the islands.

READING PASSAGE 3

*You should spend about 20 minutes on **Questions 27–40**, which are based on Reading Passage 3.*

When Tablet Turns Teacher

I remember the day, years ago, when I took an iPad home for the first time. It was a humbling experience. Within minutes, my two young daughters had seized on the device, and were handling it with far more dexterity than me. So much so, in fact, that after that, whenever I felt flummoxed by a phone or computer, I'd give it straight to my kids to sort out. And if we were ever trapped in a car, train or anything else, I was apt to hand over whatever device I was using at the time, and let them explore its functions – something people of my generation never seem to have the skill or patience to do.

But does their dexterity arise because my children are 'digital natives' – kids who have grown up in a world surrounded by mobile phones and keypads? Or is the ability to decode an electronic gadget innate to all young human brains, irrespective of where they live? These are the fascinating questions which a group of researchers from Boston in the USA have been exploring in the unlikely setting of Ethiopia. A few years ago, Nicholas Negroponte, formerly of the Massachusetts Institute of Technology, co-founded a group known as One Laptop per Child, which has been successfully distributing ultra-cheap computers to the world's poor as part of an educational campaign. But now Negroponte and Matt Keller, a fellow researcher who previously worked with the World Food Programme, have launched an experiment so bold it might be science fiction.

Six months ago, they dropped dozens of boxed iPads into two extremely remote villages in Ethiopia, where the population was completely unable to read and write and had no prior exposure to electronics. No instructions were left with the packages, aside from telling the village elders that the iPads were designed for kids aged four to eleven. They also showed one adult how to charge the iPads with a solar-powered device. Then the researchers vanished and monitored what happened next by making occasional visits and tracking the behaviour of the children via SIM cards, USB sticks and cameras installed in the iPads.

The results were thought-provoking, particularly for anyone involved in the education business. Within minutes of the iPads landing, they'd unpacked the boxes and worked out how to turn them on. Then, in both villages, activity coalesced around a couple of child leaders, who made the mental leap to explore those tablets – and taught the others what to do. In one village, this leader turned out to be a partly disabled child: although he had never been a dominant personality before, he was a natural explorer, so became the teacher.

The discovery process then became intense. When the children used the iPads, however, they didn't sit with a machine each on their laps in isolation as western kids might be expected to do. Instead they huddled together, touching and watching each other's machines, constantly swapping knowledge. Within days, they were using the pre-installed apps, with games, movies and educational lessons. After a couple of months, some were singing the 'alphabet song' in English and recognising letters – at the request of the Ethiopian government, the machines were all in English. More startling still, one group of kids even worked out how to disable a block that the Boston-based researchers had installed into the machines, which was supposed to stop them taking pictures of themselves. And all of this apparently happened without any adult supervision – and without anyone in that community having handled text on screen before.

This experiment still has much further to run, and has not been independently audited. But the researchers have already drawn three tentative conclusions. The first is that, 'no matter how remote children are, or how illiterate their community, they have the ability to figure out sophisticated technology,' as Keller says. Secondly, and leading from that first point, technology can potentially be a potent self-learning tool. And thirdly – and more controversially – Keller concludes that 'getting kids access to technology may be much more important than giving them schools.' In other words, instead of pouring money into shiny buildings and teacher training, aid groups might do better just to distribute mobile phones and laptops with those self-teaching games.

Many people would dispute that. After all, the technology world is full of hype; and some economists and development experts such as C.K. Prahalad have questioned whether poor communities can truly derive the benefits of modern technology without help. Singing an 'alphabet song' is one thing; reading calculus is quite another. But at the very least, Negroponte and Keller's experiments raise two further questions in my mind. Firstly, what is all this technology doing to our kids' neural networks and the way future societies will conceive of the world? Secondly, and more practically, could these lessons about self-learning be applied to the West? Should someone who worries about the failures of the US education system to reach the American poor, for example, be looking to iPads for a possible solution? The answers aren't clear. But the next time my kids grab my own devices, I may not feel quite so much parental guilt. Those devices may now be unleashing an evolutionary leap – with consequences that my tech-challenged generation cannot imagine.

Questions 27–33

Do the following statements agree with the information given in Reading Passage 3?

In boxes 27–33 on your answer sheet, write

YES	*if the statement agrees with the views/claims of the writer*
NO	*if the statement contradicts the views/claims of the writer*
NOT GIVEN	*if it is impossible to say what the writer thinks about this*

27 The writer accepts that young people are more adept at using electronic devices.

28 The writer is surprised that the Boston researchers chose Ethiopia for their research project.

29 The writer regards the project in Ethiopia as very ambitious.

30 The villagers in Ethiopia were unaware that the gadgets were intended for children.

31 The behaviour of the Ethiopian children was similar to that observed in western children.

32 The researchers would have preferred the textual content on the laptops to have been in the local language.

33 The researchers predicted that the children would learn how to enable the laptops' camera function.

Questions 34–37

*Complete the summary using the list of words, **A–N**, below.*

*Write the correct letter, **A–N**, in boxes 34–37 on your answer sheet.*

Although the research project is **34** .... , it is possible to identify some preliminary findings. Firstly, the ability to **35** .... the workings of digital hardware and software seems not to depend on levels of **36** .... nor on experience of using technology. What's more, faced with the challenge presented by the computers, the village children behaved in a highly **37** .... way, with leaders emerging who took on the role of teacher to the benefit of the whole community.

A	inconsequential	**B**	instruction	**C**	literacy	**D**	disrupt
E	numeracy	**F**	independent	**G**	invalid	**H**	competitive
I	co-operative	**J**	ongoing	**K**	design	**L**	intuition
M	decode	**N**	input				

Questions 38–40

*Choose the correct letter, **A**, **B**, **C** or **D**.*

Write the correct letter in boxes 38–40 on your answer sheet.

38 What do the preliminary findings suggest to Matt Keller?

   A Current educational policies may be misguided.

   B Certain teaching methods are counter-productive.

   C Technology is not as hard to understand as was thought.

   D Formal instruction may make technical subjects harder to grasp.

39 In the final paragraph the writer suggests that the project

   A has revealed dangers that young people using technology might face.

   B has overstated the case for how much can be self-taught about technology.

   C has the potential to provide a model for dealing with education elsewhere.

   D has made her re-evaluate her own attitude towards the misuse of technology.

40 In the passage as a whole, the writer's main aim is to

   A criticise the way some teachers make use of technology.

   B question the findings of one study into children's use of technology.

   C compare the effects of technology on children in various parts of the world.

   D explore the idea that young people have a natural ability to engage with technology.

TASK TYPE 1 Identifying Information (True/False/Not Given)

If there's not enough information, write NOT GIVEN.

Dunes of the Sahara Desert, Africa

A About the task

1 Read the information about the task type. Then look at some notes a student made about the task. The student has made two mistakes. Can you correct them?

The Identifying Information (True/False/Not Given) task tests your ability to find information in a reading passage, then to read it carefully to understand the details.

This task is often used to test your understanding of a factual passage about a specific subject. On the question paper, you see a set of statements that report the information from the passage. Your job is to read the passage and decide if the statements are reporting the information correctly or not. For each statement, there are three possible answers:

TRUE   *if the statement agrees with the information*

FALSE   *if the statement contradicts the information*

NOT GIVEN *if there is no information about it*

Here are the basic rules for the Identifying Information (True/False/Not Given) task:

- The statements follow the order of information in the passage.
- The statements are not exactly the same as the wording of the passage, but they contain the same information.
- The statements include some words and names that are also used in the passage. These help to locate the relevant information.
- You read this information carefully and compare it with the statement.
- You then decide if the statement reports the meaning of the passage exactly or not, and write TRUE or FALSE on the answer sheet.
- For some statements, there isn't enough information in the passage to know if the statement is correct or not. In this case, you write NOT GIVEN on the answer sheet.

Notes

1 You're mostly reading for facts and figures.

2 The questions are in the same order as the information in the passage.

3 The questions include some words you find in the passage.

4 The passage contains some information which is incorrect.

5 You have to tick (✓) the correct box on the answer sheet.

B Sample questions

2 Read the passage and answer the questions. Use the rules about the task from Section A to help you. Then check your answers. Which questions did you find difficult?

IELTS PRACTICE TASK

Measuring Snowfall

Despite the many high-tech instruments now available to scientists who study the weather, one measurement remains relatively difficult to make, and that's calculating how much snow actually falls in any particular place during a snowstorm. This explains why the National Center for Atmospheric Research (NCAR) in the USA is experimenting with new ways of achieving a greater level of accuracy in snowfall figures. As their representative Ethan Guttmann points out, 'You'd think it was just a matter of going out and sticking a ruler in the snow and measuring how much is on the ground. The problem is, if you move the ruler over just a few centimetres, you may get a different reading.'

In fact, the taking of measurements is complicated by a number of factors. For example, the first snowflakes may melt as soon as they hit warm surfaces, while others are whisked away by the wind, leaving some ground bare and other places buried under deep snowdrifts. Guttman's colleagues have been testing a number of new snow-measuring devices, including ultrasonic snow depth sensors, which send out a pulse of noise and measure how long it takes to bounce back from the surface below the snow, and laser sensors which work on the same basic principle but use light instead of sound. Another device for measuring snowfall is a type of open container with motor-vehicle antifreeze inside it. The antifreeze melts the snow as it falls and sensors measure the weight of the resulting liquid.

NCAR scientists have also experimented with using Global Positioning Satellites (GPS) to measure snow depth. It may be possible for signals sent from these satellites to measure the distance to both the surface of the snow and to the ground beneath it. Not only would this method be more cost-effective than other methods, but it might also be particularly useful for measuring the snow in remote locations such as inaccessible upland areas and the highest mountain peaks and ranges. Accurate measurement of snowfall in these areas is important as entire regions may depend on spring run-off of melted snow for their water supply.

The scientists also learned that they could improve the results of both manual and high-tech methods of snow measurement by using something known as a snow board. Basically, this is just a flat piece of white-painted wood on which snow can accumulate. Windshields placed around these can also add to the accuracy of measurements.

Questions 1–6

Do the following statements agree with the information given in the Reading Passage?

Next to each question, 1–6, write

> **TRUE**   *if the statement agrees with the information*
> **FALSE**   *if the statement contradicts the information*
> **NOT GIVEN** *if there is no information on this*

1 NCAR accepts the need for more precise methods of measuring snowfall.
2 Researchers have found ultrasonic sensors more reliable than laser sensors.
3 The device that uses motor-vehicle antifreeze measures the amount of snow both before and after it melts.
4 Using GPS technology would be more expensive than using the alternative devices being tried out.
5 GPS technology could allow snowfall to be measured across a wider range of landscapes.
6 The use of a snow board is particularly effective in areas with high winds.

C Tips and tactics

3 Work in pairs. Read the tips and tactics and discuss these questions.

    a Which tips and tactics do you think are the most useful?
    b Did you use any of these tips and tactics when you answered the sample questions in Section B?
    c Which tips will you use in the future?

    1 Before you read the passage, read the statements and think about what you're going to read. Underline key words and ideas in each statement.

    2 Remember that the questions follow the order of information in the passage. When you read the passage, you may see some words or ideas from the statements. These help you to find the relevant sections.

    3 First read the passage quickly and mark the relevant sections for each question. Write the question numbers in the margin so that you can find the sections again easily.

    4 Questions for which the answer is *NOT GIVEN* also refer to a specific section of text – so you always need to find the relevant section.

    5 Then go through the questions one by one. Read the section of the passage you have marked carefully to make sure you're in the correct place.

    6 Don't use your own knowledge of the subject to decide the answers. Use ONLY the information in the passage.

    7 If you think the answer is *TRUE*, re-read both the statement and the section of passage carefully and think about the meaning of both. Does the wording of the statement express exactly the same ideas or not?

    8 If you think the answer is *FALSE*, re-read both the statement and the section of passage carefully and think about the meaning of both. Underline the words that make the statement different from the passage.

    9 For *TRUE* and *FALSE* answers, quickly check the rest of the paragraph in the passage to make sure you haven't missed anything.

   10 If you think the answer is *NOT GIVEN*, underline the words and ideas in the statement that aren't in the passage. Read the rest of the paragraph in the passage quickly to make sure you haven't missed anything.

   11 It's especially important to check carefully whether an answer is *FALSE* or *NOT GIVEN*.

   12 Remember to write the words *TRUE*, *FALSE* or *NOT GIVEN* in the boxes on the answer sheet.

   13 Never leave a box empty. If you're not sure, always give an answer.

D Skills-building exercises

Q FOCUS

Identifying true and false statements based on a short passage

4 Read the pairs of statements (1–6). Underline the important words and ideas in each statement.

    1 A The recipes in the book *Apicius* are much older than the book itself.
       B The recipes in the book *Apicius* are 1,500 years old.
    2 A The book *Apicius* provides plenty of information about the life of Marcus Gavius Apicius.
       B The book *Apicius* provides very little information about the life of Marcus Gavius Apicius.
    3 A Apion's book about Marcus Gavius Apicius is no longer available to read.
       B Apion's book about Marcus Gavius Apicius is still popular today.
    4 A It is widely thought that Marcus Gavius Apicius wrote the recipes in *Apicius*.
       B It is widely doubted that Marcus Gavius Apicius wrote the recipes in *Apicius*.
    5 A The book *Apicius* includes recipes that are still in use today.
       B The book *Apicius* includes recipes for dishes that are familiar today.
    6 A The ingredients used in the recipes tell us the type of people the book *Apicius* was intended for.
       B The book *Apicius* uses ingredients that were commonly available in Ancient Rome.

5 Read the passage on page 79 quickly. Underline the sentences that contain the information relevant to each pair of statements in Exercise 4.

6 Go through the questions in Exercise 4 one by one. Read the passage carefully and decide which statement (A or B) is *TRUE* and which is *FALSE*.

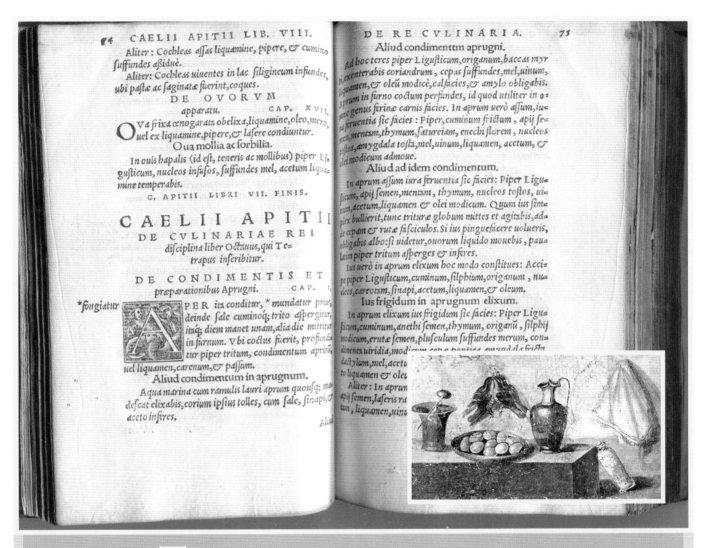

THE FIRST COOKBOOK

Apicius is the title of a collection of recipes written in Latin that is believed to be the world's oldest cookbook. The recipes were collected into a book 1,500 years ago, but they were in existence several centuries before that. The book is named after Marcus Gavius Apicius, a Roman who lived around 2,000 years ago. Not much is known about this man other than the fact that he loved good food and enjoyed a luxurious lifestyle. He himself was the subject of another book entitled *On the Luxury of Apicius*, written by the Greek grammarian Apion. This book was once famous but, unfortunately, it has since been lost. Few scholars today think Apicius was the actual author of the recipes in the book that bears his name. Some of the recipes, such as the one for *Isicia Omentata* (a kind of ancient Roman burger), would not seem strange to us today. Others call for ingredients that would have been rare and hard to come by even in Ancient Rome, such as flamingo tongues, roast ostrich and camel heels. This indicates that the book was written for wealthy Romans, as only they could have afforded such exotic ingredients. At any rate, the book gives us insight into the history of Italian cuisine long before foods such as tomatoes and pasta, now identified with that region, were available.

7 Work in pairs and answer these questions.

1 Did you and your partner underline the same sentences in the passage?
2 Are your answers all the same?
3 Discuss why the *TRUE* statements are true and the *FALSE* statements are not. Compare your ideas with another pair.

FOCUS

Deciding if the information is Given or Not Given

8 Look at the statements (1–7). Is there enough information in the passage below to know if the statements are true or false?

a Read the statements and underline the main ideas.
b Read the passage quickly and find the relevant section for each statement.
c For each statement, read the passage carefully and decide if the information is given or not given.

1 The first chess-playing machine was built in the 18th century.
2 Benjamin Franklin was able to defeat the Chess Turk.
3 Edgar Allan Poe realised that the Chess Turk was a hoax.
4 The Chess Turk was found to be operated by a human being.
5 The first chess game on a computer was played in the 1950s.
6 Deep Blue defeated Garry Kasparov in both of their two matches in 1997.
7 The first chess-playing programs available on the Internet were designed by grand masters.

MACHINES THAT PLAY CHESS

The idea of creating a chess-playing machine dates back to the 18th century. Around 1769, an Austrian inventor constructed one called the Chess Turk. This machine could play a strong game of chess against a human opponent and it became quite famous throughout Europe. In Paris, the machine played a game against the US ambassador, who at that time was the inventor and scientist Benjamin Franklin. Franklin was fascinated by the machine and said it was the most interesting game of chess he had ever played. The writer Edgar Allan Poe wrote an essay explaining how he thought the Chess Turk worked, though his theories proved to be incorrect.

It was not until the 1820s in London that the Chess Turk was revealed to be an elaborate and clever hoax. It was discovered that a living chess master was concealed within the machine, plotting the moves and operating the machinery. After that, the field of mechanical chess research was neglected until the development of the digital computer in the 1950s. One of the first games that could be played on a computer was chess.

Chess enthusiasts and computer engineers have gone on to develop chess-playing computers and software with increasing degrees of sophistication. In 1997, a chess-playing supercomputer called Deep Blue played the reigning world chess champion Garry Kasparov in two six-game matches. Kasparov won one of these matches and the computer won the other. These days, free chess-playing programs can be downloaded from the Internet that are challenging even for grand masters.

9 Work in pairs. Do you have the same answers for Exercise 8? Discuss any answers that are different.

10 Now look at the statements that you marked as 'given'. Are the statements *TRUE* or *FALSE*?

Q **FOCUS**

Identifying if the
information is False
or Not Given

11 **Read the statements (1–7) and underline the main words and ideas.**

1　The Burrunan dolphin was given its name by Australian Aborigines.
2　Both of the recently discovered populations of dolphins were found near urban areas.
3　The common bottlenose and the Indo-Pacific bottlenose are difficult to tell apart.
4　Scientists using DNA evidence immediately realised that the Burrunan was a previously unidentified species.
5　Burranan dolphins share the same colouring as other bottlenose dolphins.
6　The skeletons of two dolphins captured in 1915 have been re-examined recently.
7　The Australian government intends to put the Burrunan dolphin on the endangered list.

12 **Read the passage about new dolphin species quickly and mark the relevant sections for each statement in Exercise 11.**

13 **None of the statements is true. But are they _FALSE_ or _NOT GIVEN_? Is there enough information to know? Next to each statement, write**

FALSE　　　if the statement contradicts the information

NOT GIVEN　　if there is no information on this in the passage

New
dolphin species

Identified by DNA tests, the new mammals were right under researchers' noses.

A previously unknown species of dolphin has been identified in Australia. One of only three new dolphin species found since the 1800s, the Burrunan dolphin has been named after an Australian Aboriginal phrase that means 'large sea creature of the porpoise kind'. Only two populations have been discovered so far, both of them in the state of Victoria. Around a hundred have been located in Port Phillip Bay, a built-up area very close to Melbourne, Australia's second most populous city, while another fifty are known to frequent the saltwater coastal lakes of the rural Gippsland region, a couple of hundred miles away.

It's long been known that distinct dolphin populations roam off south-eastern Australia. But now DNA tests have shown that these dolphins are genetically very different from the other two local species, the common bottlenose and the Indo-Pacific bottlenose. The results were so surprising that the team initially thought there was a mistake and reran the tests. As Kate Charlton-Robb, a marine biologist at Monash University, says: 'The main focus of our research was to figure out which of the two known bottlenose species these dolphins belonged to. But from the DNA sequences that we got, it turned out that they were very different from either of them.'

The team also examined dolphin skulls collected and maintained by Australian museums over the last century, and determined that Burrunan dolphins have slight cranial differences that sets the species apart. And there are other observable differences too, such as the Burrunan's more curved dorsal fin, stubbier beak, and unique colouring that includes dark grey, mid-grey and white.

So how did the dolphins escape researchers' notice for so long? Physical variations in dolphins in south-eastern Australia have been reported for decades, though the new study is the first to use multiple lines of evidence to make a strong case for a distinct species. In fact, the Burrunan dolphin was almost discovered as far back as 1915, when a biologist captured and examined two very different dolphins from Australian waters. Scientists at the time concluded that both the animals were common bottlenose dolphins, and that their differences were due to one being male and the other female. After reviewing the female dolphin's skeleton recently, though, Charlton-Robb's team determined she was a Burrunan.

Because so few individuals belonging to the new dolphin species have been identified, the research team has petitioned the Australian government to list the animals as endangered. 'Given the small size of the population,' Charlton-Robb says 'it's really crucial that we make an effort to protect them.' ●

14 **Work in pairs. Do you have the same answers for Exercise 13? Discuss any answers that are different. Then compare your answers with another pair of students.**

IELTS PRACTICE TASK

What price fresh flowers?

Flowers have long been symbols of love and caring. People send them to express sympathy, to apologise, or just wish someone well. But today, floriculture – the growing and selling of flowers – is very big business, worth £2.2 billion a year in the UK alone. The majority of the cut-flowers sold there are imported, these days mostly from countries such as Colombia and Kenya. The Netherlands is the traditional centre of flower production in Europe, and remains a major supplier of flowers. In recent years, however, as labour and production costs have soared, attention there has shifted from flower production to flower trading. Meanwhile, the Kenyan cut-flower industry has grown rapidly, and now provides a vital income for around two million people. It is the country's largest agricultural foreign exchange earner after tea, producing £165 million annually.

For the environmentally conscious, it might seem wasteful that a commodity such as flowers should travel halfway around the world before arriving at a supermarket or florist shop. Just as some environmentalists say that it's better to buy fruit and vegetables grown locally, some also advocate the buying of locally-grown flowers. Thanks to globalisation, however, the UK cut-flower industry now supplies just ten per cent of the country's needs. Twenty years ago it was more like half. What's more, it is suggested that reversing this trend would actually have serious environmental consequences.

Research published in 2006 by Cranfield University in the UK showed that the production of Kenyan flowers, including delivery by air freight and truck, resulted in a carbon footprint nearly six times smaller than that caused by the production of Dutch flowers. Kenya has optimal growing conditions and the warm African sun provides heat and light, whereas growers in the Netherlands and other developed countries require significant inputs of gas and electricity to grow flowers year-round in artificial climate-controlled environments.

But there are other environmental factors to consider. A vast range of pesticides, fertilisers and fumigants are used in producing cut flowers. Lake Naivasha, the centre of Kenya's flower industry, is the ideal place to grow roses, thanks to its high altitude and abundant sunlight and water. However, environmental damage has resulted from the development that has followed in the wake of floriculture. Lake Naivasha itself has shrunk to half its original size, with water levels dropping by three metres, fish catches falling and the native hippopotamus feeling the effects of pollution.

Meanwhile, transporting flowers over long distances poses its own set of challenges. Roses, for example, have to be shipped by air rather than sea because they require constant refrigeration and wilt quickly. Transporting other types of flowers by sea can also be tricky compared to air freight. Demand is difficult to predict, which means entire shipping containers can seldom be filled with a single species, but mixing flowers is often inadvisable because some varieties emit gases that spoil others. One strategy is to opt for heartier breeds such as carnations and lilies which are easier to ship and require less refrigeration than roses.

Questions 1–8

Do the following statements agree with the information given in the Reading Passage?

Next to each question, 1–8, write

TRUE	*if the statement agrees with the information*
FALSE	*if the statement contradicts the information*
NOT GIVEN	*if there is no information on this*

1   In recent years, cut flowers have become more expensive to grow in the Netherlands.
2   More people are employed in the cut-flower industry in Kenya than in Europe.
3   Flowers represent Kenya's most valuable agricultural export.
4   The UK has seen a marked decline in the proportion of locally-grown cut flowers on sale.
5   The Cranfield study concentrated on the environmental effects of transporting cut flowers.
6   The Lake Naivasha region produces a range of cut flowers including roses.
7   Supplies of some local food items have been affected by the impact of floriculture around Lake Naivasha.
8   Transporting cut flowers by sea is generally more successful than using other means of transport.

Which statement best describes how you feel about Identifying Information (True/False/Not Given) tasks?

☐   I feel confident about doing True/False/Not Given tasks.

☐   I did OK, but I still need to do more work on True/False/Not Given tasks.

☐   I need more practice with True/False/Not Given tasks. I need to focus on …

▶▶ **For further practice, see the DVD-ROM.**

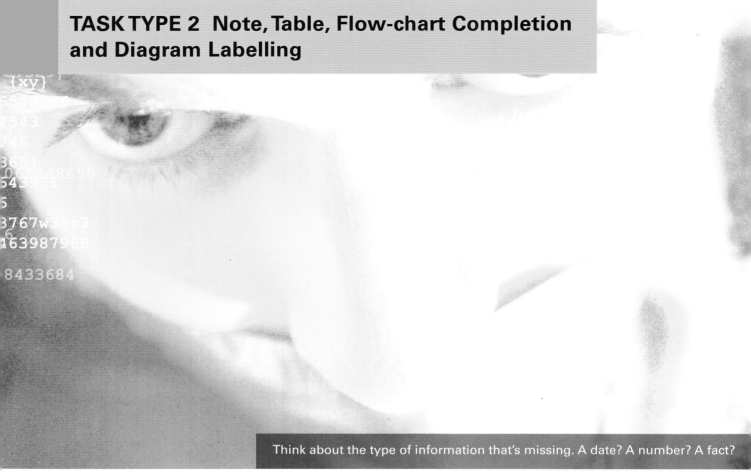

TASK TYPE 2 Note, Table, Flow-chart Completion and Diagram Labelling

Think about the type of information that's missing. A date? A number? A fact?

A About the task

1 **Read the information about the task type. Then look at the list of questions on page 85 that a classmate has emailed to you. Can you answer them?**

The Note, Table, Flow-chart Completion and Diagram Labelling task tests your ability to locate and record specific information from a reading passage. It's often used to test your understanding of a factual passage about a specific subject. You usually read facts about a subject, and you may need to write words or numbers. Some of the information from the passage is already written on the question paper; your job is to read the passage and find information to complete the gaps. On the question paper, you see a set of notes that report the information from the passage. In the notes, some key words are missing. You read and write the missing words in the gap.

The notes may take the form of:
- a set of notes under headings
- a set of notes in a table
- a diagram or flow-chart with labels

Here are the basic rules for these tasks:
- The instructions tell you how many words to write in each gap.
- The words you need to write in your answers are found in the passage.
- The information in the notes is presented in a different way from the passage, but it usually comes in the same order (diagram tasks may be in a different order).
- The words you write must be spelled correctly.
- You write the words in the same form as you see them in the passage (e.g. singular/plural) – you don't need to change them in any way.
- Write only the missing words on the answer sheet.

It's especially important to read through the notes before you read the passage, and think about the type of information you're looking for. In the passage, you may see different words that could fit logically into each gap. You have to read carefully to choose the correct information, so that the notes report the meaning of the passage exactly.

Can you answer these questions about the Note, Table, Flow-chart Completion and Diagram Labelling tasks, please?
1 Are you mostly reading for facts and figures?
2 Do you always have to write two words?
3 Do the notes always have the same format?
4 Is the information in the notes always in the same order as the information in the passage?
5 Is it important to spell words correctly?
6 Do you have to report the ideas in the passage in your own words?
7 Do you write only the missing words on the answer sheet?
Thanks!

B Sample questions

2 **Read the passage and complete the notes on page 86. Use the rules about the task from Section A to help you. Then check your answers. Which questions did you find difficult?**

IELTS PRACTICE TASK

Types of Ports

According to the World Bank, there are five distinct types of seaports: *service ports, tool ports, landlord ports, corporatized ports* and *private ports.* The basic difference between the five models is the amount of government control.

Service ports are most often found in developing countries; the port of Dakar in Senegal, for example, is a service port. At one time, most of the ports in the world were service ports. A service port is controlled by the central government, usually by the Ministry of Transportation or Communications. The government owns the land and all the port's assets – all the infrastructure and tools. A port's assets include roads, docks, terminal buildings, container facilities, vehicles and cargo handling equipment, such as cranes and forklift trucks. The dock workers who load and unload the ships in service ports are all government employees. Some supplementary services, such as food for the workers, can be in the hands of private companies. Economic inefficiencies have led to a decline in the number of service ports in recent years.

In the *tool port* model, an agency, usually called the Port Authority, owns and manages the land and assets on behalf of the city. However, the dock workers are employed by private companies. All the ports in Portugal, many in Brazil, and the French port of Le Havre are tool ports. For many ports, the tool port model represents a transitional stage on the way to becoming a landlord port. The transition generally requires that fundamental laws governing ports be changed, and that process often takes some time.

The *landlord port* represents the dominant model today, and is the one recommended by the World Bank. Landlord ports include the world's largest port, Rotterdam, the port of New York in the USA, and, since 1997, the port of Singapore. The city retains ownership of the land and the infrastructure, but leases these to a private company or companies which actually operate the port. The workers are employed by these private companies. The most common form of lease is a concession agreement where a private company is granted a long-term lease in exchange for rent. The firms that operate the port facilities agree to maintain port equipment and keep it up-to-date.

A *corporatized port* has been almost entirely privatized. The port authority is essentially a private enterprise which owns and controls the port. However, public agencies – either local or national – own a majority of the stock in the company managing the port and can use their controlling interest to steer the development of the port. As in the landlord model, the privatized port authority must keep up and improve the infrastructure, but must agree only to develop port activities. It could not, for example, turn a container storage yard into a block of luxury apartments. Corporatized ports can be found in Poland, in Australia, and elsewhere.

In the *privatized port* model, governments have no direct involvement in port activities. The land and all the assets are owned and managed by private companies, which likewise employ the dock workers. The government operates just in a regulatory capacity, making sure laws are followed. However, public entities can be shareholders. This model is in use in various ports in the United Kingdom, such as Felixstowe, and in several ports in New Zealand. The World Bank does not in general approve of this system. The bank advises against completely giving up public ownership, especially of the land.

Questions 1–9

Complete the table below.

Choose **NO MORE THAN TWO WORDS** *from the passage for each answer.*

Type of port	Role of government	Role of private companies	Comments
Service port	- owns and manages all assets - employees are public workers	may only provide **1** .... e.g. catering	fewer of these today due to **2** ....
Tool port	an agency known as a **3** .... - owns the land - manages the infrastructure	employs the workers	acts as a **4** .... between two other models

Landlord port	- government owns the land
	  and assets
	- leases them out long-term
	- receives **5** ....
		- operates the port
		- employs the workers
		- keeps **6** ....
		  in good order
			- dominant model today
			- endorsed by the World Bank

Corporatized port	government agencies own most of the port authority's **7**	- owns the land and assets - manages the port	owner agrees to restrict use to **8** ....
Privatized port	government has a **9** .... role	- owns the land and assets - management of the port	not recommended by the World Bank

C Tips and tactics

3 **Work in pairs. Read the tips and tactics and discuss these questions.**

    a **Which tips and tactics do you think are the most useful?**

    b **Did you use any of these tips and tactics when you answered the sample questions in Section B?**

    c **Which tips will you use in the future?**

    1   Before you read the passage, look at the notes and think about what you're going to read.

    2   Think about the type of information that's missing to complete the information. For example, are you looking for a name, a number, a specific term or something else?

    3   Look for clues in the notes that tell you the type of information you're looking for, e.g. headings or the words already on the page.

    4   Sometimes the wording of the notes tells you what to look for, e.g. if 'Year' is a heading, you may see references to a number of years in the passage.

    5   Most of the missing information is facts about the topic, so the words you need to write are mostly nouns. Check if the word is singular or plural in the passage.

    6   Remember that the notes follow the order of information in the passage. In tables, read the information from left to right, not up and down. In diagrams read the labels in clockwise order – the question numbers follow the order of information in the passage.

    7   Go through the numbered questions in order. Read the relevant section of the passage again and find the words to complete the gaps or answer the question.

    8   The word(s) you need to write are in the passage. Don't put the information you read into your own words.

    9   Don't just write down the first word you find that fits a gap – keep reading and think about the meaning.

   10 Remember, the instructions tell you how many words to write – if you write more, your answer will be marked wrong.

   11 Write numbers as figures, e.g. '104' – <u>not</u> as words, e.g. 'one hundred and four'.

   12 If you aren't sure, always write something. No marks are taken off for wrong answers.

D Skills-building exercises

4 Look at the words and phrases in the box. What does this vocabulary describe?

> assembly line   electronic tongs   fans   fibre discs   heavy stones   hammermill
> industrial decanter   ladders   large nets   millstones   nitrogen   wooden spoons

5 Read the passage and underline the words from Exercise 4.

Producing olive oil

in traditional and commercial ways

Olive trees can live to be hundreds of years old and produce large amounts of fruit in their lifetime. People have been making olive oil in countries around the Mediterranean Sea for many centuries, and this can be done by simply crushing the olives. Modern commercial extraction is a more complex process, although the same basic principle of crushing the fruit to release the oil is in play.

The olive harvest is the first step in making olive oil. Traditional producers use a number of low-tech means to gather the olive crop. One common method is for workers on ladders to simply pick the olives by hand and put them into baskets tied around their waists. Or workers may beat the branches with broomsticks, collecting the olives on the ground. Commercial processors use electronic tongs to strip olives off the branches and drop them into large nets spread out below the trees. It is then important to get the olives to the mill as quickly as possible, before the level of acidity becomes too great, as this can spoil the flavour of the oil.

After the harvested olives have been brought to the mill, traditional producers pick through the olives by hand to remove dirt, leaves and twigs. Commercial producers use cleaning machines to accomplish the same goal. Fans blow away the majority of smaller particles and another machine picks out any remaining larger bits. The olives are then turned into a paste as they pass through the mill. Large 'millstones' are used for this purpose by traditional makers, whereas commercial production involves the use of a mechanised alternative, known as a hammermill. Once milled, the olive paste is ready for a process called malaxation. In this stage of the process, the milled paste is stirred and mixed for 20 to 40 minutes. This is done with wooden spoons by traditional producers, while commercial producers use a mixing machine with a metal spiral blade. The stirring causes the smaller droplets of oil released by the milling process to form larger drops. The larger drops can be separated from the paste more easily. Heating the paste during the malaxation stage increases the yield of oil. However, the use of higher heat affects the taste and decreases shelf life. To compromise, commercial producers usually heat the paste to only about 27 degrees Centigrade. Oxidation also reduces the flavour, so commercial producers may fill the malaxation chamber with an inert gas such as nitrogen so the paste avoids contact with oxygen.

Next, the oil must be separated from the paste. Traditionally, the paste is spread onto fibre discs that are stacked on top of each other in a cylindrical press. Heavy stones are placed on top of the discs, squeezing out the liquid. The oil thus produced is called first press or cold press oil. The paste is then mixed with hot water or steam and pressed once more. The second press oil doesn't have such an intense flavour. The modern commercial method of olive oil extraction uses a machine called an industrial decanter to separate the oil from the paste. This machine spins at approximately 3000 revolutions per minute. The paste and oil are easily separated because of their different densities. This is essentially the same method that is used to separate milk from cream.

After the separation process, the oil is bottled, and the bottle is capped and labelled. Small, traditional producers often do this by hand, while commercial producers use assembly line techniques. The leftover paste is sometimes used for animal feed or it can be further chemically processed to extract more olive oil, which is usually blended with other oils or used for processes such as soap making.

6 Which of the words from Exercise 4 on page 87 are used to describe the traditional method? Which words are used to describe the modern commercial method?

7 Look at the flow-chart below. Choose the correct words to complete the notes. Read the passage again to make sure you have reported the meaning exactly in the notes.

*Choose **NO MORE THAN TWO WORDS** from the passage for each answer.*

HOW OLIVE OIL IS MADE

TRADITIONAL METHOD | **COMMERCIAL METHOD**

Harvesting
Manual labourers climb **1** .... to reach the olives. Picked by hand.

Harvesting
2 .... are used to remove olives from the trees.
Collected in **3** .... on the ground.

↓ ↓

Cleaning
Dirt, leaves and twigs removed by hand.

Cleaning
Mechanical methods.
4 .... remove most unwanted material.

↓ ↓

Milling
5 .... are used to turn olives into paste.

Milling
A machine called a **6** .... is used.

↓ ↓

Malaxation
Paste stirred with **7** .... to create larger drops of oil within the paste.

Malaxation
Paste mixed in a machine.
Paste heated to about 27° C.
8 .... is used to retain flavour.

↓ ↓

Pressing
Paste applied to **9** .... in a cylindrical press. **10** .... are used to force the oil out of the paste.

Pressing
An **11** .... is used to remove oil from the paste.

↓ ↓

Final stages
Oil bottled, capped and labelled by hand.

Final stages
12 .... methods are used to bottle, cap and label the oil.

---

8 Work in pairs. Look at this student's answers. Why were they marked wrong?

1   baskets
5   Milstones
11   Industry decantor
12   by hand

IELTS PRACTICE TASK 1 (Note Completion)

In 1977 the Voyager 1 and Voyager 2 spacecraft photographed the outer planets of our solar system before continuing toward interstellar space. Both are currently in the Heliosheath – the extreme outer edge of the solar system. They are currently about 1.8 billion kilometres from the sun, travelling at about 56,000 kilometres an hour.

In addition to the scientific equipment aboard these spacecraft, both carry 'Golden Records'. These are phonograph records containing sounds and images that portray life and culture on Earth. They are intended for intelligent extraterrestrial life forms who may find them and are kind of time capsules intended to communicate the story of humans on earth.

The Golden Records are 12-inch gold-plated copper disks sealed in aluminum jackets. They are accompanied by a stylus and visual instructions on how to play the record and to convert some of the information on the disk into images.

The contents of the record were selected for NASA by a committee. This was chaired by the late Carl Sagan of Cornell University. Dr Sagan and his associates assembled 115 images, greetings, musical selections and sounds, as well as printed messages from the US President and the UN Secretary General.

The 115 images are encoded in analog form. The remainder of the record is an audio recording, designed to be played at 16-2/3 revolutions per minute. (1977 was long before the era of DVDs, CD-ROMs, or MP3 files.)

The collection of images includes photographs and diagrams both in black and white and colour. The first images are mainly of scientific interest, showing mathematical and physical quantities, the solar system, DNA and human anatomy. Care was taken to include pictures not only of humanity, but also of animals, insects, plants and landscapes. Images of humanity depict a broad range of cultures. These images show food, architecture and humans going about their day-to-day lives. The audio portion begins with spoken greetings in 55 languages – six ancient languages and 49 modern ones, beginning with Akkadian, a language spoken about 6,000 years ago, and ending with Wu, a modern Chinese dialect. These greetings tell us something of the attitudes of the regions where these languages are spoken. The greeting in Farsi reads: 'Hello to the residents of far skies.' In Amoy (a Chinese dialect): 'Friends of space, how are you all? Have you eaten yet? Come visit us if you have time.' In Bengali: 'Let there be peace everywhere.' In English: 'Hello from the children of planet Earth.' In French, simply this: 'Hello everybody!'

The bulk of the recording space is taken up by music. The records have the inscription 'To the makers of music – all worlds, all times' hand-etched on its surface in the space on the record between the label and the playable surface. Musical selections were painstakingly chosen. Sagan's basic directive was that the music be 'diverse and good'. The first Earth music aliens will hear is the First Movement of Bach's *Brandenburg Concerto No. 2*. In addition to such classical pieces, rock is represented by Chuck Berry's *Johnny B. Goode* and jazz by a Louis Armstrong song. Sagan wanted to include the Beatles' song *Here Comes the Sun*. The Beatles agreed to the idea, but for some reason their publishing company refused.

The rest of the musical section is predominantly what we would call 'world music' today. It is one of the most diverse compilations of music ever put together. It includes Navajo Indian chants, panpipe music from Peru, a men's house song from New Guinea, Australian aboriginal didgeridoo music, and the initiation song of Pygmy girls from the Congo.

The final portion of the audio recording features a variety of sounds from the planet Earth, both natural and man-made; the sounds of thunder and volcanoes; the sounds of wind and rain; the songs of humpback whales and the chatter of chimpanzees; of automobiles, tractors, horse-drawn carts, jet planes and rockets. The final sound is that of a kiss.

Although not aimed at any particular stars, Voyager I will pass relatively close to Gliese 445, and Voyager 2 will drift past the star Ross 248 – in about 40,000 years. Some scientists estimate that by that time, collisions with micro-particles in deep space will have made the Golden Record unplayable. At any rate, since the probes are extremely small compared to the vastness of interstellar space, the probability of an extraterrestrial civilization encountering them is infinitesimal, especially since the probes will stop emitting any kind of electromagnetic radiation by 2025. Carl Sagan noted that, 'The spacecraft will be encountered and the record played only if there are advanced space-faring civilizations in interstellar space. But the launching of this "bottle" into the cosmic "ocean" says something very hopeful about life on this planet.' Thus, the record is best seen as a symbolic statement rather than a serious attempt to communicate with extraterrestrial life.

Questions 1–10

Complete the notes below.

Choose **TWO WORDS AND/OR A NUMBER** *from the passage for each answer.*

The Golden Records

Location
- on Voyager spacecraft
- in the area known by the name **1** ....
- travelling into outer space

Appearance
- discs made mostly of **2** ....
- covered by **3** ....

Content
- chosen by **4** ....
- divided into four sections

Section 1: Images
- begins with images of a **5** .... nature
- others show humans from a variety of **6** ....

Section 2: Spoken Greetings
- a total of **7** .... are represented

Section 3: Music
- begins with an example of the **8** .... genre of music
- majority of examples can be defined as **9** ....

Section 4: Final section
- dedicated to a variety of sounds
- ends with a sound made by a **10** ....

IELTS PRACTICE TASK 2 (Diagram Labelling)

The giraffe towers above all other mammals in the world.

Roaming the African grasslands on long, thin legs, an adult male can reach a maximum height of six metres. But only about half of that height comes from its lower body – the rest is accounted for by the neck. The giraffe uses its height to feed on leaves and buds in treetops that few other animals can reach. The leaves of acacia trees are a favourite; these trees typically grow to be six or seven metres tall. And the giraffe has yet another tool to expand its reach – its tongue can stretch as far as forty-six centimetres. A giraffe spends most of its time eating, consuming hundreds of kilograms of leaves per week and travelling long distances in search of food. The animal's height also helps it to keep a sharp lookout for predators across the wide expanse of the African savannas, and it can move its head through 180 degrees in order to see what is behind it.

But it is the giraffe's neck that is its most noticeable feature. The neck has seven bones called the cervical vertebrae, and these are joined together by what are known as ball-and-socket joints – of the sort that join human arms and shoulders. These joints allow movements through 360 degrees. Another key anatomical feature is the giraffe's thoracic vertebrae – the ones that join the neck to the back. These have the same type of joints as the cervical vertebrae, which gives the giraffe great flexibility, as well as explaining why it has its characteristic hump. These bones support muscles that hold the neck upright, in the same way that cables hold up a crane on a construction site.

The giraffe has the highest known blood pressure among animals because it must pump blood, against gravity, all the way up its long neck to the brain. To pump blood on that long journey to their heads, giraffes have enormous hearts, weighing up to twelve kilograms. Their enlarged lungs compensate for the length of their tracheas. The giraffe also has a high concentration of red blood cells and tight skin, especially around the legs, which prevents blood from pooling in the limbs. It serves the same purpose as the G-suit worn by astronauts who are subjected to excessive G forces, or tight elastic stockings worn by people with leg circulation problems.

While giraffes don't need to drink very often – they mostly get water from the leaves that they eat – they do need to do so every few days. To do this, giraffes must splay out their legs and lower their heads. The extremely high blood pressure, coupled with gravity, could cause a potentially lethal rush of blood to giraffes' brains when they bend their heads. This doesn't happen because of one-way valves that stop excess blood from flowing too quickly down their necks to their heads.

The giraffe's neck is also integral to the animal's movement and moves back and forth with its stride. That's because the weight and motion of the neck guides the animal's centre of gravity. The giraffe also tosses its neck to and fro to help it rise to a standing position on its spindly legs. This is comparable to the way people swing their arms up over their heads to pull themselves out of bed in the morning.

Questions 1–7

Label the diagram below.

*Choose **NO MORE THAN THREE WORDS AND/OR A NUMBER** from the passage for each answer.*

The Anatomy of Giraffes

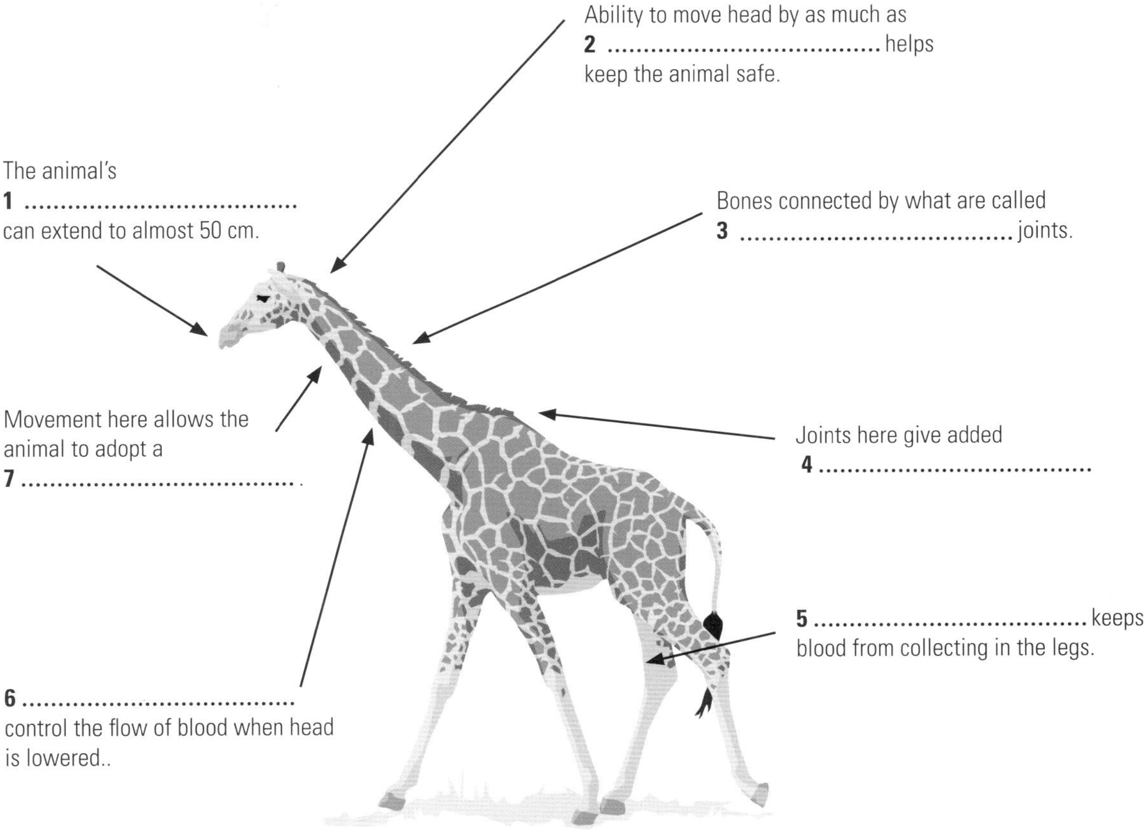

Ability to move head by as much as
2 .... helps
keep the animal safe.

The animal's
1 ....
can extend to almost 50 cm.

Bones connected by what are called
3 .... joints.

Movement here allows the
animal to adopt a
7 ....

Joints here give added
4 ....

5 .... keeps
blood from collecting in the legs.

6 ....
control the flow of blood when head
is lowered..

Which statement best describes how you feel about Note, Table, Flow-chart Completion and Diagram Labelling tasks?

- [ ] I feel confident about doing these tasks.
- [ ] I did OK, but I still need to do more work on these tasks.
- [ ] I need more practice with these tasks. I need to focus on …

▶▶ **For further practice, see the DVD-ROM.**

TASK TYPE 3 Short Answer Questions

When you read the passage, you see the words that you need to write.

Visitor views Chugach Mountains, Alaska

A About the task

1 **Read the information about the task type. Then look at some notes two of your classmates made about the task. For each point, who is right: Classmate A or Classmate B? Choose the correct answer.**

The Short Answer Questions task tests your ability to answer questions on factual information using words taken from the passage.

It's often used to test your understanding of a factual passage about a specific subject. You usually read facts about a subject, and you may be asked to write words or numbers. On the question paper, you see a set of questions about the passage. Your job is to read the passage and find information to answer the questions.

Here are the basic rules for the Short Answer Questions task:

- The questions follow the order of information in the passage.
- The instructions tell you how many words to write in each answer.
- The wording of the questions includes some words and ideas that you can find in the passage.
- The words you need to write in your answer are found in the passage.
- You write the words in the same form as you see them in the passage (e.g. singular/plural) – you don't need to change them in any way.
- Spelling counts! The words you write must be spelled correctly.

It's especially important to read through the questions before you read the passage, and think about the type of information you're looking for. You have to read the passage carefully to find the correct information.

Short Answer Questions

1 Classmate A You are mostly reading for facts and figures.

    Classmate B You are reading to understand the writer's opinions.

2 Classmate A The questions sometimes follow the order of the passage.

    Classmate B The questions always follow the order of the passage.

3 Classmate A You have to check the instructions to see how many words you can write.

    Classmate B You always have to write two words.

4 Classmate A You have to use your own words to explain the ideas in the passage.

    Classmate B You have to write the exact words you find in the passage.

5 Classmate A All answers must be spelled correctly.

    Classmate B Small spelling mistakes are not penalised.

B Sample questions

2 Read the passage and answer the questions. Use the rules about the task from Section A to help you. Then check your answers. Which questions did you find difficult?

IELTS PRACTICE TASK

A Crack in the Earth

Researchers working off the coast of Portugal in western Europe have discovered what could be the birth of a new subduction zone. Subduction zones happen when the large tectonic plates that make up the Earth's crust crash into one another, and one slides, or subducts, below the other.

According to a report published in the journal *Geology*, this new subduction zone could signal the start of an extended cycle that fuses continents together into a single land mass – or supercontinent – and then forces them apart again. This process has occurred at least three times during Earth's approximately four-billion-year history, with the most recent evidence coming from the splitting up of the single land mass called Pangaea about 200 million years ago. In the distant future, the Earth's continents could 'look very much like Pangaea,' says researcher João Duarte, a geoscientist at the University of Monash in Australia.

The recently discovered subduction zone is located in the Atlantic Ocean about 200 kilometres off the southwest coast of Portugal. It is made up of six distinct segments that together span a distance of about 300 kilometres. The subduction zone is actually a newly formed crack in the Eurasian plate, which is one of the main tectonic plates making up the Earth's crust. The Eurasian plate contains all of Europe and most of Asia. In this case, 'the Eurasian plate is breaking in two,' says Duarte.

Scientists have long suspected that a new subduction zone was forming near the western margin of the Eurasian plate, off the coast of Portugal. Part of the reason is that the region has been the site of significant earthquakes. Over the past 20 years, several scientific teams from different countries have been mapping the region's seafloor. As part of his research project while at the University of Lisbon, Duarte gathered together the data from these different mapping projects and combined them to create a new tectonic map of the seafloor off the coast of Portugal. This provided the first conclusive indication that the ocean floor off the coast of Iberia is indeed beginning to fracture, and that a new subduction zone is starting to form. 'It is not a fully developed subduction, but an embryonic one,' says Duarte.

The evidence collected by Duarte's team suggests that the Eurasian plate could eventually split into separate oceanic and continental sections. If this happens, the oceanic section – which is made of denser rock – will dive beneath the continental section, causing the Atlantic Ocean to shrink and pulling North America and western Europe closer together. Other studies have indicated that geologic activity in the region could also pull Africa and Europe together, causing the Mediterranean Sea to vanish. 'Eventually North America and Europe will be together again, and the collision will give origin to new mountain chains,' says Duarte.

Questions 1–8

Answer the questions below.

*Choose **NO MORE THAN THREE WORDS** from the passage for each answer.*

1 What term describes the situation in which a single land mass exists on Earth?
2 How long has it been since the last single land mass existed?
3 What is the size of the area affected by the new subduction zone?
4 What happened to make scientists think that the new subduction zone existed?
5 What name is used for the type of image Duarte produced of the region's seabed?
6 Which word does Duarte use to indicate the new subduction zone's stage of development?
7 According to Duarte, which section of the Eurasian plate is likely to move?
8 According to researchers, what might disappear as a result of the new subduction zone?

C Tips and tactics

3 Work in pairs. Read the tips and tactics and discuss these questions.

   a Which tips and tactics do you think are the most useful?
   b Did you use any of these tips and tactics when you answered the sample questions in Section B?
   c Which tips will you use in the future?

1 Before you read the passage, look at the questions and think about what you're going to read.
2 Underline the most important words in the questions and think about the type of information you're looking for. For example, are you looking for a name, a number, a specific term or something else?
3 Most of the answers are facts about the topic, so many of the words you need to write are nouns. Check if words are singular or plural in the passage.
4 Read the passage quickly. Remember that the questions follow the order of information in the passage.
5 Then go through the questions one by one. Use the underlined words to help you find the relevant sections of the passage. Read these sections in detail and find the information to answer the question.
6 The word(s) you need to write are in the passage. Don't put the information you read into your own words. Copy the spelling of the words exactly and check it carefully.
7 Don't just write down the first word you find that fits the gap – keep reading and keep thinking about the meaning.
8 Remember, the instructions tell you how many words to write – if you write more, your answer will be marked wrong.
9 Write numbers as figures, e.g. '104' – <u>not</u> as words, e.g. 'one hundred and four'.
10 If you aren't sure of an answer, always write something. No marks are taken off for wrong answers.

Q FOCUS

Understanding the focus of Short Answer Questions

D Skills-building exercises

4 Read the questions and look at the underlined words. What type of information are you looking for to answer each question?

1 <u>Who discovered</u> that white light breaks into component colours?

2 <u>Which part</u> of the <u>human eye</u> is sensitive to colour?

3 <u>How many colours</u> is the human eye able to distinguish?

4 <u>Which colours</u> are dogs unable to perceive?

5 <u>What type</u> of light can bees see that humans can't see?

6 <u>Which animal</u> has the most complicated colour vision?

5 Now underline the other important words in each question in Exercise 4.

6 Work in pairs. Discuss what each question focuses on and what kind of information you would look for in the reading passage. (NB There is no reading passage for these questions.)

Eadweard Muybridge

(1830–1904)

Today we know exactly what features of their physical make-up allow animals to move at speed. Less well-known is the role of motion photography in helping us to understand these features. Before moving images could be captured on film, it was difficult to know exactly how animals' bodies moved at speed. This was because the movements happened too quickly for the human eye to perceive them. An understanding of the processes involved only came in the 1880s with the pioneering work of Eadweard Muybridge (1830–1904), who was a pioneer in the development of early motion photography.

Muybridge was an Englishman who went to the USA at the age of 20 in search of fame and fortune. By 1855, this search had taken him as far as California, which in those days was perceived as the land of opportunity. The region had just seen the rapid development associated with the Gold Rush, which attracted many ambitious young men like Muybridge to the region. San Francisco was at the centre of this boom and Muybridge initially set himself up as a bookseller in the city. He also took up photography, working for a commercial photographer, and soon began to develop a reputation for his images of the local landscape, in particular those of the Yosemite Valley. This led, in 1868, to his appointment to a US government post as Director of Photographic Surveys. As part of his new role, Muybridge travelled to Alaska, which had just become US territory, to produce a photographic record.

The work for which Muybridge is best remembered, however, began in 1872, the year when a racehorse owner, Leland Stanford, asked Muybridge to try and establish whether or not all four of a racehorse's hooves left the ground when it was running. Muybridge rose to the challenge, realising that photography could provide the necessary evidence. But his first efforts, using wet-plate techniques, were not conclusive because the images were not clear enough. As he worked on the problem, however, Muybridge's fascination with the idea of rapid motion photography grew and its further development now became his main work. In his next experiment, he positioned 50 cameras alongside the track before a horserace took place. Through the use of devices called electrically-controlled shutters, Muybridge was able to capture a split-second image from each camera as the horse ran past. His findings answered Stanford's question definitively: all four hooves leave the ground at the same time, as could be seen from the photographic images.

What's more, by projecting the images on to a screen, and showing them one after another at great speed, the horse's actual movements could be recreated. Muybridge's public demonstration of this technique in 1882, using a device called a zoopraxiscope which he also invented, is credited with being the birth of the moving picture industry.

For the remainder of his life, Muybridge concentrated on the further development of the techniques he had developed, and is regarded as having inspired Thomas Edison, who was to invent the cinecamera. Indeed, Muybridge's groundbreaking work paved the way for a new art form, making it just as important as Josheph Niépce's pioneering still photography had been back in 1825.

7 **Read the passage on page 95 and the questions (1–8) below. Put a tick (✓) next to the correct answers. Put a cross (X) next to incorrect answers and write the correct answer.**

1   What historical event had just ended when Muybridge arrived in San Francisco?
The Gold Rush

2   What was Muybridge's first job in San Francisco?
commercial photographer

3   What type of photographs did Muybridge originally become well-known for?
landscape

4   Where did Muybridge serve as a government photographer?
Alaska

5   What method did Muybridge use to take his first photos of moving racehorses?
electrically-controlled shutters

6   What was the purpose of the zoopraxiscope?
projecting the images

7   When was the first moving picture show seen by the public?
in 1872

8   Who was influenced by Muybridge?
Josheph Niépce

8 **Work in pairs. Discuss why you marked some answers incorrect.**

IELTS PRACTICE TASK

Staying cool … naturally

With heatwaves gripping much of the planet every summer, electricity companies worry that they may not be able to generate enough energy to meet demand during the warmest months because air-conditioning systems use a tremendous amount of energy. However, one group of forward-thinking designers believe that they may be able to find the answer by studying the way other creatures function. Through a process known as biomimicry, they aim to use designs inspired by the natural world to address human problems.

The idea is that over billions of years, nature itself has solved many problems which are similar to those that humanity faces today. In natural systems, nothing is wasted, since everything can be used by something else. Human manufacturers, on the other hand, use large inputs of non-renewable energy, produce toxic chemicals as by-products and then ship finished goods across the globe. Nature makes what it needs, where it needs it, using water-based chemistry. The following designs are examples of how this approach might be applied to the issue of air-conditioning:

1 Ventilation inspired by termites

Perhaps the most famous example of biomimicry when it comes to heating and cooling is ventilation inspired by termites. A few years ago, scientists observed that big termite mounds in Africa stay remarkably cool inside, even in blistering heat. The insects accomplish that feat by creating air pockets in strategic places in the mounds they inhabit. This clever design creates a natural ventilation system, driving air through the mound through the process of convection. Architect Mick Pearce and engineering firm Arup borrowed that idea to build the Eastgate Centre, a large office and shopping centre in Zimbabwe that is cooled with the outside air. The system uses only 10% as much energy as conventional air-conditioning.

2 Countercurrent heat exchange inspired by birds

Penguins that live in cold climates have an innovative adaptation that helps them survive in frigid water. The veins and arteries in their feet have a countercurrent configuration, which ends up warming the blood that is closer to the animal's core and cooling the blood at its extremities. By keeping cooler blood closer to the snow and icy water, such birds lose less body heat overall. Heat exchangers in industrial-scale heating and cooling systems use a similar type of principle to maximize efficiency.

3 Moisture absorption inspired by ticks

A system called a liquid desiccant dehumidifier is designed to pull humidity from the air inside a building (traditional air-conditioning also reduces humidity). It uses a liquid salt solution – something similar to the liquid that a parasitic insect called the brown dog tick secretes to absorb water from the air.

4 Efficient fans inspired by whales

In another take on better fan design, a company called WhalePower is developing fan blades that produce greater lift, and therefore move more air, thanks to an idea inspired by the bumpy design of a humpback whale's flipper. WhalePower says its fans move 25% more air than conventional fans while using 20% less energy. The company is also working on more powerful wind turbine blades.

Questions 1–8

Answer the questions below.

*Choose **NO MORE THAN THREE WORDS** from the passage for each answer.*

1   What name is given to the idea of taking ideas from nature to serve human needs?
2   What do industrial processes consume in a wasteful way?
3   What do termites create in order to cool their mounds?
4   In which part of a penguin's body does warmer blood circulate?
5   What mechanism used by air-conditioning units is inspired by penguins?
6   Which creature produces a fluid that can take moisture from the air?
7   Which feature of one species of whale do WhalePower fans copy?
8   How much more effective are WhalePower fans?

Which statement best describes how you feel about Short Answer Questions tasks?

  ☐ I feel confident about doing Short Answer Questions tasks.
  ☐ I did OK, but I still need to do more work on Short Answer Questions tasks.
  ☐ I need more practice with Short Answer Questions tasks. I need to focus on …

▶▶ **For further practice, see the DVD-ROM.**

Collocation

1 Read the information about collocations.

When two or more words go together frequently, it's called a collocation. There are several different types of collocation made from combinations of verbs, nouns, adjectives, etc. Some of the most common types are:

- adverb + adjective: *completely wrong*
- adjective + noun: *a golden opportunity*
- noun + noun: *a bunch of bananas*
- verb + noun: *play the guitar*

Collocation: verb/noun/adjective + preposition

2 Many verbs, nouns and adjectives are frequently followed by certain prepositions. Look at the sentences about the text on page 79. Complete the sentences with the correct preposition.

after	for	into (x 2)	to	with

1 The recipes were **collected** .... a book 1,500 years ago.
2 The book is **named** .... Marcus Gavius Apicius.
3 The foods are familiar. They would not seem **strange** .... us today.
4 They **call** .... ingredients that we don't have today.
5 The book gives us **insight** .... Italian cuisine.
6 The recipes are **identified** .... that region.

Go back to the text on page 79 and check your answers, or use a dictionary.

Collocation: verb + noun

3 There are also verb + noun collocations (*play the guitar*). Match the verbs (1–8) with the nouns in the box to make collocations. Then go back to the text on page 80 to check.

machinery   a match   moves   a program from the Internet   an essay
a game of chess   a chess-playing machine   (chess-playing) computers

1 develop
2 download
3 create
4 play
5 operate
6 write
7 plot
8 win

4 Write your own sentences with these collocations.

1 download from the Internet
2 win/play a game
3 write an essay

5 Look at the verbs. Which weather word do they collocate with? Go back to the text on page 77 and check. Then write your own sentences with the collocations.

1 fall
2 melt
3 freeze

Collocation: adjective + noun

6 **Many adjectives and nouns form collocations too (*a golden opportunity, a lucky break, a bitter argument*). Complete the sentences with an adjective from the box. The noun in bold that follows forms the collocation.**

basic	controlling	developing	direct	distinct	private

1 Burma is a .... **country**.
2 There are public companies and .... **companies**.
3 The government has .... **involvement** in port activities.
4 The majority stock holder has a .... **interest** in the company.
5 This .... **type** of bag is very easy to distinguish from others available.
6 The .... **difference** is the size.

7 **Go back to the text on page 85 and find the collocations in the text. Then choose three or four of these collocations and write your own examples.**

Common IELTS topic: History

Suffixes

8 **Complete the sentences below. Form the words by choosing the correct suffix from the box for the words in brackets.**

-al	-ally	-ion	-ity	-ment

1 The steam engine was perhaps the most significant ....*invention*.... of its time (invent).
2 The most important consideration for the country at that period of its history was economic .... rather than political reform. (develop)
3 The technologies available at the time were not .... friendly, which led to serious air and water pollution. (environment)
4 The country's .... allies offered immediate support after the disaster. (tradition)
5 In some western countries, the idea of expressing your own .... gained popularity among young people during the 1960s. (individual)
6 When the explorer set sail, he had a clear .... from the government regarding what route to take. (instruct)
7 The government adopted a .... economic policy, with a different focus for each part of the country. (region)
8 Some colleagues questioned the .... of our approach, but I believe that our success has proved it was the right course to take. (valid)
9 Most people agree that the .... of so many respected experts was one of the conference's major achievements. (involve)
10 The owner .... asked for a meeting with the finance director. (specific)

Wordbuilding

9 **Complete the sentences using the word in brackets in the correct form. Add a prefix and/or a suffix, and make changes to spelling where necessary.**

1 It seems _unbelievable_ (believe) to us today that ancient structures like the Pyramids were built using the resources that were available at the time.
2 The country's vast supply of natural resources including coal and oil were .... (essence) to its recovery after the economic downturn.
3 The majority of shareholders were opposed to the scheme and their .... (approve) ultimately persuaded the managing director to review it.
4 The .... (create) of the new port was the most important reason for the region's economic development.
5 The growing sense of .... (secure) led to tighter airport security controls.
6 By the end of the century many of the country's older industries had become .... (economy) because consumers were no longer buying these products.
7 People never know when the next bus will come because the timetable is highly .... (regular).
8 Scientists were able to develop new .... (vary) of pest-resistant plants and this had a huge impact on farming.

TASK TYPE 4 Matching Headings

The words in the heading reflect the main ideas in the passage.

Footbridge reflected on a canal surface, Yunnan Province, China

A About the task

1 Read the information about the task type. Then look at a quiz about the task from a website. Choose the correct options to complete the sentences.

The Matching Headings task tests your ability to read and understand the main ideas in a passage. On the question paper, you see a set of headings that report information and ideas from the passage. Your job is to read the passage and decide which of the headings best describes the information and ideas in each paragraph or section of the passage.

Here are the basic rules for the Matching Headings task:

- The list of headings in the box are in random order.
- There are more options in the box than you need to answer all the questions.
- You can use each heading once only.
- The words in the headings summarise the main ideas in the passage, but do not use exactly the same words or phrases.
- You read each paragraph or section of the passage carefully and find the main idea.
- You then decide which of the headings in the box reports that idea exactly and write the correct Roman numeral (e.g. i, ii, iii, iv, etc.) on your answer sheet.

MATCHING HEADINGS
1 You *can* / *cannot* use the headings more than once.
2 You should read the passage *quickly* / *carefully*.
3 There are *more* / *fewer* headings than paragraphs.
4 You are *likely* / *unlikely* to see the words in the headings repeated in the passage.
5 You write a *letter* / *numeral* on the answer sheet.

B Sample questions

2 Read the passage and answer the questions. Use the rules about the task from Section A to help you. Then check your answers. Which questions did you find difficult?

IELTS PRACTICE TASK

Questions 1–5

The Reading Passage has five paragraphs, **A–E**.

*Choose the correct heading for paragraphs **A–E** from the list of headings below.*

*Write the correct number, **i–viii**, next to questions 1–5.*

i	A wrong assumption regarding the qualities of medical gloves	**1** Paragraph **A**	....
ii	Comparison of the qualities of rival brands of medical gloves	**2** Paragraph **B**	....
iii	Main reasons why medical gloves are necessary	**3** Paragraph **C**	....
iv	Health problems arising from the wearing of medical gloves	**4** Paragraph **D**	....
v	Events leading to the development of medical gloves	**5** Paragraph **E**	....
vi	Varieties of medical gloves for specific purposes		
vii	Evidence for the effectiveness of medical gloves		
viii	Resistance to a policy promoting the use of medical gloves		

Medical Gloves

A

Medical gloves are disposable gloves that are worn to help reduce cross-contamination between doctors, nurses and other health professionals and patients during surgery, physical examinations and other medical procedures. When health professionals use gloves, they protect their patients from infection more effectively than if they simply wash their hands or, in the case of surgical teams, scrub up before operations. Likewise, health professionals are protected from being infected by their patients.

B

Not all medical gloves are the same, however. Surgical gloves have more precise sizing than exam gloves, for example, as well as greater sensitivity. They are also less prone to ripping or tearing. Exam gloves are available as either sterile or non-sterile, while surgical gloves are always sterile. Both exam and surgical gloves can be made of natural materials, such as latex, or synthetic materials, such as vinyl, neoprene or nitrile rubber. Surgical gloves can be unpowdered or powdered with cornstarch, which makes them easier to put on the hands. Cornstarch has mostly replaced powders such as talc, which are more likely to cause irritation, but since even cornstarch can impede healing if it gets into tissues during surgery, unpowdered gloves are now becoming more commonly used during surgery. A manufacturing process called chlorination has made unpowdered surgical gloves somewhat easier to slip on.

C

A significant innovation involving medical gloves occurred at Johns Hopkins Hospital in Baltimore, USA in the 1880s. Following the advice of the British physician Joseph Lister, Chief Surgeon W. S. Halsted directed surgeons and surgical nurses to disinfect their hands with carbolic acid to reduce the rate of infection during operations. One of his nurses, Caroline Hampton, was sensitive to the chemical and found it was damaging the skin on her hands, and considered abandoning her career at the hospital. Dr Halsted contacted the Goodyear Tire and Rubber Company, asking if they could make a rubber glove that could be dipped in carbolic acid. That short letter has become known as 'the most important paragraph in the history of surgical literature'. The gloves that Goodyear produced proved to be very satisfactory, and soon all of Dr Halsted's nurses and assistants were required to routinely use sterilized rubber gloves.

D

Strangely enough, Dr Halsted and his fellow surgeons didn't, at first, wear gloves themselves. The wonderfully named Dr Joseph Bloodgood, Halsted's pupil, began using gloves during surgery in 1896. 'Why shouldn't the surgeon use them as well as the nurse?' he asked. In 1899, Bloodgood published a report on over 450 surgeries with a near 100 per cent drop in the infection rate brought about by using gloves. Halsted wrote at the time, 'Why was I so blind not to have perceived the necessity for wearing them all the time?'

E

The first disposable medical gloves came onto the market in the 1960s. These gloves have a range of clinical uses, as well as non-medical uses. Workers in the hospitality industry wear them, as do some janitorial and sanitation workers. Criminals have also been known to wear these gloves while committing their crimes, believing that they will conceal their identities. Ironically, because of the thinness of these gloves, fingerprints may actually pass through the material as glove prints, thus transferring the wearer's prints onto whatever surface is touched or handled.

C Tips and tactics

3 **Work in pairs. Read the tips and tactics and discuss these questions.**

a Which tips and tactics do you think are the most useful?
b Did you use any of these tips and tactics when you answered the sample questions in Section B?
c Which tips will you use in the future?

1 Before you read the passage, read the list of headings and underline the key words.
2 Read the passage quickly to get an idea of the type of information and ideas it contains.
3 Now read each paragraph or section of the passage carefully. Think about the main idea or the main point that the writer is making in each paragraph.
4 After reading each paragraph or section, look at the list of headings and choose the one that best reports the main idea.
5 When you read the passage, you may see some words or phrases that appear in the headings. Be careful. The correct heading for each paragraph uses different words to express the main ideas.
6 Don't use your own knowledge of the subject to help you choose the heading. The headings need to report the ideas in the passage.
7 Quickly read the paragraph or section again to make sure you haven't missed anything.
8 Remember to write only the correct Roman numeral on the answer sheet.
9 Always answer all the questions, even if you're not sure of the answer.

D Skills-building exercises

Q FOCUS

Identifying an appropriate heading for paragraphs in a passage

4 **Read the passage on page 103. Look at these headings. Which of the headings (i or ii) best reflects the content of each paragraph (1–6)?**

1 i What is special about the Rafflesia?
ii Why scientists find the Rafflesia interesting
2 i Unusual features of the Rafflesia
ii Unusual features of the Tetrastigma vine
3 i How to identify the plant
ii How the plant spreads
4 i The conservation status of the plant
ii How the plant should be protected
5 i Threats to the plant from tourism
ii How the plant is regarded
6 i Similarities and differences with the Titan arum
ii Why the Rafflesia's position is being challenged by the Titan arum

5 **Work in pairs. Answer the questions.**

1 Did you and your partner choose the same headings?
2 Discuss why each of the headings you have chosen is correct and the other one is wrong.
3 Compare your ideas with those of another pair.

The world's biggest flower

1

The Rafflesia is not only the world's largest flower – it is also one of the most bizarre. There are several species of Rafflesia that grow in the rainforests of Southeast Asia. The largest is the *Rafflesia arnoldii*, which produces a flower a metre in width and can weigh up to 11 kilograms. This species has been found only on the islands of Sumatra, Borneo and Java in Southeast Asia, in particular in the Malaysian states of Sabah and Sarawak.

2

The Rafflesia lives as a parasite on the *Tetrastigma vine*, which grows only in primary (undisturbed) rainforests. Rafflesia lacks any observable leaves, branches, or even roots, yet is still considered a vascular plant. The plant grows as thread-like strands of tissue completely embedded within the vine that hosts it. Unlike most plants, the Rafflesia has no leaves and no chlorophyll, so it cannot photosynthesize and make its own food. Because it lacks roots, it cannot obtain water and minerals from the ground. All of its water and nutrients come from the Tetrastigma vine.

3

Rafflesia can only be seen when it is ready to reproduce. Then, a tiny bud forms outside the root or stem of its host and develops over a period of a year. The cabbage-like head that develops eventually unfolds, revealing a massive, fleshy, reddish-brown flower. A foul smell of spoiled meat attracts flies and beetles to pollinate the plant. To pollinate successfully, the flies or beetles must visit both the male and female plants, in that order. The fruit produced contain many thousands of hard seeds that are eaten and spread by ground squirrels and tree shrews.

4

It is not known how many individual plants exist; they are rare and hard to spot except when they are in bloom, and the blossom only exists for a few days. However, all species of Rafflesia are classified as threatened or endangered. The remaining primary forests where the Rafflesia live are disappearing. To make matters worse, the flower of the Rafflesia is collected and used as an ingredient in traditional medicines for women to promote their recovery from childbirth.

5

This strange and smelly parasitic plant has attracted eco-tourists eager to see the world's largest flower. Landowners have been urged to preserve the flowers and charge tourists a fee to see them. The flower of *Rafflesia arnoldii* has become an iconic symbol of the Southeast Asian rainforest, and is often used on the covers of tourist brochures to symbolize the rich biodiversity of the region's forests. The flower has also been depicted on Indonesian postage stamps on several occasions.

6

There are some plants with flowering organs bigger than the flower of the Rafflesia. The enormous *Titan arum*, also found in Indonesia, can reach a height of three metres and can weigh an incredible 75 kilograms. Like the Rafflesia, the Titan arum emits an unpleasant, rotting smell to attract pollinators. Technically, however, the Titan arum is not a single flower. It is a cluster of many tiny flowers, called an inflorescence. So the Rafflesia holds the record for the largest individual flower.

Q FOCUS

Choosing between
possible headings
for paragraphs in a
passage

6 **Look at the passage and the list of headings. Choose the best heading (i, ii, iii or iv) for the two paragraphs (A and B).**

A
i   Where the name 'Little Ice Age' came from
ii Scientists' ideas about why the Little Ice Age started are confirmed
iii New evidence may explain why the Little Ice Age didn't last
iv Researchers put forward a new explanation for the Little Ice Age

B
i   How a theory was disproved
ii How evidence supporting a theory was gathered
iii The key role of technology in developing a theory
iv How evidence from the past could help us predict the future

LITTLE ICE AGE

A

For more than a millennium, up to the late Middle Ages, temperate regions of the northern hemisphere enjoyed generally balmy weather. Then it got cooler and a period that climatologists today call the Little Ice Age set in. There has been little scientific consensus about the onset of the Little Ice Age – either its timing or cause. Some experts believe an important factor was a slight reduction in the amount of solar energy reaching Earth.

But an international study, led by scientists from the University of Colorado, Boulder, suggests that the cooling started quite rapidly, with a series of four huge volcanic eruptions between 1275 and 1300. These eruptions blasted vast amounts of sulphates and dust particles into the upper atmosphere, reflecting solar energy back into space for a few years. This led to an expansion of Arctic ice and a related change in Atlantic Ocean currents, which prolonged the cooling for several centuries.

B

'This is the first time anyone has clearly identified the specific onset of the cold times marking the start of the Little Ice Age,' says Gifford Miller, lead author of the study published in *Geophysical Research Letters*. The researchers reached their conclusions by analysing ancient samples of dead plants collected from beneath the margins of what are today receding ice caps on Canada's Baffin Island. They found a cluster of 'kill dates' between 1275 and 1300, showing that the plants were quickly engulfed by expanding ice. Confirmation came from ice cores of Iceland's Langjokull ice cap, which suddenly thickened over the same period. Then computer modelling showed how this cold shock could persist for centuries, even without further volcanic cooling. 'If the climate system is hit again and again by cold conditions over a relatively short period – in this case from volcanic eruptions – there appears to be a cumulative cooling effect,' Miller says.

7 **Work in pairs. Answer the questions.**

1   Discuss why each of the other headings is wrong.
2   Underline the information in the paragraph that helped you decide which was the correct heading.

IELTS PRACTICE TASK

Questions 1–5

The Reading Passage on page 105 has five paragraphs, **A–E**.

*Choose the correct heading for paragraphs **A–E** from the list of headings below.*

*Write the correct number, **i–viii**.*

i	A long-standing mystery is now partially explained
ii	A comparison that confirms a theory
iii	Evidence suggesting a high level of skill
iv	A possible explanation why similar finds haven't been made elsewhere
v	A reason to doubt the claims made for a new discovery
vi	A lack of evidence to show the precise way in which the find was used
vii	Disagreement about the age of some implements
viii	The age of a find is established

1	Paragraph **A**	....
2	Paragraph **B**	....
3	Paragraph **C**	....
4	Paragraph **D**	....
5	Paragraph **E**	....

The World's Oldest Fish Hook

A

Digging in the Jerimalai cave on the Southeast Asian island of East Timor, Professor Sue O'Connor of the Australian National University in Canberra and a team of scientists uncovered over 38,000 fish bones from 2,843 fish – dating back 42,000 years. More significant, though, was the unearthing of fish hooks made from seashells which date back up to 23,000 years, according to radiocarbon dating of the charcoal in the soil surrounding the specimens. The oldest previously known fish hooks are associated with the beginnings of agriculture, which in Southeast Asia was around 5,500 years ago, says O'Connor.

B

The find means early modern humans were sophisticated hunters, using tools to catch their dinner rather than using their hands or spears. The bones were of both inland and deep sea species. 'That these types of fish were being routinely caught 40,000 years ago is extraordinary,' says O'Connor. 'It requires complex technology and shows that early modern humans in Southeast Asia had amazingly advanced maritime skills.' It seems certain that the ancient inhabitants of Jerimalai used sophisticated fishing technology and watercraft to fish in offshore waters. 'They were expert at catching species of fish that are challenging even today, such as tuna.' Capturing such fast-moving fish requires a lot of planning and complex maritime technology, suggesting that early humans developed these abilities earlier than previously thought.

C

Such fish were clearly a primary food source for these people, since there were 'only rats, bats, snakes, lizards and small birds available on land,' according to O'Connor. However, researchers can only speculate about exactly how these ancestral fishermen managed to catch the deep-sea fish. 'It's not clear what method the islanders of Jerimalai used to capture the fish,' O'Connor says.

D

Far older fish bones have been found at sites in southern Africa – those at the Blombos Cave in South Africa, for example, date from 140,000–150,000 years ago – but those bones belonged to freshwater inland species; catching such fish would require less complex technology. The oldest known fishing equipment from that vicinity dates from around 12,000 years ago, but it includes only bone gorges (straight hooks less sophisticated than curved hooks), and was probably used exclusively in rivers, lakes and streams. O'Connor thinks that African coastal sites might have provided more evidence of early maritime technology in Africa, but that these areas may have disappeared owing to a rise in sea levels over time. The Jerimalai site – which was preserved because it perches high up on the edge of an uplifted coastline – provides a 'window into what early modern humans were capable of,' she says.

E

The discovery of these ancient fish hooks has shed new light on one of the great puzzles of human migration: the question of how and when Australia was first colonised. Recent research indicates that the ancestors of the aboriginal people migrated from Africa through Asia about 75,000 years ago, and that they arrived in Australia over 50,000 years ago. 'We have known for a long time that Australians' ancient ancestors must have been able to travel hundreds of kilometres by sea because they reached Australia at least 50,000 years ago,' according to O'Connor. 'When we look at the watercraft that indigenous Australians were using at the time of European contact, however, they are all very simple, like rafts and cones. So how people got here at such an early date has always been puzzling. Fishing skills would have helped early modern humans to cross the ocean to Australia by allowing them to efficiently exploit coastlines and survive on the open sea,' says O'Connor. 'These new finds from the Jerimalai cave go a long way towards solving that puzzle.'

Which statement best describes how you feel about Matching Headings tasks?

☐ I feel confident about doing Matching Headings tasks.

☐ I did OK, but I still need to do more work on Matching Headings tasks.

☐ I need more practice with Matching Headings tasks. I need to focus on …

▶▶ **For further practice, see the DVD-ROM.**

TASK TYPE 5 Matching Information

The statements often tell you the type of information you're looking for.

Dates, apricots and nuts for sale in a market, Marrakesh, Morocco

A About the task

1 **Read the information about the task type. Then look at the notes about the task you read on a blog. There are three mistakes. Can you correct them?**

The Matching Information task tests your ability to read a passage carefully and understand the main ideas as well as detailed information and arguments. On the question paper, you see a set of numbered statements. Your job is to read the passage and find the information and ideas that match the statements.

Here are the basic rules for the Matching Information task:

- The passage is divided into paragraphs and each paragraph has a letter written above it.
- The lettered paragraphs are in the correct order.
- The numbered list of statements is in random order.
- The statements do not use exactly the same words and phrases as the passage, but they do refer to the same information and ideas.
- The statements often tell you the type of information you are looking for, for example. a comparison or a description.
- The answer to each question is the letter that appears above the relevant paragraph.
- Some letters may not be used if those paragraphs include no answers.
- Sometimes a letter may be used more than once because some paragraphs may include more than one answer. (The instructions tell you if this is possible.)
- You decide which of the paragraphs contains the information in each statement.
- You write the correct letter on the answer sheet.

ABOUT THE MATCHING INFORMATION TASK

1   You are only reading to check facts and figures.
2   The paragraphs in the passage are numbered.
3   The numbered statements are in random order.
4   The statements include the same words that you find in the passage.
5   You don't have to use all the letters.
6   You can sometimes use the letters more than once.
7   On the answer sheet, you write one letter for each question.

B Sample questions

2 Read the passage and answer the questions. Use the rules about the task from Section A to help you. Then check your answers. Which questions did you find difficult?

IELTS PRACTICE TASK

Do Animals Laugh?

A

According to a recent study, laughter and joy may not be unique to humans. Ancestral forms of play and laughter existed in other animals long before they did in humans. Jaak Panksepp, a professor of psychobiology at Washington State University and the author of the study, says, 'Human laughter has robust roots in our animal past.'

B

While humans are the only creatures that tell jokes, it's long been suspected that some animals like to laugh. In his 1872 treatise, *The Expression of the Emotions in Man and Animals*, Charles Darwin pointed out that 'very many kinds of monkeys, when pleased, utter a reiterated sound, clearly analogous to our laughter.' In an experiment Panksepp had performed earlier, he found that when chimpanzees play and chase each other, they make noises strikingly like human laughter, and that dogs have a similar response.

C

Panksepp notes that children who are too young to laugh at verbal jokes tend to shriek and laugh during rowdy play. Panksepp found in his recent study that when young rats are playing, they also make sounds – they chirp, although people can't hear them. These chirps are ultrasonic sounds, far too high-pitched for the human ear. Researchers must use special electronic receivers that convert the chirps to sounds that humans can hear. Rats also chirp when they are playfully tickled by researchers. During the course of the experiment, it was discovered that rats are especially ticklish in the area around the back of the neck, which is also the area young rats tend to nip each other during chases and play.

D

According to Panksepp, the chirps resemble our giggles, and are a primitive form of laughter. Rats who have been tickled before seem to bond socially with their human ticklers. The animals seek out specific human hands that had tickled them previously and seek to be tickled more.

E

In studying laughter, scientists have focused mostly on related issues – humour, personality, health benefits, social theory – rather than laughter itself. New research, however, shows that circuits for laughter exist in very ancient regions of the human brain. The capacity to laugh appears early in childhood, as anyone who has tickled a baby knows. As humans have incorporated language into play, we may have developed new connections to parts of our brains that evolved before the cerebral cortex, the outer layer associated with thought and memory. In separate experiments, scientists have scanned subjects' brains with magnetic resonance imaging as they took part in activities that made them laugh. The two types of humour – verbal and non-verbal – lit up different parts of the brain. Non-verbal, physical humour apparently appeals to some of the brain's more 'primitive' parts.

F

Indeed, some scientists say that other mammals, just like humans, are capable of many feelings. 'The recognition by neuroscientists that the brain mechanisms underlying pain, pleasure and fear are the same in humans and other mammals underscores our similarity to other species and is extremely important,' said Tecumseh Fitch, a psychology lecturer at the University of St Andrews in Scotland. Science has traditionally held that humour is exclusively a human trait, and many scientists believe that more research is required before the rats' chirping sounds can be considered real laughter. Panksepp believes that, through a study of laughter in rats, the human sense of humour can be more fully understood.

Questions 1–7

The Reading Passage has six paragraphs, **A–F**.

Which paragraph contains the following information?

*Write the correct letter, **A–F**, next to each statement.*

***NB** You may use any letter more than once.*

1. examples of situations in which different animal species produce a kind of laughter
2. mention of the point in human development when the ability to laugh develops
3. a description of the method used to capture certain noises
4. a reference to earlier research conducted by the author of the new study
5. the idea that humans were not the first species to develop laughter
6. the realisation that one species has a particularly sensitive region of its body
7. the idea that people and animals may share a range of emotional responses

C Tips and tactics

3 Work in pairs. Read the tips and tactics and discuss these questions.

  a **Which tips and tactics do you think are the most useful?**
  b **Did you use any of these tips and tactics when you answered the sample questions in Section B?**
  c **Which tips will you use in the future?**

1 Before you read the passage, read the title and the list of statements and think about what you're going to read.
2 Read the passage quickly to get an idea of the type of information and ideas in each paragraph. Mark any sections that contain the type of information and ideas indicated in the list of statements.
3 Write the number of the statement next to these sections. You probably need to mark more than one section for each statement at this stage.
4 Then read the numbered statements in order, and read the sections you have marked with that number carefully to decide which section contains exactly the information or idea in the statement.
5 Remember that the statements don't use exactly the same words and phrases as you see in the passage.
6 Quickly read the paragraph or section again to make sure you haven't missed anything.
7 When you are sure you have found the correct section, write only the correct letter on the answer sheet.
8 Remember that some sections may contain two answers and some none at all.
9 Always answer all the questions, even if you're not sure of the answer.

D Skills-building exercises

Q FOCUS

Identifying language features in a passage and matching them to words indicating function

4 Look at the list of language functions (1–10) and match each one to the phrase that best introduces that function (A–J).

1	an explanation	A	Research has shown that …
2	an example	B	Unlike others of its type, …
3	a finding	C	To my mind, …
4	a prediction	D	As Dr Smith suggested, …
5	a description	E	There are four stages, the first of which …
6	a personal opinion	F	The reason for this is that …
7	a claim	G	I would like to put forward the idea that …
8	a comparison	H	A similar pattern can be found in …
9	a contrast	I	For instance, when the …
10	a reference	J	There are likely to be considerable …

5 Look at the passage about elephants' teeth on page 109. Look at the underlined sections of the passage. For each section, choose the best match (A, B or C).

1 A detailed information supporting a claim
   B a physical description of an animal
   C a reference to a piece of research

2 A a comparison with other species
   B an explanation of how something works
   C reasons to doubt a theory

3 A a comparison with another species
   B reasons why something happens
   C a reference to a similar process

4 A a worrying prediction
   B mention of a drawback
   C a finding that contradicts a theory

ELEPHANTS' TEETH

In terms of its long-term wellbeing and survival, an elephant's teeth are a vital part of its anatomy. [1] An African elephant consumes around 100 kilograms of vegetation a day. To process that quantity of food, the animal needs to chew constantly. Each tooth is worn down until it is no longer usable, at which point it falls out.

[2] Whereas most animals have two sets of teeth in their lifetime, an elephant gets through six. Each set – one tooth on the top and on the bottom – lasts about three years in a young animal, but up to ten later in life. [3] Unlike human teeth, which sprout from the gum line, elephants' teeth start at the back of the mouth and move forward like a conveyor belt.

It's an effective system until there aren't any teeth left. [4] Elephants that live to an old age – about 70 years in captivity – often succumb to starvation, because they are unable to chew.

Q FOCUS

Identifying information in a passage

6 **Look at the passage below about quinoa. Underline the sections in the passage that contain the following ideas (1–6).**

1 a prediction regarding the future
2 an unfortunate consequence of a development
3 a statement of an aim
4 an example illustrating a point
5 a possible positive result of a development
6 evidence of expanding production

Quinoa

A

Quinoa is a food that has been a staple of South American cuisine for millennia. The grain which people eat is in fact the seed of a plant species that originated around Lake Titicaca in Peru and Bolivia. Since the turn of the century, other cultures have developed a taste for it too, with imports to the US rising from 3 million kilograms per year to 30 million.

B

The growing appetite is affecting South America, however, where farmers are struggling to meet demand, and some urban populations are unable to afford the resultant price increases. To cash in on the crop's popularity, countries on other continents have begun moving from customer to cultivator. There are now quinoa farms in 56 countries, including France, Thailand, Australia and the US. Quinoa is also being grown in Africa, because the UN hopes its high protein content will help to alleviate hunger.

C

The long-term objective is diversity, says Kevin Murphy, a plant breeder at Washington State University. 'There are hundreds of varieties of quinoa, and our goal is to develop the ideal one for each climate.' For now, most retail stores in the US remain stocked with South American quinoa. With continued crop experimentation, though, Murphy adds, it won't be long before locally grown – and less expensive – quinoa becomes an everyday option.

7 **Work in pairs and answer the questions.**

1 Did you and your partner underline the same sections of the passage?
2 Are your answers all the same? Compare your ideas with another pair.

IELTS PRACTICE TASK

Leonardo's lost mural

A

According to historical records, in 1502 Florentine statesman Piero Soderini commissioned the artist Leonardo da Vinci to paint a fresco on the inside wall of the Hall of the Five Hundred – a room named after the 500 members of the Republic of Florence's Grand Council – which now serves as the city hall. The painting, six metres long and three metres tall, was to depict the scene of the knights of the Italian League defeating an army from Milan near the Tuscan town of Anghiari. Da Vinci, it is said, used the opportunity to try out a new oil-painting technique, but it was not very successful, possibly because of the high humidity in the hall. He never completed the mural.

B

In the 1550s, biographer and artist Giorgio Vasari was commissioned to remodel the Hall of the Five Hundred and paint several enormous murals, each four or five metres high. One mural – picturing the same battle – was to be painted over Leonardo's unfinished work, but at least one source describes Vasari as a Leonardo fan who couldn't bring himself to destroy the work.

C

Maurizio Seracini, an art diagnostician at the University of California, San Diego, has spent around 40 years on a quest to find out what happened to da Vinci's painting. He has said, 'I'm convinced it's there.' A break came in the 1970s, when he climbed a scaffold in front of Vasari's painting and spied two words inscribed on a banner one of the knights is carrying: 'cerca trova,' it said, which roughly translates as 'seek and find'. Seracini took it as a clue that rather than doing what had been asked, Vasari had built a false wall in front of da Vinci's work and painted his mural on that surface instead.

D

A team led by Seracini eventually got permission to scan the entire building with high-frequency surface-penetrating radar. The scanning revealed some sort of hollow space directly behind the section of mural where the inscription had been found. To peek behind Vasari's fresco, the team planned to drill 14 strategically located centimetre-wide holes in the work. But an outcry ensued after journalists publicised the project. Some 300 Italian scholars petitioned the mayor of Florence to halt the work. 'But the team was making little boreholes some nine to twelve metres above the ground,' said art historian Martin Kempof of Oxford University, who wasn't involved in the work. 'That kind of damage can be repaired invisibly.'

E

Despite the public protests, in late 2011 Seracini and his team were given permission to continue their work – but not in the 14 spots they'd originally hoped to investigate. To avoid damaging original portions of Vasari's painting, museum curators permitted them to drill only into existing cracks and recently restored spots. This time the researchers struck gold: a hollow space behind 17 centimetres of fresco and brick. They inserted an endoscopic camera into the space and took video footage of rough masonry work as well as spots that appear to have been stroked by a brush. A substance removed from the void was analysed with x-rays, and the results suggested it contained traces of black pigment.

F

Based on the x-ray data, Seracini thinks the black pigment, which is made up of an unusual combination of manganese and iron, is similar to those found in brown glazes of what is probably da Vinci's most famous painting, *La Gioconda* (*Mona Lisa*). That Seracini found components unique to Renaissance painting leads him to call the results 'encouraging evidence', yet he complained that further samples couldn't be collected because he was only permitted to work on the project within a very narrow time period. 'Unless I get hold of a piece of it, and prove that it is real paint, I cannot say anything definite, and that's very frustrating,' he said.

fresco (n) a painting done directly in the wet plaster of a wall; a type of mural

Questions 1–8

The Reading Passage has six paragraphs, **A–F**.

Which paragraph contains the following information?

*Write the correct letter, **A–F**, next to each statement.*

NB *You may use any letter more than once.*

1   a compromise that allowed work to continue
2   a connection that lends weight to a theory
3   a report that suggests great professional respect
4   a restriction that prevented a conclusion from being reached
5   evidence of instructions not being followed
6   a long-term commitment to an investigation
7   an experiment that failed to produce satisfactory results
8   an independent opinion on a contentious issue

Which statement best describes how you feel about Matching Information tasks?

☐   I feel confident about doing Matching Information tasks.
☐   I did OK, but I still need to do more work on Matching Information tasks.
☐   I need more practice with Matching Information tasks. I need to focus on …

▶▶ **For further practice, see the DVD-ROM.**

Read the sections carefully to see if the ideas match precisely.

Family celebrating Chinese Lunar New Year, Vancouver, Canada

A About the task

1 Read the information about the task type. Then look at the list of questions about the task which your friend has emailed to you. Can you answer them?

The Matching Features task tests your ability to read a passage carefully and understand the main ideas as well as detailed information and arguments. There are two different types of Matching Features task. They look slightly different, but they both test the same reading skills in the same way.

Type 1: On the question paper, you see a set of numbered statements. There is also a box containing a set of options – these could be a list of people's names, organisations or any other feature that is found in the passage. Your job is to read the passage and match the information and ideas in the statements to the options.

Here are the basic rules for the Matching Features task (Type 1):

- The list of numbered statements is in random order.
- The statements do not use the same words and phrases as the passage, but they do refer to the same information and ideas.
- The answer to each question is the letter that appears next to the feature in the box.
- You should use all the letters.
- The letters may be used more than once.
- You then decide which of the lettered features in the box each statement refers to.

Type 2: On the question paper, you see a set of numbered features – these could be a list of people's names, organisations or any other feature that is found in the passage. There is also a box containing a number of options. This is also a list of features, for example a list of theories mentioned in the passage. Your job is to read the passage and match the features, for example. the person's name to the theory they are connected with.

Here are the basic rules for the Matching Features task (Type 2):

- The features in the numbered questions are in the same order as they first appear in the text.
- The answer to each question is the letter that appears next to the option in the box.
- You decide which of the lettered options in the box matches each feature in the numbered list.

---

1 Are you only reading to check facts and figures?
2 Are the numbered statements in random order in Type 1?
3 Do the statements in Type 1 include the same words that you find in the passage?
4 Do you have to use all the letters?
5 Can you use the letters more than once?
6 On the answer sheet, do you write one letter for each question?

B Sample questions

2 Read the passage and answer the questions. Use the rules about the task from Section A to help you. Then check your answers. Which questions did you find difficult?

IELTS PRACTICE TASK

Underground railways are an essential part of life in some of the world's largest cities. There are, for example, 275 stations on the London underground and 450 on New York's subway system. Although the Paris metro can only boast 275, it is said that wherever you live in the city, you're never more than 500 metres from a station. In all three cities, the railways move enormous numbers of people around every day, while making little impact on the visual appearance of the cityscape.

Many of the world's most famous underground railways date back to the period around the beginning of the twentieth century. The first metro trains in Paris ran in 1900, while New York's subway dates from 1904. They came into existence as the development of railway building technology coincided with an enormous influx of people into the world's largest cities, part of a general urbanisation associated with both population growth and industrial development. Underground railways facilitated the expansion of cities without placing more strain on their already overcrowded surface transportation systems – a forward-thinking conclusion reached by city leaders in London, whose system was inaugurated some 40 years before developments in Paris and New York. Today, there are more than 160 subway systems around the world that have followed that model.

Tunnelling under a city, however, is easier said than done. In the early days, there was a reliance on manual labour, and it was tough work. Around 8,000 people were involved in the construction of the first lines in New York, while the original tunnelling in London was marked by a high level of both injuries and fatalities. A variety of techniques has since been developed for use in the excavation of tunnels, and each system has its own particular needs and challenges. For example, in Paris, soft mud rather than hard rock is the main headache for tunnelling engineers, whose solution has been to freeze it using calcium chloride so that it can be removed more easily.

In New York City, the subway system is currently in the middle of a massive renovation project that involves boring a number of new tunnels, using what's known as a tunnel-boring machine (TBM). This enormous piece of equipment cuts through the earth beneath the city slowly but safely, and is especially important in New York where the hard bedrock is not far below the surface. This method of construction is very different to those in use when the first underground railways were built.

New tunnels are currently being dug beneath London to reduce overcrowding on a system that already carries in excess of seven million passengers a day. The tunnelling has unearthed archaeological remains of great interest, a factor that held up the construction project. Sometimes, however, archaeology can work in the builders' favour, as in Paris where the metro was able to take advantage of deep quarries which were first excavated by the Ancient Romans.

Whether it's solid rock in New York or ancient remains in Europe, tunnelling is never without its challenges. But the benefits of underground railways certainly outweigh the cost and challenge of building them.

Questions 1–6

Look at the following statements (Questions 1–6) and the list of railway systems below.

*Match each statement with the correct railway system, **A**, **B** or **C**.*

*Write the correct letter, **A**, **B** or **C**, next to each question.*

***NB** You may use any letter more than once.*

1 Construction of tunnels in the city was delayed by unexpected discoveries.
2 The city authorities were pioneers in the development of these railway systems.
3 The city is taking advantage of available technology to update its system.
4 An impressive claim is made regarding the ease of access to the city's system.
5 This system has to deal with the problem of tunnelling in difficult soil conditions.
6 Safety of the workforce was an issue during the initial construction of this system.

> **List of Railway Systems**
> **A** Paris Metro
> **B** New York City Subway
> **C** London Underground

C Tips and tactics

3 **Work in pairs. Read the tips and tactics and discuss these questions.**

a Which tips and tactics do you think are the most useful?
b Did you use any of these tips and tactics when you answered the sample questions in Section B?
c Which tips will you use in the future?

1 Before you read the passage, read the list of statements and features and think about what you're going to read.
2 Read the passage quickly to get an idea of the information and ideas in each paragraph. Underline the names of the features where they occur.
3 Mark any sections that contain the ideas in the statements (Type 1). Write the number of the question next to these sections.
4 You probably need to mark more than one section for each statement or option. This is OK. You can read them again carefully later and choose which one is correct.
5 Now go through the numbered questions one by one and read the sections you have marked with the question number. Look for the underlined features in this section.
6 Read the sections carefully to see if the ideas match precisely.
7 Remember that the statements in Type 1 use different words and phrases from the passage. You are looking for the information and ideas.
8 When you are sure you have found the correct section, write the correct letter on the answer sheet.
9 Quickly read the paragraph or section again to make sure you haven't missed anything.
10 Remember to write only the correct letter on the answer sheet.
11 Always answer all the questions, even if you're not sure.
12 Remember in Type 2, you have two sets of features. You need to underline both sets of features in the passage, and then match them, e.g. the numbered achievements to the lettered names.

D Skills-building exercises

Q FOCUS

Locating the main features in a passage (Type 1)

4 **Read the passage on page 115 and look at the underlined names. For each name, decide which are**

a academics.
b professional writers.
c other people.

5 **Read the passage again and answer the questions.**

According to the writer, which person
1 has a mistaken view of the effects of communications technology?
   A John Humphrys
   B John McWhorter
   C Clare Wood
2 has done research which accounts for the success of social media?
   A John McWhorter
   B Clare Wood
   C Laura Mickes
3 would have approved of recent developments in writing?
   A Tom White
   B George Orwell
   C Jane Austen

6 **Read the passage again and underline all the references to email, texts, blogs and social media. Then answer the questions.**

According to the writer, which form of communication
1 began the changes in writing habits he describes?
2 became commonplace remarkably quickly?
3 has been shown to help young children learn key skills?
4 is characterised by the omission of unnecessary language features?
5 is written in a style that makes it easier to remember the content?
6 allows original ideas to reach a wider audience?

How Communications Technology Has Improved Writing Skills

Day by day, written communications are becoming more like speech, and writing that reads like conversation is a very modern phenomenon. What's more, social media, blogs and emails have hugely improved the way we write, and made it more relevant. I remember the term at school when we were taught to write essays. Most of my classmates just endured it. They'd never written down their extended thoughts before, and were confident they'd never need do it again.

Email kicked off an unprecedented expansion in writing. We're now in the most literate age in history. I remember in 2003 asking Tom White, a fellow journalist, 'What's a blog?' By 2006, the analysis firm NM Incite had identified 36 million blogs worldwide; five years later, there were 173 million. Use of online social media rises every month. In fact, writing is overtaking speech as the most common form of interaction. Ofcom, the UK's communications regulator, says Britons now text absent friends and family more often than they speak to them on the phone or in person.

Pessimists like to call this the death of civilisation: a vision of mute youths exchanging semi-literate messages. John Humphrys, the BBC broadcaster, once dismissed texters as 'vandals' intent on destroying the language. He's wrong. As the linguist John McWhorter points out, pedants have been lamenting the decline of language since at least 63 AD. Clare Wood, development psychologist at Coventry University, says very little research exists to back up claims such as Humphrys'. Her own study of primary school students suggested that texting improved their reading ability. Texters, after all, are constantly practising reading and spelling. Sure, children tend not to punctuate text messages. But most of them grasp that this genre has different rules from, say, school exams. That's a distinction we adults are slowly learning: I've only just begun dropping commas from texts.

But texts, blogs, emails and Facebook posts are infecting other kinds of writing, and mostly for the good. They are making journalism, books and business communications more conversational. Social media offer a pretty good model for how to write. First, the writers mostly keep it short. People on Twitter often omit redundant words which waste space, and use vocabulary which is more succinct. Likewise, bloggers say 'but' instead of 'however', and the writing is usually unpolished, barely edited – but that's its great strength.

A recent study by Laura Mickes and others published in the journal *Memory & Cognition*, found that people were much better at remembering casual writing like Facebook posts than lines from books or journalism. One possible reason: 'The relatively unfiltered and spontaneous production of one person's mind is just the sort of thing that is readily stored in another's mind.' That's probably why Twitter and Facebook are so successful.

The unfiltered productions of people's minds are often banal, but they don't have to be. Nobel prize-winning scientists tweet too. You can express quite thought-provoking new concepts in everyday language, and conversational prose actually improves your chances of being heard and understood. True, other styles are valid too. The novelist Jane Austen wrote beautiful formal prose. But for an average writer with no particular gift, the conversational model works better. The other tip for getting a point across is to tell a human story, as I always want to tell conference speakers who speak in diagrams.

Of course, bad writing still exists. But mostly, social media have done wonders for writing. Back in 1944, the essayist George Orwell lamented the divide between wordy, stilted, written English and much livelier speech. 'Spoken English is full of slang,' he wrote. 'It is abbreviated wherever possible.' His ideal was writing that sounded like speech. It seems that, thanks to modern communications technology, we're getting there at last.

7 **Look at the list of people A–E. Read the passage and underline the names.**

List of People	List of Achievements
A Aristotle	**1** saw the brain as a type of cooling system
B Cajal	**2** drew the first visual representation of the brain
C Golgi	**3** realised all parts of the brain were interconnected
D Lichtman	**4** identified the role of individual brain cells
E Willis	**5** developed computer models of brain cells

8 **Look at the list of achievements 1–5. Read the passage carefully and match each person with his achievement.**

9 **Work in pairs. Answer the questions.**

    a   Did you and your partner underline the same section of the passage?

    b   Are your answers all the same?

    c   Look at the sections where there are two names. How did you know which is correct?

The Science of the Brain

Scientists are learning so much about the brain now that it's easy to forget that for much of history we had no idea at all how it worked or even what it was. In the ancient world, physicians believed that the brain was made of mucus. The Greek philosopher Aristotle looked on it as a refrigerator, taking the heat out of a fiery heart. From his time through to the 17th century, anatomists declared with great authority that our perceptions, emotions, reasoning and actions were all the result of what they called animal spirits – in other words mysterious, unknowable vapours that swirled through cavities in our head and travelled through our bodies.

The scientific revolution in the 17th century began to change that. The British physician Thomas Willis recognized that the tissue of the brain was where our mental world existed. To understand how it worked, he studied the brains of sheep, dogs and other animals, producing an accurate map of the organ, something which hadn't previously been attempted.

It would take another century for researchers to grasp that the brain is an electric organ and that voltage spikes travel through it and out into the body's nervous system. Still, even in the 19th century scientists knew little about the paths those spikes followed. The Italian physician Camillo Golgi argued that the brain was a web – with all of its parts linked together. Building on Golgi's research, the Spanish scientist Santiago Ramón y Cajal tested new ways of staining individual neurons to trace their tangled connections. Cajal recognized what Golgi did not: that each neuron was a distinct cell, separate from every other one, and that signals, triggered by a mix of chemicals, are transmitted to neighbouring neurons.

Jeff Lichtman, a neuroscientist, is the current Ramón y Cajal Professor of Arts and Sciences at Harvard, carrying Cajal's project into the 21st century. Instead of making pen-and-ink drawings of neurons by hand, he and his colleagues are creating extremely detailed three-dimensional images of neurons on screen, revealing their every detail. By looking at the fine structure of individual nerve cells, they may finally get answers to some of the most basic questions about the nature of the brain.

IELTS PRACTICE TASK

Read the passage and answer the questions.

Reading the game

Thirty-five years ago, a hundred tennis-playing children were tested for general athleticism. One girl was rated by the psychologist leading the analysis as 'the perfect tennis talent'. She outperformed her contemporaries at every tennis drill, as well as general motor skills. Her lung capacity suggested that she could have become a European champion at 1,500 metres. The girl's name? Steffi Graf, who went on to win 22 Grand Slams.

I was reminded of Graf's innate sporting talent during a recent conversation with the geneticist and former *Economist* journalist Matt Ridley. We were discussing the common argument that greatness, even genius, is the result of 10,000 hours of dedicated practice. This has been the sales pitch of several widely read books, the subtitles of which include 'The genius in all of us' and 'Greatness isn't born, it's grown'.

If nurture is so dominant and nature such an irrelevance, then an unavoidable question follows: how many people, of all those born in 1756, had the potential, if they were given the right opportunities, to be as good as Mozart? Or in this case, how many women, of all those born in 1969, had the potential to become as good at tennis as Graf? According to the logic that a genius lurks in all of us, the answer must lie somewhere between 'most' and 'many'.

Ridley's answers were a bit different: four Mozarts and about 30 Grafs. There was mischief, of course, in attaching numbers to such hypothetical questions. But his answer rang true.

The surprise here is that the idea of talent finds itself on the ropes, beaten and bruised by those who believe in nurture alone. Acknowledging a role for genes, any role, can feel almost immoral. When I was quizzed by a newspaper about the genetic arguments in my book *Luck*, the interviewer sounded surprised – even though he agreed – that I dared to take on the gene-denial industry. His reticence was understandable. The anti-genes lobby often suggests that it is a short hop from recognising the existence of genetic talent to believing in eugenics. Personally, I'm pretty confident we can distinguish between the two.

The role of innate talent in elite sport, just as it has been written out of the causal narrative, is actually in the ascendant out on the pitch. Consider the example of modern tennis. In the late 1970s and 1980s, tennis was still catching up with the implications of professionalism. John McEnroe enjoyed going for a burger much more than going to the gym. It fell to the underrated Ivan Lendl, a less talented all-round player than his elite rivals, to dedicate his whole life to the pursuit of self-improvement. To protect his joints, Lendl pioneered aerobic training on bikes rather than road running. He even installed an exact replica of the court at Flushing Meadows, home of the US Open, in his own back garden in Connecticut. Less gifted than McEnroe, Lendl relied on being fitter and more prepared. He used nurture, if you like, to make up for a shortfall in nature. And it worked. Lendl overhauled his rivals and spent 270 weeks as the world number one.

One up for nurture. But what if all the top players hire nutritionists, masseurs and specialist coaches? That is what happened within 20 years. The upshot was that for 302 weeks between 2004 and 2009, the world number one was Roger Federer, widely rated the most talented player ever to pick up a racket. This view hardly needs anecdotal support, but if you're sceptical, perhaps you can take his greatest rival's word for it: 'His DNA,' Rafael Nadal says, 'seems perfectly adapted to tennis.'

During the amateur era and the early decades of professionalism, tennis players came in all shapes, sizes and training regimes. So it was possible to gain a significant edge through sheer hard work. But when a sport becomes fully professional and global, and nurture equilibrates, nature once again has the upper hand.

The **Grand Slam** *tournaments are the four most important international tennis events, including Wimbledon and the US Open.*

Questions 1–6

Look at the following statements (Questions 1–6) and the list of tennis players below.

*Match each statement with the correct player, **A**, **B**, **C**, **D** or **E**.*

*Write the correct letter, **A**, **B**, **C**, **D** or **E**, next to each question.*

NB *You may use any letter more than once.*

1	This player's level of achievement was successfully predicted.
2	This player's innate ability was not matched by a commitment to training.
3	This player was responsible for innovations in training procedures.
4	This player's level of success would seem to support the idea that talent can be developed through training.
5	This player has acknowledged the superior talent of a rival.
6	This player's achievements support Epstein's view regarding the innate nature of talent.

List of Tennis Players
A Roger Federer
B Steffi Graf
C Ivan Lendl
D John McEnroe
E Rafael Nadal

Which statement best describes how you feel about Matching Features tasks?

☐ I feel confident about doing Matching Features tasks.
☐ I did OK, but I still need to do more work on Matching Features tasks.
☐ I need more practice with Matching Features tasks. I need to focus on …

▶▶ **For further practice, see the DVD-ROM.**

Prefixes and suffixes

1 Read the information about prefixes and suffixes.

There are different prefixes and suffixes in English that, when added to words, change their meaning or word class. Prefixes go at the start of a word and change its meaning. Suffixes go at the end of a word and change its word class. For example:

- the prefix *un-* gives the word an opposite meaning: *fashionable*/**un***fashionable*
- the suffix *-able* changes a noun to an adjective: *fashion*/*fashion***able**

In the IELTS exam, particularly the reading paper, you will certainly come across vocabulary that you do not know. Using your knowledge of prefixes and suffixes can be a useful tool in helping you to understand the likely meaning of unknown words.

Suffixes

2 Look at the words (1–7). Match the words with the correct suffix from the box.

| -able | -al | -ion | -er | -ity | -ly | -ion | -ness |

strange + -ly   strangely

1	dispose	5	strange
2	sensitive	6	thin
3	easy	7	clinic
4	irritate		

3 Go back to the text on page 101 and check your answers. Highlight the words in the text. Then identify the word class in each case.

strange (adjective) – strangely (adverb)

Negative prefixes

4 Read the information about negative prefixes.

One of the most common uses of a prefix is to change a word to its opposite meaning. There are a number of prefix forms used to make a word negative. These include: *in-, un-, im-* and *non-*.

5 Look at the following words and negative prefixes. Some of the words come from the text on page 101. Match the prefixes with the words.

| il- | im- (x 2) | in- | non- (x 2) | un- |

sterile – non-sterile

1	probable	5	appropriate
2	powdered	6	legal
3	medical	7	modest
4	sterile		

6 Use the examples in Exercise 5 to complete the general rules.

1 The prefix *im-* is often used before words starting with the letters … and …
2 The prefix *il-* is often used before words starting with the letter …

Synonyms and paraphrases

7 **Read the information about synonyms.**

A synonym is a word or phrase with the same meaning. Sometimes the difference is in formality. A paraphrase is when a word or phrase is expressed in a different way. There are many synonyms! In the IELTS test, questions often require you to know a number of synonyms or to recognise a phrase that expresses a similar meaning, e.g. *very good / excellent.*

8 **Complete the sentences (1–7). Choose the correct synonym or word with a similar meaning from the box which matches the word in bold.**

> bizarre   depicted   endangered   foul   lack   ~~largest~~   rare

1 The **biggest** flower is found in Sarawak, in Malaysia. It is the <u>largest</u> species of its kind.
2 The flowers are **strange**. They are ....
3 The flowers **have no** leaves. They .... leaves.
4 They emit an extremely **unpleasant** smell. They emit a .... smell.
5 The flowers are **very uncommon**. They are ....
6 They are **threatened**. They are ....
7 They are often **shown** on tourist brochures. They are often .... on tourist brochures.

Go back to the text on page 103 and check the meaning of the words in context or use a dictionary.

Antonyms

9 **Read the information about antonyms.**

An antonym is a word or phrase with the opposite meaning. Recognising antonyms is useful in the IELTS test, particularly when answering reading and listening questions. Words may have different antonyms, depending on the context.

*very **good** / very **bad***
*a **mature** cheese / a **mild** cheese*
*a **mature** person / an **immature** person*

10 **Look at the words in column A, which come from the text on page 104, and match them with their opposite meaning in column B.**

A		B	
1	balmy	a	increase
2	consensus	b	gradually
3	onset	c	conclusion
4	reduction	d	cool
5	rapid	e	disagreement
6	suddenly	f	slow

Dependent prepositions

11 **Read the information about dependent prepositions.**

Certain prepositions must be used according to the verbs or nouns they follow. In the IELTS exam, it's important to recognise and use the correct prepositions. Try to memorise the correct prepositions in combination with the words they follow.
- verb + preposition: *It depends on the weather.*
- noun + preposition: *He's a friend of mine.*

12 **Read the summary of the text on page 105 below. Complete the summary text with the correct preposition. Underline the verb or noun that the preposition depends on.**

about	at	of (x 3)	on	~~to~~

This text <u>refers</u> **1** ....to.... research in Australia. According to the researchers, early modern humans were sophisticated hunters. It is not known what method **2** .... hunting they used. Researchers can speculate **3** .... methods but they have no evidence. It seems the hunters were experts **4** .... catching fish such as tuna, which are hard to catch even today. The bones found show hunters were capable **5** .... catching these fish much earlier than previously thought. This evidence sheds new light **6** .... the puzzle of how Australia was first colonised. Other evidence has been destroyed as a consequence **7** .... rises in the sea level.

13 **Write your own sentences using the following expressions.**

1 shed light on   2 be an expert at   3 refer to

Wordbuilding

14 **Read the information about wordbuilding.**

Recognising the grammatical form of words can help you in many aspects of the IELTS test. Using prefixes and suffixes as well as organising words into families is helpful. When recording new words in your notebook, include the word class (noun, verb, etc.) and any special features.

15 **Look at the mind map with words to do with happiness. Complete the sentences with words from the mind map.**

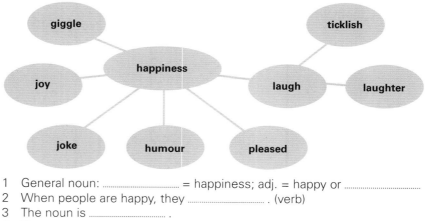

1 General noun: .... = happiness; adj. = happy or ....
2 When people are happy, they .... (verb)
3 The noun is ....
4 To .... is to laugh in a childish way. (also a noun)
5 People laugh when you tell them a .... (also a verb – to make ....s).
6 The abstract noun is ....(to have a sense of ....)
7 If people also laugh when you tickle them, we say they are .... (adj)

16 The mind map in Exercise 15 is about 'happiness'. Try and create your own word diagram for words about 'sadness'.

Common IELTS topic: Industry and technology
Collocation: adjective + preposition

17 Choose the correct prepositions to complete the sentences.

at	by	for	from	of	to	with

1 Older cars can be prone .... rust, especially if they are not kept in a garage.
2 The factory is capable .... producing over 10,000 components a day.
3 The use of solar power is beneficial .... the environment and saves on electricity bills.
4 Not all software will be compatible .... older hardware.
5 Japan is known .... its innovation in the field of robot design.
6 This earthquake-proof building is typical .... the ones being constructed all over the city.
7 The gadget is sensitive .... a person's eye movements, and can track what they are reading.
8 Our team is responsible .... checking the durability of the products.

Collocation: verb + noun

18 Match the verbs and the nouns that they collocate with.

conclusion	hold	implement	maintain	meet	perform	place	solve

1 Rogers and Black still .... the record for the longest time spent in zero gravity.
2 Researchers have yet to reach a .... about the reason for the programme failure.
3 The manufacturers are working hard to .... the demand for the product.
4 The question is how can governments .... their carbon-reducing policies?
5 More funding is required to .... the same experiment in different environments.
6 Both Simpson and Mallory .... the view that science should be compulsory in high school.
7 The high demand for new buildings will .... even more strain on the construction industry.
8 What is causing the machine to malfunction? We need to .... the puzzle before it affects profits.

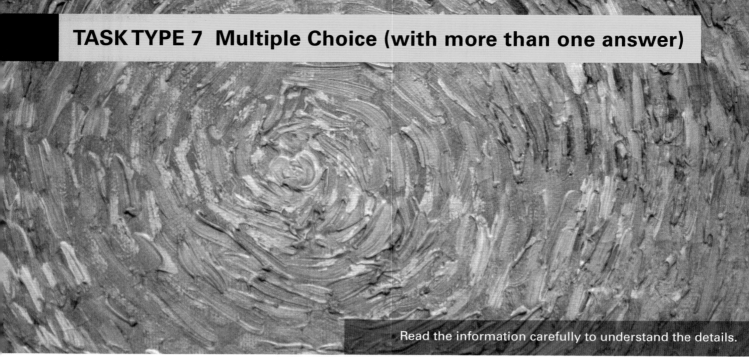

Read the information carefully to understand the details.

Brushwork in *Road with Cypress and Star* by Vincent van Gogh

A About the task

1 Read the information about the task type. Then look at a quiz you have been given to do. Choose the correct options to complete the sentences.

The Multiple Choice (with more than one answer) task tests your ability to find information in a reading passage, and then to read it carefully to understand the details. It's often used to test your understanding of a factual passage about a specific subject. On the question paper, you see a question with a set of five statements that refer to the information and ideas in the passage. Your job is to read the passage and decide which of the five statements matches the information and ideas in the passage. For each question, there are two correct options and three incorrect options.

Here are the basic rules for this type of Multiple Choice task:

- There are two or three sets of statements (A–E).
- Each set contains two correct answers and three wrong answers.
- The statements in each set follow the order of information in the passage.
- All five statements refer to information in the passage, but only two of them match the exact meaning of the passage.
- The wording of the correct statements is not exactly the same as the wording of the passage, but they contain the same information.
- When you read the statements, you see some words and ideas that are also used in the passage. These help you to find the information.
- You write the letters of the correct statements on the answer sheet.

Multiple Choice QUIZ

1 You have to choose *two* / *three* of the five options in each set.

2 The statements in each set are in *random order* / *the same order* as the information in the passage.

3 The wrong statements refer to information you *can* / *cannot* find in the passage.

4 You are *likely* / *unlikely* to see the words in the statements repeated in the passage.

5 You write a *letter* / *numeral* on the answer sheet.

B Sample questions

2 Read the passage and answer the questions. Use the rules about the task from Section A to help you. Then check your answers. Which questions did you find difficult?

IELTS PRACTICE TASK

The Perfect Protein

There may be a profound way for the oceans to forgive our ecological mistakes: by providing us with lots of food. That's the premise of a recently published book, *The Perfect Protein*, by Andy Sharpless, the head of Oceana, a non-profit conservation organization. Sharpless says that there's a lot of unused potential protein swimming in the ocean. Fish are 'the healthiest, cheapest, and most environmentally friendly source of animal protein.' If we manage the way fish are caught, and choose wisely which fish we eat, there should be plenty of food for the growing number of mouths on the planet. Larger species, however, like Atlantic cod and bluefin tuna, aren't thriving because overfishing has devastated their populations. Although numerous international conferences have been held to urge countries to reduce fishing levels and allow fish stocks to regenerate, little progress has been made.

Andy Sharpless tries to get above the country-to-country debate to make a simple point: countries don't necessarily have to agree. Most of the world's edible fish aren't found in the deep seas. They're within the shallower waters 320 kilometres off coastlines, areas generally controlled by a single national government. If about 25 countries with long shorelines set limits on fishing within these areas, there would be plenty of fish to go around.

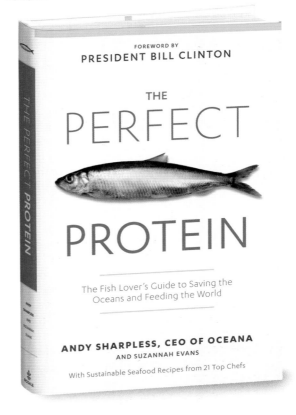

FOREWORD BY
PRESIDENT BILL CLINTON

THE
PERFECT
PROTEIN

The Fish Lover's Guide to Saving the Oceans and Feeding the World

ANDY SHARPLESS, CEO OF OCEANA
AND SUZANNAH EVANS

With Sustainable Seafood Recipes from 21 Top Chefs

More and more of the fish available as food today is farmed – the result of aquaculture. When assessing the benefits, Sharpless says it depends on what kind of fish is being bred. Fish farmers take small, highly nutritious, fast-growing species such as anchovies, mackerel and sardines and feed them to more popular – and profitable – species such as salmon. A farmed salmon can consume as much as two kilograms of small fish in order to produce about half a kilogram of protein. Aquaculture should, in Sharpless' view, add protein to the planet, not reduce it. For example, farmed shellfish such as oysters, mussels and clams, which eat algae, don't compete with people for food. Smaller fish also contain fewer harmful pollutants such as mercury, and also contain high levels of healthy Omega-3 acids.

If feeding more people around the world is the goal – and how could it not be? – changing people's tastes so that they eat more of these species and fewer of the big ones could result in much more edible protein in the human food supply. To this end, Sharpless includes recipes from celebrity chefs like Mario Batali and José Andres in his book. Whether you can get excited about sardine tartare or sautéed mackerel is a matter of taste, but the argument seems sound.

Questions 1 and 2

*Choose **TWO** letters, **A–E**.*

Which **TWO** of these points about Andy Sharpless' book does the reviewer make?

A Sharpless believes that fish should be used more as food.
B Bluefin tuna are being protected by new regulations.
C Sharpless favours stronger regulations in international waters.
D Sharpless regards the fishing of salmon as a waste of resources.
E Sharpless is keen to restrict the farming of shellfish.

1 ....
2 ....

C Tips and tactics

3 Work in pairs. Read the tips and tactics and discuss these questions.

   a Which tips and tactics do you think are the most useful?
   b Did you use any of these tips and tactics when you answered the sample questions in Section B?
   c Which tips will you use in the future?

   1 Before you read the passage, read the five statements in the questions and underline the main words and ideas.
   2 Use the words and ideas you've underlined to help you find the relevant sections of the passage.
   3 Read the passage quickly and mark the relevant sections for each question. Write the question numbers in the margin so that you can find the sections again easily.
   4 The statements in each set follow the order of information in the passage. When you read the passage, you may see some words or ideas from the statements. These help you to find the relevant sections.
   5 Go through the statements one by one. Read the section of the passage you have marked carefully to make sure you are in the correct place.
   6 For each statement, decide if the wording of the statement expresses exactly the same ideas that are in the passage or not.
   7 There are two correct answers in each set. However, you should check all the statements carefully to make sure you have the right ones. Find reasons why the incorrect statements are wrong.
   8 Don't use your own knowledge of the subject to decide the answers. Use ONLY the information in the passage.
   9 Remember to write the correct letters on the answer sheet.
   10 Always write two letters. If you're not sure, always give an answer.

D Skills-building exercises

Q FOCUS

Deciding if sentences match the information in the text

4 Read the pairs of statements (1–3). Underline the important words and ideas in each statement.

   1 A BMI is widely used in medical studies to decide if a person is underweight.
     B BMI is widely respected as a reliable method of deciding if a person is overweight.
   2 A BMI provides information about the total level of fat in a person's body.
     B BMI gives no information about the distribution of fat in a person's body.
   3 A BMI provides a numerical measure of obesity in adults.
     B BMI provides an unreliable measure of obesity in children.

5 Read the passage below quickly. Mark the sections that contain the information relevant to each pair of statements in Exercise 4.

6 Go through the statements in Exercise 4 one by one. Read the passage carefully and decide which statement (A or B) best matches the information in the text and which does not.

BMI

Body mass index (BMI) is often used as a way of establishing whether a person's weight should be regarded as normal or not, and it is used to categorize individuals as underweight or overweight. But there are doubts as to its reliability and questions about how good a measure it is of good or bad health. Although it is common for medical studies to use BMI, it's acknowledged that it may not be particularly accurate. One reason for this is that BMI neither measures fat, nor gives any information about where fat might be located in the body. The importance of this should not be underestimated because if, for example, fat is located near vital organs, then there is an increased risk of heart disease and conditions such as diabetes. Peripheral fat, which is found in other parts of the body, poses much less of a threat.

To find an adult's BMI it is necessary to do a simple calculation. You take the individual's weight in kilograms and divide this by their height in metres, squared. A BMI reading under 18.5 is deemed underweight, 18.6 to 24.9 normal, while 25 to 29.9 is regarded as overweight, and the term obese is applied to people with readings over 30. A similar principle is applied to obtaining a BMI for children, but different values are used.

Q FOCUS

Recognising
why sentences
don't match the
information in the
text

7 Read the statements (1–5). Underline the important words and ideas in each statement.

1 BMI was developed by a physician from Belgium.
2 Quetelet's main aim was to define what represented an obese person.
3 BMI takes into account the differences in weight between body fat and muscle.
4 BMI has been shown to vary in people from different ethnic backgrounds.
5 Trefethen thinks that Quetelet's formula is most accurate when used with taller people.

8 Read the first two paragraphs of the passage below quickly. Mark the sections that contain the information relevant to each of the statements (1–5) in Exercise 7.

9 Look at the statements in Exercise 7 again. Read the first two paragraphs carefully. Decide which words in each statement make it different from the meaning of the passage.

BMI was developed in 1832, at a time when much less was known about human health, and was the work of neither a physician nor a biologist, but of a Belgian statistician named Adolphe Quetelet. He devised the equation as part of his quest to define the 'normal person' in terms of everything from average arm strength to the age of marriage, a project which had nothing to do with obesity-related diseases.

Another reservation about the use of BMI is that it doesn't distinguish between body fat and muscle mass, which weighs more than fat. Many powerful athletes could be considered 'obese' because of their high BMI, when they actually have a low percentage of body fat. On the other hand, elderly people may have a low BMI because they have lost height and their muscle mass has deteriorated with age. In some cases, a low BMI may result from illness. BMI does not take into consideration other physical factors, such as bone density or the size of a person's frame, and doesn't consider ethnic differences. Nick Trefethen, Professor of Numerical Analysis at Oxford University Mathematical Institute in the UK, believes that the Quetelet formula divides the weight by too much in short people and by too little in tall individuals, with the result that short people tend to appear underweight and tall people overweight.

Because the BMI is expressed as a number between 1 and 100 and derives from a mathematical formula, it carries an air of scientific authority. The use of precise measurements suggests that there are distinct categories: underweight, normal, overweight, and obese, with sharp boundaries between them. According to Dr Rexford Ahima, a medical professor, however, there's no single number that can represent a healthy weight, as that depends on too many factors.

Since the early 20th century, studies have linked obesity and health problems. Many studies have shown that people with a BMI higher than 30 are at increased risk of diseases such as diabetes, cancer, etc. But in the last few years, studies have suggested that in some cases, a BMI which is slightly higher than normal can actually protect a person from certain types of heart and kidney failure because when someone has a chronic illness, body fat can provide additional energy reserves. Further studies show that a very low BMI – in other words, being severely underweight – can be as dangerous as an extremely high BMI. Scientists need to start looking more closely at the undoubtedly complex relationship between body fat and disease. Ahima asks: 'What is it about being obese that makes one unhealthy? We need to understand the molecular mechanisms.'

This raises the question of why BMI is still so widely used and why physicians continue to recommend it. 'Because it's simple,' says Ahima, and it is also cheap and non-invasive. Trefethen points out that in the 1830s there were no calculators or computers, which probably explains why Quetelet opted for such a simple system. Other methods have their drawbacks as well. Computer tomography, magnetic resonance imaging, and bone densitometry scans can all accurately measure body fat, but they are very expensive. Even accurate waist measurements require slightly more time and training than it takes to record a BMI reading, and they don't come with any official cut-offs that can be used to make easy assessments. All this explains why BMI continues to be the standard.

10 Read the statements (A–E). Underline the important words and ideas in each statement.

A The fact that BMI produces a numerical score leads people to assume that it is accurate.
B A link between a high BMI and certain diseases has never been clearly established.
C Some benefits of having a high BMI have recently been recognised by researchers.
D Ahima and Trefethen predict that more up-to-date methods will soon replace BMI.
E BMI remains widely used because it is quick and inexpensive to administer.

11 Read the last three paragraphs of the passage quickly. Mark the sections that contain the information relevant to the statements (A–E) in Exercise 10.

12 Go through the statements in Exercise 10 again. Read the last three paragraphs carefully and decide which TWO statements match the information in the text.

IELTS PRACTICE TASK

Our Vanishing Night

If humans were nocturnal creatures, the night-time world would be as visible to us as it is to the vast number of nocturnal animals on this planet. The light of the stars and moon would supply all the light that was needed. But humans are a diurnal species, with eyes adapted to the sunlight. In order to extend human activity into the hours of darkness, humans have created artificial light.

As with all kinds of human intervention in the natural environment, there are environmental consequences – what is often called light pollution. Ill-designed lighting lessens the darkness of night and radically alters the light levels and rhythms to which various animal species, including nocturnal predators, have adapted.

For most of human history, the expression "light pollution" would have meant little to people. Today, nearly all of night-time Europe is a nebula of light, as is most of the United States and all of Japan. In the south Atlantic, the glow from a single fishing fleet – squid fishermen luring their prey with metal halide lamps – can be seen by satellites in space, burning brighter than Buenos Aires or Rio de Janeiro. The sky as seen from most cities looks as though it has been emptied of stars, leaving behind a haze known as "skyglow". People have grown so used to this pervasive orange haze that the original glory of an unlit night is wholly beyond their experience, and professional astronomers have been forced to set up observatories in the few places beyond its reach, such as the Atacama Desert in South America.

Light is a powerful biological force and acts as a magnet to many species and triggers certain types of behaviour. For example, birds are attracted by artificial light, causing them to sing at unnatural hours. Scientists think that artificially long days and short nights may induce early breeding in birds, and while a longer day allows for longer feeding, it can also affect migration schedules. Migration, like most other aspects of bird behaviour, is a precisely timed biological process. Leaving early may mean arriving too soon for the optimum nesting conditions, which may have an effect on breeding rates.

Light pollution doesn't just affect animals – it takes a biological toll on people as well: sleep deprivation, increased incidence of headaches, fatigue, stress and anxiety have all been attributed to light pollution by researchers. At least one recent study has suggested a correlation between higher rates of certain types of cancer and the night-time brightness of residential areas.

Light pollution, however, is perhaps the most easily remedied of all the man-made pollutants that affect the natural world. Simple changes in lighting design yield immediate changes in the amount of light spilt into the atmosphere and often represent energy savings. What's more, this can be achieved by using inexpensive technology which is already available. For example, wasteful mercury lamps can be replaced with LED, sodium or halide lamps. Timers and sensors can turn off artificial lighting when it is not needed. Illuminated outdoor advertising, for example, doesn't have to operate all night. Meanwhile, well-designed streetlamps can encase bulbs from above and to the side, channeling light where it is needed. Known as "cutting off light at the horizontal", this ensures that light is used to illuminate the ground, not the sky.

In the end, humans are trapped by light. We have cut ourselves off from the light of the stars and the rhythms of day and night. Light pollution causes us to lose sight of our place in the universe, to forget the scale of our being, which is best measured against the dimensions of a deep night with the Milky Way arching overhead.

Questions 1 and 2

The list below gives some effects of light pollution.

Which **TWO** of these are mentioned by the writer?

A   Light pollution has a negative effect on fishing activities.
B   Light pollution obscures people's view of man-made objects in the night sky.
C   What is called 'skyglow' now affects all parts of the world to some extent.
D   Light pollution has affected the reproductive success of certain bird species.
E   There is growing evidence to suggest light pollution affects human health.
1   ....
2   ....

Questions 3 and 4

Which **TWO** of these points related to remedies for light pollution does the writer make?

A   It takes time for the benefits of new types of lighting to be felt.
B   New types of lighting can save money as well as reducing light pollution.
C   New types of lighting can be expensive to install.
D   Automated systems can be programmed to reduce light pollution.
E   Street lighting can easily be redesigned to use less electricity.
3   ....
4   ....

Which statement best describes how you feel about these Multiple Choice tasks?

☐   I feel confident about doing these Multiple Choice tasks.
☐   I did OK, but I still need to do more work on these Multiple Choice tasks.
☐   I need more practice with these Multiple Choice tasks. I need to focus on …

▶▶ **For further practice, see the DVD-ROM.**

TASK TYPE 8 Sentence Completion

The Sentence Completion task tests your ability to locate and record specific information.

A About the task

1 **Read the information about the task type. Then look at a quiz you found on a website. Choose the correct options to complete the sentences.**

The Sentence Completion task tests your ability to locate and record specific information from a reading passage. It's often used to test your understanding of a factual passage about a specific subject. You usually read facts about a subject, and you may be asked to write words or numbers to complete sentences. Some of the information from the passage is already written on the question paper. Your job is to read the passage and find information to complete the gaps. On the question paper, you see a set of sentences that report the information from the passage. In each sentence, one, two or three key words are missing. You read the passage and write the missing words in the gap.

Here are the basic rules for the Sentence Completion task:

■ The sentences follow the order of information in the passage.
■ The instructions tell you how many words to write in each gap.
■ The wording of the sentences in the questions is not exactly the same as the wording in the passage, but they contain the same information.
■ When you read the passage, you see the words that you need to write.
■ You write the words in the same form as you see them in the passage (e.g. singular/plural) – you don't need to change them in any way.
■ Spelling counts! The words you write must be spelled correctly.

It's especially important to read through the sentences before you read the passage, and think about the type of information you're looking for. In the passage, you see different words that could fit logically into each gap. You have to read carefully to choose the correct information, so that the sentence reports the meaning of the passage exactly.

How well do you know IELTS?
SENTENCE COMPLETION TASKS

1 You are mostly reading for *facts and figures / ideas and opinions.*
2 The questions are in *random order / the same order as the information in the passage.*
3 You always have to write *two words / the number of words indicated in the instructions.*
4 You have to use *words from the passage / your own words* to fill the gaps.
5 You have to *find words which already fit / change the words you find so that they fit* the grammar of the sentence.
6 Correct spelling is *not important / important.*

B Sample questions

2 Read the passage and answer the questions. Use the rules about the task from Section A to help you. Then check your answers. Which questions did you find difficult?

IELTS PRACTICE TASK

First Publication of Newton's Principles

You have probably never heard of the book entitled *History of Fish*, even though it played quite a key role in the history of scientific thought. The book, written by John Ray and Francis Willughby, was in fact an impressive collection of wood engravings, depicting various types of marine creatures, with an accompanying text. It was first published in 1686 by the Royal Society in London, the world's oldest scientific academy, and was justly recognised as a seminal work in the study of natural history. The heavy cost involved in producing such a lavish work, however, meant committing a large portion of the Society's funds to it. When, therefore, the book failed to sell quite as many copies as predicted, the Society found itself in financial difficulties. Almost bankrupt, it was obliged to withdraw an offer to publish Sir Isaac Newton's masterpiece *Mathematical Principles of Natural Philosophy*.

But luck was on Newton's side. One of his earlier publications, *Law of Universal Gravitation* (1684) was much admired by a man called Edmond Halley. Halley is chiefly known today for his discovery in 1705 of the famous comet that is named after him. At this time, however, Halley was a humble clerk employed by the Royal Society. On hearing that Newton's latest work was not to be published, he decided to take it on as his personal project. He managed to raise sufficient financial backing to allow the Society to publish it after all in 1687. So near was the Society to bankruptcy that Halley didn't even get paid as an employee that year, receiving instead unsold copies of Ray and Willughby's book to the value of his annual salary.

Featured in Newton's work were his three laws of motion which, together with his law of universal gravitation, explain the orbits of planets. The book is still widely regarded as one of the most significant scientific works by both physicists and mathematicians. It seems odd to us to think that the Royal Society nearly missed the chance to publish it because it was more impressed by a book about fish.

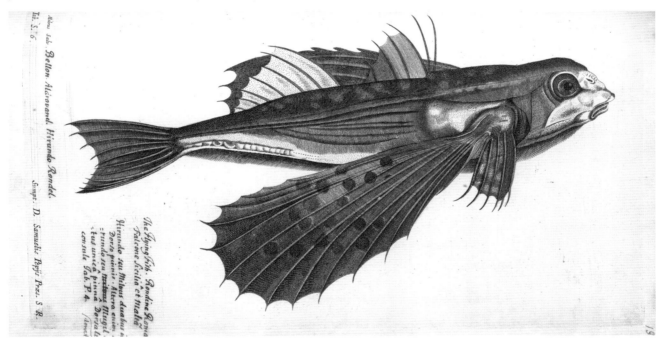

Questions 1–5

Complete the sentences below.

Choose **NO MORE THAN TWO WORDS AND/OR A NUMBER** from the passage for each answer.

1 Ray and Willughby's book featured a type of illustration which are known as ....
2 Ray and Willughby's book was regarded as important in the field of ....
3 The Royal Society was nearly .... as a result of publishing Ray and Willughby's book.
4 At the time the books were published, Halley was working as a .... at the Royal Society.
5 Newton's greatest work was eventually published in the year ....

C Tips and tactics

3 Work in pairs. Read the tips and tactics and discuss these questions.

    a Which tips and tactics do you think are the most useful?
    b Did you use any of these tips and tactics when you answered the sample questions in Section B?
    c Which tips will you use in the future?

1. Before you read the passage, look at the sentences and think about what you're going to read.
2. Think about the type of information that's missing in each sentence. For example, are you looking for a name, a number, a specific term or something else?
3. Look for clues in the sentence that tell you the type of information you're looking for, e.g. 'in the field of …' and 'working as a …'.
4. Sometimes the sentence tells you what to look for, e.g. 'in the year …', but you may see a number of years in the passage. Read carefully to find out which is correct.
5. Most of the missing information is facts about the topic, so the words that you need to write are mostly nouns. Check if the word is singular or plural in the passage.
6. Read the passage quickly. Remember that the sentences follow the order of information in the passage.
7. Then go through the sentences one by one. Read the relevant section of the passage again and find the words to complete the sentences.
8. Remember, the word(s) you need to write are in the passage. Don't put the information you read into your own words.
9. Don't just write down the first word you find that fits the gap – keep reading and keep thinking about the meaning.
10. Remember, the instructions tell you how many words to write – if you write more, your answer will be marked wrong. Most answers are single nouns, e.g. 'clerk', or compound nouns that include two words, e.g. 'wood engravings'.
11. Write numbers as figures, e.g. '104' – <u>not</u> as words, e.g. 'one hundred and four'.
12. If you aren't sure, always write something. No marks are taken off for wrong answers.

D Skills-building exercises

Q FOCUS

Identifying what type of information is missing

4 Read the sentences (1–6). Can you predict the type of information which is missing in each of the gaps? (There is no passage to refer to.)

1. Johnson was working as a .... by the time his original work was published.
2. Johnson's original work was first published in a journal called ....
3. Johnson decided to visit .... in order to do further research.
4. Johnson got funding from a .... to help pay for his further research.
5. Johnson had difficulty with .... during the research project.
6. Johnson's breakthrough came when he began studying .... rather than larger animals.

5 Read the passage on page 131 and make a note of the following information.

1. Three occupations are mentioned in the first paragraph. Write the words here.

    ....

2. 'Cavities' is a plural noun. There are five more plural nouns in the second paragraph. Write the words here.

    ....

3. There are four types of taste mentioned in the article. Which two are mentioned in the paragraph about Hanig's work?

    ....

4. In the paragraph about Boring's work, there are three terms for pictures. Write these terms here.

    ....

6 **Look at the sentences (1–4). Read the passage again carefully and complete the sentences. Use your answers from Exercise 5 to help you. Write *NO MORE THAN TWO WORDS AND/OR A NUMBER* for each answer.**

1 The idea of the four basic tastes had its origin in the work of a ....
2 Close observation of the tongue revealed small cavities that looked like ....
3 Hanig's experiments suggested a link between the front of the tongue and .... tastes.
4 Boring preferred to use the word .... for the picture of the tongue he produced.

THE FOUR BASIC TASTES

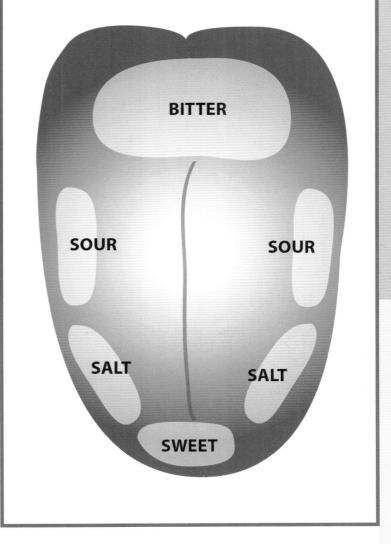

When humans eat, they use all of their five senses – sight, hearing, smell, touch and taste – to form judgments about their food. But as every cook knows, and scientists have long confirmed, it is taste that is most influential. Indeed, it was the Ancient Greek philosopher Democritus who first formulated the notion that people could perceive four primary tastes – sweet, sour, salty and bitter – which couldn't be replicated by mixing together any of the others.

When tongue cells were studied under a microscope in the late 19th century, they appeared to resemble tiny keyholes, and scientists put forward the idea that these cavities came in four different shapes, each corresponding to one of the primary tastes.

Then, in 1901, a German scientist named D.P. Hanig set out to measure the relative sensitivity of the tongue to the four known basic tastes. He concluded that this varied in different parts of the tongue, with sweet sensations peaking in the tip and salty ones more prevalent at the sides.

In 1942, Edwin Boring, a psychologist at Harvard University, took Hanig's raw data and created a visual image, what he termed a map of the tongue, showing which areas were most sensitive to which taste. The concept is easy enough to refute with a home experiment. Place salt on the side of your tongue and you'll taste salt. Place sugar on the other side and you'll taste sweet. But for some unknown reason, scientists never bothered to do this, and Boring's ideas and accompanying diagram continued to be widely accepted.

7 **Read the sentences (1–4). What type of information is missing in each of the gaps?**

1 <u>Escoffier</u> lacked the <u>scientific knowledge</u> to identify the .... of the new taste he had developed.
2 <u>Ikeda</u> first identified the fifth taste in <u>a dish</u> made from .... , which he analysed.
3 <u>Ikeda</u> was also responsible for developing <u>a product</u>, which is <u>widely used</u> as a ....
4 <u>Collings' research</u> showed that there are .... in various <u>parts of the mouth</u>.

8 **Look at the words and phrases that are underlined in the sentences in Exercise 7. Then do the following:**

a Read the passage quickly and underline the names of three people when you see them.
b Read the text around each name and find the underlined idea in each question Remember that the passage may use different words to express these ideas.
c Find the information you need to complete the sentence and write the word or words in the gap. Write *NO MORE THAN TWO WORDS AND/OR A NUMBER* for each answer. Be careful to copy the spelling exactly.

The fifth taste

In fact, taste is more complicated than sweet, sour, salty and bitter, and most scientists today agree that there's a fifth distinct taste. In the late nineteenth century, an influential cookbook entitled *The Guide Culinaire* was published. Its author, a distinguished French chef called Auguste Escoffier, created meals that tasted unique – like no combination of salty, sour, sweet and bitter before achieved. Not being a scientist, however, he wasn't able to analyse the chemical composition of the unique quality he had created.

It was Kikunae Ikeda, a professor at Tokyo Imperial University, who eventually managed to do that in 1908. He had noticed that the flavour of a seaweed soup was quite distinct from the four primary tastes, and went on to discover that various chemical compounds known as glutamates were responsible for its distinct taste. He named this taste *umami*, a Japanese word meaning delicious or yummy. Umami is common in a number of Japanese foods, as well as in mushrooms, cheeses, fish, soy sauce and various cured meats.

The taste of umami itself is subtle and blends well with other tastes to expand and round out flavours. It is also present in monosodium glutamate, a food additive which Ikeda isolated and patented for commercial use. Most people don't recognize umami when they encounter it, but it plays an important role in making various types of food taste good, and monosodium glutamate is still used to flavour many types of processed food today.

In 1974, a scientist named Virginia Collings published findings demonstrating that all tastes can be detected anywhere there are taste receptors – around the tongue, on the soft palate at the back roof of the mouth, and even in the epiglottis, the flap that prevents food from entering the windpipe. In 2002, scientists agreed that humans do have specific receptors in the tongue for umami. Even so, some textbooks continue to print Boring's tongue map and neglect to mention the fifth taste. And so the debate continues.

9 **Work in pairs.**

a Check your answers for Exercise 7. If they are different, try to decide which answer is better.
b Underline the sections of the text that you needed to answer each of the sentence completion questions in the passage.
c Discuss why some words from the passage fit the gaps and others do not.

10 **Look at this student's answers. Why were they marked wrong?**

Exercise 7

1 unique quality
2 seaweed soup
3 food adittive
4 taste receptors in the tongue

IELTS PRACTICE TASK

Predicting Volcanic Eruptions

Predicting a volcanic eruption is hard even in developed countries such as Italy, Iceland and the USA, where there is intensive monitoring to detect movements beneath the surface. But in the developing world the majority of active volcanoes, including some that pose a high risk to large populations, have no local monitoring or warning system.

Help is on the way, however, from the sky. Earth-observing satellites, such as the European Space Agency's Envisat, can detect unrest in unmonitored volcanoes using a technique called Interferometric Synthetic Aperture Radar (InSAR). InSAR is the most revealing way to show slight deformations in the ground due to movements of molten rock below. It works by combining satellite radar images of the same place taken at different times. This is displayed in the form of rainbow-coloured interference patterns, or interferograms as they are known, in which the arrangement of coloured bands shows the direction and extent of ground deformation. InSAR is particularly useful for tropical volcanoes, where cloud cover can obscure visual observations, because the radar beam can see through it.

As a result, many volcanoes previously thought to be dormant are now known to be showing signs of unrest. The resources for acquiring more detailed, ground-based monitoring can now be targeted at such volcanoes. A recent review of InSAR technology in the journal *Science* gave Mount Longonot, Kenya, as an example. Radar data from Envisat showed a nine-centimetre uplift over two years in the volcano, which was previously thought dormant.

While InSAR has enormous potential, it is still a new technique that relies on frequent observations and long-duration space missions. A series of Earth-observing satellites called Sentinel is expected to provide the data continuity required for serious InSAR volcano modelling. Sentinel is expected to observe all land masses regularly, with a six-day cycle in operation for the next two decades.

'InSAR is a growing field,' says Juliet Biggs of Bristol University, co-author of the *Science* paper. 'In the past ten years of my involvement … the community has gone from a small handful of specialists to a wide range of practitioners.'

Of course, early warning of eruptions still faces challenges, as scientists try to work out how to tell whether a period of volcanic unrest will lead to eruption. Unrest usually subsides without an eruption, and false alarms can undermine public trust. But consistent InSAR monitoring will give vulcanologists a clearer picture of potentially threatening behaviour.

Questions 1–8

Complete the sentences below.

Choose **NO MORE THAN THREE WORDS** *from the passage for each answer.*

1 There is relatively little monitoring of most active volcanoes located in ....
2 InSAR techniques can indicate pieces of land where .... may be moving beneath the surface.
3 The term .... is used to describe the coloured patterns produced by InSAR techniques.
4 InSAR can be used in places where .... makes other methods problematic.
5 The type of movement measured at Mount Longonot is described as ....
6 InSAR techniques depend on space flights of .... in order to function.
7 Regular data for InSAR modelling will be provided on a .... by Sentinel.
8 The writer is concerned about the effects of .... on people's attitude towards predicting volcanic activity.

Which statement best describes how you feel about Sentence Completion tasks?

☐ I feel confident about doing Sentence Completion tasks.
☐ I did OK, but I still need to do more work on Sentence Completion tasks.
☐ I need more practice with Sentence Completion tasks. I need to focus on …

▶▶ **For further practice, see the DVD-ROM.**

TASK TYPE 9 Summary Completion (1)

Spelling counts! The words you write must be spelled correctly.

A glyph (ancient symbol) on a Mayan pot

A About the task

1 Read the information about the task type. Then look at some notes about the task you found in a blog. There are three mistakes. Can you correct them?

The Summary Completion task tests your ability to locate and record specific information from a reading passage. It's often used to test your understanding of a factual passage about a specific subject. You usually read facts about a subject, and you may be asked to write words or numbers. On the question paper, you see a short summary on the same subject as the reading passage. The summary usually includes the main points of information from one section of the passage. Your job is to use information from the passage to complete the gaps in the summary.

Here are the basic rules for the Summary Completion task:

- The summary reports the main ideas from the passage, but the information may not be presented in the same order.
- The instructions tell you how many words to write in each gap.
- The wording of the summary isn't exactly the same as the wording in the passage, but it contains the same information.
- When you read the passage, you see the words that you need to write.
- You write the words in the same form as you see them in the passage (e.g. singular/plural) – you don't need to change them in any way.
- You write the missing words or numbers on the answer sheet.
- Spelling counts! The words you write must be spelled correctly.

1	The information in the summary always comes in the same order as the information in the passage.
2	You have to only write one word in each gap.
3	You should copy the words that you find in the passage exactly.
4	Some of the answers could be numbers.
5	Minor spelling mistakes are ignored.

B Sample questions

2 **Read the passage and answer the questions. Use the rules about the task from Section A to help you. Then check your answers. Which questions did you find difficult?**

IELTS PRACTICE TASK

The Effect of the Full Moon on Sleep

There has long been a popular belief that human sleep patterns are affected by the moon. People complain, for example, that they sleep badly, or that their sleep is disturbed, when there is a full moon. Some people put this down to the bright glow that is created in the sky when the moon is full, whilst others look for an explanation in the gravitational pull of the Earth's closest neighbour. A recent study at the University of Basel in Switzerland put these theories to the test.

Christian Cajochen and his colleagues were discussing these beliefs when they suddenly realised they already had data that might give them the answer. In an earlier, unrelated study, conducted between 2000 and 2003, researchers in Basel had collected detailed observations of some thirty men and women of various ages who had slept for three days at various times of the month in the university's sleep lab. The amount of light in this lab is artificially controlled to ensure that anyone sleeping there cannot perceive the changes in light that occur at different times of the night and day.

Cajochen decided to revisit the data collected during the study to see what it might reveal about the effects of the phases of the moon on sleeping patterns. What he found was that when the moon was full, there was a reduction in brain activity related to deep sleep of around thirty per cent. He also found that people were taking five minutes longer to drop off to sleep, and that the overall time spent asleep fell by twenty minutes. It is also recorded that participants reported feeling that they'd slept less well at the time. What's more, they seemed to have reduced levels of melatonin, a hormone known to regulate sleep. It was the first time that a link had been established between lunar cycles and human sleep patterns. The lunar cycle seems to influence human sleep, even when the moon itself cannot be observed.

While conceding that the findings may not be replicated by larger-scale studies, Cajochen says it would be interesting to investigate the idea that there might be what he calls a circalunar clock in the brain, and whether the moon also has power over other aspects of human behaviour, such as cognitive performance and mood.

Questions 1–8

Complete the summary below.

Choose **NO MORE THAN TWO WORDS AND/OR A NUMBER** *from the passage for each answer.*

For a long time it has been commonly believed that people sleep less well when there is a full moon, either because of the light it creates or because of the **1** .... influence that the moon has over the Earth. Christian Cajochen of Basel University has shown that human sleep is affected by the lunar cycle, even when the moon itself cannot be seen. To do this, he studied existing data collected in the university's **2** .... where subjects were kept in **3** .... conditions so that they had no idea if it was light or dark outside. Cajochen knew that certain types of **4** .... are associated with deep sleep, and discovered that this fell by around **5** .... when the moon was full. He also found that the onset of sleep was delayed by as much as **6** .... and that there was a fall in the amount of a hormone called melatonin which is understood to **7** .... sleep patterns in the body. Cajochen is now keen to see if there is such a thing as a **8** .... in the brain and whether the moon affects other aspects of human behaviour.

C Tips and tactics

3 Work in pairs. Read the tips and tactics and discuss these questions.

 a Which tips and tactics do you think are the most useful?
 b Did you use any of these tips and tactics when you answered the sample questions in Section B?
 c Which tips will you use in the future?

1 Before you read the passage, read the summary and underline the main words and ideas.
2 Think about the type of information that's missing in each gap. For example, are you looking for a name, a number, a specific term or something else?
3 The summary usually relates to one section of the passage, but may also report the meaning of the whole passage.
4 Read the passage and find the main words and ideas you underlined in the summary.
5 Then go through the summary, gap by gap, and read the relevant sections of the passage.
6 Look for clues in the summary that tell you the type of information you're looking for. For example, the phrase 'delayed by as much as' indicates that you're looking for a period of time.
7 Sometimes the wording of the summary tells you what to look for, for example 'this fell by around …' , indicates you are looking for a number but you may see various numbers in the passage. Read carefully to know which is correct.
8 Don't just write down the first word you find that fits the gap – keep reading and keep thinking about the meaning.
9 The word(s) you need to write are in the passage. Don't put the information you read into your own words.
10 Remember, the instructions tell you how many words to write – if you write more, your answer will be marked wrong. Most answers are single words, e.g. 'regulate', or short phrases, e.g. 'artificially controlled'.
11 Write numbers as figures, e.g. '104' – <u>not</u> as words, e.g. 'one hundred and four' because this may go over the word limit.
12 If you aren't sure, always write something. No marks are taken off for wrong answers.

Q FOCUS

Identifying the missing information

D Skills-building exercises

4 Read the summary and think about the type of information that is needed to complete each gap. Which gaps are likely to need:

 a a number? **b** a place name? **c** a specific term? **d** a plural noun?

Summary
*Write **NO MORE THAN TWO WORDS AND/OR A NUMBER** in each gap.*

Around 50,000 years ago, Australia was inhabited by as many as **1** .... different giant animal species, which included both mammals and **2** .... For many years, scientists have linked their extinction to the arrival of humans on the continent, who may have started **3** .... and also hunted the animals for food. But recent research suggests that climate change is a more likely explanation.

Evidence suggests that Australia's climate gradually changed into the type known as **4** .... , and a process of **5** .... followed as a result. This process destroyed the natural habitat of the giant animals whose diet consisted mostly of **6** .... Evidence for this change in climate has come from research carried out in **7** .... as well as in Australia itself. It is thought that as **8** .... became less abundant, so did the animals' source of food and these species became increasingly confined to an area in **9** .... Australia. As few as **10** .... of these species are thought to have been in existence by the time the first humans arrived.

5 Underline the main words and ideas in the summary, for example: *humans, climate change, natural habitat, research,* etc.

6 Read the passage on page 137 quickly to get a general idea of its content, and mark the parts where these main ideas are discussed.

7 Look at the gaps in the summary in Exercise 4. Find the relevant section of the passage and read it carefully to find the exact word(s) you need. Remember, the information may come in a different order, and you may need to read more than one section of the passage.

AUSTRALIA'S GIANT ANIMAL SPECIES

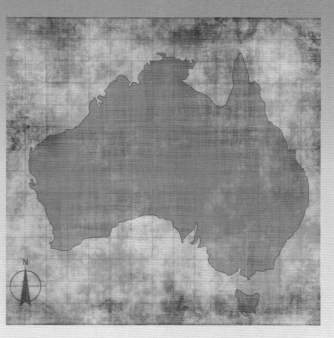

Around 50,000 years ago, Australia was a strange and hostile place with a vast, expanding desert core which was dominated by giant animals. These included mammals such as the Diprotodon, a giant wombat the size of a rhinoceros, short-faced kangaroos weighing more than 200 kilograms, and massive flightless birds. Around 90 of these gigantic species and subspecies once existed.

Finding an explanation for exactly why these creatures became extinct has locked scientists in a heated debate since the nineteenth century. According to one hypothesis, the arrival of humans, who hunted them down and caused bush fires, could account for their demise. Humans arrived in Australia around 45,000 years ago, but new research seems to show that most of the giant species had already disappeared from the continent before that. It's now thought that no more than 15 per cent of these species overlapped in time with humans.

At the end of the last Ice Age, Australia's climate changed from what is termed cold-dry to warm-dry. As a result, surface water became scarce. Most of the vast inland lakes dried up and forests and grasslands turned to desert. The giant species mostly ate plant matter and so lost both their natural habitat and their main source of food. They tended, therefore, to retreat to a narrow band of land in eastern Australia, where there was permanent water and better vegetation. The evidence for this ongoing desertification of Australia over time has become firmer, thanks to new and mounting data from scientists studying ice cores in Antarctica. This data shows a marked drying, beginning at around 50,000 years ago, which is around the same time that humans arrived in Australia, and this is consistent with evidence for the decline of inland lakes there.

Many questions remain. The claim that humans played a role in the extinction of the species that were still present when they arrived cannot be entirely dismissed. However, it is increasingly clear that the disappearance of giant species took place over tens of thousands of years primarily because of the influence of climate change, and that at the time the first humans arrived, the environmental conditions that were favourable to giant species had already deteriorated.

8 **Work in pairs. Look at the passage again and discuss the following.**

a   How does the wording of the summary relate to the order of information in the passage?

b   Why do some words you read fit the gaps and others do not?

9 **Look at this student's answers. Why were they marked wrong?**

Notes

3   caused fires
4   cold-dry
5   drought
6   Grassland
7   Ice of Antarctica
8   Serface waters

IELTS PRACTICE TASK

In Pursuit of the Perfect Tomato

For supermarket shoppers, the tomato symbolises what has been lost in terms of taste and texture, in exchange for being able to buy cheap vegetables and fruit all year round. But a fight-back for flavour is under way – and its scientific champion is Harry Klee, horticulture professor at the University of Florida in the USA. 'The big problem with the modern commercial tomato is that growers are not paid for flavour, they're paid for yield and extended shelf life,' says Klee. He thinks that the answer is to 'put together an integrated system that starts with the consumer and what they want. We have come up with a recipe to breed a really great tomato, but a lot of work will be needed to get it into the commercial system, which has other priorities.'

Klee's research started with what are sometimes called heritage tomatoes, which date back to the period before mass commercialisation, and compared these with modern varieties. He found that, in general, the loss of flavour coincided with the intensive breeding that began in the second half of the twentieth century. 'Since flavour started going down, yields of tomatoes have gone up by three hundred per cent,' says Klee.

Biochemical analysis of the best-flavoured varieties – with input from many tasting panels – identified sixty-eight flavour-associated compounds. Most important are 'volatiles', many of which also contribute strongly to the enticing smell of freshly-picked tomatoes. Some chemicals, such as cis-3-hexanal, which scientists had previously thought important for taste were not, while others such as geranial, which had been regarded as marginal contributors, were actually key.

At the same time, scientists are discovering the genetics of tomato flavour, appearance and durability. One particular mutation, favoured because it gives ripe tomatoes a beautifully even scarlet surface, turns out to reduce the biosynthesis of flavouring compounds. Now the Florida researchers have bred a tomato which is half-way between the great-tasting tomatoes of the past and modern commercial lines. 'People love the taste of this hybrid and it is easier to grow,' Klee says. 'I'd say we have a hundred per cent of the flavour of old varieties and eighty per cent of the performance of modern ones – but we need a hundred per cent of the performance before commercial growers will take them up.'

Although Klee worked for a large chemical company until 1995, developing genetically modified (GM) crops, he does not see a role for GM technology in breeding better tomatoes, because of public resistance and because it would be too costly and time-consuming to obtain regulatory approval. 'We can do it through conventional breeding, using modern genetics and flavour chemistry,' he says.

Questions 1–8

Complete the summary below.

*Choose **NO MORE THAN TWO WORDS** from the passage for each answer.*

Summary

Professor Harry Klee of the University of Florida recognises that today's mass-produced tomatoes, although cheap and available throughout the year, are lacking in both flavour and **1** .... He identifies the reason for this as the fact that growers are encouraged to grow tomatoes that have a high yield and will have a long **2** .... in the supermarket. His solution to this problem is a new approach to tomato growing that has **3** .... preferences as its starting point. Klee compared modern tomatoes with so-called **4** .... varieties and found the latter more flavoursome. He put the blame for the loss of flavour on intensive breeding techniques.

Klee found that compounds known as volatiles gave tomatoes a distinctive **5** .... as well as a good flavour and that a chemical called **6** .... was more important in this respect than had been previously thought. Klee's team have now produced what he calls a **7** .... tomato that combines the qualities of old and new varieties. It tastes good but cannot yet compete on yield. Klee thinks that **8** .... tomatoes are unlikely to be developed, however, predicting that traditional breeding techniques will eventually produce a tomato that is both tasty and commercially viable.

Which statement best describes how you feel about Summary Completion (1) tasks?

☐ I feel confident about doing Summary Completion (1) tasks.

☐ I did OK, but I still need to do more work on Summary Completion (1) tasks.

☐ I need more practice with Summary Completion (1) tasks. I need to focus on …

▶▶ **For further practice, see the DVD-ROM.**

Academic vocabulary

In the IELTS exam you have to listen to speakers in academic situations and read academic texts. You also use academic vocabulary in your writing for IELTS.

Scientists **have long confirmed** *that lifestyle affects life expectancy.* (= Scientists **have said that something is true**.)

Linking words and phrases

1 **Read the information about linking words and phrases.**

Understanding linking words and phrases helps you understand the whole text more fully. Being able to use linking words to organise your writing is a strength, particularly in writing tasks with strict word limits, such as Task 1 and Task 2 in the IELTS Writing paper.

2 **Match the sentence halves to make complete correct sentences.**

1	<u>According to</u> Ahima,	a	BMI continues to be the standard.
2	<u>Since</u> the early twentieth century	b	why BMI is widely used.
3	<u>Further studies show</u>	c	there's no single number that can represent a healthy weight.
4	<u>This raises the question of</u>	d	studies have linked obesity and health.
5	Other methods	e	<u>that</u> a low BMI can be dangerous.
6	All this <u>explains why</u>	f	<u>have their drawbacks</u> as well.

Look back at the text on page 125 and check your answers.

3 **Use the underlined phrases in Exercise 2 in your own examples. Write about one of the following areas or choose your own: health, fitness and longevity, lifestyle.**

Content words

4 **Read the sentences. Match the words and expressions in bold with a word or expression from the box that has a similar meaning.**

different	had an idea	holes	look like	named/called	notice	proposed

1 Democritus **formulated the notion** that people could **perceive** four primary tastes.
2 The cells appeared to **resemble** tiny keyholes.
3 Scientists **put forward** the idea that …
4 The **cavities** came in four different shapes.
5 He **termed** it a map of the tongue.
6 The flavour was quite **distinct**.

Which of the expressions are more formal/academic and likely to be written?

5 **Go back to the text on page 131 and highlight the expressions in the text.**

Affixes

6 **Read the information about affixes.**

An affix is a prefix (added to the start of a root word) or suffix (added to the end of a root word) which changes the meaning of the root word. Being able to guess words by recognising the meaning added by a prefix or suffix is a useful skill for dealing with new words. Affixes can add different meanings, so use the context to help you decide what the new meaning may be.

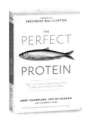

7 **Look at the sentences. Identify the meaning added by the underlined prefix or suffix. Choose from the meanings in the box.**

| again   full of   not (x 2)   too much   you can |

Word	Affix	Meaning
profitable	-able	you can

1   Oceana is a <u>non</u>-profit organisation.
2   There's a lot of <u>un</u>used potential protein swimming in the ocean.
3   <u>Over</u>fishing has devastated the fish population.
4   Countries are urged to allow fish stocks to <u>re</u>generate.
5   More profit<u>able</u> species such as salmon.
6   Smaller fish also contain fewer harmf<u>ul</u> pollutants.

Go back to the text on page 123 and check the words in context. Highlight the words in the text.

Common IELTS topic: Human behaviour

Affixes: Changing verbs to nouns

8 **Complete the paragraph by choosing a verb and a suffix from the box.**

| Verb: assess   avoid   develop   disturb   establish   find   perform   surround   work
Suffix: -ings   -ance   -ment |

Over the last few decades psychologists and neurologists have made remarkable discoveries about the mysterious **1** .... of the human brain, and how its **2** .... may be affected by genetic and external factors. One aspect of psychological behaviour that both groups are still exploring is that of irrational fear – in other words, phobias. While the reason for the **3** .... of these phobias in people is still a matter of debate, it can clearly be seen that some are more common than others. Arachnophobia, or a 'fear of spiders', is at the top of the list, followed by a fear of snakes and heights. Some people have strategies to manage their phobias; they avoid disruptions to their routines and **4** .... in their daily lives by ensuring that the object of their fear will not be encountered in their immediate **5** .... and environment. People with *ornithophobia*, for example, will often choose routes where there are few birds on the path. These kinds of **6** .... strategies, however, are not always successful. Professor Mark Hopkins is well known in the field of phobia research. Since the **7** .... of his clinic in 2001, his team has seen over 8,000 patients. When a new patient is referred to him, he will carry out a detailed **8** .... of the person's personality and background. His **9** .... then enable him to work out the most appropriate treatment.

Relationships and connection

9 **Complete the sentences by choosing the correct endings.**

1   Our strong desire for sugar may derive
2   A lack of sleep will often lead
3   Low energy levels are often symptomatic
4   The lack of exposure to natural light has an impact
5   A seasonal increase in pollen is known to contribute
6   Researchers are looking at how mood is affected
7   It has been proven that there is a clear correlation
8   The occurrence of arthritis in our joints will often stem

a   of the early stages of diabetes.
b   by fluctuations in hormone levels.
c   between obesity and heart disease.
d   from our ancestors' continual search for sources of energy.
e   to the incidence of allergies in spring and summer.
f   from untreated injuries in early life.
g   on the eyesight of young children.
h   to increased levels of stress and anxiety.

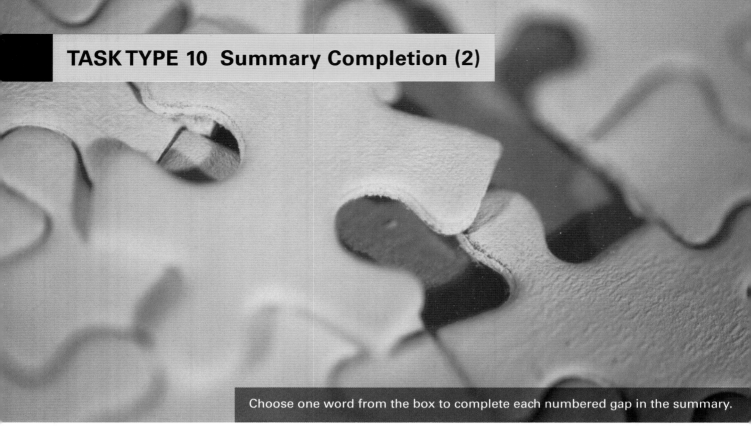

TASK TYPE 10 Summary Completion (2)

Choose one word from the box to complete each numbered gap in the summary.

A About the task

1 Read the information about the task type. Then look at some notes about the task you found on an exam website. Are the sentences true or false? Correct the false sentences.

The Summary Completion task tests your ability to locate ideas in a reading passage and use them to complete a summary of that passage. This task is often used to test your understanding of a passage where different ideas about a subject are presented. On the question paper, you see a short summary on the same subject as the long reading passage. The summary usually includes the main points of information from one section of the passage. Your job is to read both the passage and the summary and choose which words from a list complete the gaps in the summary.

Here are the basic rules for the Summary Completion task:

- The summary reports the main ideas from the relevant section of the passage, but the information may not be presented in the same order.
- The missing words are listed in a box (A–K). You choose one word from the box to complete each numbered gap in the summary.
- The wording of the summary isn't exactly the same as the wording in the passage, but it contains the same information and ideas.
- When you read the passage, you sometimes see the words from the box, but sometimes the words are different from those used in the passage because the summary is reporting the main ideas using different language.
- You write the correct letter on the answer sheet.

1 You are mostly reading for facts and figures.
2 The words in the box all come from the passage.
3 The summary always relates to one section of the passage.
4 The questions are never in the same order as the information in the passage.
5 You have to write the missing words on the answer sheet.

B Sample questions

2 Read the passage and answer the questions. Use the rules about the task from Section A to help you. Then check your answers. Which questions did you find difficult?

IELTS PRACTICE TASK

Biophilia in the city

Biophilia, as defined by evolutionary biologist E.O. Wilson, is 'the human bond with other species', and the idea was elaborated in his work *Biophilia*, published in 1984, in which he argues that our very existence depends on this close relationship with the natural world. The concept of biophilia with reference to whole cities is, however, a 21st-century phenomenon, as evidenced by the communiqué released at the end of the Copenhagen Climate Summit in 2009 which stated: 'the future of our globe will be won or lost in the cities of the world.'

Climate change has probably been the single greatest influence on this debate. This idea has been further fuelled by the United Nations identifying cities as the source of 75% of greenhouse gas emissions, which have an environmental impact around the world. Cities are also the consumers of 75% of the world's natural resources, the extraction of which affects many habitats across the globe.

Since 2009, work has been going on around Europe and beyond to encourage city leaders to adapt their policies to the reality of climate change in a concerted manner. One group of cities has gone a step further and formed the Biophilic Cities Network, which recognises people's need to access and respond to nature as part of their daily lives.

Any city joining the network is asked to commit to the following aims:

- Work diligently to protect and restore nature within their boundaries and to forge new links with the natural world wherever possible.
- Share information and insights about tools, techniques, programmes and projects which have been successfully applied in the city.
- Assist other cities outside the group, which are also striving to become more biophilic, offering help in data collection and analysis, sharing technical expertise and knowledge, and other forms of professional support for the expansion of urban nature.
- Meet periodically as a group to share experiences and insights and provide mutual support and guidance in advancing the practice of biophilic urbanism.

Questions 1–6
*Complete the summary using the list of words, **A–K**, below.*
*Write the correct letter, **A–K**.*

Biophilia Cities Network

Biophilia is the idea that human existence relies on maintaining a close relationship with the natural world, and it has recently been acknowledged that cities play a key part in this. The United Nations identified that cities are responsible for creating 75% of greenhouse gas emissions whilst at the same time consuming around the same
1 .... of the world's natural resources.

This led to the **2** .... of the Biophilic Cities Network, a group of city governments that has made a
3 .... to work together in addressing not only the issue of climate change, but also the need for their citizens to have access to nature as part of their everyday lives.

Each city in the group will work towards the **4** .... of its own natural environment, as well as restoring nature wherever possible. Through co-operation with the other members, cities will share information about
5 .... which have worked. They will also help non-members to achieve the same goals through the sharing of both skills and **6** .... Regular meetings of the group will help to further these aims.

A initiatives	**B** formation	**C** commitment	**D** impact
E protection	**F** management	**G** non-members	**H** expertise
I proportion	**J** insights	**K** collection	

C Tips and tactics

3 Work in pairs. Read the tips and tactics and discuss these questions.

a Which tips and tactics do you think are the most useful?
b Did you use any of these tips and tactics when you answered the sample questions in Section B?
c Which tips will you use in the future?

1 Before you look at the passage, read the summary and underline the main words and ideas.
2 Think about the type of information that's missing in each gap. For example, are you looking for a name, a number, a specific term or something else?
3 Read the passage and find the main words and ideas you underlined in the summary.
4 The summary usually relates to one section of the passage, but may also report the meaning of the whole passage.
5 Go through the summary, gap by gap, and read the relevant sections of the passage.
6 A number of words from the box will fit each gap logically and grammatically. You have to choose the one that reports the meaning of the passage exactly.
7 Don't just choose the first word you find that fits the gap – keep reading and keep thinking about the meaning.
8 Remember that some of the words you need may not be in the passage, e.g. *initiatives* summarises the idea of programmes and projects.
9 Remember that sometimes you may need to choose a word that has a different form to the way it is used in the passage to complete the summary, e.g. *commit -> commitment.*
10 If you aren't sure, always write something. No marks are taken off for wrong answers.

D Skills-building exercises

Q FOCUS

Identifying what information is missing

4 Read the summary and think about the type of information that is needed to complete each gap. Which gaps are likely to need:

a a verb form?   b a singular noun?   c a plural noun?   d an adjective?

Summary

The Ancient Romans used large **1** .... jars called amphorae to **2** ....
liquid goods such as olive oil from one part of their empire to another. The cone-shaped amphorae were not **3** .... , however, and most ended up in rubbish heaps. In Rome, for example, there is a hill, fifty metres in height, that is composed almost entirely of **4** .... amphorae, whereas in the port city of Arles in what is now southern France, they tended to end up in the River Rhône.

Two thousand years ago, Arles was an important port where goods were **5** ....
from ocean-going vessels to river boats before continuing their journey inland. Little is left of the Roman port today, however, although it is still possible to identify a **6** .... under the water that indicates where the Roman rubbish dump used to be. In 2004, a diver spotted an interesting wooden **7** .... , which turned out to be part of a thirty-metre barge that was largely still **8** .... Archaeologists later discovered the boat's final **9** .... as well as some of the crew's personal **10** ....

5 Underline the main words and ideas in the summary, for example: *jars, Rome,* etc.

6 Read the passage on page 145 quickly to get a general idea of its content, and mark the parts where the main ideas are discussed.

7 Look at each gap in the summary in Exercise 4. Find the relevant section of the main passage and read it carefully to find the information you need.

8 Look at the gaps (1–5) in the summary and choose the best word to complete them.

1 clay ship olive oil
2 make transport barge
3 re-used drained opened
4 re-used tossed broken
5 transported transferred reloaded

9 Complete the rest of the summary (6–10) using the list of words, A–K, below.

A intact	**B** layers	**C** rubbish	**D** shadow
E financed	**F** possessions	**G** object	**H** cargo
I sheltered	**J** boat	**K** excavations	

10 Work in pairs. Check your answers for Exercises 8 and 9. Underline the sections of the passage that you needed to answer each of the questions in the summary. Then compare your answers with another pair.

11 Look at the passage again and discuss these questions.

  1 How did the wording of the summary help you to find the correct information?
  2 Why do some words in the box fit the gaps and others do not?

12 Look at this student's answers. Why are they wrong?

6 F   7 J   8 H   9 C   10 G

ANCIENT ROMAN RUBBISH

The Ancient Romans had a serious rubbish problem, though by our standards it was good-looking rubbish. Their problem was amphorae. These were jars made of clay and the Romans needed millions of them to ship liquids like olive oil and fish sauce around the empire. Often, they didn't recycle their empties. Sometimes they didn't even bother to open them—it was quicker to cut off the neck or the pointy base, drain the thing, then throw it away. In Rome there's a hill rising to fifty meters called Monte Testaccio, that consists almost entirely of shattered amphorae, mostly seventy-liter olive oil jars from Spain. They were tossed out the back of warehouses along the River Tiber. Spanish archaeologists who've been digging into the dump believe its rise probably began in the first century, as the empire itself was rising toward its greatest heights.

Around that time in Arles, on the Rhône River in what is now southern France, port workers did things a bit differently: they threw their empties into the river. Arles in the first century was the thriving gateway to Roman Gaul. Freight from all over the Mediterranean was unloaded from sea-going vessels and reloaded into riverboats, before being hauled up the Rhône by teams of men to supply the northern reaches of the empire. "It was a city at the intersection of all roads, which received products from everywhere," says David Djaoui, an archaeologist at the local antiquities museum. In the city centre today, on the left bank of the Rhône, you can still see the amphitheatre that seated 20,000 spectators for gladiator fights. But of the port that financed all this, and that stretched half a mile or more along the right bank, not much remains—only a shadow in the riverbed that reveals the presence of the Roman rubbish.

Rubbish to them, not to us. In the summer of 2004 a diver surveying the dump for archaeological riches noticed a large lump of wood sticking out of the mud at a depth of four meters. It turned out to be the side of a thirty-meter barge. The barge was almost intact; most of it was still buried under the layers of mud and amphorae that had sheltered it for nearly 2,000 years. Subsequent archaeological excavations revealed that it had held on to its last cargo and even to a few personal effects left behind by its crew. It can now be seen in a brand-new wing of the Arles Museum of Antiquity.

IELTS PRACTICE TASK

Gannet feeding territories

The gannet, with its two-metre wingspan, is the largest European seabird. Unlike many other species, gannets have been increasing in number in recent years. Scientists studying gannet colonies around the coasts of Britain and Ireland have made a surprising discovery about the feeding habits of these huge seabirds. Each colony has its own fishing territory where the birds feed undisturbed by intruders from neighbouring colonies. These divisions persist even though gannets do not engage in aggressive territorial behaviour. Birds entering from a neighbouring colony could fish unhindered – but choose not to do so.

'The accepted view is that exclusive foraging territories are associated with species such as ants, which aggressively defend the feeding areas around their colonies, but this opens the door to a completely new way of thinking about territory,' says Ewan Wakefield of Leeds University in the UK, joint leader of the study published in the journal *Science*. 'We found the gannet colonies also had adjoining, but clearly defined, feeding areas,' he says. 'Gannets may be a byword for gluttony in popular folklore, but clearly they don't eat off each other's plates.'

Researchers from 14 institutions tracked 200 gannets flying from 12 colonies around Britain and Ireland. Instead of criss-crossing flight paths from neighbouring colonies as the birds headed out to fish, a tightly defined non-intersecting pattern emerged. The Irish colonies at Bull Rock and Little Skellig are within sight of each other, but their inhabitants always head off in opposite directions. The explanation seems to be that each colony started fishing in the closest waters, and this preference has been reinforced by cultural transmission between generations.

'Finding such separation between colonies, even when visible from each other, indicates that competition for food cannot be the only explanation and suggests cultural differences between gannet colonies may be important,' says Thomas Bodey of Exeter University. 'As with humans, birds have favoured routes to travel, and if new arrivals at a colony follow experienced old hands then these patterns can quickly become fixed, even if other opportunities potentially exist.'

For Stuart Bearhop, also at Exeter, this raises the question of how many other species show segregated feeding patterns. 'We understand an awful lot about what seabirds like these do on land, but until recently we knew shockingly little about what they do at sea. The technology is now allowing us to leave the coast with them and we are discovering more and more of these amazing and unexpected patterns. The answer will be important for formulating conservation strategies.'

Questions 1–6

*Complete the summary using the list of words, **A–K**, below.*

*Write the correct letter, **A–K**, in spaces 1–6 below.*

Scientists studying the feeding habits of gannets, Europe's largest seabirds, were surprised to discover that each group or 'colony' of birds has its own clearly defined feeding territory. Other species which exhibit such behaviour, such as ants, tend **1** .... their territories aggressively, but this is not so in the case of gannets. According to Ewan Wakefield of Leeds University, we need **2** .... traditional ideas about both gannets and territorial animals in general. Researchers taking part in the study have suggested that knowledge about the territories is passed on to members of the gannet colony through a process of **3** .... Thomas Bodey of Exeter University suggests that new arrivals in a colony may prefer **4** .... existing members rather than find new feeding areas. Stuart Bearhop predicts that other seabirds may have similar **5** .... and that such knowledge could be useful when **6** .... are drawn up.

A popular folklore	**B** conservation strategies	**C** to defend	**D** to respect
E feeding patterns	**F** opposite directions	**G** flight paths	**H** to rethink
I to fix	**J** to follow	**K** cultural transmission	

1 ....

2 ....

3 ....

4 ....

5 ....

6 ....

Which statement best describes how you feel about Summary Completion (2) tasks?

[ ] I feel confident about doing Summary Completion (2) tasks.

[ ] I did OK, but I still need to do more work on Summary Completion (2) tasks.

[ ] I need more practice with Summary Completion (2) tasks. I need to focus on …

▶▶ **For further practice, see the DVD-ROM.**

TASK TYPE 11 Matching Sentence Endings

There are more options in the box than you need to answer all the questions.

Belly General Store, Atlanta, USA

A About the task

1 Read the information about the task type. Then look at a quiz you found on a website. Choose the correct options to complete the sentences.

The Matching Sentence Endings task tests your ability to identify the views of the writer and claims made in a passage. It's often used to test your understanding of a passage in which the writer is presenting an argument or where different ideas about a subject are compared and analysed. On the question paper, you see a set of numbered incomplete sentences that report information and ideas from the passage. You only see the beginning of the sentence. There is also a box which contains different sentence endings. Your job is to read the passage and decide which of the options in the box completes each of the numbered sentences. The complete sentence must report the ideas and information from the passage exactly.

Here are the basic rules for the Matching Sentence Endings task:

- The numbered sentence beginnings follow the order of information in the passage.
- The options in the box are in random order. There are more options in the box than you need to answer all the questions.
- The wording of the sentence beginnings and options is not exactly the same as the wording in the passage, but they contain information and ideas from the passage. .
- The sentence beginnings include some words and names that are also used in the passage. These help you to find the relevant section.
- You read this section carefully and think about the writer's views and claims.
- You then decide which of the sentence endings in the box reports the writer's views and claims exactly and write the correct letter on your answer sheet.
- All of the options create grammatically correct sentences, but only one of the endings creates a sentence that reports the meaning of the passage exactly.

Matching Sentence Endings

1 You're mostly reading for *facts and figures / ideas and opinions*.
2 The numbered sentence beginnings are in *random order / the same order as the passage*.
3 There are *more / fewer* options than questions.
4 The sentence beginnings *never / sometimes* include the same words that you find in the passage.
5 On the answer sheet, you write one *letter / number* for each question.
6 *Some / None* of the options will create grammatically incorrect sentences.

B Sample questions

2 **Read the passage and answer the questions. Use the rules about the task from Section A to help you. Then check your answers. Which questions did you find difficult?**

IELTS PRACTICE TASK

Loblolly Pines and Carbon Dioxide

Scientists at North Carolina's Duke University in the US have been studying how plants react to higher levels of carbon dioxide in the atmosphere. The researchers collected, counted and analysed seeds produced at the Duke Free Air CO_2 Enrichment (FACE) site in Duke Forest, near the university's campus. Loblolly pine trees there have been receiving elevated amounts of carbon dioxide (CO_2) around the clock for over a decade, in a US Department of Energy funded project designed to simulate natural growing conditions. This is important research because many people predict that there will be significantly higher levels of the gas everywhere by the middle of this century.

The Carolina researchers have shown that loblolly pine trees grown for twelve years in air one-and-a-half times richer in CO_2 than today's levels produced twice as many seeds as those grown under normal conditions. Their analysis found the high CO_2 loblolly seeds were similar in nutrient content, germination and growth potential to seeds from trees growing under present-day CO_2 concentrations. As one researcher said: 'If anything, they actually seem to be slightly better seeds rather than more seeds of poorer quality.' This is particularly interesting since a previous study established that grasses and other herbaceous plants tend to produce a greater number of seeds under high CO_2, but of inferior quality.

This means that some woody tree species could, in the future, out-compete grasses and other herbaceous plants. 'Even if both groups were producing twice as many seeds, if the trees are producing high-quality seeds and the herbaceous species aren't, then competitively you can get a shift,' said Danielle Way, a Duke post-doctoral researcher.

The ultimate competitive outcome will depend on how other comparable trees respond to high CO_2 levels, admits James Clark, another Duke biology professor who also participated in the study. 'We don't know that yet, because we only have estimates for loblolly pines,' he adds.

Questions 1–5
*Complete each sentence with the correct ending, **A–G**, below.*
*Write the correct letter, **A–G**.*

1 It is widely predicted that plant species all over the world could
2 Research in North Carolina has established that loblolly pine trees would
3 Previous research had established that herbaceous plant species would
4 Danielle Way makes the point that trees like the loblolly pine could
5 James Clark concedes that the loblolly pine trees could

A	produce greater quantities of good seeds if CO_2 levels were higher.
B	benefit from rising CO_2 levels at the expense of other similar species.
C	be untypical in the way they respond to higher CO_2 levels.
D	eventually have a competitive advantage over other plant species.
E	face uniformly high levels of CO_2 by 2050.
F	be adversely affected by rising CO_2 levels in unforeseen ways.
G	produce poorer quality seeds if CO_2 levels were higher.

---

1 ....
2 ....
3 ....
4 ....
5 ....

C Tips and tactics

3 Work in pairs. Read the tips and tactics and discuss these questions.

   a Which tips and tactics do you think are the most useful?
   b Did you use any of these tips and tactics when you answered the sample questions in Section B?
   c Which tips will you use in the future?

1   Before you read the passage, look at the numbered sentence beginnings and think about what you're going to read. Don't look at the options in the box yet.
2   For each sentence beginning, underline names, key words and main ideas.
3   Remember that the questions follow the order of information in the passage.
4   Read the passage quickly and use the words you've underlined to help you to find the relevant sections for each question. Write the question numbers in the margin so that you can find the sections again easily.
5   Go through the questions one by one. Read the section of the passage you have marked carefully to make sure you are in the correct place.
6   When you are sure you have understood the section of the passage, look at the options in the box and choose the one that reports what you have understood.
7   Re-read the complete sentence you are creating with the option. Does the wording of the new sentence report the writer's views or the claims made in the text accurately?
8   Don't use your own knowledge of the subject to help you choose the option. You need to report the views and claims you read in the passage.
9   Quickly check the rest of the paragraph in the passage to make sure you haven't missed anything.
10   Remember to write only the correct letter in each box on the answer sheet.
11   Never leave a box empty. If you're not sure, always give an answer.

Q FOCUS

Identifying whether sentences report the writer's views or claims made in the passage

D Skills-building exercises

4 Read the pairs of sentences (1–5). Underline the important words and ideas in each sentence.

1 A   The experiment set up in Dublin in 1944 sought to disprove a popular misconception.
     B   The experiment set up in Dublin in 1944 sought to demonstrate that an accepted principle was correct.
2 A   When Professor Parnell set up his experiment, he was hoping to show that the pitch would drop within a given period of time.
     B   When Professor Parnell set up his experiment, he was unaware how long the pitch would take to drop.
3 A   John Mainstone's experience shows that the original experiment was based on a miscalculation.
     B   John Mainstone's experience shows that it is impossible to make very precise predictions about when the drop will occur.
4 A   Shane Bergin's innovation was designed to prove a point to rival scientists.
     B   Shane Bergin's innovation was designed to share an experience more widely.
5 A   The writer feels that the public may have a better opinion of science thanks to the experiment.
     B   The writer feels that the public may fail to appreciate the wider significance of the experiment.

5 Read the passage on page 151 quickly. Mark the section that contains the information relevant to each pair of sentences in Exercise 4.

6 Go through the sentences in Exercise 4 one by one. Read the passage carefully and decide which sentence (A or B) accurately reports the writer's view or a claim made in the passage.

7 Work in pairs. Answer the questions. Then compare your ideas with another pair of students.

1   Did you and your partner underline the same section of the passage?
2   Are your answers all the same?
3   If these sentences were part of a matching sentence endings task, where do you think they would be divided? Why?

WAITING
FOR THE DROP

In 1944, in a physics lab at Trinity College in Dublin, Ireland, a scientist (whose name, sadly, has been lost to history) set up an experiment. He took several lumps of tar pitch, heated them, and placed them in a funnel. After giving the pitch time to settle, he left the apparatus alone. Not for minutes or days or even years, but for decades. Pitch is a thick black material which appears to be solid at room temperature. In fact, if hit with a hammer, it shatters. The point of the experiment, however, is to prove the long-held belief that, over a long period of time, pitch actually has some liquid properties and is capable of flowing – albeit extremely slowly.

The Trinity experiment is only one of a number of similar experiments. The earliest and most famous one was initiated in 1927 by Professor Thomas Parnell of the University of Queensland in Brisbane, who wanted to see if his calculations regarding the viscosity of pitch were correct. Parnell poured a heated sample of pitch into a sealed funnel and allowed it to settle for three years, after which the seal at the neck of the funnel was cut, allowing the pitch to start flowing. A glass dome covers the apparatus which has been on display outside a lecture theatre ever since. Over time, a large droplet of pitch forms and eventually falls out of the funnel. This event, known as a pitch drop, was predicted to occur about once a decade.

The Queensland experiment, however, has demonstrated that calculating the exact moment when a drop is likely to occur is hardly an easy matter. In 1979, John Mainstone, the professor by then in charge of the experiment, skipped one of his usual Sunday campus visits and missed the drop. In 1988, Mainstone went for a cup of tea and when he returned, he found he had missed the drop by five minutes. In 2000, Mainstone set up a video camera to catch the drop, but the camera malfunctioned, and he saw nothing.

Little wonder, therefore, that the Trinity College drop was being eagerly awaited. In April of 2013, Physics professor Shane Bergin set up a webcam so that the world at large could witness a pitch drop. And the event the scientists were looking for came in the form of a momentary, yet momentous, happening: the pitch, rendered elastic, succumbed to gravity and leaked through the funnel, and dropped to the bottom of the jar. The event occurred at 5.00 p.m. local time on 11 July 2013. This time, the camera equipment didn't

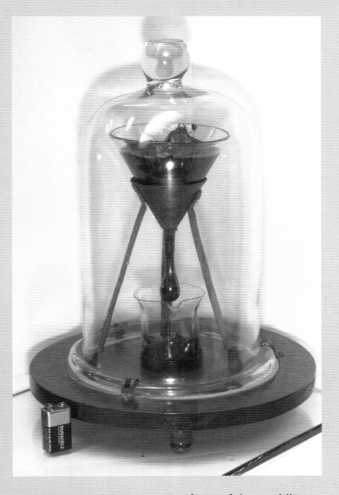

malfunction and the outcome of one of the world's longest running experiments was finally observed by human eyes.

All this has given these lumps of pitch something of a cult following – one that has been amplified by the Internet. Thanks to which, you may be able to watch the momentous event yourself next time. And when it comes, the drop may not be the most significant scientific event of its time, but it may be one of the more exciting ones. Science, in the public imagination, is often perceived as data-driven and analytical, by design divorced from human emotion. But this split-second falling of a lump of liquid pitch is a nice reminder of the excitement that can be embedded in even the dullest of experiments. The pitch drop when it comes may simply prove what we already know. But it is the result the world has been waiting for.

IELTS PRACTICE TASK

The meaning of dreams

We are fascinated by our dreams. And it is usually our own dreams we're fascinated by. When another person launches into a lengthy exposition of the dreams that graced their night, our eyes are liable to glaze over quickly. But for many of us, our own dreams provide an endless source of intrigue.

Nowadays we are less likely than our ancestors to believe that dreams have a predictive function. But it is probably part of the 20th-century neurologist Sigmund Freud's lasting legacy that we can't quite shake off the idea that they somehow hold the key to our hidden hopes and desires. Incredibly enough, the idea that the symbolic meaning of our dream is there, waiting to be interpreted, remains very appealing.

There are, of course, alternative views, including the one that dreams have no meaning whatsoever and result instead from the brain's attempts to make sense of neural processes that occur during sleep. But adopting such a scientific attitude to dreams doesn't imply that they are no longer a source of fascination to us. We could simply relate to them differently. Instead of seeking to decipher the symbols that our unconscious is supposedly messaging to us, we could use them as a starting point for reflection.

Whether or not the content of our dreams actually reflects our waking concerns, thinking about them could be a helpful way of exploring our own thoughts. While we may be disappointed that we can't consult a dream dictionary to explain what the things we've dreamt about mean, by thinking about them we might gain insights into our own lives. In other words, the important thing is not what the dream means in an absolute sense, but what it means to us personally.

Questions 1–4

*Complete the summary using the list of words **A–G**, below.*

*Write the correct letter, **A–G**, for each question.*

1   The idea that dreams can foretell the future
2   Freud's idea that it's possible to interpret the meaning of dreams
3   The idea that dreams have no meaning at all
4   The idea that it is worth thinking about our own dreams

A	has been the subject of extensive scientific research.
B	shouldn't make them any less interesting.
C	is no longer taken as seriously as it used to be.
D	seems more relevant when we hear about other people's dreams.
E	may be a useful one for the individual to pursue.
F	has never gained wide acceptance.
G	is still surprisingly influential today.

1   ....
2   ....
3   ....
4   ....

Which statement best describes how you feel about Matching Sentence Endings tasks?

☐   I feel confident about doing Matching Sentence Endings tasks.
☐   I did OK, but I still need to do more work on Matching Sentence Endings tasks.
☐   I need more practice with Matching Sentence Endings tasks. I need to focus on …

▶▶ **For further practice, see the DVD-ROM.**

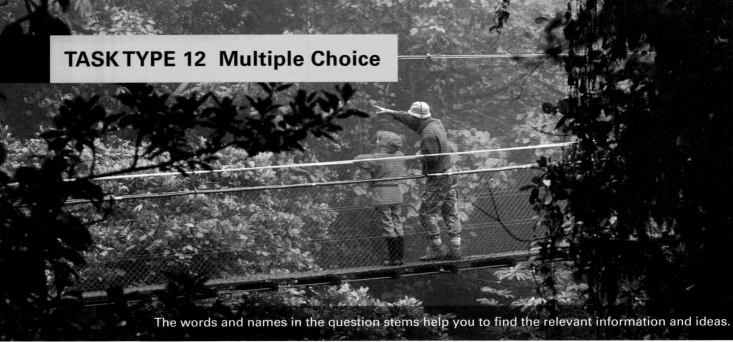

TASK TYPE 12 Multiple Choice

The words and names in the question stems help you to find the relevant information and ideas.

Canopy walkway, Monteverde Cloud Forest Rreserve, Costa Rica

A About the task

1 **Read the information about the task type. Then look at some notes about the task made by two of your classmates. For each point, decide who is right (Classmate A or Classmate B).**

The Multiple Choice task tests your ability to read a passage carefully and understand detailed information and arguments. It's often used to test your understanding of a passage in which the writer is presenting an argument or where different ideas about a subject are compared and analysed. On the question paper, you see a set of question stems with four possible answers. Your job is to read the passage and decide which of the four options correctly answers the question.

There are two types of question:

- A question which has four different answers (A, B, C or D).
- An incomplete sentence that has four possible endings (A, B, C or D).

Here are the basic rules for the Multiple Choice task:

- The questions follow the order of the information in the passage.
- The wording of the options is not exactly the same as the wording in the passage.
- When you read the question stems, you see some words and names that are also used in the passage. These help you to find the relevant information and ideas.
- You read the whole passage quickly to find the information and ideas you need to answer each question.
- You then read this section carefully and compare the information and ideas with the four options.
- You have to decide which option correctly answers the question or completes the sentence.
- You write the correct letter on the answer sheet.

		Notes	
1	Classmate A	You are reading mostly for facts and figures.
	Classmate B	You are reading to understand the writer's views and claims.
2	Classmate A	There are two different types of question stem.
	Classmate B	The question stems always end in a question mark.
3	Classmate A	The questions always follow the order of the passage.
	Classmate B	The questions sometimes come in random order.
4	Classmate A	The question stems probably include words from the passage.
	Classmate B	The question stems never include words from the passage.
5	Classmate A	You copy out the correct answer onto the answer sheet.
	Classmate B	You only write the correct letter on the answer sheet.

B Sample questions

2 Read the passage and answer the questions. Use the rules about the task from Section A to help you. Then check your answers. Which questions did you find difficult?

IELTS PRACTICE TASK

The Svalbard Seed Bank

Modern agriculture is primarily focused on maximising profit. This means that a small number of specially selected plant varieties are grown throughout the world, and these have replaced the wide diversity of local varieties that once existed. This approach guarantees consistently high yields under normal conditions, but it also harbours a hidden danger. Essentially, every single commercially grown plant is a clone of one of only a few specially selected pieces of genetic material, known as cultivars. This leads to a lack of genetic diversity, leaving crops more exposed to any disease which attacks that single cultivar. With corn, wheat and rice being grown worldwide in this way, there is a concern that a fungal infection could wipe out an entire world crop in a matter of months, causing massive food shortages.

There are many types, or cultivars, of any given agricultural product, each one a special variety, developed to have particular characteristics and given a special name. Various cultivars come in and out of favour over the years. For example, almost all bananas in the world today are now of the Cavendish variety. But in the mid-20th century, the Gros Michel was the dominant banana cultivar consumed in North America and Europe. Around 1950, however, this variety became virtually extinct due to the rapid spread of a fungal infection that attacked the roots of the banana plant, with the result that the Gros Michel was replaced with the more resilient but notably less tasty Cavendish cultivar.

In order to preserve gene diversity of major food crops, international institutions have established a series of national gene banks, which store samples of various strains of each plant species. On a remote island north of the Arctic Circle, however, there is a sort of master gene bank for all the world's plants. The Svalbard seed bank serves as a reserve of last resort and the popular press has emphasized the use of the seed bank as an insurance policy in case of a major global catastrophe. To date, it has more frequently been accessed when national gene banks lose samples due to accident, equipment failures, natural disasters and, all too often, mismanagement.

The bank is located in an old copper mine on the remote northern island of Spitsbergen in Norway. The facility has a capacity to conserve 4.5 million seed samples. Under the current temperature conditions in the vault (similar to those in a kitchen freezer) the seed samples for many fruits and vegetables can remain viable for hundreds of years. Some seeds, including those of important grains, can survive far longer, anywhere from 2,000 to 20,000 years. The bank functions like a safety deposit box in a commercial bank. While the bank owns the building, the individual depositor owns the contents of his or her box, and the access to individual specimens is regulated by their respective depositors. No depositor has access to any other depositor's seeds. The seed samples stored in the bank are copies of samples stored in the depositing gene banks. Researchers, plant breeders, and other groups wishing to access seed samples cannot do so through the seed bank; they must request samples from the depositing gene banks.

The main storage vault is dug into a sandstone mountain, on a seismically inactive island. The bank employs a number of robust security and preservation systems: seeds are packaged in special packets and heat-sealed to exclude moisture; a local coal mine and power plant supply the electricity for refrigeration control and crucially the remote northern location also serves as a natural fridge. In the case of complete power failure, at least several weeks will elapse before the temperature inside the vault rises to the temperature of the surrounding sandstone bedrock. By locating the site 130 metres above sea level, the designers have even ensured that the site will remain dry if the polar icecaps melt.

Questions 1–6

*Choose the correct letter, **A**, **B**, **C** or **D**.*

1 The hidden danger referred to in line 4 is

   A changing growing conditions.
   B local variations reducing crop yields.
   C crops being more at risk from disease.
   D poor selection of original genetic material.

2 What does the Cavendish banana cultivar serve as an example of?

   A a cultivar that is preferred by consumers
   B a cultivar that is resistant to fungal infection
   C a cultivar that was previously facing extinction
   D a cultivar that offers good flavour but low yield

3 In the third paragraph, what is implied about the use of the Svalbard seed bank to date?

    A It's mostly been used in response to situations which could have been avoided.

    B It's generally been used in situations resulting from natural disasters.

    C It hasn't been used as much as has been suggested in the media.

    D It's been used more by some countries than by others.

4 According to the fourth paragraph, people requiring access to the seeds at Svalbard should

    A apply directly to the seed bank itself.

    B contact those who originally deposited the seeds.

    C visit the building where the seeds are held in person.

    D ask for samples to be transferred to them by secure means.

5 Which aspect of the Svalbard seed bank's security does the writer regard as most important?

    A the absence of volcanic activity in the region

    B the local availability of fossil fuel resources

    C the prevailing temperature at the site

    D the height of the site above sea level

6 The writer's main point in writing this passage is to

    A trace several recent developments in agricultural science.

    B discuss the dangers facing various national gene banks.

    C show why reliance on one cultivar can be dangerous.

    D explain the role of the master seed bank in Norway.

C Tips and tactics

3 Work in pairs. Read the tips and tactics and discuss these questions.

    a Which tips and tactics do you think are the most useful?

    b Did you use any of these tips and tactics when you answered the sample questions in Section B?

    c Which tips will you use in the future?

1 Before you read the passage, read the question stems and underline the most important words and ideas. Don't look at the options (A, B, C and D) yet.

2 Remember that the questions follow the order of the information in the passage.

3 When you read the passage, you may see some words or ideas from the question stems. These help you to find the relevant sections.

4 Read the passage quickly and mark the relevant sections for each question. Write the question numbers in the margin so that you can find the sections again easily.

5 Go through the questions one by one. Read the section of the passage you have marked carefully to make sure you are in the correct place.

6 When you feel you have understood the passage completely, then read the four options (A, B, C and D). Choose the option that answers the question or completes the sentence to match the meaning of the text.

7 Remember, the correct answer reports the meaning of the passage, but doesn't use the same words and expressions.

8 Don't use your own knowledge of the subject to help you choose an option. Remember, you are being tested on your understanding of the reading passage.

9 When you have chosen your answer, read the other options again, and re-read the passage to be sure that they are wrong.

10 Remember to write only one letter on the answer sheet.

11 Always answer all the questions, even if you're not entirely sure.

D Skills-building exercises

Q FOCUS

Locating the focus
of each question

4 **Look at the question stems (1–5) and underline the main words and ideas. Use these to help you find the relevant information and ideas in the passage.**

1 What does the writer think about the analysis of the data from the landing?
2 The writer mentions a ball to give us an idea of ...
3 What does Stefan Schroder suggest about the stone which the probe hit?
4 The writer quotes the words of Erich Karkoschka in order to ...
5 The dust-like material mentioned in the final paragraph provides evidence that ...

5 **Read the passage. Mark the sections which contain the information relevant to each question. Read each section carefully. What do you think the answer is going to be?**

Secrets of the Titan landing

The landing of the Huygens probe on Titan, Saturn's moon, in January 2005 was the most spectacular single event to date in exploration of the outer solar system. Huygens was made by the European Space Agency and brought to Titan by NASA's Cassini spacecraft, which is still orbiting Saturn. It took seven years for mission scientists to work out exactly what happened during what was then the most distant touchdown of a man-made spacecraft. Their analysis, however, was worth waiting for. It reveals that the twenty-kilogram probe 'bounced, slid and wobbled its way to rest in ten seconds' after parachuting down through the moon's thick and hazy atmosphere, and provides us with fascinating insights into an alien world.

Scientists reconstructed the chain of events by analysing data from all the instruments active during the landing. Their data was compared with computer simulations and tests that had been carried out using a model of Huygens. The probe hit the ground with an impact speed similar to a ball dropped from about a metre on Earth. On first contact Huygens dug a shallow hole about twelve centimetres deep, then bounced out and slid for thirty-five centimetres across the surface. At its final resting place it wobbled back and forth five times, till all motion ceased.

'A spike in the acceleration data suggests that during the first wobble, the probe probably encountered a stone protruding by around two centimetres from the surface of Titan, and may have even pushed it into the ground, suggesting a substance with the consistency of soft, damp sand,' says Stefan Schroder of the Max Planck Institute for Solar System Research in Germany. Had the probe hit a wet, mud-like substance, its instruments would have recorded a 'splat', with no further indication of bouncing or sliding. The ground must, therefore, have been soft enough to allow the probe to make a sizeable depression, but hard enough to support Huygens rocking back and forth. 'It's like snow that has been frozen on top,' says Erich Karkoschka of the University of Arizona. 'If you walk carefully, you can walk on it as on a solid surface, but if you step on the snow a little too hard, you break in very deeply.'

The landing data also shows evidence of a dry, dust-like material thrown up by the impact. Although liquid hydrocarbons (methane and ethane) sometimes fall from Titan's clouds – forming streams, rivers and lakes and giving the landscape a surprisingly Earth-like appearance – it had evidently not rained on the landing site for some time.

6 Look at the questions and the options (A or B) for each question. Read the passage on page 157 carefully. Which option (A or B) is correct? Why is the other option wrong?

1 What does the writer think about the analysis of the data from the landing?
   A It has produced very interesting findings.
   B It took an unacceptably long time to perform.

2 The writer mentions a ball to give us an idea of
   A how far the probe had travelled.
   B how quickly the probe was travelling.

3 What does Stefan Schroder suggest about the stone which the probe hit?
   A It may have given a false impression about the surface of Titan.
   B It has provided clear evidence about the surface of Titan.

4 The writer quotes the words of Erich Karkoschka in order to
   A give us a clearer idea of the consistency of the ground.
   B offer a different interpretation from that given by Schroder.

5 The dust-like material mentioned in the final paragraph provides evidence of
   A the dryness of the precise area where Titan landed.
   B weather patterns affecting the area where Titan landed.

Q FOCUS

Identifying the writer's views and claims

7 Look at the statements (1–6). For each statement, decide what the writer is doing (A, B or C).

   A giving factual information
   B giving his/her personal view
   C giving the ideas of others

1 A total solar eclipse is a compelling and life-changing sight that begins with the strangest light you have ever seen.
2 It takes just over two hours for the moon to cover the sun until only a ring of light remains.
3 Tour operators report a surge in interest in eclipse viewing sparked by 'the eclipse of the century' in July 2009.
4 Scientists agree that no two eclipses are identical.
5 Professor Jay M Pasachoff of Williams College, Masachusetts has seen fifty-five eclipses in the course of his work.
6 'The appeal of eclipse tourism looks set to increase,' says Simon Grove.

8 Look at the questions (1–5) and underline the main words and ideas. For each one decide what you will look for in the passage (A, B or C).

   A factual information
   B the writer's point of view
   C other people's ideas

1 What is the writer doing in the first paragraph?
2 What do we learn about the eclipse seen in China in 2009?
3 What does Simon Grove suggest about eclipse tourists?
4 What is Jay Pasachoff keen to stress?
5 What is suggested about partial eclipses?

9 Look at the passage on page 159 and mark the relevant sections of the passage for the question stems (1–5) in Exercise 8.

10 Read each section of the passage on page 159 carefully and find your own answer to the questions in Exercise 8.

In pursuit of the solar eclipse

A total solar eclipse is a compelling and life-changing sight that begins with the strangest light you have ever seen; a unique grey dusk in the middle of the day. The shadows get sharper and the onlookers grow quieter as the crescent sun gets smaller. It takes just over two hours for the moon to cover the sun until only a ring of light remains, often supplemented by a bright flash through some valley on the moon's rim. This is the so-called 'diamond ring', a moment which romantics have used for marriage proposals. Then, for several minutes, the most beautiful sight in the known universe is yours. The sun's atmosphere, the corona, springs into view as soon as its far brighter surface is blocked off. Twisted into bizarre shapes by the sun's magnetic field, the corona is a white light seen in a dark daytime sky against a backdrop of stars and planets.

For a growing band of eclipse tourists, the corona is an experience that cannot be repeated often enough. Tour operators report a surge in interest in eclipse viewing, sparked by the 'eclipse of the century' in July 2009, which was visible across large parts of China and lasted six minutes thirty-nine seconds – the longest eclipse until 2132. Alongside the growth in formal tours, thousands of people find their way to eclipses under their own steam. They aim to get as close as possible to the point of greatest totality, and to the centre of the eclipse track for a longer total eclipse, and seek a spot where the odds of clear weather are at their best.

'The appeal of eclipse tourism in general has increased in recent years and looks set to increase further,' says tour operator Simon Grove. 'Part of the joy of this hobby is that the moon's shadow can fall anywhere on the Earth's surface. This means eclipse-chasing needs careful planning, but also that eclipse-lovers end up in places they would never visit otherwise, including Easter Island and the Antarctic in the past few years. Happily for their finances, the solar system is laid out so that they can only have the experience at most once in a typical year. Although eclipse-watchers fly long distances, the growth of the hobby also taps into enthusiasm for more natural and less commercialised forms of tourism.'

Scientists agree that no two eclipses are identical. Professor Jay M Pasachoff, of Williams College, Massachusetts has spent decades trying to work out why the corona is at a temperature of more than one million degrees while the visible surface of the sun, the photosphere, is at a mere six thousand. In the course of this research he has seen fifty-five eclipses, but refuses to name a favourite. As he says: 'They are all good and each is intriguing in its own way. The corona varies in shape over the twenty-two year sunspot cycle.'

Nor do the so-called umbraphiles, as serious eclipse watchers are known, limit their scope to total eclipses. More frequent are partial eclipses, which occur when the moon is too far away in its orbit to cover the sun completely, so a ring of the solar surface is left visible and the corona does not appear. These eclipses are spectacular, and people travel long distances to see them, but they cannot compare to the sheer beauty and drama of a total eclipse in a clear sky.

11 Choose the correct option (A, B, C or D). Decide why your answer is correct and the other options are wrong.

1 What is the writer doing in the first paragraph?
   A accounting for different people's reactions to a total eclipse
   B describing his own emotions on first seeing a total eclipse
   C explaining exactly what can be seen during a total eclipse
   D encouraging readers to go and see a total eclipse

2 What do we learn about the eclipse seen in China in 2009?
   A It lasted for longer than others in living memory.
   B It made more people want to experience seeing one.
   C It left enthusiasts feeling dissatisfied with organised tours.
   D It benefited from particularly favourable climatic conditions.

3 What does Simon Grove suggest about eclipse tourists?
   A They are happy for some aspects of their trips to be left to chance.
   B The number of possible destinations sometimes surprises them.
   C They share certain attitudes with other groups of travellers.
   D The cost of long-haul air travel often limits their activities.

4 What is Jay Pasachoff keen to stress?
   A Some eclipses are more interesting than others.
   B Not all eclipses provide him with useful data.
   C Studying eclipses can be very frustrating.
   D Every eclipse is worthy of his attention.

5 What is suggested about partial eclipses?
   A They are just as exciting to watch as full eclipses.
   B They lack some of the key elements of full eclipses.
   C They attract people who cannot gain access to full eclipses.
   D They are not popular with the most serious eclipse enthusiasts.

IELTS PRACTICE TASK

The Internet Archive

Brewster Kahle is the founder of the Internet Archive, a not-for-profit digital library dedicated to preserving the Internet's past for the use of future historians. 'In the past, if you wanted to study the evolution of language for a PhD or the roles of women in different eras, you had to do all the groundwork with references and citations all done by hand,' he says. 'Now it can be done by machine at an astonishing rate.' Kahle explains that one of the biggest drivers behind the idea was his fear that culture and history would be lost to future generations if they were not preserved online. 'The web is locked in the perpetual present. It's what people want you to see right now and that's not good enough – that's not how you run a society or open culture,' he says. 'The best of the web is already not online.' Clearly, this is a golden age for librarians, historians and scholars and it is the work of men such as Kahle that ensures the extensive data posted on the web is not lost.

The archive is located in a quiet corner of San Francisco. Flashing servers are stacked high, not unlike old books, each blue blink a signal that someone somewhere is trying to reach a webpage frozen in time in its archive. It's one of just a handful of institutions, including parts of the British Library and the Library of Congress in the USA, trying to ensure that what is online now is saved for the future. It does this by capturing more than a billion web pages a week, though it doesn't try to archive every page of every website – on the fast-moving web the average page is changed every hundred days – or any social media. This snapshot of the web has been taken every two months since 1996 and the gateway to the archive, the 'Wayback Machine', is deservedly one of the most popular sites online.

Niels Brügger, director of the Centre for Internet Studies at Aarhus University in Denmark, recalls his frustration at the way the object of his study used to disappear before his eyes. Now, using the Danish national web archive, which takes a snapshot of all '.dk' websites four times a year, he can track how the Internet as a whole is developing in his country, from the different types of websites to the balance between text and images.

He is surprised at how few historians make use of the Internet as a source but expects that to change rapidly in five or ten years as a new generation of scholars better understands its potential and acquires the tools for rigorous data analysis, which are required to study such an ocean of information. 'It really is an astonishing new source for future historians,' he says. 'It gives us a great opportunity to study the daily life of people. It is as if we had a tape recorder on the marketplace in the fifteenth century.' It's a most intriguing parallel.

At the University of Leicester in England, Ruth Page, a lecturer in linguistics, has already made sources such as Wikipedia central to her work. She studies how entries in the online encyclopedia are edited as a particular event unfolds. Page believes that historians will have to transform the way they work. 'I'm an empiricist so I like data. It is like being let loose in a very large sweet shop,' she says. 'But the days of the lone scholar are gone; in my personal opinion we really need to embrace creative ways to work collaboratively.'

The Long Now Foundation, an organisation founded in 1996 to promote long-term thinking, wants to create a space to persuade people to stop and think about how the decisions they make now will affect the next 10,000 years. Laura Welcher, the foundation's director of operations, says for years they have feared a 'digital dark age' where resources kept only online disappear. Initially, the project looked at ways to help people constantly migrate their files to ensure, for example, old Microsoft Word documents were still readable in the newer versions. Then, they got much more ambitious, building a new version of the Rosetta Stone, a silicon disc inscribed with thousands of pages documenting human languages. 'We were very purposeful about creating a future artefact, even if the intentional migration of information into the future is much harder digitally,' she says. Yet she, too, is refreshingly positive about the chances of being able to both create and preserve your own space online. 'I think keeping a story of an individual or of a cultural group is more egalitarian because access to archiving your stuff is easier,' she says. 'It is a very new thing to have your voice out there like never before.'

Questions 1–6

*Choose the correct letter, **A**, **B**, **C** or **D**.*

1 Brewster Kahle originally founded the Internet Archive
   A as a by-product of an online business venture.
   B in connection with his doctoral research project.
   C as part of a study of social interaction on the web.
   D as a way of safeguarding data for future researchers.

2 From the second paragraph, we understand that the Internet Archive
   A is just one of a large number of similar initiatives.
   B is edited to remove outdated content on a regular basis.
   C is an attempt to keep a comprehensive record of all webpages.
   D is designed to provide a representative sample of available data.

3 Niels Brügger predicts that historians will soon begin
   A paying more attention to the visual data available online.
   B making a study of how the Internet has developed in Denmark.
   C developing the skills needed to take full advantage of the Internet.
   D using the resources on the Internet to understand past centuries better.

4 According to Ruth Page, future historians will need to
   A spend more time contributing to popular websites.
   B make more of an effort to co-operate with each other.
   C be willing to change their view of past events more often.
   D be prepared to analyse the language used to record past events.

5 The overall aim of the Long Now Foundation is to encourage
   A the keeping of key data in a non-digital format.
   B a move away from short-term decision making.
   C people to manage their data files more effectively.
   D the long-term retention of data in a variety of languages.

6 In the text as a whole, the writer reveals that she feels
   A optimistic about the future potential of online data.
   B concerned about whether lost data can be recovered online.
   C frustrated at the difficulty of monitoring online data effectively.
   D convinced that enough is being done to preserve online data indefinitely.

Which statement best describes how you feel about Multiple Choice tasks?

   I feel confident about doing Multiple Choice tasks.
   I did OK, but I still need to do more work on Multiple Choice tasks.
   I need more practice with Multiple Choice tasks. I need to focus on …

▶▶ **For further practice, see the DVD-ROM.**

TASK TYPE 13 Identifying the Writer's Views and Claims (Yes/No/Not Given)

For some statements there isn't enough information in the passage to know ...

A About the task

1 Read the information about the task type. Then look at some questions about the task a student in your class has emailed to you. Can you answer them?

The Identifying the Writer's Views and Claims (Yes/No/Not Given) task tests your ability to identify the views and claims of the writer in a passage. It's often used to test your understanding of a passage in which the writer is presenting an argument or where different ideas about a subject are compared and analysed. On the question paper, you see a set of statements that report information and ideas from the passage. Your job is to read the passage and decide if the statements are reporting the information and ideas correctly or not. For each statement, there are three possible answers:

YES   if the statement agrees with the views/claims of the writer
NO   if the statement contradicts the views/claims of the writer
NOT GIVEN   if it is impossible to say what the writer thinks about this

Here are the basic rules for the Identifying the Writer's Views and Claims (Yes/No/Not Given) task:

- The statements follow the order of information in the passage.
- The wording of the statements is not exactly the same as the wording in the passage, but they contain the same information and ideas.
- The statements include some words and names that are also used in the passage. These help to locate the relevant information and ideas.
- You read this section of the passage carefully and compare the writer's views and claims with the statement.
- You then decide if the statement reports those ideas exactly or not, and write *YES* or *NO* on the answer sheet.
- For some statements, there isn't enough information in the passage to know whether the writer's views or claims are being reported exactly or not. In this case, you write *NOT GIVEN* on the answer sheet.

> Hi there,
> I've got some questions for you about the Yes/No/Not Given task.
> 1 Is this the task where the answers are all facts and figures?
> 2 Do the statements come in the same order as the information in the passage?
> 3 Do the statements include words from the passage?
> 4 What do you have to write on the answer sheet?
> 5 If the information is *NOT GIVEN* , do you leave the box blank?
> Thanks!

B Sample questions

2 Read the passage and answer the questions. Use the rules about the task from Section A to help you. Then check your answers. Which questions did you find difficult?

IELTS PRACTICE TASK

Addicted to Tech?

Smartphones, social networking and the Internet are destroying our identities and ruining our lives. At least, that is what two new books, *iDisorder* by Larry Rosen and *Digital Vertigo* by Andrew Keen, would have you believe. I'm not so sure.

Rosen, a psychologist at California State University, argues that over-reliance on technology can cause psychological problems, the *'iDisorders'* of the book's title, but I struggled to find any causal link in chapter after chapter of correlations. He describes how overuse of hand-held devices and general exposure to technology can cause various psychological disorders. But of course, the disorders existed before these technologies, and Rosen fails to convince that their incidence is on the rise.

Digital Vertigo is equally unconvincing. Keen, whose previous book *The Cult of the Amateur* spoke out against user-generated content, states that privacy 'is being dumped into the dustbin of history', warning that we cannot trust the large corporations that run the Internet with our precious personal data. It's a viewpoint I'm entirely sympathetic with, but Keen's argument, woven between name-dropping anecdotes from Silicon Valley conferences and well-known quotes from the film *The Social Network*, left me unconvinced. As Keen points out, we must all take personal responsibility for the information we put online. However, social media needn't inevitably lead to the problems he suggests. I have found Twitter, Facebook and other online services essential for initiating and maintaining major social connections. In fact, without social networking, I would be short one wife, one job and at least half a dozen close friends.

These technologies are tools, and like all tools they must be used correctly. Cars are far more dangerous to society than Facebook. According to the World Health Organization, 1.2 million people die in road traffic accidents each year. As a society we accept this because of the benefits that cars offer, and we work to mitigate the downsides. It should be the same with smartphones and social networking. If you can't go five minutes without a status update then, yes, you should probably step away from the touchscreen, but let's not ignore the great opportunities these technologies offer for fear of some unproven and unrealised disaster. People used to worry about the effects of the telephone on society, but 150 years on, we seem to be managing just fine.

Questions 1–6

Do the following statements agree with the information in the Reading Passage?

Next to each statement, write

> **YES**   *if the statement agrees with the views/claims of the writer*
>
> **NO**   *if the statement contradicts the views/claims of the writer*
>
> **NOT GIVEN** *if it is impossible to say what the writer thinks about this*

1 Rosen has demonstrated a connection between overuse of technology and certain psychological conditions.
2 Rosen provides evidence that the conditions he describes are becoming more common.
3 Keen's previous book has been very influential.
4 Keen is right to warn about the threat to privacy posed by the Internet.
5 An international body is concerned that social networking might be addictive.
6 There may be people who are over-dependent on electronic devices.

C Tips and tactics

3 Work in pairs. Read the tips and tactics and discuss these questions.

   a Which tips and tactics do you think are the most useful?
   b Did you use any of these tips and tactics when you answered the sample questions in Section B?
   c Which tips will you use in the future?

1 Before you read the passage, read the statements in the questions and think about what you're going to read.
2 Don't use your own opinions or knowledge of the subject to decide the answers. Use ONLY the views of the writer of the passage.
3 For each statement, think about the names, key words and main ideas you're looking for in the passage to help you locate the relevant section.
4 First read the passage quickly and mark the relevant sections for each question. Write the question numbers in the margin so that you can find the sections again easily.
5 Remember that the questions follow the order of information in the passage. When you read the passage, you may see some words or ideas from the statements. These help you to find the relevant sections.
6 Questions where the answer is *NOT GIVEN* also refer to a specific section of text – so you always need to find the relevant section.
7 Go through the questions one by one. Read the section of the passage you have marked carefully to make sure you are in the correct place.
8 If you think the statement agrees with the writer's views, re-read both the statement and the section of passage carefully and think about the meaning of both. Does the wording of the statement express exactly the same ideas or not?
9 If you think the statement contradicts the writer's view, re-read both the statement and the section of passage carefully and think about the meaning of both. Underline the words that make the statement different from the passage.
10 For *YES* and *NO* answers, quickly check the rest of the paragraph in the passage to make sure you haven't missed anything.
11 If you think the answer is *NOT GIVEN,* underline the words and ideas in the statement that aren't in the passage. Read the rest of the paragraph in the passage quickly to make sure you haven't missed anything.
12 Remember to write the words *YES, NO* or *NOT GIVEN* in the boxes on the answer sheet.
13 Never leave a box empty. If you're not sure, always give an answer.

D Skills-building exercises

Q FOCUS

Identifying whether statements report the writer's claims or views as expressed in the passage or not

4 Read the pairs of statements (1–5). Underline the important words and ideas in each statement.

1 A I first heard about the particular properties of mycelium at college.
  B I discovered the particular properties of mycelium by chance.

2 A The idea of making packaging materials from mycelium was the result of a joint effort.
  B I needed help to develop my idea of making insulation material from mycelium.

3 A Our packaging is generally no more expensive to produce than its synthetic rivals.
  B Our packaging is generally much cheaper to produce than its synthetic rivals.

4 A We aim to make our products even more environmentally friendly.
  B Our products are already extremely environmentally friendly.

5 A It's encouraging that we can't meet the growing demand for our products.
  B It's worrying that we can't meet the growing demand for our products.

5 Read the passage on page 165 quickly. Mark the sections that contain the information relevant to each pair of statements in Exercise 4.

6 Go through the questions in Exercise 4 on page 164 one by one. Read the passage carefully and decide which statement (A or B) agrees with the writer's claims or views, and which one contradicts it. Write *YES* if the statement agrees with the writer's claim or view, and *NO* if it contradicts it.

7 Work in pairs and answer the questions.

1 Did you and your partner mark the same section of the passage?
2 Are your answers all the same?
3 Discuss why the *YES* statements agree with the writer's claims and views and the *NO* statements do not. Compare your ideas with another pair.

Mushroom Man

Mushrooms are the new styrofoam, says the entrepreneur who is growing everything from packaging material to ocean buoys.

I grew up on a farm in Vermont and I just happened to notice one day that mycelium – that's essentially the 'roots' – of mushrooms – had an unusual quality: it made chips of wood stick together. Years later, at Rensselaer Polytechnic Institute, I was working to develop a better insulation material. I remembered the bonding ability of mushrooms and began to think about industrial applications. After making a few samples, I teamed up with Gavin McIntyre and our professor, Burt Swersey, to figure out how this could work as a product. Packaging materials made from mushroom waste were the outcome.

The strength of our products comes from the mycelium, which consists of millions of tiny fibres. The fibres bond with chitin – a natural plastic produced by mushrooms. Together, these act like a glue, fusing agricultural waste such as seed husks into solid forms. Our materials basically self-assemble; the organism is doing most of the work.

In general, we are cost competitive with synthetic packaging materials such as expanded polystyrene and polyethylene. But that's not our only advantage. Plastics start with expensive, finite raw materials derived from oil or natural gas, whereas we're using waste from farms. For over a century, humans have been using petrochemicals to make plastics. Eventually we will run out, and if we aren't careful toxic waste will choke our oceans and landfills. Biomaterials like ours are sustainable, non-polluting and need little outside energy to make. They also dissolve back into the earth at the end of their useful lives.

As well as packaging, we're also developing materials for the construction industry. We have found that if we take our material and compress it, we can create products that are similar to engineered woods like fibreboard and particle board. Current engineered wood products use toxic resins to hold the wood particles together. In our process, we're using mycelium as the resin. We're also developing materials to replace the plastic foams used in insulation and acoustic tiles. We even grew a miniature house from mushrooms to test our insulation product!

Our key challenge at the moment is an enviable one: scaling up to meet the growing demand. We're coping with it. Restore™ Mushroom® Packaging is now being made widely available, from our Upstate Green Island plant and a manufacturing facility in Cedar Rapids, Iowa through our partnership with Sealed Air Corporation.

Q FOCUS

Identifying if there is a view or claim about the statement in the passage or not

8 Is there enough information in the passage to know if the statements (1–6) agree with the writer's views or not? Do the following:

a Read the statements (1–6) and underline the main ideas.
b Read the passage quickly and find the relevant section for each statement.
c For each statement, read the passage carefully and decide if an opinion about this point is given or not given.

1 The book *The Hidden Persuaders* is still worth reading today.
2 Packard's background in psychology made people take his book seriously.
3 The title of Packard's book may have contributed to its success.
4 Packard should be credited with coining the term 'subliminal advertising'.
5 Vicary's research findings should no longer be considered valid.
6 There is evidence to suggest that subliminal advertising is still in use.

THE BIRTH OF SUBLIMINAL ADVERTISING

These days most people are very aware of the attempts of advertisers and marketing professionals to influence their consumer habits, but this wasn't always the case. The first serious critique of questionable marketing techniques came in 1957 in Vance Packard's celebrated book *The Hidden Persuaders*. It remains one of the best books around for demystifying the deliberately mysterious arts of advertising. Packard argued that advertisers used the techniques of applied sociology and psychology to make consumers perceive a need to buy certain products, whether they really needed them or not. Packard's book was a great success, his impeccable choice of a very catchy title revealing just how well he understood at least one of the basic rules of marketing. In the book, Packard described a number of methods advertisers used to take advantage of consumers' unconscious fears and desires. Although the term was yet to be coined, one such method is what we now know as subliminal advertising.

A notorious experiment involving this technique was conducted by marketing researcher James Vicary in 1956. If popular legend is to be believed, during a showing of a movie called *Picnic* in New Jersey, Vicary used a special projector to flash a subliminal message onto the screen. The message appeared every five seconds, but only remained there for a fraction of a second, far too fast for the human eye to read. The message read, 'Hungry?

Eat popcorn', and the experiment went on for six weeks. The result? According to Vicary, popcorn sales jumped by a whopping 57.8%. The public panicked, thinking this technique could be used for all kinds of sinister purposes. However, in 1962, psychologist Dr Henry Link challenged Vicary to repeat his experiment under controlled conditions. This time, there was no increase in popcorn sales. Vicary later admitted that he'd made up the original sales figures. In fact, it's likely that he never even conducted the first experiment, so his findings deserve to be disregarded. Despite his confession, however, the media and the public continued to focus only on the sensational original story and the idea that subliminal advertising works is still widely believed.

9 Work in pairs. Do you have the same answers for exercise 8? Discuss any answers that are different.

10 Look at the statements Yents where a view is given. Does each statement agree with the writer's view or not? Write *YES* if the statement agrees with the writer's view, and *NO* if it contradicts it.

🔍 **FOCUS**

Identifying if the view in the statement contradicts the writer's view or claim, or if no information is given about it

11 **You are going to identify whether the views in the statements contradict the writer's views or claims, or if no information is given.**

a Read the statements (1–6) and underline the main words and ideas.
b Read the passage quickly and mark the relevant sections for each statement.
c None of the statements agrees with the writer's views or claims. But does each statement contradict the writer's view? Is there enough information to know? Next to each statement, write

NO   *if the statement contradicts the writer's view or claim*
NOT GIVEN   *if it is impossible to say what the writer thinks about this*

1 The majority of steel shipping containers currently in Amsterdam are unlikely to go to sea again.
2 Various solutions to Amsterdam's housing shortage have been tried.
3 The suggested way of repurposing used steel shipping containers is not a new idea.
4 The poor condition of some of the containers means they cannot be reconditioned.
5 Once rehabilitated, the containers sell for relatively low prices.
6 Reconditioned shipping containers could meet the growing housing needs of developing nations.

12 **Work in pairs. Did you get the same answers for Exercise 11? Discuss any which are different. Then compare your answers with those of another pair.**

CARGOTECTURE

About eighteen million steel shipping containers are currently moving cargo on seas and roadways around the world. But, especially in countries where imports outnumber exports, such as the Netherlands, mountainous stacks of them pile up in the ports. Some two million steel containers sit idle at any given time, and some of these will eventually be retired.

In the densely populated city of Amsterdam there is a pressing need for student and other low-cost housing. One innovative suggestion for meeting this need is to repurpose used steel shipping containers. A growing number of steel containers are being cleaned and refurbished and then used to house people instead of products. It's an idea that could catch on.

This creative, green style of housing costs only a fraction of what it costs to build standard houses, and requires less energy and new materials. Freight containers are available for just a few thousand dollars before they are rehabilitated. Despite their uniform size and shape, they can be used in a nearly endless number of configurations because they fit together like real-world building blocks. After years at sea, the containers are often dented and beat up, but they can be reconditioned to look remarkably attractive. The interiors are compact but can be made into cosy living spaces.

Today, half of the Earth's population lives in cities, and that figure will reach sixty per cent by 2030. Nearly all of this urban expansion is likely to occur in the sprawling cities of the developing world, which already suffer from a lack of decent, affordable housing.

More than eight hundred million people now live in urban slums and that number is expanding. Slum housing often lacks basic necessities for human health, including running water and proper sanitary facilities. Steel shipping containers can be economically fitted with necessities like modern bathrooms and other amenities for a fraction of traditional construction costs. Although cargo containers cannot by themselves solve the urban housing needs of developing nations, they may provide a useful resource.

IELTS PRACTICE TASK

Fieldwork on the final frontier

What is it like to work in the remote forests of Papua New Guinea? Biologist Vojtech Novotny knows better than most.

Let me tell you about our work in Papua New Guinea. We've built a research station on the northern coast. About five per cent of all species live in Papua New Guinea. With the Amazon and the Congo, it is one of the three largest areas of rainforest still left.

Papua New Guinea has about 800 different languages, a really amazing diversity, and there are 20 different ones within a 20 mile radius of our station. Because different tribes speak such different languages, they also speak one universal language, pidgin English. Once you learn that – and Europeans usually manage this in less than six months – you can speak directly to the local people. This is socially very rewarding because there is a coming together of tribal culture and high-level academic culture.

We have a team of what we call para-ecologists. These are people we train in scientific methods and pay to work with us. The local people are perfect for this. They not only have an intimate knowledge of the local geography, they also have an extensive knowledge of taxonomy, especially of the trees. We connect the Latin names with their local language names and then explain that we need caterpillars from this list of trees, and ask them to collect them for us. On one occasion, we were studying tiny larvae that bore tunnels in leaves. I put a fairly high reward for every live insect. We were expecting that our collectors might earn £5 a day, which is reasonable by Papua New Guinea standards and by our budget. But embarrassingly, they found so many that we had to lower the rate because otherwise we would have gone bankrupt.

This collaboration with local people helps our research because it opens up possibilities that others don't have. For instance, we have contacts with people who own the forest that they cut down for their subsistence, using traditional 'slash-and-burn' agricultural methods. We always like to shock our fellow biologists at conferences by describing how we are cutting down tropical forests so that we can survey insects from the canopy. But that's exactly what we are doing. When local people were clearing their part of the forest, we worked with them, slowly taking the forest apart, collecting caterpillars, ants, everything.

We have devised a 3D structure of insects and plants in the forest. Our inventory came up with about 9,500 insect species feeding on 200 species of tree, and they do it in 50,000 different ways. Even for us ecologists, this is a mind-boggling complexity. However, ecologists also tend to get overexcited by the huge diversity we see in rainforests and extrapolate it to unrealistic numbers of species for the entire planet. Previous estimates put the number of insect species worldwide at 30 million. We put it at six million. We found that a tree species has about the same number of insect species feeding on it whether it grows in Papua New Guinea or Europe: tropical forests are so rich in insects only because they have so many species of tree.

Questions 1–6

Do the following statements agree with the claims of the writer in the Reading Passage?

Next to questions 1–6, write

YES   *if the statement agrees with the claims of the writer*

NO   *if the statement contradicts the claims of the writer*

NOT GIVEN   *if it is impossible to say what the writer thinks about this*

1   The range of languages in the region makes communication difficult for Europeans.
2   The training of para-ecologists costs less in Papua New Guinea than in Europe.
3   Reducing the rate of pay offered to specimen collectors can reduce their effectiveness.
4   The fact that some local collaborators are also landowners is an advantage.
5   The researchers try to discourage the use of destructive agricultural practices.
6   There is a tendency for scientists to underestimate the diversity of species in existence in the world.

Which statement best describes how you feel about Identifying the Writer's Views and Claims (Yes/No/Not Given) tasks?

☐   I feel confident about doing Yes/No/Not Given tasks.
☐   I did OK, but I still need to do more work on Yes/No/Not Given tasks.
☐   I need more practice with Yes/No/Not Given tasks. I need to focus on …

▶▶ **For further practice, see the DVD-ROM.**

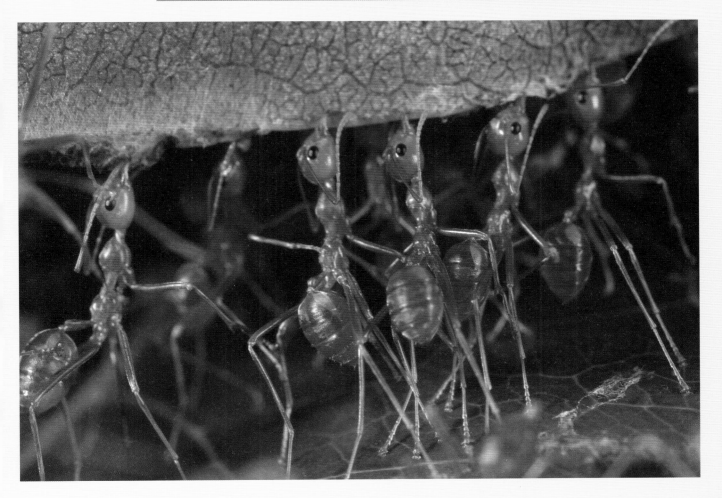

Identifying the writer's views and claims

1 Read the information about identifying the writer's views and claims.

In the IELTS exam you need to read carefully to identify the views of the writer. As well as recognising phrases used to express views, it helps to pay close attention to linking words such as *however* and the grammar of the sentence (affirmative or negative).

2 Decide if the expressions in bold suggest the writer is in favour of or against an argument or point of view. Write the expression in the appropriate column.

1 Rosen argues that over-reliance on technology can cause problems, but **I struggled to find a causal link**.
2 Rosen **fails to convince** their incidence is on the rise.
3 *Digital Vertigo* **is equally unconvincing**.
4 It's a viewpoint **I'm entirely sympathetic with**.
5 Keen's argument **left me unconvinced**.

In favour of	Against
	I struggled to find a causal link.

Go back to the text on page 163 and check the expressions in context, or use a dictionary.

Collocation: adjective + noun

3 Match the adjectives (1–7) with the nouns (a–g) to make collocations. Look at the text on page 152 to help you.

1	endless	a	hopes
2	lasting	b	concerns
3	hidden	c	view
4	symbolic	d	meaning
5	appealing	e	source of intrigue
6	alternative	f	legacy
7	waking	g	idea

Commonly confused words

4 Look at the word pairs and think about how they differ in meaning. For more context, find one word from each pair in the text on page 151.

1	thick/fat	4	hardly/hard
2	eventually/lastly	5	momentary/momentous
3	decade/decayed	6	reminder/remember

5 Choose the correct option in each sentence.

1 Pitch is a *thick / fat* material.
2 A large droplet *eventually / lastly* falls out of the funnel.
3 He left the apparatus alone for *decades / decayed*.
4 You may be able to watch the *momentary / momentous* event yourself.
5 It's *hardly / hard* an easy matter.
6 It's a nice *reminder / remember* of the excitement caused.

Synonyms

6 Match the words (1–9) with words or phrases with a similar meaning from the box.

> big   careful   change totally   development   equal   interesting   keep
> never-ending   remember

1	evolution	4	recall	7	transform
2	perpetual	5	rigorous	8	preserve
3	extensive	6	intriguing	9	egalitarian

Antonyms

7 Match the words (1–8) with words or phrases with an opposite meaning from the box.

> ancient   different   include   minimise   nearby   slow   tiny   weak

1	modern	3	massive	5	resilient	7	similar
2	maximise	4	rapid	6	remote	8	exclude

To help you, go back to the text on page 155 and check the words in context. A form of all words appears in the text.

8 Complete the sentences with words from Exercise 7.

1 Modern agriculture aims to .... profit, to make the most money possible.
2 The loss of an entire crop would cause .... food shortages.
3 The Cavendish is a more .... banana cultivar.
4 The seed bank is located on a .... island, miles from anywhere.
5 Seeds are packaged to .... moisture so as to keep the seeds dry.

Common IELTS topic: Agriculture
Commonly confused words

9 Choose the most suitable options to complete the sentences.

1 Humans no longer spent so much time hunting once they had *tamed / domesticated* cattle, sheep and chicken.
2 Soil quality cannot be *sustained / supported* if farmers re-use the same land year after year.
3 Seeds from the trees may be *circulated / distributed* by the wind, birds and animals.
4 Experts *assess / estimate* that 90% of cotton produced in the USA comes from genetically-modified plants.
5 China now *consumes / utilizes* twice the amount of meat that it did ten years ago.
6 The number of apple varieties has been *declining / reducing* over the last few centuries.
7 More and more people are *excluding / rejecting* gluten from their diet.
8 By keeping the seeds safe, scientists hope to *ensure / insure* against future famines.
9 Certain plant species are unable to *exist / survive* the warmer temperatures brought on by global warming.
10 To prevent the growth of bacteria, meat must be *saved / stored* in the refrigerator.

Collocation: adjective + noun

10 Complete the sentences with an adjective from the box.

> controlled   excess   exact   fresh   hard   primary   severe   top

1 The government needs to take a .... approach to reducing food waste.
2 The recent drought has resulted in a .... shortage of corn and wheat.
3 The .... crop which is grown in the region is rice.
4 Scientists must find ways to prevent .... moisture from ruining the seeds.
5 Researchers carried out the experiment in a .... environment in a laboratory.
6 Many people prefer working in cities to making a living from .... labour.
7 The .... layer of soil has been gradually eroded by flooding.
8 The .... source of the disease is unknown, but it has affected many trees.

READING PASSAGE 1

*You should spend about 20 minutes on **Questions 1–13,** which are based on Reading Passage 1.*

The Return of the Leech

A leech is a type of freshwater worm that attaches itself to people and animals which enter rivers and ponds. The leech is a parasitic creature, which takes blood from its host in order to survive. It has long been recognised that leeches have therapeutic effects on their hosts that can be useful in medicine. Meanwhile, throughout history there has been a widespread belief that removing blood from the body through a procedure known as bloodletting is effective in the treatment of illnesses, and leeches were an easy way of achieving this.

The earliest recorded use of leeches being used for this purpose dates back 3,500 years to paintings of medicinal leeches found in tombs in ancient Egypt, but the practice is probably much older, and medical treatment with leeches is also thought to have been practised in ancient China. In classical Greece and Rome, bloodletting with leeches was believed necessary to restore the body's essential balance, even in perfectly healthy people, whilst in medieval Europe, doctors and chemists made extensive use of leeches to treat all manner of diseases. In the days before antibiotics and sterile surgery, bloodletting was one of the few tools available to combat infections and treat wounds, although in many cases, the treatment was ineffective and often even dangerous.

The practice of bloodletting by leeches reached its peak in the 1830s and leeches were used to treat a wide variety of disorders, ranging from headaches to yellow fever. Medical bloodletting was so popular that the commercial trade in leeches became a major industry. In France, for example, the domestic supply was insufficient to meet demand and in 1833 alone, 4.1 million leeches were imported from places as far away as India and Africa, although the best leeches were said to come from Sweden and Hungary. Leeches were harvested by collectors who would walk through the water, allowing the creatures to attach themselves to their legs. A good collector could gather up to 2,500 leeches in a day. Indeed, so many leeches were harvested that the creature was in danger of becoming extinct, and leech farms were established in France and Germany to ensure a continued supply.

By the early 20th century, hirudotherapy – the medical use of leeches – was considered old-fashioned and somewhat barbaric. This all changed in the 1980s thanks to Joseph Upton, a surgeon based at Harvard University in the USA. Upton wrote an article about his successful use of hirudotherapy to treat a condition called venous insufficiency, where blood pools under the skin. Not only can leeches remove the excess blood quickly, but their saliva contains a natural anti-coagulant called hirudin that prevents blood from clotting.

In fact, the saliva of leeches is a useful pharmaceutical substance in other respects too. It acts as a local anaesthetic because it contains a chemical that numbs its host so that the person doesn't know that a leech has attached itself. Leech saliva also contains both a chemical that brings down swelling, and bacteria that produce a natural antibiotic substance to prevent their host picking up other infections. Hirudotherapy has been found to have a range of uses. For example, a clinic in Germany has reported that it is useful in treating arthritis, a painful condition that affects the knees and other joints.

Scientists at the University of Wisconsin and elsewhere have been trying to develop a mechanical leech that would avoid the risk of infection and be effective over longer periods. Real leeches only feed for 15 to 30 minutes before they become full and detach themselves from the host. Hopefully, patients who are bothered by the thought of biological leeches might be better able to tolerate the mechanical kind.

Questions 1–8

Do the following statements agree with the information given in Reading Passage 1?

In boxes 1–8 on your answer sheet, write

> **TRUE**   *if the statement agrees with the information*
>
> **FALSE**   *if the statement contradicts the information*
>
> **NOT GIVEN** *if there is no information on this*

1 The first historical evidence for the use of leeches in medicine comes from China.

2 In Ancient Rome, leeches were used to treat people who were not ill.

3 In medieval Europe, bloodletting may have done more harm than good.

4 In the 19th century, more leeches were used in France than in any other country.

5 Wild leeches are quite difficult to catch in large quantities.

6 Leech farming was developed in the 19th century in response to a shortage of wild leeches.

7 In the early 20th century, the use of leeches was prohibited in the USA.

8 Joseph Upton struggled for many years to prove that hirudotherapy was effective.

Questions 9–13

Complete the notes below.

Choose **NO MORE THAN TWO WORDS** from the passage for each answer.

Write your answers in boxes 9–13 on your answer sheet.

Modern Medical Use of Leeches

<u>**Properties of leech saliva**</u>

Stops blood **9** ....

Works as a **10** .... (host unaware)

Contains a substance that reduces **11** ....

Contains bacteria that act as a **12** ....

Also helps patients suffering from **13** ....

READING PASSAGE 2

*You should spend about 20 minutes on **Questions 14–26**, which are based on Reading Passage 2.*

Driverless Cars

A Autonomous vehicles that require no driver at the wheel have become the hottest new thing in the car industry as technology companies and carmakers race to build vehicles that will revolutionise the way we travel, commute, work and own cars. The idea may sound futuristic but its proponents think the benefits are tangible and will come soon.

B 'There are no limits. We're pushing cars beyond anything people thought possible before,' says Professor Alberto Broggi, a self-driving pioneer from Parma in Italy. He's been driving autonomous cars for more than fifteen years without mishap. But for most of that time the technology has been on the sidelines. 'The first test we did was back in 1998 when no one was talking about autonomous cars … the media was treating it as one of those things crazy professors do,' says Broggi. 'When we made it to the national news, our drive was broadcast after an item about the fattest cat in the world.' Although much of the technology exists in many cars today in devices such as parking cameras and electronic steering, it was only Google's demonstration of self-driving technology in 2010 that brought serious attention. That demonstration, says Andy Palmer, Nissan's head of product planning, 'put a rocket under the industry'.

C The most obvious effect of letting cars control themselves is reclaiming time for drivers. In the USA, people who commute by car spend about fifty minutes a day at the wheel, says Ragunathan Rajkumar, a professor at Carnegie Mellon University. Saving those dead hours 'enhances the productivity of the individual', he says. Carmakers dream of commuters spending the time replying to emails or school runs where parents help their kids with their homework.

D A second effect could come with quicker travel. No longer under the control of slow-reacting humans, cars can travel much closer together without the danger of collisions. 'The majority of traffic jams are caused by the mismatch of speeds between different vehicles,' says Prof Rajkumar. 'Autonomous vehicles don't have to speed up or slow down.' Also, by driving close together in narrow lanes at a constant speed, autonomous cars could pack themselves far more tightly into the same amount of road space. This could also have a telling impact on urban planning and reduce the need for new roads as the world's population rises, particularly in cities in developing countries in danger of being throttled by traffic. The average US citizen spends thirty-eight hours a year stuck in traffic, whilst cars spend ninety per cent of their lives parked up. Such inefficiency would be eliminated if cars ruled the road, and passengers could get on with their lives.

E Another significant benefit could be a big reduction in accidents, most of which are caused by human error. 'Our vision is very simply that cars shouldn't crash,' says Toscan Bennett, a product planner at Volvo, which builds cars programmed to spot and avoid large animals such as moose. 'And one of the ways to prevent cars from crashing is to actually take the human out of the equation.' Despite a capacity to save many lives, however, automated cars may still struggle for social acceptability. Even a small number of mishaps would raise difficult questions about the technology. 'People aren't comfortable with robots killing them,' says Bryant Walker Smith, of Stanford University in the USA. Meanwhile, insurers have nightmares about court cases involving crashes for which responsibility lies with a defective microchip rather than a person. Carmakers say these difficult questions will not stop them. 'There are many things that have to be solved,' says Alan Mulally of Ford. 'But we're absolutely committed to the technology.'

F   Meanwhile, marketing experts are looking at the economics. In the early days, high costs will mean few people can afford the vehicles. Ford's self-driving prototypes cost about $500,000. Although these costs would fall once a vehicle goes into production, most buyers would be priced out of the market. To spread the cost, autonomous cars will simply have to work harder, says Paul Saffo, a Silicon Valley commentator, touring the streets endlessly to justify their costs by ferrying more people around – operating more like taxis than private vehicles and making some forms of public transport such as buses redundant.

G   Indeed, the impact in social, economic and personal terms promises to be far-reaching. If the industry's visionaries are to be believed, it will mean a complete rethink of the car – many people's second most valuable possession after their home. The role of the car as a status symbol would be under serious threat. Ultimately, with the development of automated cars, there may be no reason to own a vehicle at all, no matter how low prices fall. If it can be summoned with nothing more than the tap of a smartphone app, then discarded after dropping a passenger off, why bother to own a car outright? 'People won't buy robotic cars, they'll subscribe to them,' says Mr Saffo.

H   But it will be humans who determine whether driverless cars become the norm. Habits and cultural norms do not change quickly – particularly when they concern an object that has become a conspicuous part of daily life. A study by the UK's Automobile Association found that sixty-five per cent of people liked driving too much to want an autonomous car. It may take a generational change to overcome such deeply ingrained beliefs. Mr Saffo, who came of age in California in the second half of the 20th century – the golden age of the car – says: 'For my age group, personal freedom was a car.' But of the students he teaches now at Stanford University, he says: 'For them, a smartphone fulfils that function.' The desire to be liberated rather than enslaved by technology will be the decisive factor.

Questions 14–20

Reading Passage 2 has eight paragraphs, A–H.

Which paragraph contains the following information about driverless cars?

*Write the correct letter, **A–H**, in boxes 14–20 on your answer sheet.*

Some letters may be used more than once.

14 An example of a particular manufacturer already using some related technology.

15 Evidence that confirms that the idea of the cars wasn't always taken seriously.

16 Mention of an event that changed attitudes towards the idea of the cars.

17 The idea that the cars would need to be used more intensively.

18 An example of how an individual might gain access to a driverless car.

19 Mention of the determination of those in the industry to overcome legal complications.

20 The suggestion that there is great competition between manufacturers to be the first to produce them.

Questions 21–24

Complete the summary below.

*Choose **NO MORE THAN TWO WORDS** from the passage for each answer.*

Write your answers in boxes 21–24 on your answer sheet.

How automated cars will make road travel more efficient.

Ragunathan Rajkumar predicts that people travelling to work or **21** .... by car will be able to make more efficient use of the time if they use autonomous cars. The time spent travelling could also be reduced thanks to the technology. Drivers tend to be rather **22** .... which means that cars have to keep a safe distance from one another. Driverless cars can use the available road space more efficiently because they do not need such wide **23** .... and can travel at a **24** .... which doesn't vary.

Questions 25–26

*Choose **TWO** letters, **A–E**.*

Write the correct letters in boxes 25 and 26 on your answer sheet.

The list below includes some predictions made about the impact of driverless cars.

Which **TWO** are mentioned by the writer?

A They may not be suitable for all the world's cities.

B They would be too expensive for most individuals to buy.

C The technology might not be totally reliable.

D Most people would find using them enjoyable.

E People will come to see them as a symbol of personal freedom.

READING PASSAGE 3

*You should spend 20 minutes on **Questions 27–40**, which are based on Reading Passage 3.*

Ultraconserved Words

The idea that it is possible to trace the relationship between languages by comparing words with similar sounds and meanings seems obvious today, but there was little research in this field until the 1780s. That is when William Jones noted the similarity between Latin, Greek and Sanskrit, and proposed that they all derived from a common ancestral language. This idea is the basis for historical linguistics and has been used to trace the movements of people from place to place. For instance, by comparing Romany with various Indian languages, it was possible to prove that India was the original homeland of the Roma people living in Europe.

Traditionally, linguists have believed that it was impossible for words to exist in a recognisable form for more than nine thousand years. Recently, however, evolutionary biologist Mark Pagel and colleagues from the University of Reading in the UK claim to have traced a group of common words back to the language used by hunter-gatherers some fifteen thousand years ago.

The team from Reading published a report in the *Proceedings of the National Academy of Sciences* indicating that they had found a group of what they termed 'ultraconserved' words that have survived since the last Ice Age. The researchers studied some two-hundred cognates – words that have a similar sound and a similar meaning in more than one language. For example, the English word *mother* has cognates in numerous languages, including *madre* in Spanish, *mutter* in German, *mater* in Latin, *matar* in Sanskrit, and *mathair* in Irish. The researchers examined commonly used words, because these are the ones which are less likely to change over time.

Seven major language families were studied, which together comprise over seven hundred individual modern languages: Altaic, which includes modern Turkish and Mongolian; Chukchi-Kamchatkan, which includes the languages of north-eastern Siberia; Dravidian, which includes languages spoken in southern India; Inuit-Yupik, which includes languages spoken in Alaska and other Arctic regions; Kartvelian, which includes Georgian and other languages spoken in the Caucasus region; and Uralic, which includes Finnish and Hungarian. About half of the world's current population speaks one of the languages in these seven families, but the individual languages make for quite a diverse group; they do not sound alike, use a range of different alphabets and their speakers are widely separated geographically.

When the researchers found cognates, they tried to translate these into 'proto-words' which they believed to be the common ancestral item of vocabulary. This required a knowledge of how sounds change when words move from one language to another; for example, the *p* sound in Romance languages (*pisces* in Latin and *pesce* in Italian) becomes an *f* in Germanic languages (*fisch* in German and *fish* in English). The team then looked at these proto-words in relation to the languages in the seven families, and were gratified to find twenty-four that were shared by at least four of the language families, although frustratingly only one (*thou*) that was found in all seven. According to Pagel, however, all this points to the existence of a proto-Eurasiatic language, which was the ancestor of all the languages in these families. 'We've never heard this language, and it's not written down anywhere,' he says, 'But this ancestral language was spoken and heard. People sitting around campfires used it to talk to each other.'

Some of the twenty-three ultraconserved words on the list are unsurprising: *mother, you, me, this, what, not, man, fire*. Others are rather unexpected: *bark, worm, to spit, ashes*. Pagel found the inclusion of the verb *to give* on the list heartwarming. 'I was really delighted to see it there,' he says. 'Our society is characterised by a degree of cooperation and reciprocity that you simply don't see in any other animal. Verbs tend to change fairly quickly, but that one hasn't.'

The study's conclusions are not without critics. Linguist Sarah Thomason from the University of Michigan in the USA is unconvinced and finds a number of flaws in it. She writes: 'This is the latest of many attempts to get around the unfortunate fact that systematic sound-meaning correspondences in related languages decay so much over time that even if the words survive, they are unrecognisable as cognates ... This means that word sets that have similar meanings and also sound similar after fifteen thousand years are unlikely to share those similar sounds as the result of inheritance from a common ancestor.' William Croft, a linguist at the University of New Mexico in the USA, is more sympathetic than many to the idea, and says that the use of methods from evolutionary biology makes the idea of a Eurasiatic superfamily more plausible. 'It probably won't convince most historical linguists to accept the Eurasiatic hypothesis, but their resistance may soften somewhat.'

Questions 27–32

Do the following statements agree with the views/claims of the writer of Reading Passage 3?

In boxes 27–32 on your answer sheet, write

> **YES** *if the statement agrees with the views of the writer*
>
> **NO** *if the statement contradicts the views of the writer*
>
> **NOT GIVEN** *if it is impossible to say what the writer thinks about this*

27 William Jones was a pioneer in the field of historical linguistics.

28 Study of Romany has shown that it is most closely related to other European languages.

29 Linguists had overestimated how long words might exist in a recognisable form.

30 The National Academy of Sciences was impressed by Pagel's research methods.

31 Pagel's team studied words that begin with the same sound in various languages.

32 Pagel's team concentrated on words which occur very frequently in the languages studied.

Questions 33–37

*Complete each sentence with the correct ending **A–H** below.*

*Write the correct letter, **A–H**, in boxes 33–37 on your answer sheet.*

33 The languages in the families studied by Pagel's team are

34 Dravidian is given as an example of a group of languages which are

35 The proto-words which Pagel's team initially identified were

36 Pagel's team was pleased to find a number of proto-words which are

37 Pagel's team was disappointed not to identify more proto-words which were

---

A also the ancestor of the rest of the world's languages.

B common to all of the larger groups under consideration.

C currently spoken by a significant proportion of the world's inhabitants.

D derived from cognates found across groups of languages.

E likely to have similarities in their written form.

F currently spoken in one specific geographical area.

G marked by similarities in the way they are pronounced.

H found in the majority of the language groups studied.

Questions 38–40

*Choose the correct letter, **A**, **B**, **C** or **D**.*

Write the correct letter in boxes 38–40 on your answer sheet.

38 Pagel was particularly pleased to find that '*to give*' was an ultraconserved word because

  A it was one of the few verbs on the list.
  B it was one that he wouldn't have predicted.
  C it reflects an enduring aspect of human behaviour.
  D it proves that some word classes are less likely to change.

39 Sarah Thomason is critical of Pagel's study because

  A she doubts that it has looked at enough cognates to be valid.
  B she feels that it is merely replicating previous work on cognates.
  C she feels that more research is needed on the subject of cognates.
  D she thinks it is based on a wrong idea about which words are cognates.

40 William Croft puts forward the view that Pagel's research

  A may help to make historical linguists more open to his ideas.
  B has made linguists more sympathetic to interdisciplinary studies.
  C puts forward a convincing case for a Eurasiatic superfamily of languages.
  D should have made more use of study methods from evolutionary biology.

A The Test

Academic Writing	Description	Suggested time	Minimum length	Marks
Task 1	Describing visual information	20 minutes	150 words	1/3 of total
Task 2	Expressing and justifying an opinion	40 minutes	250 words	2/3 of total

The IELTS Academic Writing Test is designed to test your ability to write in clear, coherent, and well-organised English. There are two Writing tasks, and you have one hour to complete both tasks. The instructions advise you to spend about 20 minutes on Task 1 and 40 minutes on Task 2. You can decide how to organise your time, but it's best to follow this advice.

In Task 1, you see some visual information on the question paper. For example, there may be a chart, a graph, a table, a diagram or a map/plan. Your job is to describe this visual information in your own words. There is no need to give your opinion about the data or to interpret the information in any way, because only a simple description is required.

In Task 2, a point of view or argument is presented on the question paper. Your job is to comment on this, giving your own opinions with examples from your own knowledge and experience.

In Task 2 you have to write more words, have more time and more marks are available. This doesn't mean that Task 1 is easier to write, however. In fact, you may have more experience of writing opinion essays and so you may find this easier than describing visual information. The main difference between Tasks 1 and 2 is that Task 1 only calls for a simple description, whereas in Task 2 you're expected to give your opinion.

Task 1

For Task 1, you see some sort of visual information which you need to describe. There may be, for example, a map or a diagram showing a process or how something works, or statistical information may be presented in the form of line graphs, bar charts, tables or pie charts. This information often describes how something has changed over time, and there may be two sets of visual information to compare.

Your job is to describe the most important points in the statistical or diagrammatic information in your own words. For statistical tasks, you usually need to select and report on the most important features of the charts, to identify trends, and to compare and contrast data. For map tasks, you often have to compare the features of a place over time, for example, a map of a town today compared with one of the same town twenty years ago. In diagram tasks, you usually have to describe a process, for example, how a product is made or how a piece of equipment functions.

There are seven Task 1 Writing lessons, which deal one by one with the seven possible variations in Task 1.

Task 2

In Task 2, you're asked to give your opinion about a contemporary issue, and to support your opinion with reasons and examples. The issue that you have to write about is given on the question paper, and there is no choice of topic. But the issues included are familiar ones that most students already know quite a lot about. Not all tasks are the same, however, and you may, for example, be asked to present a solution to a problem, present and justify an opinion, or to compare and contrast evidence and the opinions of other people.

The task on the question paper often takes the form of a brief, general statement and you have to say to what extent you agree or disagree with it. The task may, however, present two sides of an argument and ask you to discuss these views before giving your own opinion. A third type of task presents you with a problem and asks you to describe possible causes and solutions.

You don't need any special knowledge to do any of these tasks and you're marked on your use of language rather than your opinions. Some typical Task 2 topics include: technology, culture, education, family, health, friendship, transportation, the environment, travel, crime, work and entertainment.

There are three Task 2 Writing lessons, which deal one by one with the three possible variations in Task 2.

B Marking criteria

Writing tasks are marked by trained examiners according to very detailed criteria. The two tasks are marked separately, and each is given a band score from 0–9. Half-band scores such as 4.5 are also possible. Task 2 accounts for two thirds of your overall Writing score, and Task 1 accounts for one third.

Tasks are marked according to four criteria. Each of these criteria counts equally towards your score for each task.

Task Achievement (Task 1)

Here the examiner assesses whether you have fulfilled the task. For example, have you included all the relevant information in your own words? Did you write at least 150 words?

Task Response (Task 2)

Here the examiner assesses whether you have fulfilled the task. For example, have you addressed all the points in the task? Are your ideas supported by examples and reasons? Did you stay on topic? Did you write at least 250 words?

Coherence and Cohesion

Here the examiner assesses your ability to write a coherent and cohesive answer. For example, is your answer organised in a clear and logical way? Is there a smooth flow of ideas? Have you used paragraphs effectively? Are your paragraphs, sentences and clauses joined together with appropriate linking words and phrases?

Lexical Resource

Here the examiner assesses your ability to use a wide range of vocabulary accurately and appropriately. For example, do you know enough words to answer the question fully? Have you used formal words? Have you spelled words correctly and used the correct form of words?

Grammatical Range and Accuracy

Here the examiner assesses your ability to use a range of grammatical structures accurately. In other words, do you know which grammatical structures to use to write your answer? Does your answer use a wide range of simple and complex grammatical structures? Is the grammar of your sentences generally accurate?

For the IELTS Writing Band Descriptors for Task 1 and Task 2, see pages 331 and 332.

C Strategies

Before the test

•   It's a good idea to familiarise yourself with the format of the Writing test. Make sure you know exactly what you have to do in both parts of the test – then you can feel confident and prepared on the day of the test. For example, you could read some examples of students' writing tasks and see what marks they were given and why.

•   Practise doing the writing tasks within the time limit. Students often spend too long on Task 1 because they try to include too much information. This leaves them with too little time to complete Task 2.

•   For Task 1, it's important to look at the visual material and understand it fully before you start writing. Practise looking at charts, tables, etc, to see how the information is typically laid out. Practise identifying the most important pieces of information.

•   For Task 1, expressing ideas clearly in a few words is a key skill. Use the exercises in this section to practise comparing trends and ideas within the same sentence and between short sentences by using linking words and phrases, e.g. *whereas, although, on the other hand*, etc.

•   When you practise writing the tasks, use a stopwatch app on your phone or computer to time yourself.

•   When thinking about possible Task 2 topics, it's a good idea to choose a topic, brainstorm some ideas, and then make a note of them. Do this with as many topics as possible.

•   For Task 2, practise writing plans for different types of questions before you answer them. Make sure you plan to include an introduction, two or three paragraphs on different aspects of the topic and a conclusion.

•   Read in English as often as you can. Use the Internet to keep up with the latest news and current affairs in English. While you're reading, think about your opinions on the issues. This can help you find something to say about a variety of different topics.

•   As you read about current issues, make a list of words and phrases that relate to that topic. Make a note of how words are spelled and used, for example, idiomatic expressions they are used in, prepositions and other words they collocate with, etc.

During the test

•   In the test, the tasks appear on the question paper and you write your answers on a separate answer sheet. There is a specific space on the answer sheet for you to write each of the two tasks. You can write on the question paper if you like, but only the answer sheet counts. The question papers are collected in and destroyed.

•   Write clearly so that the markers can read your writing easily. You can write in cursive style (*example*) or you can print (*example*). You can make corrections and changes if you like, but make sure it is clear what you want the examiner to read as part of your answer.

•   Remember to divide your work into paragraphs and to make this clear to the examiner by leaving spaces between paragraphs or by indenting the first word of each paragraph.

•   Make sure you write more than the minimum number of words for each task – 150 words for Task 1 and 250 words for Task 2. There is no maximum number of words, but you should focus on writing a clear and correct answer rather than a long one.

•   Don't waste time counting words during the test. Always check the number of words you write when you do practice tasks – this helps you to develop a feel for how much you need to write during the actual exam.

•   Remember that the two tasks are not timed separately, but that the question paper advises you to spend 20 minutes on Task 1 and 40 minutes on Task 2. It's best to follow this advice. There is always a clock in the exam room that everyone can see.

•   Remember not to spend too long on Task 1.

After the test

•   It's a good idea to reflect on how you performed in the test, but don't waste time and energy worrying about any mistakes that you may have made.

WRITING TASK 1

You should spend about 20 minutes on this task.

> *The graph below gives information from a report about the purpose and frequency of Internet use by medical students in 2009 in one country.*
>
> *Summarise the information by selecting and reporting the main features and make comparisons where relevant.*

Write at least 150 words.

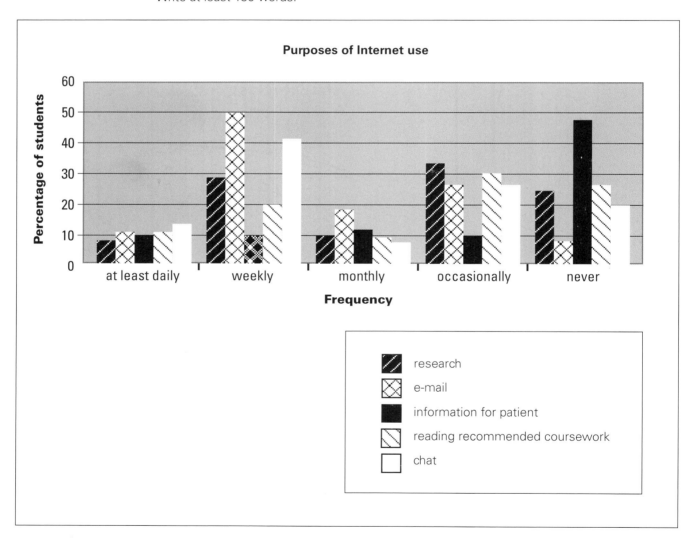

WRITING TASK 2

You should spend about 40 minutes on this task.

Write about the following topic:

> *On balance, advertising is more harmful than beneficial.*
>
> *To what extent do you agree or disagree?*

Give reasons for your answer and include any relevant examples from your own knowledge or experience.

Write at least 250 words.

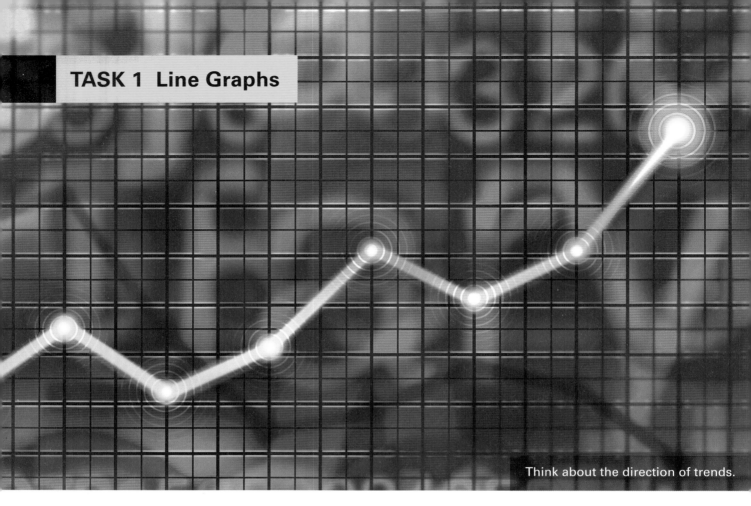

TASK 1 Line Graphs

Think about the direction of trends.

A About the task

1 Read the information about the task.

Task 1 tests your ability to look at visual information in a graph, chart, table or diagram, and identify and report the most important information in your own words.

One common way to present visual information is in the form of a line graph. On the question paper, you see a line graph with a title. The instructions for writing your response appear in a box above the graph. There is also a brief description of the information in the line graph in the box. There is usually a key (legend) which helps you to distinguish the lines on the graph and tells you what each line represents. Your job is to look at the graph and select, summarise and describe the most important information.

Line graphs typically show *trends*. A trend is a movement of data in a general direction over time. On a line graph, trends are represented by the direction of the lines. Trends can be upward or downward or they can remain at the same level. An important part of your response is to describe trends and to compare them.

The horizontal axis usually involves units of time: days, months, years, and so on. Usually the time represented in the task is in the past, but some graphs include projections about the future. The vertical axis can show almost any kind of data: costs, temperatures, rainfall, amounts of some commodity, population figures, and so on.

It's important to examine the graph before you write your answer, and to think about what the graph is telling you. You have to look and think carefully and choose what information to include so that your response reports only the key information.

Here are the basic rules for writing about a line graph:

- Look at the graph carefully and decide what the most important information and striking features are.
- Write a well-organised overview.
- Include data to support the key points.
- Use an academic register or style.
- Write at least 150 words.
- Complete the task in about 20 minutes.
- Include only the key points. Minor details or irrelevant data can be left out.
- Don't do any calculations or give your opinion about the information.

2 Work in pairs. Complete the sentences (1–9) with the correct ending (A–I).

1   Your overall task is to identify and write about
2   You should write
3   You aren't required to write
4   The graph usually has
5   The text box above the graph includes
6   The numbers on the horizontal axis usually represent
7   The key on a line graph provides
8   The direction of the lines on a line graph shows
9   You have about

A information about what each line represents.
B units of time.
C over 150 words.
D trends, which can be rising, falling, or level.
E an explanation or analysis of the information on the graph.
F the most important information shown in the line graph.
G 20 minutes to complete the task.
H a title above it.
I instructions and some information about the graph.

B Sample question

3 Read the instructions and answer the question. Use the rules about the task from Section A to help you. Then look at the sample answer on page 334. Which aspects of the task did you find difficult?

IELTS PRACTICE TASK

You should spend about 20 minutes on this task.

> *The graph below gives information about the technology that households in one US city used for watching television between 2004 and 2014.*
>
> *Summarise the information by selecting and reporting the main features, and make comparisons where relevant.*

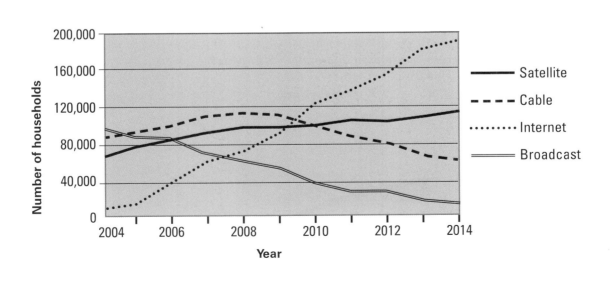

C Tips and tactics

4 Work in pairs. Read the tips and tactics and discuss these questions.

    a Which tips and tactics do you think are the most useful?
    b Did you use any of these tips and tactics when you answered the sample question in Section B?
    c Which tips will you use in the future?

1   The first step is to look carefully at the information in the line graph. Don't rush through this step. Make sure you understand the graph before you start to write.

2   Underline important words in the question and circle important points on the graph.

3   Identify what key information is being presented in the graph and which important dates, figures or striking features you'll need to write about.

4   Plan your writing. You can usually divide it into three paragraphs: introduction, first main paragraph and second main paragraph.

5   If the line graph has more than two lines, try to arrange the data into two or three groups. For example, you could divide the data into rising trends and falling trends.

6   Look carefully at the timeframe that the graph covers and work out what tenses you need to use (past, present, present perfect or future).

7   Begin with an introductory sentence that describes the graph in general terms, but don't repeat the exact wording of the question.

8   Then describe one or two general trends shown in the graph. Don't go into detail; just report the most important trends you see when you look at the graph.

9   In the first main paragraph, select and write about the features that are most important and interesting, for example, rising or falling trends, or where lines intersect, and include relevant data to support the points you make.

10   Focus on the general direction of a trend; don't write about each change in direction of a line.

11   Don't try to write about all the data in the line graph and don't include details that are irrelevant to the main trends.

12   Remember, don't try to analyse or explain the information in the graph, or do any calculations; just describe and report it.

13   Keep track of the time. Don't spend more than 20 minutes on Task 1.

14   Make sure your handwriting is clear and legible.

15   Keep in mind the criteria that the examiners use to mark your response. (For marking criteria, see About the Academic Writing Test, page 180.)

D Skills-building exercises

INTRODUCTORY VERBS

indicate *The graph **indicates** the growth in the service sector and the decline in the manufacturing sector.*

show *This graph **shows** how two programs performed over a ten-year period.*

compare *The graph **compares** changes in the annual rainfall in four cities.*

provide/give information *Information **is provided/is given** in this graph about the gradual growth of productivity for several firms.*

provide data *This graph **provides data** about three trends: … , … , and … .*

FOCUS

Writing introductory
sentences to
describe the graph
in general terms

5 Look at the title and the graph about average temperatures in Paris, Dubai and
Melbourne. Write four introductory sentences about the graph using introductory
verbs from the box on page 186. Try to use different sentence structures and
vocabulary in each sentence.

1 This graph shows the average temperatures in three cities over a two-month period.

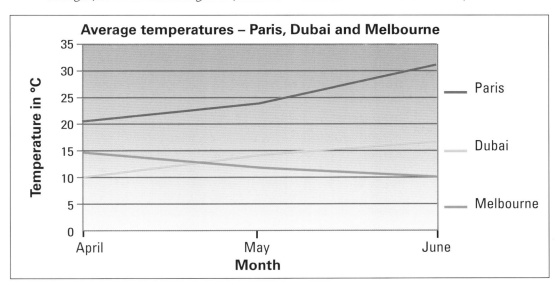

DESCRIBING TRENDS

UP ↗

rise (v) Production costs **rose** to their highest level of the year in July.

rise (n) There was a **rise** in production costs to the highest level of the year in July.

go up (v) Between 1900 and 2000, the population **went up** by over a million people.

grow (grew, grown) (v) The number of first-time users **grew** rapidly in 2015.

growth (n) There was a rapid **growth** in the number of first-time users in 2015.

increase (v) The numbers of cyclists **increased** between 2005 and 2010.

increase (n) There was an **increase** in the number of cyclists between 2005 and 2010.

DOWN ↘

decline (v) The construction of new homes **declined** for ten years in succession.

decline (n) There was a **decline** in the number of new homes for ten years in succession.

go down (v) After a brief rise, imports **went down** again.

decrease (v) Average test scores **decreased** at three of the schools.

decrease (n) There was a **decrease** in test scores at three of the schools.

drop (v) In 2008, foreign investment **dropped** by over 20%.

drop (n) In 2008, there was a **drop** in foreign investment of over 20%.

fall (fell, fallen) (v) The number of overseas students **fell** in 2013.

fall (n) There was a **fall** in the number of international students in 2013.

SAME →

stay the same The company's market share **stayed the same**.

remain constant For three months, the percentage **remained constant**.

UP AND DOWN ↘ ↗ ↘

fluctuate (v) The number of seasonal workers employed by the company **fluctuates** each
year.

fluctuation (n) There have been **fluctuations** in the number of seasonal workers employed
by the company.

go up and down (v) Fares **have gone up and down** over the last few months.

PREPOSITIONS OF TIME

at (+ time of day) **at** *noon;* **at** *8 a.m.*

on (+ date/day of the week) **on** *1st October;* **on** *Mondays*

in (+ month/season/year/decade/century) **in** *June;* **in** *the summer;* **in** *2014;* **in** *the 1990s;* **in** *the 21st century*

for (a period of time) **for** *ten years;* **for** *the next several months*

by (before or at a specific point in time) **by** *10th April;* **by** *the end of 2016*

until (up to a certain point) **until** *December 31;* **until** *2020;* **until** *the beginning of 2014*

from ... to/between ... and (starting points and ending points) **from** *2001* **to** *2015;* **between** *1st January* **and** *31st June*

before/after (+ point in time) **before** *5:00 p.m.;* **after** *the 19th century*

around (+ period of time or point in time) **around** *1997; for* **around** *six months*

during (for the duration of a period of time) **during** *the 1980s;* **during** *the winter;* **during** *April*

▶▶ For more information and practice of prepositions, see Grammar Resource Bank page 327.

Q FOCUS

Describing general trends and main features

6 Look at the graph about the number of university applications. Write sentences with the words in brackets. Write about main trends or important points.

1 (rise / from ... to)
 The number of applications received by Atherton University rose from 1980 to 2005.
2 (climb to / by)
3 (fall to / in)
4 (a decline in / during)
5 (fluctuate / between ... and)
6 (level off / around)
7 (reach a peak / around)
8 (drop / after)
9 (stay the same / from ... to)

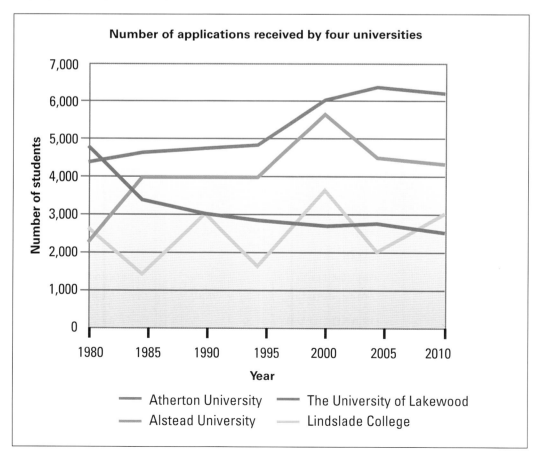

ADVERBS AND ADJECTIVES

UP OR DOWN QUICKLY ↑↓

rapidly (adv) *The number of smartphones in use has risen* **rapidly** *over the last ten years.*

rapid (adj) *In this decade, there was a* **rapid** *increase in smartphone use.*

suddenly (adv) *Employment figures dropped* **suddenly** *during the following ten years.*

sudden (adj) *The next decade saw a* **sudden** *decrease in employment figures.*

sharply (adv) *The price of textbooks rose* **sharply**.

sharp (adj) *There was a* **sharp** *rise in the price of textbooks.*

dramatically (adv) *Exports fell* **dramatically** *last year.*

dramatic (adj) *There was a* **dramatic** *fall in exports last year.*

significantly (adv) *Property taxes rose* **significantly** *in 2014.*

significant (adj) *There was a* **significant** *rise in property taxes in 2014.*

steeply (adv) *The number of people attending the event increased* **steeply** *in 2013.*

steep (adj) *The year 2013 saw a* **steep** *increase in the number of people attending the event.*

major (adj) *A* **major** *expansion of the company's marketing department is expected in the next few years.*

UP OR DOWN MORE SLOWLY ↗↘

steadily (adv) *The number of tourists visiting the park rose* **steadily**.

steady (adj) *The park experienced a* **steady** *increase in the number of tourists.*

gradually (adv) *The population of the province* **gradually** *declined.*

gradual (adj) *There was a* **gradual** *decline in the population of the province.*

slightly (adv) *Bus fares may go up* **slightly**.

slight (adj) *A* **slight** *increase in bus fares is expected.*

minor (adj) *There were* **minor** *fluctuations in the value of raw materials.*

▶▶ **For more information and practice of adjectives and adverbs, see Grammar Resource Bank pages 313–315.**

7 **Look at the graph about students studying languages at university. Write two sentences about each language. Use vocabulary from any of the language boxes on pages 186–189 to help you. Try to write about main trends or significant features.**

French

1   <u>The number of students studying French increased somewhat from 1990 to 1995.</u>

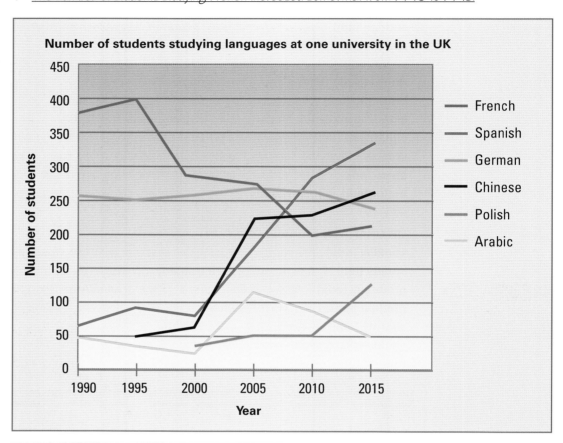

Number of students studying languages at one university in the UK

— French
— Spanish
— German
— Chinese
— Polish
— Arabic

DESCRIBING PROJECTIONS

Some line graphs make predictions about the future. When you are describing a projection, you should use language that indicates that these activities take place in the future and that the data is uncertain.

***might* + infinitive**   *The costs of doing business in Country B **might rise** next year.*

***may* + infinitive**   *Government revenues **may go down** again during the next quarter.*

***will* + *probably* + infinitive**   *According to the graph, the number of websites **will probably double** over the next few years.*

***is* + *probably* + *going to* + infinitive**   *There **is probably going to be** an increase in the number of television dramas this autumn.*

noun + *is predicted*   *A sudden **increase in tourism is predicted**.*

***is predicted* + *to* + infinitive**   *The number of tourists **is predicted to rise**.*

noun + *is expected*   *A decline in the **average age is expected**.*

noun + *is expected* + *to* + infinitive   *The **average age is expected to go** down.*

***It is expected that* + clause**   ***It is expected that** the average age will decrease.*

▶▶ **For more information and practice of future tenses, see Grammar Resource Bank pages 304–306.**

FOCUS

Using the right tense to describe projections

8 Look at the graph showing worldwide rice consumption. Write sentences about the four projections. Remember to use language from the box on page 190 to indicate that the data is uncertain.

1 <u>According to Projection 1, rice consumption around the world is expected to grow to over 520 metric tonnes.</u>

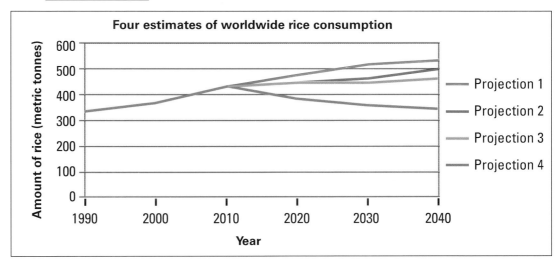

FOCUS

Understanding the task

9 Work in pairs. Look at the line graph below and answer the questions.

The graph below gives information about marriage and divorce in the United Kingdom from 1956 to 2006.

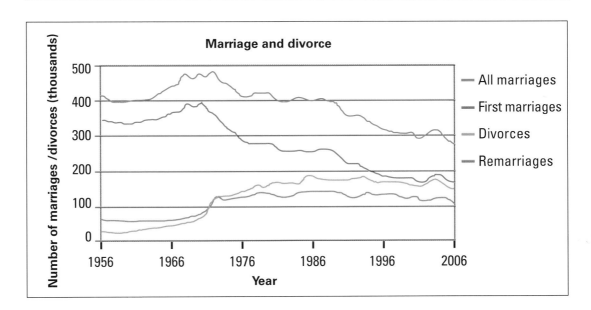

1 What basic information does the graph provide?
2 What do the four lines on the graph indicate?
3 What is measured on the vertical axis? What unit of measurement is used?
4 What is measured on the horizontal axis?
5 What trends do you see in the graph?
6 What are some of the most important features of this graph?
7 Should you try to report on all the changes in direction that you see in the graph? Why?/Why not?

10 Look at the graph about marriage and divorce on page 191 again. Answer the questions.

1 Which of these statements about the graph (A or B) do you think is the best introductory sentence? Why is it better?

A This graph provides information about marriage and divorce in the United Kingdom from 1956 to 2006.

B This graph indicates the changing nature of marriage, divorce and remarriage over a period of five decades.

2 Which of these statements best describes the main trends of the graph? Why is it better?

A In general, we see that the number of marriages declined dramatically over this period, while the number of divorces and remarriages slightly increased.

B Overall, the marriage rate went from about 405,000 per year to less than 300,000 a year, while the number of divorces went from about 30,000 a year to about 150,000.

11 Look carefully at the graph below and answer the questions. (3–5 minutes)

1 What is the overall purpose of the graph?

2 What are one or two important points about the population in:
a the United States? b Nigeria? c Japan?

3 What points of comparison can you make about changes in population in these three countries?

> *The graph below gives historical information and projections about changes in population in the United States, Nigeria and Japan.*

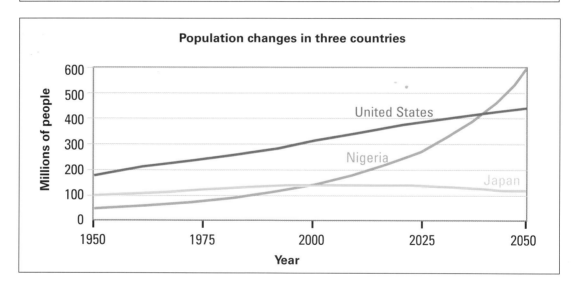

Population changes in three countries

12 Now write your answer. (10–15 minutes)

1 Write an introductory statement (based on the information in the text box above the graph) and describe the main trends shown in the graph in paragraph 1.

2 Give details about changes in population in the three countries in the next paragraph. Remember to use the appropriate tenses (past and future for predictions).

3 Compare the population changes in the third paragraph.

13 Check your work. Look for mistakes in spelling, punctuation and grammar. Make sure that you have used the correct tenses, and used a good variety of language for describing graphs. (3–5 minutes)

14 Work in pairs. After you have finished, look at the model answer on the DVD-ROM. Compare your answers with the model answer and think about the marking criteria. (See page 180 for marking criteria.)

IELTS PRACTICE TASK

You should spend about 20 minutes on this task.

> *The graph below gives information about how teenagers (aged 12–19) in one state in the United States communicated with each other.*
>
> *Summarise the information by selecting and reporting the main features, and make comparisons where relevant.*

Write at least 150 words.

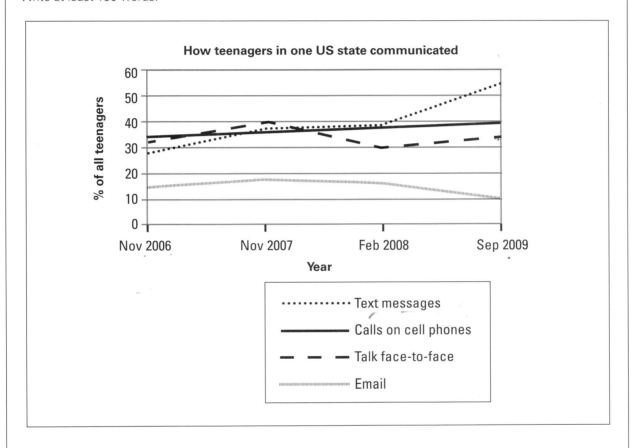

Which statement best describes how you feel about Task 1 Line Graphs tasks?

☐ I feel confident about writing responses for Task 1 Line Graphs.
☐ I did OK, but I still need to do more work on writing responses for Task 1 Line Graphs.
☐ I need more practice with writing responses for Task 1 Line Graphs. I need to focus on …

▶▶ **For further practice, see the DVD-ROM.**

TASK 1 Bar Charts

Think about the big picture.

Whale sharks swimming at the Churaumi Aquarium, Okinawa, Japan

A About the task

1 Read the information about the task.

This version of Task 1 tests your ability to look at and identify the most important and relevant information and trends in a bar chart, and then report the information in your own words.

On the question paper, you see a bar chart with a title. The instructions for writing your response appear in a box above the chart. There is also a brief description of the information in the bar chart in the box. There is usually a key (legend) that explains what each bar represents. Your job is to look at the chart and select, summarise and describe the most important information.

Bar charts represent different values with rectangular bars. They present the same sort of information that is found in line graphs but in a different form. Typically, one axis represents some numerical value such as costs, income, birth rates, temperatures, etc. The other axis can represent many different types of information: units of time, different countries or cities, means of travel, sources of energy, and types of people (male and female; employed and unemployed; teenagers and adults, etc.).

Bar charts are often used to compare things and many bar charts show *trends* – changes in numbers in a certain direction over time. You should describe these trends and compare and contrast them in your response. However, be aware that not all bar charts show consistent trends.

There may also be *exceptions*. For example, a chart may show that the number of people who use smart phones has been growing annually except for one year.

It is important to look at the bar chart carefully and think about the information in the chart. You shouldn't write about all of the information; you have to choose the points to write about carefully.

Here are the basic rules for writing about a bar chart:

■ Look at the chart carefully and decide what the most important information and striking features are.
■ Write a well-organised overview.
■ Include data to support the key points.
■ Use an academic register or style.
■ Write at least 150 words.
■ Complete the task in about 20 minutes.
■ Include only the key points. Minor details or irrelevant data can be left out.
■ Don't do any calculations or give your opinion about the information.

2 **Work in pairs. Look at the bar chart and answer the questions.**

1 What topic does it provide information about?
2 What is meant by the term 'trends'?
3 What trends do you see in this chart?
4 What is meant by the term 'exception'?
5 What exception do you see in this chart?
6 Which are the lowest and highest bars in the chart?

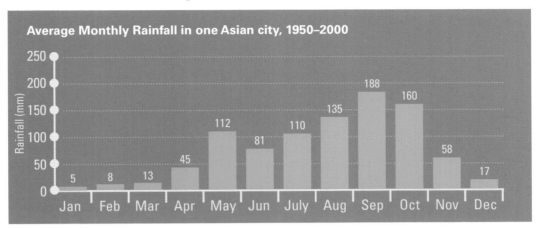

B Sample question

3 **Read the instructions and answer the question. Use the rules about the task from Section A to help you. Then look at the sample answer on page 334. Which aspects of the task did you find difficult?**

IELTS PRACTICE TASK

You should spend about 20 minutes on this task.

> *The chart below gives information about how commuters travelled to work in one city in New Zealand.*
>
> *Summarise the information by selecting and reporting the main features, and make comparisons where relevant.*

Write at least 150 words.

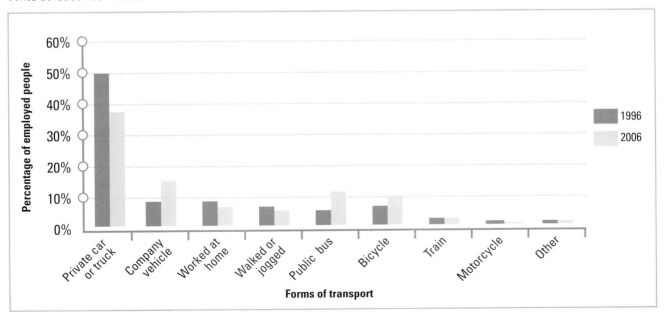

C Tips and tactics

4 Work in pairs. Read the tips and tactics and discuss these questions.

a Which tips and tactics do you think are the most useful?
b Did you use any of these tips and tactics when you answered the sample question in Section B?
c Which tips will you use in the future?

1 The first step is to look carefully at the information in the bar chart. Don't rush through this step. Make sure you understand the chart before you start to write.
2 Underline important words in the question and circle important points in the bar chart.
3 Identify what key information is being presented in the bar chart and which important dates, figures or striking features you'll need to write about.
4 Plan your writing. You can usually divide it into three paragraphs: introduction, first main paragraph and second main paragraph.
5 Look carefully at the timeframe that the bar chart covers and work out what tenses you need to use (past, present, present perfect or future).
6 Begin with an introductory sentence that describes the bar chart in general terms, but don't repeat the exact wording of the question.
7 Then describe one or two general trends or features shown in the bar chart. Don't go into detail; just report the most important trends and features you see when you look at the chart.
8 In the first main paragraph, select and write about the features that are most important and interesting, and include relevant data to support the points you make.
9 When selecting key information, look for the highest and the lowest bar. Look for any trends and exceptions to those trends.
10 Don't try to write about all the data in the bar chart and don't include details that are irrelevant to the main trends.
11 Remember, don't try to analyse or explain the information in the chart, or do any calculations; just describe and report it.
12 Be careful when talking about quantities. If you're unsure about exact figures, it's better to give an approximate figure, e.g. *Factory A produced around 5,000 units.*
13 Keep track of the time. Don't spend more than 20 minutes on Task 1.
14 Make sure your handwriting is clear and legible.
15 Keep in mind the criteria that the examiners use to mark your response. (For marking criteria, see About the Academic Writing Test, page 180.)

D Skills-building exercises

APPROXIMATION

around *The population grew by **around** a million people in that decade.*

about *According to the chart, **about** 45% of all people surveyed believe in UFOs.*

roughly ***Roughly** 300,000 units were manufactured in factory A in 2005.*

approximately ***Approximately** 4,000 more people attended this year's parade.*

almost *The vacancy rate for hotel rooms is **almost** zero in August.*

nearly ***Nearly** 90% of people in the country agreed with this decision.*

just over ***Just over** 2.5 billion people worldwide own digital cameras.*

just under *This state has **just under** 300 days of sunshine a year.*

NUMBERS AND AMOUNTS

the number of
***The number of** serious storms to affect New England rose to 21 this year.*

the amount of
***The amount of** natural gas produced this year increased sharply.*

more than
*There was **more** rainfall in April **than** in May.*

fewer than
*The chart indicates that **fewer** people visited this website in 2012 **than** in 2011.*

less than
*The factory produced **less** pollution during 2010 **than** in the previous year.*

(about) the same as
*The amount of time it takes to complete task A is **(about) the same as** the amount of time it takes to complete task B.*

To make these expressions stronger, you can use *many, much, far*: **many** more than, **much** more than, **far** less than

To make these expressions weaker, you can use *slightly* or *a little*: **slightly** more than, a **little less** than

twice as many as
*There were nearly **twice as many** accidents at the factory this year **as** last year.*

twice as much as
*According to the chart, there was about **twice as much** coal mined in this county in the 1940s **as** in the 1990s.*

(nearly/almost) doubled
*The amount of milk produced at this dairy farm **nearly doubled** over the five year period.*
*The number of runners in the race **almost doubled** between 2000 and 2015.*

half as many as
*There were only about **half as many** applications for jobs received in January **as** there had been in July.*

half as much as
*A dollar in 1980 was worth around **half as much as it** had been in 1967.*

amount + times + as many as *There were, on average, about **three times as many** pages in newspapers in country A **as** in country B.*

amount + times + as much as
*There was around **four times as much** traffic in city X **as** in city Y.*

Comparing numbers
and amounts using
approximation

5 Look at the chart about world production of bicycles and cars. Write sentences about
the information in the chart using these phrases:

1 the number of
   The number of cars produced rose to its highest point in 2000 to about 50 million.
2 slightly more / than
3 roughly three times as many / as
4 far fewer / than
5 about twice as many / as
6 only half as many / as

> *The chart compares worldwide production of bicycles and cars over a fifty-year period.*

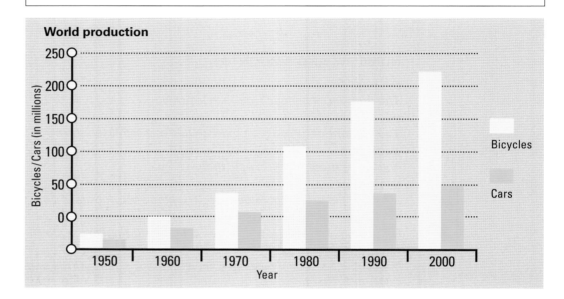

6 Look at the chart about snowfall in Canadian ski resorts. Then write complete
sentences with information from the chart. Use the expressions in the language boxes
on page 197.

1 Viking Mountain / November / December
   Viking Mountain had slightly less snow in November than in December.
2 Viking Mountain / Snowbury / November
3 Snowbury / Viking Mountain / December
4 Powder Peak / December / November

> *The chart shows the amount of snowfall at three Canadian ski resorts over a two-
> month period.*

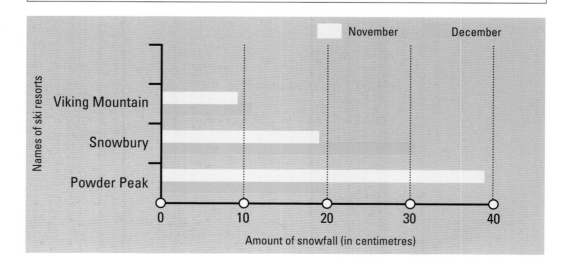

7 Look at the chart below. Use information from the chart to write sentences with these words and phrases.

1 the most expensive
   The Beijing Olympics in 2008 were the most expensive.
2 the second most expensive
3 the least expensive
4 slightly higher than
5 much less costly than
6 far more expensive

> *The chart shows the initial estimate of costs and the actual costs for the Summer Olympics from 1976 to 2012.*

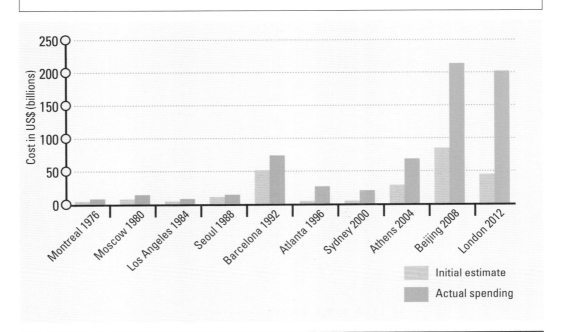

▶▶ **For more information and practice of comparatives and superlatives, see Grammar Resource Bank pages 315–316.**

The chart below provides information about student accommodation at one US university in 2013.

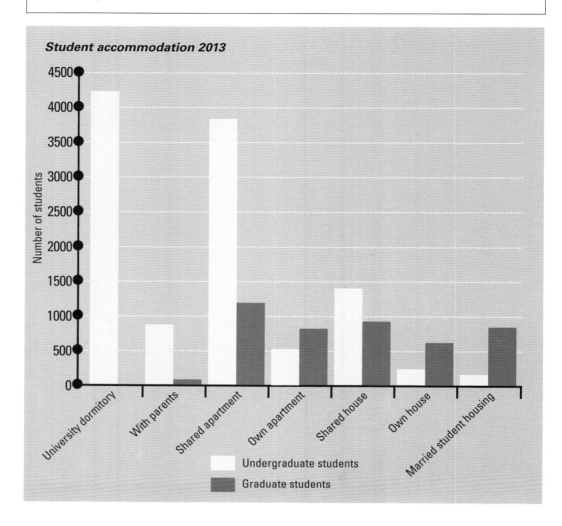

Student accommodation 2013

GLOSSARY

dormitory (n) student accommodation provided by a university

8 Look carefully at the chart and the instructions and answer the questions. (3–5 minutes)

1 What is the overall idea of the chart?
2 What are two important points about undergraduate student accommodation?
3 What are two important points about graduate student accommodation?
4 What points of comparison can you make between undergraduate and graduate student accommodation?

9 Now write your answer. (10–15 minutes)

1 Write an introductory statement (based on the information in the text box above the chart) and describe the overall idea or main trend shown in the chart in paragraph 1.
2 Write two or three important points about undergraduate student accommodation.
3 Write two or three important points about graduate student accommodation.
4 Compare the information about graduate and undergraduate student accommodation. Give examples to support your answer.

10 Check your work. Look for mistakes in spelling, punctuation and grammar. Make sure you have used comparative and superlative forms correctly, and used a good variety of language to describe charts. (3–5 minutes)

11 Work in pairs. After you have finished, look at the model answer in the answer key on the DVD-ROM. Compare your answers with the model answer and think about the marking criteria. (See page 180 for marking criteria.)

IELTS PRACTICE TASK

You should spend about 20 minutes on this task.

> *The chart below gives information about the purpose of visits to five cities in the UK in 2013.*
>
> *Summarise the information by selecting and reporting the main features, and make comparisons where relevant.*

Write at least 150 words.

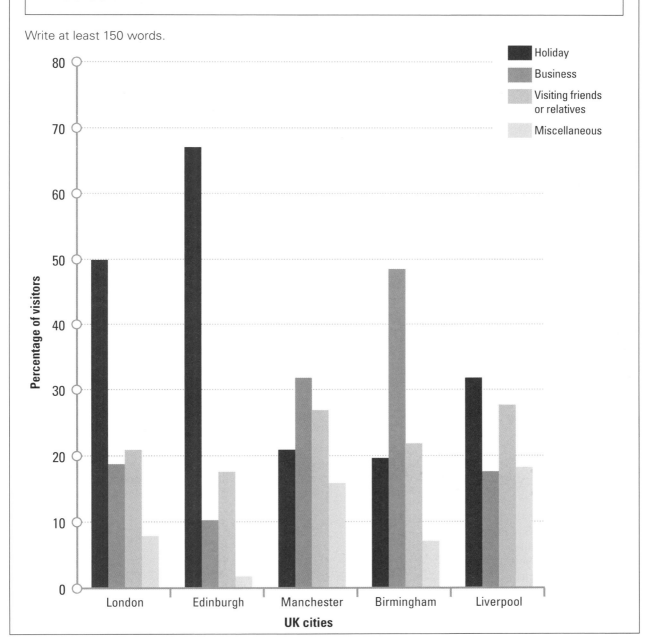

TASK 1 Tables

Decide what the most important information and striking features are.

A climber on limestone pinnacles, Madagascar

A About the task

1 Read the information about the task.

This version of Task 1 tests your ability to look at and identify the most important information in a table, and then report the information in your own words.

On the question paper, you see a table with a title. The instructions for writing your response appear in a box above the table. There is also a brief description of the information in the table in the box. Your job is to look at the table and select, summarise and describe the most important information.

The columns and rows in the table may represent different time periods, different types of people, different countries and so on. Each box in the table contains numbers. There may be certain trends (a general direction in which something is developing or changing), sharp increases or decreases, or exceptions. Your task is to identify the most important and interesting points, and write a well-organised overview, comparing and contrasting where appropriate.

Here are the basic rules for writing about a table:

- Look at the table carefully and decide what the most important information and striking features are.
- Write a well-organised overview.
- Include data to support the key points.
- Use an academic register or style.
- Write at least 150 words.
- Complete the task in about 20 minutes.
- Include only the key points. Minor details or irrelevant data can be left out.
- Don't do any calculations or give your opinion about the information.

2 Work in pairs. Look at the table on page 203 and answer the questions.

1 What information does the table provide?
2 Look at the text shaded in darker blue across the top of the table. What information does this give you?
3 Look at the text shaded in darker blue in the left-hand column. What information does this give you?
4 What trends can you see in the table?
5 What exceptions to the trends can you see in the table?
6 How much time would you have to write about a table like this in an IELTS exam?
7 How long (how many words) should your answer be?

Monthly mobile phone usage by age in one Australian city

Age group	2007		2012	
	Minutes used	Texts sent/received	Minutes used	Texts sent/received
younger than 18	760	1004	322	1898
18–24	728	705	401	1392
25–34	640	530	633	854
35–44	516	252	502	590
45–54	577	134	568	304
55–64	478	103	442	202
older than 64	405	32	578	18

B Sample question

3 Read the instructions and answer the question. Use the rules about the task from Section A to help you. Then look at the sample answer on page 335. Which aspects of the task did you find difficult?

IELTS PRACTICE TASK

You should spend about 20 minutes on this task.

> *The table below gives information about passenger arrivals and departures at the six main airports serving London for the year 2012.*
>
> *Summarise the information by selecting and reporting the main features and make comparisons where relevant.*

Write at least 150 words.

Passengers in and out of London's airports, 2012

Airport	Number of passengers (in millions)	Change from 2011	% of total passengers	Distance from central London
Heathrow	70.0	+ 0.9%	52%	22km
Gatwick	34.2	+ 1.7%	25%	48km
Stansted	17.4	- 3.2%	13%	64km
Luton	9.6	+ 1.1%	7%	57km
London City	3.0	+ 0.8%	2%	11km
Southend	1.2	+ 135%	1%	64km
Total	**135.0**	**+ 1.0%**		

C Tips and tactics

4 Work in pairs. Read the tips and tactics and discuss these questions.

   a   Which tips and tactics do you think are the most useful?
   b   Did you use any of these tips and tactics when you answered the sample question in Section B?
   c   Which tips will you use in the future?

1   The first step is to look carefully at the information in the table. Don't rush through this step. Make sure you understand the table before you start to write.

2   Underline important words in the question and circle important information in the table.

3   Identify what key information is being presented in the table and which important figures or striking features you'll need to write about.

4   Plan your writing. You can usually divide it into three paragraphs: introduction, first main paragraph and second main paragraph.

5   Look carefully at the timeframe that the table covers and work out what tenses you need to use (past, present, present perfect or future).

6   Begin with an introductory sentence that describes the table in general terms, but don't repeat the exact wording of the question.

7   Then describe one or two general trends or features shown in the table. Don't go into detail; just report the most important features you see when you look at the table.

8   In the main paragraph, select and write about the features that are most important and interesting, and include relevant data to support the points you make.

9   When selecting key information, look for the highest and the lowest figures in each set of figures, and the range between them.

10   Look for similarities and differences in the information in the table and try to divide the information in the table into groups. Write about each main point.

11   Don't try to write about all the data in the table and don't include details that are irrelevant to the main trends.

12   Remember, don't try to analyse or explain the information in the table, or do any calculations; just describe and report it.

13   Keep track of the time. Don't spend more than 20 minutes on Task 1.

14   Make sure your handwriting is clear and legible.

15   Keep in mind the criteria that the examiners use to mark your response. (For marking criteria, see About the Academic Writing Test, page 180.)

D Skills-building exercises

Q FOCUS

Using the correct wording to describe the categories or figures in a table

5 Look at the table on page 205 about sources for films. Then look at the sentences (1–5). Choose the best option to complete the sentences.

1   *Based on original screenplay / Films based on an original screenplay* had the highest *per cent / percentage* of market share.

2   *Films based on books or plays / Books and plays* represented about a third of all the films made during this period.

3   There were slightly more *based on fact / movies based on fact* made than *on TV / movies based on TV shows*, and *based on fact / films based on fact* had a higher total gross.

4   *Legend and fairy tale / Films that were based on legends and fairy tales* represented just under two per cent of all movies made in this period.

5   *Theme park rides / Movies based on theme park rides* had the lowest *percentage of market share / market share per cent* but had by far the highest average gross.

> **The table shows the source material on which Hollywood movies were based from 1995 to 2013.**

	Movies	Total gross ($ billions)	Average gross ($ millions)	Market share (%)
1 Original screenplay	4,972	77.5	15.6	47.2
2 Based on books/plays	1,087	49.2	116.2	29.9
3 Remake	264	10.9	36.4	5.8
4 Based on TV	180	8.8	48.7	5.3
5 Based on fact	188	11.2	41.3	6.8
6 Based on legend and fairy tale	43	1.7	40.1	1.1
7 Based on theme park ride	7	1.4	196.0	0.8

6 Write four more sentences based on the information in the table. Make sure you correctly identify the category you are writing about.

USING THE CORRECT TENSE

Present simple: If no definite time periods are given, you should use the present simple. *People over the age of 65 **send** and **receive** the lowest number of text messages.*

Past simple: When a table gives definite past time periods, you should use the past tense. *In the 1950s, about half the population of the United States **lived** in urban areas.*

Present perfect: If you are looking back from now to actions or situations at an earlier time in the past that are in some way connected to the present, you should use the present perfect tense. *The number of internet users **has increased** significantly since 1998.*

Past perfect: You can use the past perfect tense when you are talking about two periods of time in the past. *Only about 15% of the population lived in cities in 1850, but by 2000, that number **had reached** nearly 70%.*

Possibility in the future: If the table involves projections about the future, use verb forms that express possibility in the future. *The urban population **may reach** 70% by 2025.*

▶▶ For more information and practice of tenses, see Grammar Resource Bank pages 303–308.

🔍 **FOCUS**

Identifying the timeframe to help you choose the correct tense

7 Read the box above about using the correct tense. Then look at the two tables below about car colours and answer the questions.

1 Write five sentences about the information in the first table.
2 Write five sentences about the information in the second table. Use the correct verb tense in each sentence.

Overall preference for car colours in four countries/regions (% of total new cars sold)

	White	Black	Silver	Blue	Grey	Red	Green	Other
North America	20	17	17	13	12	11	3	7
Brazil	11	25	31	3	16	8	2	4
Europe	10	26	20	13	18	7	2	4
South Korea	18	26	44	2	8	1	0	1

Preference for car colours globally (% of total new cars sold)

	1994	2004	2014	2024 (estimated)
White	21	20	27	25
Black	11	13	16	15
Silver	15	25	20	25
Blue	9	9	8	9
Grey	10	6	13	8
Red	12	7	4	15
Green	8	6	4	1
Other	14	14	8	3

ACADEMIC WRITING 205

8 **Rewrite the following sentences. Replace the underlined words using words or expressions with a similar meaning.**

1 The amount of goods <u>moved</u> by rail has increased over the years.
2 According to the table, more bicycles are <u>made</u> in China than in the European Union.
3 <u>About</u> $10 million of luxury goods are imported every year.
4 The data <u>shows</u> that more types of materials are being recycled.
5 The income from oil exports <u>went down</u> in 2012 and then again in 2014.
6 The data from the year 1995 is quite <u>interesting</u>.
7 Farmers in this province <u>grow</u> fruit and vegetables.
8 Some of these changes were <u>important</u>, but others were less so.
9 <u>These numbers</u> changed radically in the early 1900s.
10 Brazil's performances in World Cup matches have generally been <u>very good</u>.

9 **Look at the table below about milk production in Australia and answer the questions. (3–5 minutes)**

1 What is the main point of the table?
2 What overall trend do you see?
3 Are there any exceptions to this general trend?
4 What are one or two important points about Australian milk production in 2001/2002?
5 What about in 2010/2011?
6 What points of comparison can you make between these two years?

> *The table below provides information about milk production in Australia in millions of litres.*
>
> *Summarise the information by selecting and reporting the main features, and make comparisons where relevant.*

Australian milk production

	2001/2002	**2010/2011**
July	590	590
August	630	710
September	830	1050
October	920	1350
November	840	1120
December	790	1060
January	730	970
February	550	740
March	570	730
April	580	690
May	590	640
June	610	590

10 **Now write your answer. (10–15 minutes)**

    1 Write an introductory statement (based on the information in the text box above the table) and describe the overall idea or main trend shown in the table in paragraph 1.

    2 Give details about 2001/2002 and 2010/2011 in paragraph 2.

    3 Compare statistics about milk production during these two periods.

11 **Check your work. Look for mistakes in spelling, punctuation, and grammar. Make sure that you have used the correct tenses, and used a good variety of language for tables. (3–5 minutes)**

12 **Work in pairs. After you have finished, look at the model answer on the DVD-ROM. Compare your answers with the model answer and think about the marking criteria. (See page 180 for marking criteria.)**

IELTS PRACTICE TASK

You should spend about 20 minutes on this task.

> *The table below gives information about the languages that high school students speak at home in one school district in the USA.*
>
> *Summarise the information by selecting and reporting the main features, and make comparisons where relevant.*

Write at least 150 words.

Languages which high school students speak at home

	Number of students 2008	Number of students 2014
Spanish	15,110	28,816
Korean	3,029	2,735
Vietnamese	2,557	1,467
Chinese	1,875	4,670
Arabic	430	1,302
Russian	414	1,656
Hindi	375	430
Tagalog	138	512
Polish	110	82
Nepalese	95	439

Which statement best describes how you feel about Task 1 Tables?

☐ I feel confident about writing responses for Task 1 Tables.

☐ I did OK, but I still need to do more work on writing responses for Task 1 Tables.

☐ I need more practice with writing responses for Task 1 Tables. I need to focus on …

▶▶ **For further practice, see the DVD-ROM.**

TASK 1 Pie Charts and Multiple Charts

The graphs will always be related in some way.

Ring-tailed lemurs, Berenty Reserve, Madagascar

A About the task

1 Read the information about the task.

This version of Task 1 tests your ability to look at and identify the most important and relevant information in pie charts, or to compare the information in one type of chart with that in another type of chart or graph, and then report the information in your own words.

On the question paper, you see a pie chart, or multiple charts. The instructions for writing your response appear in a box above the chart(s). There is also a brief description of the information in the chart(s) in the box. Your job is to look at the chart(s) and select, summarise and describe the most important information.

A pie chart is a circular graph that is divided into segments. It looks like a pizza cut into uneven slices. It shows the relationship between the parts and the whole. The circle itself represents 100 per cent of something and each slice represents a certain percentage of that thing. There is usually a key (legend) that explains what each segment represents.

Pie charts

Here are the basic rules for writing about pie charts:

- Look at the chart carefully and decide what the most important information and striking features are.
- Write a well-organised overview.
- Include data to support the key points.
- Use an academic register or style.
- Write at least 150 words.
- Complete the task in about 20 minutes.
- Include only the key points. Minor details or irrelevant data can be left out.
- Don't do any calculations or give your opinion about the information.

Multiple charts and graphs

In Task 1 there will often be two or three pie charts to compare. Often, these charts represent different time periods. You may also see other types of graphs or charts. They may be the same type – two line graphs, for example – or there may be two different types – a pie chart and a table, or a line graph and a bar chart.

The basic rules for writing about multiple charts are the same as for writing about single charts. However, you need to look at and report on <u>both</u> charts/graphs, and understand the relationship between them.

2 **Work in pairs. Look at the two charts below and answer the questions.**

1 What kind of chart is the first chart? And the second?
2 What is the topic of the two charts?
3 What geographical areas do they cover?
4 What time frame does each chart cover? Are they the same or different?
5 Which of the two charts shows a trend?
6 In the pie chart, which country generates the most electricity?
7 What verb forms should you use to describe the fourth bar in the second chart?

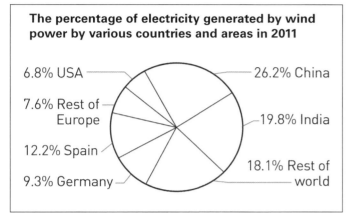

The percentage of electricity generated by wind power by various countries and areas in 2011

6.8% USA
7.6% Rest of Europe
12.2% Spain
9.3% Germany
26.2% China
19.8% India
18.1% Rest of world

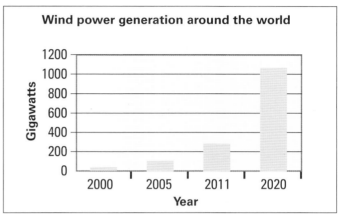

Wind power generation around the world

B Sample question

3 **Read the instructions and answer the question. Use the rules about the task from Section A to help you. Then look at the sample answer on page 336. Which aspects of the task did you find difficult?**

IELTS PRACTICE TASK

You should spend about 20 minutes on this task.

The visuals give information about the number of hours students spent preparing for an admission test for an Asian university and their subsequent performance in that test.

Summarise the information by selecting and reporting the main features and make comparisons where relevant.

Write at least 150 words.

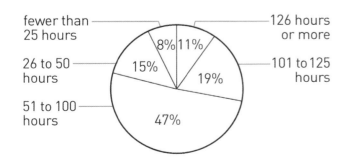

Hours studied

fewer than 25 hours
26 to 50 hours
51 to 100 hours
8% 11%
15%
19%
47%
126 hours or more
101 to 125 hours

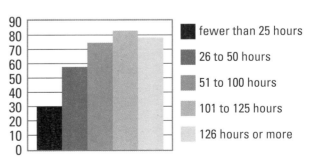

Average number of correct responses students scored (out of 100 questions) in relation to the number of hours they studied.

fewer than 25 hours
26 to 50 hours
51 to 100 hours
101 to 125 hours
126 hours or more

C Tips and tactics

4 **Work in pairs. Read the tips and tactics and discuss these questions.**

a **Which tips and tactics do you think are the most useful?**
b **Did you use any of these tips and tactics when you answered the sample question in Section B?**
c **Which tips will you use in the future?**

1 The first step is to look carefully at the information in the graphs/charts. Don't rush through this step. Make sure you understand the charts before you start to write.
2 Underline important words in the question and circle important information in the graphs/charts.
3 Identify what key information is being presented in the graphs/charts and the features or figures you'll need to write about.
4 If there is more than one pie chart, look for similarities and differences between them. If there are two or more different graphs/charts, try to work out the relationship between them.
5 Plan your writing. You can usually divide it into three paragraphs: introduction, first main paragraph and second main paragraph.
6 Choose the most significant and interesting information to comment on, for example, the largest segment, the smallest, and the main differences between the pie charts.
7 If the charts/graphs include information about time period, look for trends – numbers that go up, down, fluctuate, or stay the same over time.
8 Begin with an introductory sentence that describes the graphs/charts in general terms, but don't repeat exactly the words from the question.
9 Then describe one or two general trends or features shown in the graphs/charts. Don't go into detail; just report the most important features you see when you look at the graphs/charts. If there are two different types of chart, identify the type of chart/graph and use a connecting word between the two sentences. For example, *The pie chart shows … ; On the other hand, the bar graph illustrates …*
10 In the main paragraphs, select and write about the features that are most important and interesting, and include relevant data to support the points you make.
11 When selecting key information from pie charts, look for the largest and smallest segments. Look for any trends and exceptions to those trends across the pie charts.
12 Be careful with numbers when you are writing about pie charts. The numbers usually represent percentages but may also represent actual numbers.
13 Look carefully at the timeframe that the graphs/charts covers and think about which tenses you need to use (past, present, present perfect or future).
14 If there are different types of charts charts/graphs which cover the same categories, you can focus firstly on the more important categories in each chart/graph and secondly on other categories in each of the charts/graphs.
15 If the charts/graphs do not deal with the same categories, it is better to focus one paragraph on the information in one chart/graph and the second paragraph on information in the other chart/graph.
16 You may write a conclusion briefly explaining any relationship between the graphs/charts and summarising the main information in one sentence.
17 Don't try to write about all the data in the graphs/charts and don't include details that are irrelevant to the main points.
18 Remember, don't try to analyse or explain the information in the graphs/charts, or do any calculations; just describe and report it.
19 Keep track of the time. Don't spend more than 20 minutes on Task 1.
20 Make sure your handwriting is clear and legible.
21 Keep in mind the criteria that the examiners will use to mark your response. (For marking criteria, see About the Academic Writing Test, page 180.)

D Skills-building exercises

PERCENTAGES

These words can be useful when talking about percentages and about segments of a pie chart.

per cent/percent (used after a number) *About seventy **per cent** of the population of Singapore is of Chinese ancestry.*

percentage (used without numbers) *An important **percentage** of Canada's electricity is generated by hydroelectric power.*

proportion *A larger **proportion** of the national budget is spent on the military than on anything else.*

portion *The family spends a significant **portion** of their income on rent.*

share *Two or three companies control a large **share** of the paper-product market.*

segment *Only a small **segment** of the population agrees with this idea.*

fraction *A tiny **fraction** of the total number of applicants to this university are accepted.*

FRACTIONS

When writing about pie charts, you may also refer to fractions as well as percentages.

 three quarters / 75 per cent / three out of four

 a half / one half / 50 per cent / one out of two / one in two

 a third / one third / one out of three / one in three

 a quarter / 25 per cent / one out of four / one in four

a tenth / one tenth / 10 per cent / one out of ten / one in ten

You can combine these words with words such as *about, around, approximately, just over, just under,* etc.

OTHER USEFUL EXPRESSIONS

account for *Rice **accounts for** about a third of their diet.*

make up *Poisonous snakes **make up** only about ten per cent of all snakes.*

represent *Accidents that occur when drivers are texting **represent** about a quarter of the total number of car accidents.*

constitute *Rental properties **constitute** about a third of all the company's assets.*

FOCUS

Using percentages and fractions to talk about pie charts

5 Look at the expressions in the language boxes on page 211. Then look at the chart showing total exports from one European country. Write five sentences about the country's exports.

1 <u>Motor vehicles made up a large proportion of all exports.</u>

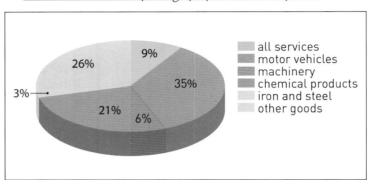

Total exports from one European country in 2012

NUMBERS AND AMOUNTS

a large proportion *Property taxes make up **a large proportion** of the city's income.*

a major portion ***A major portion** of this country's economy is fuelled by oil exports.*

a significant majority ***A significant majority** of the roads in this district are unpaved.*

a large percentage ***A large percentage** of the cars in this country are made in Japan.*

a tiny fraction *The journal can only publish **a tiny fraction** of the articles it receives.*

a mere + number or per cent ***A mere five per cent** of the people in this country had cell phones in 1995.*

a small minority *Just **a small minority** of people agree with this idea.*

a small percentage *Only **a small percentage** of earthquakes cause major damage.*

▶▶ **For more information and practice of countable and uncountable nouns, see Grammar Resource Bank pages 311–312.**

FOCUS

Using other expressions to describe numbers and amounts in pie charts

6 Look at these two pie charts. Write six descriptive sentences about the information in the pie charts. Use the expressions in the language boxes on pages 212 and 213.

The pie charts show the crops grown in one US county in 1990 and 2010.

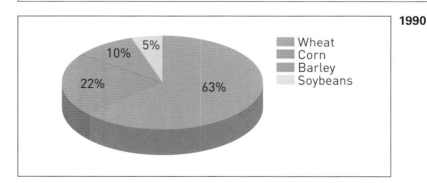

1990

2010

LINKING WORDS

COMPARISON (SIMILARITIES)

likewise *The inflation rate in Japan was fairly low in 2010;* ***likewise****, the rate in Switzerland did not go up much.*

similarly *The money that the government spends on the arts represents only a tiny portion of the total budget.* ***Similarly****, only a small amount is spent on social services.*

CONTRAST (DIFFERENCE)

however *The number of male faculty members stayed the same.* ***However****, six new female faculty members were hired.*

on the other hand *The number of radio stations playing classical music declined;* ***on the other hand****,* two new news stations opened.

in contrast *In 2010, the average age in Japan was 44.6 years;* ***in contrast****, in Yemen, the average age was only 16.4 years.*

whilst / while *Whilst the price of gold shot up in September, the price of silver remained about the same.*

although ***Although*** *health care remained a significant portion of families' budget in 2005, it wasn't as high as in 2004.*

whereas *The number of marriages declined during that period,* ***whereas*** *the number of divorces increased.*

but *California had a dry winter,* ***but*** *there was a lot of snow in the Rocky Mountain states.*

LIKE, UNLIKE, ALIKE

Like *the cost of shipping, the cost of packaging has gone up.*
Meat, ***like*** *fish, contains a lot of protein.*

Unlike *some members of the European Union, the UK does not use the euro as its currency. The US,* ***unlike*** *Japan, does not have a system of high-speed trains.*

... and ... are alike (in that) *The health care industry* ***and*** *information technology* ***are alike in that*** *they are both adding new jobs.*

▶▶ **For more information and practice of comparison, see Grammar Resource Bank pages 315–316.**

INTRODUCTIONS AND CONCLUSIONS

First, ...
First, let's consider the data in the bar chart.

Let's first ...
Let's first look at the line graph.

Turning to ...
Turning to the pie chart, ...

Next, ...
Next, let's examine the data in the second chart.

Having considered ... , let's ...
Having considered the bar chart, let's look at ...

Meanwhile, ...
Meanwhile, the information in the second graph shows that ...

It's clear ... that ...
It's clear from the data in the chart that ...

It's obvious that ...
It's obvious that an overwhelming number ...

It's easy to see ...
It's easy to see which country produces the most ...

In conclusion, ...
In conclusion, the relationship between the two graphs is ...

In brief, ...
In brief, the two graphs tell us that ...

On the whole, ...
On the whole, these graphs show that ...

To conclude, ...
To conclude, while the first graph tells us that ...

From the information ...
From the information in the two charts, it's clear that ...

As a final point, ...
As a final point, we can say that by comparing the data in these two charts, ...

7 Read the task and look at the two charts about crude oil imports and consumption. Then complete the sample answer with these words.

40%   accounted   conclusion   however   less   majority   percentage   quarter
significant   turning to   under   was   while

Both these charts deal with the amount of crude oil that is exported to the US from other countries and the amount that is produced domestically. The pie chart explains where the oil consumed in the US in one year (2012) came from, **1** .... the bar chart shows the declining percentage of imported oil used in the US over an eight-year period.

The US imports around 60% of its crude oil, but percentages have been declining since 2005. The pie chart clearly shows that a **2** .... proportion of oil was produced from wells in the US. Canada's share **3** .... just under a **4** .... of oil imports. Oil from the Middle East **5** .... for the next largest share. Latin America and African countries contributed **6** .... than 10%. The amount imported from countries not listed on the chart was a very small **7** .... (3%).

8 .... the bar chart, we see a steady decrease in the percentage of imported oil. In 2005 and 2006, imported oil made up a significant **9** .... of the oil consumed in the US. By 2010, that amount had dropped to **10** .... 50%. The decline continued. In 2012, imported oil constituted only **11** .... of the total.

In **12** .... , the US still imports oil from around the world. **13** .... , the percentage of internationally produced oil consumed in the US has shrunk dramatically.

> *The charts below give information about the origin of crude oil imports to the US in 2012 and about the percentage of imports as a share of US crude oil consumption.*
>
> *Summarise the information by selecting and reporting the main features, and make comparisons where relevant.*

Origin of crude oil imports to the US in 2012

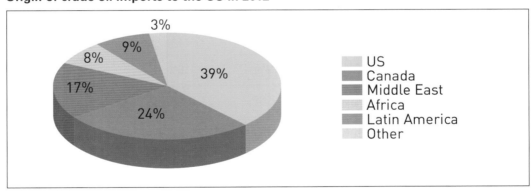

Percentage of imports as a share of US crude oil consumption

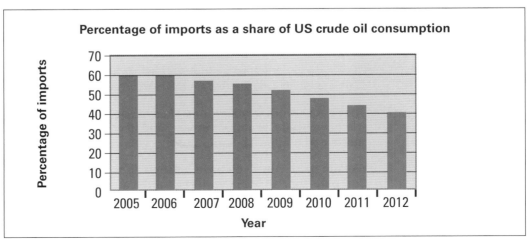

8 **Work in pairs. Read the instructions and look at the charts about office rents and office vacancy rates. Then answer the questions (1–9). (3–5 minutes)**

1 Look at the bar chart. What information does it provide?
2 Look at the table. What information does it provide?
3 Look at the bar chart. What trend do you see?
4 Are there any exceptions to the general trend?
5 What are some striking features in the bar chart?
6 Look at the table. What trend do you see?
7 Are there any exceptions to this trend?
8 What are some striking features in the table?
9 What relationship do you see between the data in the bar chart and the data in the table?

The chart shows annual office rents in five international cities in 2008 and 2013 ($US / square metre). The table shows office vacancy rates in those cities.

Summarise the information by selecting and reporting the main features, and make comparisons where relevant.

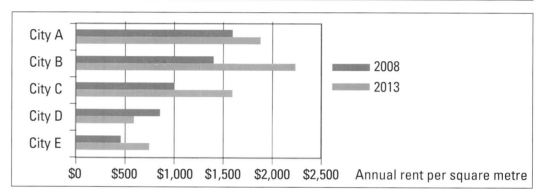

	2008	2013
City A	6%	4%
City B	7%	2%
City C	9%	6%
City D	10%	23%
City E	16%	9%

9 **Now write your answer. Use the following stages to help you. (10–15 minutes)**

1 Write an introductory statement (based on the information in the text box) and describe the general trends in the bar chart and the table in the introductory paragraph.
2 In the first main paragraph, describe the trends that you see in the costs of office rentals in those five cities and point out any interesting and important features in the bar chart.
3 In the second main paragraph, describe the trends you see in the vacancy rate and provide important and interesting details about the details in the table.
4 In a brief conclusion, explain the relationship between rents and vacancy rates.

10 **Check your work. Look for mistakes in spelling, punctuation, and grammar. Make sure you have used the correct tenses, and used a good variety of language for comparing charts and graphs. (3–5 minutes)**

11 **Work in pairs. After you have finished, look at the model answer on the DVD-ROM. Compare your answers with the model answer and think about the marking criteria. (See page 180 for marking criteria.)**

IELTS PRACTICE TASK

You should spend about 20 minutes on this task.

> *The visuals give information about the number of spacecraft launched by various national governments between 1957 and 2007 and the purpose of each mission.*
>
> *Write a report for a university lecturer summarising the most important information in the visuals.*

Write at least 150 words.

The number of spacecraft launched by national governments, 1957–2007

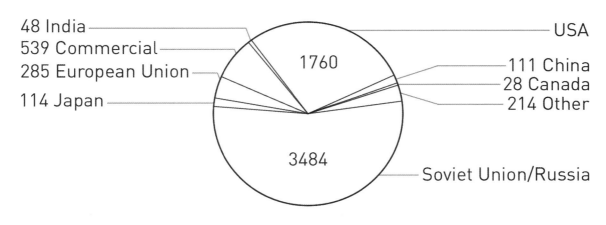

The purposes for which spacecraft were launched, 1957–2007

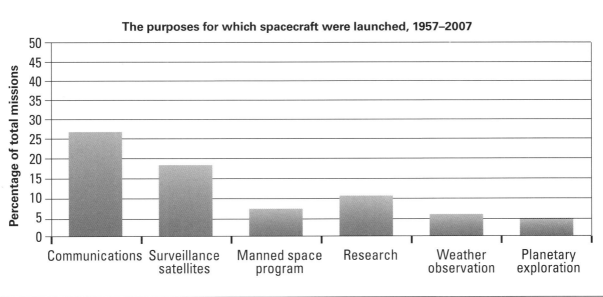

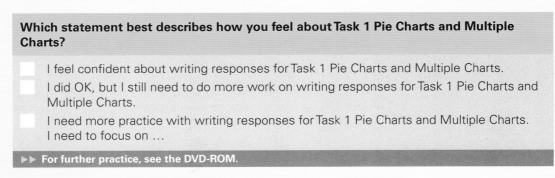

Which statement best describes how you feel about Task 1 Pie Charts and Multiple Charts?

- I feel confident about writing responses for Task 1 Pie Charts and Multiple Charts.
- I did OK, but I still need to do more work on writing responses for Task 1 Pie Charts and Multiple Charts.
- I need more practice with writing responses for Task 1 Pie Charts and Multiple Charts. I need to focus on …

▶▶ **For further practice, see the DVD-ROM.**

TASK 1 Diagrams

Look at the diagram carefully and decide what the most important steps are.

A About the task

1 Read the information about the task.

This version of Task 1 tests your ability to look at and identify the most important information in a diagram, and then report the information in your own words.

On the question paper, you see a series of pictures that are connected by arrows. There are often labels that explain the pictures. There is a title and instructions for writing your response. There is also a brief description of the information in the diagram. The pictures and text illustrate some kind of process. It might be an industrial process (e.g. how plastic is made), a biological process (e.g. the lifecycle of a snail), a physical process (e.g. the water cycle or the rock cycle) or an intellectual process (e.g. how decisions are made at one company). Your job is to write a well-organised overview of the process from the pictures and text provided.

There are several types of diagram. You may see a diagram with a clear beginning and a clear end, a diagram involving alternative stages, a diagram which shows two processes (one that follows another) or a cyclical diagram.

Here are the basic rules for writing about a diagram:

- Look at the diagram carefully and decide what the most important steps are.
- Write a well-organised overview.
- Mention all the steps in the process in your response, although you can omit minor details.
- Use an academic register or style.
- Write at least 150 words.
- Complete the task in about 20 minutes.

2 Work in pairs. Look at the diagram below and answer the questions.

1 What process is illustrated in the diagram?
2 What type of diagram is this?
3 How could you summarise the entire process in one sentence?
4 How many steps are shown?
5 Should you write one sentence for each of the steps?
6 What step should you mention first?

Recycling glass

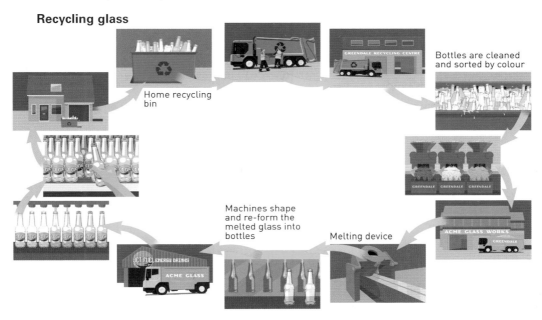

B Sample question

3 Read the instructions and answer the question. Use the rules about the task from Section A to help you. Then look at the sample answer on page 337. Which aspects of the task did you find difficult?

IELTS PRACTICE TASK

You should spend about 20 minutes on this task.

The diagram shows the way in which wind-powered energy is created and transported to the consumer. Write a report for a university lecturer describing the process.

Write at least 150 words.

Generating electricity with wind power

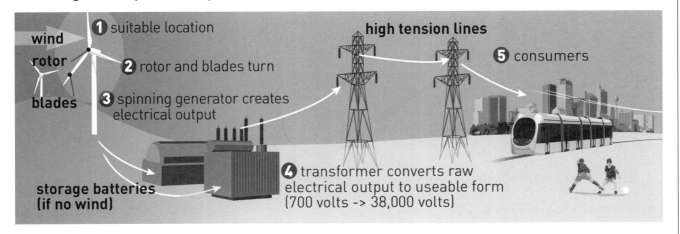

C Tips and tactics

4 Work in pairs. Read the tips and tactics and discuss these questions.

a Which tips and tactics do you think are the most useful?
b Did you use any of these tips and tactics when you answered the sample question in Section B?
c Which tips will you use in the future?

1 The first step is to look carefully at the diagram. Look at each picture or stage. Don't rush through this step. Make sure you understand the diagram before you start to write.
2 Underline important words in the question and identify what process is being presented in the diagram.
3 Plan your writing. You can usually divide it into three paragraphs: introduction, first main paragraph and second main paragraph.
4 Begin with an introductory sentence that describes the diagram or process in general, but don't repeat the exact wording of the question.
5 Then write a sentence about the entire process, for example, write about the number of steps and the beginning and ending of the process. Don't go into detail; just write about the whole process. For example: *The diagram shows the seven major stages involved in …*
6 Next, divide the steps shown in the diagram into two paragraphs. If the diagram shows a single process, choose a logical point – one of the major stages in the process – and divide your answer into two parts there.
7 You should try to mention all the steps in a process, but you can omit minor details.
8 Follow the order of the steps in the process. Usually, it's clear where a process begins. In the case of cyclical processes, choose the most logical starting point in the process.
9 Use sequencing words and phrases to separate the steps of the process, e.g. *First of all, …; Next, …; Finally …*, etc.
10 You should generally use present passive verbs (*is/are done*) or passive modal verbs (*should be done, can be done*) to describe the steps in the process.
11 For important steps, you may want to provide examples or offer more explanation. (*Next, … should be done. In other words, …*)
12 You can reuse technical terms from the labels on the diagram but write them in your own sentences.
13 No concluding paragraph is necessary for this type of response.
14 Remember, don't try to explain why the information in the diagram appears the way it does or give your opinion about the process.
15 Keep track of the time. Don't spend more than 20 minutes on Task 1.
16 Make sure your handwriting is clear and legible.
17 Keep in mind the criteria that the examiners use to mark your response. (For marking criteria, see About the Academic Writing Test, page 180.)

D Skills-building exercises

SEQUENCING WORDS AND PHRASES

These words or phrases can be used to describe the steps or stages of a process.

First, ... *First*, a suitable location must be found.

First of all, ... *First of all*, the water must be purified.

The first step/stage ... *The first step* in starting a business is to write a business plan.

The process of ... begins with ... *The process of* mining **begins with** locating a rich source of the mineral.

Next, ... *Next*, the raw materials are cleaned.

The next step ... *The next step* is to test the machine.

Then ... *Then* the tank is filled with water / The water is first filtered and **then** poured into the tank.

Following this ... *Following this,* the valve must be opened.

The following step ... *The following step* is to collect as much information as possible.

After ... *After* the two types of materials have been separated, they are stored in large containers.

After this, ... *After this*, you need to pre-heat the oven.

Once ... *Once* funds have been deposited, customers can write checks or withdraw cash.

Finally, ... *Finally*, the adult female lays eggs and the process begins again.

The final step/stage ... *The final step* is to make sure that all the parts are correctly connected.

The last step/stage ... *The last step* in applying to the university is to submit your application before the deadline.

Q FOCUS

Using appropriate sequencing words and phrases

5 Look at the diagram about drying out a mobile phone. Then rewrite the steps in the process using expressions in the language box to help you.

Step 1: The phone must be removed from the water as soon as possible.

Step 2: The phone should be placed on paper towels.

Step 3: The case should be removed and the back of the phone taken off.

Step 4: The phone should be dried with a soft cloth.

Step 5: The battery and the SIM card should be removed. They should be dried off. (Write this as one sentence.)

Step 6: A vacuum cleaner can be used to remove remaining water from the inner sections of the phone.

Step 7: The phone can be placed in a bag of uncooked rice overnight to soak up any remaining water.

Drying out a mobile phone

Act quickly!

Leave in bag at least 24 hours

battery

SIM card

VERB FORMS FOR PROCESS DIAGRAMS

In most process diagrams, the emphasis is on the action, not on the person. Therefore, you will generally use verbs in the passive in your response.

Present passive *The pigments* **are** *then* **mixed** *with oil.* (Used to describe industrial, agricultural, or business processes.)

Present perfect passive *After a bill* **has been signed** *by the president, it becomes law. Once the students' papers* **have been graded**, *the results are recorded.* (In clauses beginning with the signal words *Once* ... or *After* ...)

is + to + infinitive *The first step* **is to take** *the patient's temperature. The final step* **is to send** *the email.*

Present simple active *An adult butterfly* **emerges** *wet and shaky from its cocoon.* (For biological or other natural processes.)

Passive modal verbs *Next, the can of paint* **should be** *thoroughly* **shaken**. *The two holes* **must be lined up** *carefully.* (In a response to a 'how to' process: how to paint a room, how to change the oil in your car, etc.)

Imperative (Command) form *First,* **break** *the eggs in a bowl and then* **add** *milk. Next,* **heat** *the oil or butter in a pan.* (Can also be used in responses to 'how to' processes.)

▶▶ **For more information and practice of passives, see the Grammar Resource Bank, pages 319–321.**

6 Look at the diagram which shows the steps involved in producing coffee. Then complete the sentences describing the process. Use the correct verb forms.

1 The first step ....
2 Then, the seedlings ....
3 Next, what are called the cherries ....
4 The following step ....
5 Once the green coffee .... in bags, it can ....
.... in container ships.
6 Green coffee is next ....
7 After the coffee beans ....
8 Coffee must .... by professional tasters.
9 After that, the ground coffee .... in cans or bags
and then it .... in stores.
10 The final steps .... and to enjoy it.

GLOSSARY

*Cherries are the red fruit of the coffee plant.
*After coffee has been milled and before it has been roasted, it is known as green coffee

The pictures show the steps involved in producing coffee.

Planting coffee seeds

Replanting seedlings outdoors

Harvesting the cherries *

Drying the cherries

Milling: This removes the outer coating of the cherry.

Packing and transporting the green coffee *

Roasting: This transforms green coffee into aromatic brown beans

Grinding the beans

Tasting: Professional tasters check coffee for quality and taste

Packing and selling

Brewing

Enjoy!

7 Look at the diagram about the metamorphosis of a frog. (Metamorphosis is the process by which an animal changes its form as it matures.)

a Write sentences for each of the steps in the process.
b Use an appropriate form of the verb given and use words that signal sequence.

1 produce
2 emerge
3 start
4 transform into
5 develop into

First, an adult female frog produces an egg mass.

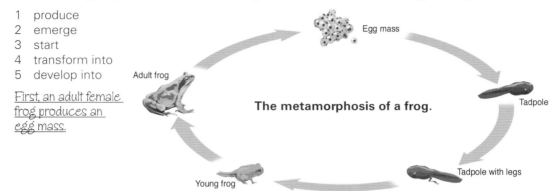

The metamorphosis of a frog.

Adult frog
Egg mass
Tadpole
Tadpole with legs
Young frog

SIGNAL WORDS FOR ALTERNATIVE STEPS

Sometimes a diagram will show two or more ways to complete a process. You should use signal words to indicate that a process can follow two possible directions.

either / or *At this point, **either** ... **or** ... can take place.*

Alternatively *The next step is for D2 to happen. **Alternatively**, D3 might occur.*

If *If B1 happens, then C1 occurs. However, if B2 takes place, C2 happens.*

Q FOCUS

Identifying alternative steps in a process and using the appropriate signal words

8 Look at the diagram about the life cycle of a star. Answer these questions.

1 What process is shown?
2 What alternatives are shown in the diagram?
3 How many stages are there in the life of an average star?
4 How many stages are there in the life of a massive star?

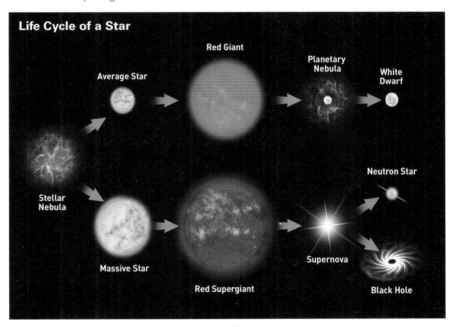

Life Cycle of a Star

Average Star
Red Giant
Planetary Nebula
White Dwarf
Stellar Nebula
Neutron Star
Massive Star
Red Supergiant
Supernova
Black Hole

9 Complete the paragraph to describe the process in the diagram. Use signal words for the alternative steps.

A stellar nebula may either **1** ... or **2** ... . If **3** ... , it next changes into a red giant. **4** ... it is transformed into a planetary nebula. **5** ... a white dwarf.

If **6** ... , it later becomes a red supergiant and then may eventually experience a supernova. **7** ... , a neutron star may be formed. **8** ... , the supernova may create a black hole.

Q **FOCUS**

Selecting and reporting the main features and writing your response.

10 **Look at the pictures which show the steps involved in operating a hot air balloon. Then answer the questions (3–5 minutes).**

1 What process is pictured in the diagram?
2 How many stages are shown?
3 How could you divide your response into paragraphs?
4 What verb forms should you mainly use in your answer?

> *The diagram below shows how to operate a hot air balloon.*
>
> *Summarise the information by selecting and reporting the main features, and make comparisons where relevant.*

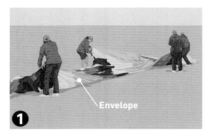

11 **Now write your answer. (10–15 minutes)**

1 Write an introductory statement (based on the information in the text box) and describe the overall process in the introductory paragraph.
2 In the first main paragraph, explain the first stages of operating a hot air balloon.
3 In the second main paragraph, explain the next stages in operating a hot air balloon.

12 **Check your work. Look for mistakes in spelling, punctuation and grammar. Make sure you have used sequence vocabulary and the correct verb forms. (3–5 minutes)**

13 **Work in pairs. After you have finished, look at the model answer on the DVD-ROM. Compare your answers with the model answer and think about the marking criteria. (See page 180 for marking criteria.)**

IELTS PRACTICE TASK

You should spend about 20 minutes on this task.

The diagram below explains how to change a tyre.

Summarise the information by selecting and reporting the main features, and make comparisons where relevant.

Write at least 150 words.

   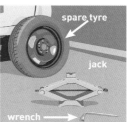

spare tyre

jack

Hazard lights

wrench

Find a safe place to pull over.

hub cap

wheel nut

15cms

Don't remove wheel nuts at this time; just loosen them.

Don't tighten all the way.

Tighten each one halfway, then continue until all are tight.

Don't leave anything on the side of the road.

Which statement best describes how you feel about Task 1 Diagrams?

- I feel confident about doing Task 1 Diagrams.
- I did OK, but I still need to do more work on Task 1 Diagrams.
- I need more practice with Task 1 Diagrams. I need to focus on …

▶▶ **For further practice, see the DVD-ROM.**

TASK 1 Maps and Plans

Your job is to describe the changes that took place at that location during the time period.

A About the task

1 Read the information about the task.

This version of Task 1 tests your ability to look at visual information presented in maps and plans, and describe the information in your own words.

On the question paper, you see one or two maps or plans with a title. You may see maps of a city or town, a university, a park, or an island. You may also see plans – for a shopping centre, an office building or a factory floor. The instructions for writing your response appear in a box above the maps. There is also a brief description of the map in the box. There is usually a key (legend) that explains what certain features and symbols on the maps mean. The maps may also include the scale (distance marker) of the map (e.g. in kilometres), and a compass arrow to show direction (*North/South/East/West*).

Typically, there are two maps or plans showing the same site at two different points in time. The maps and plans indicate the time periods that they represent with labels. Your job is to describe the changes that took place at that location during that time period. There are a number of changes from the earlier map to the later one. For example, on a map these might involve the building of new roads, the replacement of one building with another, or the movement of one feature to another part of the map.

Here are the basic rules for writing about maps and plans:

- Look at the maps or plans carefully and note the most important features and changes.
- Select the most important differences in the two maps to write about first.
- Write a well-organised overview.
- Include information from keys, the scale (distance marker) or compass arrows.
- Use an academic register or style.
- Write at least 150 words.
- Complete the task in about 20 minutes.
- Don't give your opinion about the maps or any changes to the maps.

2 **Work in pairs. Look at the maps below and answer the questions.**

1 What information do the maps provide?
2 How many changes do you see? What are they?
3 What information does the key on the first map provide?
4 What information does the key on the second map provide?
5 What time labels do you see on these maps? Why are they important?
6 Do the maps include a scale? What does it tell you?
7 Should you use verbs in the passive form to describe the maps? Why?

> *The two maps below show a park in Canada before and after a renovation project.*

1995

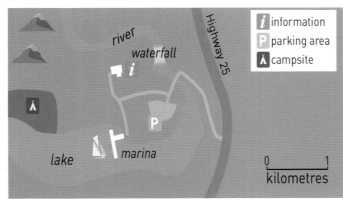

2015

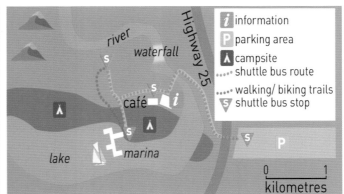

B Sample question

3 **Read the instructions and answer the question. Use the rules about the task from Section A to help you. Then look at the sample answer on page 338. Which aspects of the task did you find difficult?**

IELTS PRACTICE TASK

You should spend about 20 minutes on this task.

> *The two plans below show the City Library in 2004 and 2014.*
> *Summarise the information by selecting and reporting the main features, and make comparisons where relevant.*

Write at least 150 words.

City Library 2004

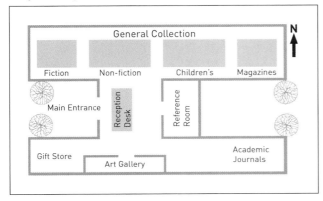

City Library 2014

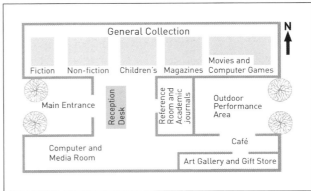

C Tips and tactics

4 Work in pairs. Read the tips and tactics and discuss these questions.

  a Which tips and tactics do you think are the most useful?
  b Did you use any of these tips and tactics when you answered the sample question in Section B?
  c Which tips will you use in the future?

1 The first step is to look carefully at the maps/plans. Don't rush through this step. Make sure you understand the maps/plans before you start to write.

2 Underline important words in the question and look for differences between the first map/plan and the second and mark these differences on the map/plan. Look at the key and the scale, if there is one. Decide which changes are the most important.

3 Plan your writing. You can usually divide it into three paragraphs: introduction, first main paragraph and second main paragraph.

4 Look carefully at the time period for each map/plan and work out what tenses you need to use (past, present, present perfect or future).

5 Begin with an introductory sentence that describes the maps/plans in general terms, but don't repeat the exact wording of the question.

6 Then describe one or two of the main changes. Don't go into detail; just report the most important changes you see when you look at the chart, e.g. *In 2010, the town of Southport was considerably larger and more urbanized than it was in 1980.*

7 In the first main paragraph, write about the most important changes first. Choose the most significant changes in the second map and compare it with the first map.

8 In the second main paragraph, describe the remaining changes and again compare the first map with what you see in the second.

9 You should generally use the passive form to describe changes that occur to rooms, buildings, roads, parts of a town, etc.

10 Use information from the key in your response and use the scale, if there is one, to estimate distances, e.g. *The new library is located about a kilometre north of the old one.*

11 Remember, don't try to explain the changes, or give your opinion; just describe and report them.

12 Keep track of the time. Don't spend more than 20 minutes on Task 1.

13 Make sure your handwriting is clear and legible.

14 Keep in mind the criteria that the examiners use to mark your response. (For marking criteria, see About the Academic Writing Test, page 180.)

D Skills-building exercises

USING THE CORRECT TENSE

Present simple *In the first map, there* **is** *no development on the northern part of the beach. However, in the second map, there* **is** *a large hotel on this section of the beach.*

Past simple and past perfect *In 1950, there* **was** *a coffee shop on the corner of 4th Street and Oak Avenue. However, in 1975, a hotel* **stood** *on that corner.*
By 2010, a bridge across the river **had been built**.

Past simple/present simple, present perfect, used to *In 2000, King Street* **was** *a two-way street, but it* **is** *a one-way street today.*
The trees **have been cut** *down and the forest* **has been replaced** *with a paved parking area.*
The shop that **used to be** *on the south side of the street* **was relocated** *to the north side.*
There **was** *formerly a large playground in the park.*

Present/future times *At the moment, there* **is** *one sports centre, but three years from now* **there will be** *four sports centres in the area.*

▶▶ **For more information and practice of tenses, see Grammar Resource Bank pages 303–308.**

COMPASS POINTS

One common way to locate features on maps is to use compass points.

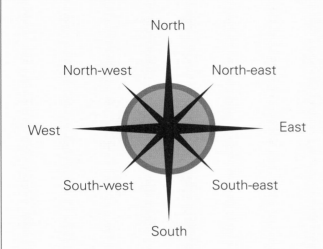

A new public swimming pool was built **to the north of** the tennis courts.

A bandstand has been constructed **in the centre of** the park.

There was formerly an industrial zone **in the south-east** of the city.

The word *just* can be used to indicate that two things are close to each other:

The public gardens are **just** west of Albert Street.

DESCRIBING MAPS AND PLANS

POSITION

be The town hall **is** in the centre of town. There **is** now a high-speed train linking the two towns.

lie The town of Greendale **lies** 20 kilometres east of Fallsbrook.

is located The new student residence **is located** on the east of the campus.

can be found / can be seen A bookstore **can be found** on the second floor of the complex.

stand (used mainly for buildings) The opera house once **stood** on the corner of Charles Avenue and Rose Street.

CHANGE

build A shopping mall **has been built** just outside of town.

construct An elementary school **was constructed** where the factory used to be.

expand The science lab **was** greatly **expanded**.

add on to A new wing **has been added on to** the art museum.

demolish Several houses **were demolished** when the road was constructed.

become The open space west of the business park **became** a residential neighbourhood.

remove The first two rows of seats in the theatre **were removed** when the stage was expanded.

convert (to) The factory **was converted to** a museum.

transform (into) The old barn **will be transformed into** an antique shop.

move to The gift shop **was moved to** another part of the art museum.

relocate By 2008, the fire station **had been relocated**.

ROADS, BRIDGES, ETC

pass through A highway now **passes through** the centre of town.

run A railway used to **run** between the two towns.

link The two skyscrapers **are linked** by a walkway on the 30th floor.

connect A bridge **connects** Travis Island with the mainland.

extend The light rail system **will be extended** all the way to the airport next year.

at the junction with There is a hospital on Cooper Street **at the junction with** Blake Avenue.

cross Cars used to **cross** the river at Pembroke Street, but now they **cross** the river at Castle Street.

Q **FOCUS**

Summarising the
main differences
and describing
specific changes

5 **The maps below show a section of a university campus in 1990 and now. Look carefully at the maps and then follow these instructions.**

1   First, write a sentence that describes what the maps show in your own words.
2   Next, write one sentence that summarises the changes shown on the two maps.

6 **Make notes on the specific changes that have taken place on the campus since 1990. Use your notes to write sentences about these changes with the words provided. Make sure you use the correct tenses.**

1	link	3	expand	5	demolish	7	relocate
2	convert	4	construct	6	build		

1990

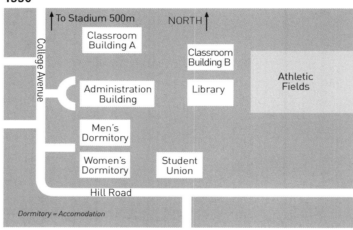

Now

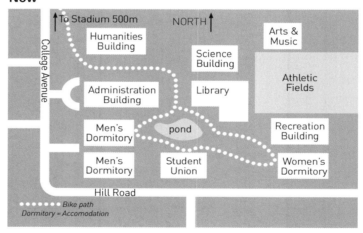

PREPOSITIONS OF PLACE

behind *Behind the supermarket, there is a cinema.*

opposite / across … from *A discount store was **opposite** the medical centre on High Street. A discount store was **across** the street **from** the medical centre.*

between *Today, there is a clothing store **between** the two coffee shops.*

next to *A laundry used to be **next to** the pharmacy.*

in front of *There is a news stand **in front of** the office building.*

at one end … and at the other *At one end of the street there was once a bank, **and at the other** was the City Hall.*

inside *Inside the courtyard you can see a garden.*

outside *There used to be some vending machines **outside** the hotel.*

in the middle of *A small island lies **in the middle of** the lake.*

▶▶ **For more information and practice of prepositions, see Grammar Resource Bank page 327.**

7 **Look at the map of the university campus again. Write six sentences to talk about location.**

1 recreation building … next to
  A recreation building has been built next to the athletic fields.
2 bike path … between
3 library … central
4 new Arts and Music classroom … north-eastern
5 women's dormitory … east of
6 science building … between

8 **Look carefully at the maps of the shopping centre below. Complete the following stages.**

1 First, write a sentence that gives the information in the instructions in your own words.

2 Next, write one sentence that summarises the changes shown on the two maps.

3 Then make notes on the specific changes that have taken place between 1985 and 2005. Use your notes to write sentences about these changes with the words below. Make sure you use the correct verb forms.

> at one end … and at the other   opposite   between   next to   in front of
> inside   in the middle of

The maps show a shopping centre in 1985 and in 2005.

1985

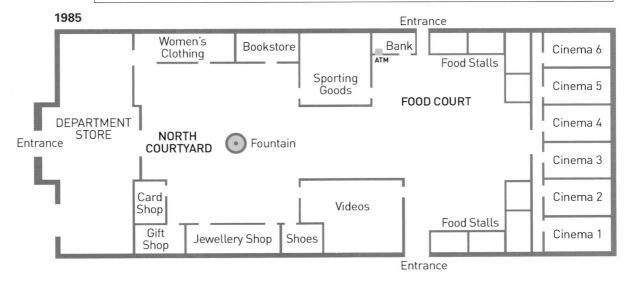

2005

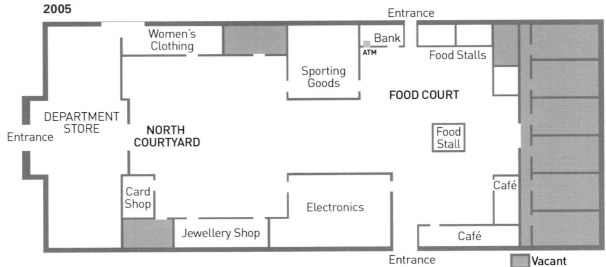

9 **Look carefully at the maps and answer the questions. (3–5 minutes)**

1 What is the overall idea of the maps?
2 What is the overall purpose of the development project?
3 What are TWO of the most important changes that took place during the development project?
4 What are some other changes that took place during the development project?

> *The maps show the waterfront section of a city before and after a development project.*

Before

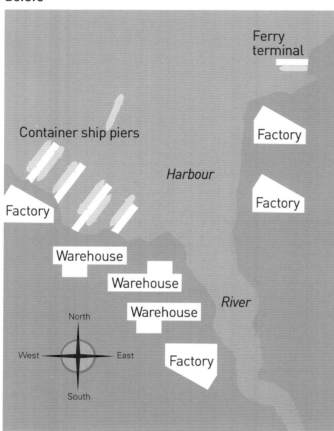

After

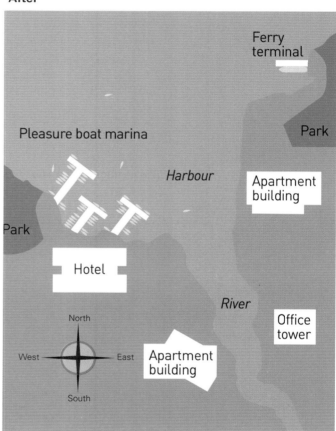

10 **Now write your answer to the task. (10–15 minutes)**

> *Summarise the information by selecting and reporting the main features, and make comparisons where relevant.*

1 Write an introductory statement (based on the information in the text box) and outline the main changes that took place.
2 Describe two of the most important changes that took place during the development project. Give details about the location of some of the features on the maps. Compare the way the waterfront looked before the project and after the project.
3 Describe two more changes that took place during the development project. Give details about the location of some of the features on the maps.

11 **Check your work. Look for mistakes in spelling, punctuation and grammar. Make sure you have used the correct tenses, and used a good variety of language for describing maps. (3–5 minutes)**

12 **Work in pairs. After you have finished, look at the model answer on the DVD-ROM. Compare your answers with the model answer and think about the marking criteria. (See page 180 for marking criteria.)**

IELTS PRACTICE TASK

You should spend about 20 minutes on this task.

> *The two maps show Tilden Airport and the surrounding area in 1985 and 2015.*
>
> *Write a report for a university lecturer summarising the information shown in the maps.*

Tilden Airport 1985

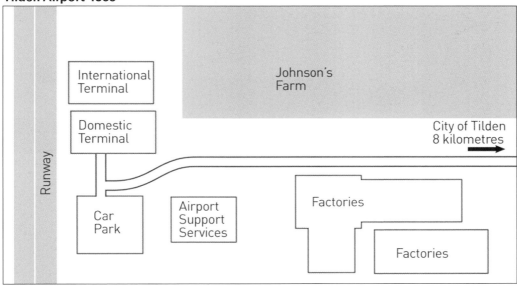

Tilden International Airport 2015

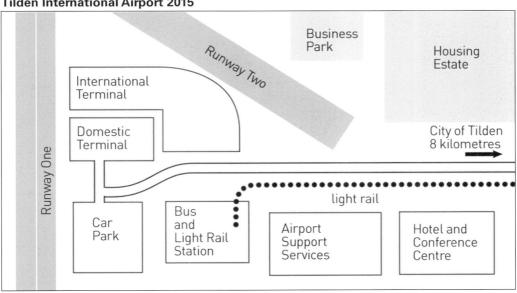

Which statement best describes how you feel about Task 1 Maps and Plans?

☐ I feel confident about writing responses for Task 1 Maps and Plans.

☐ I did OK, but I still need to do more work on writing responses for Task 1 Maps and Plans.

☐ I need more practice with writing responses for Task 1 Maps and Plans. I need to focus on …

▶▶ **For further practice, see the DVD-ROM.**

TASK 2 An Agree/Disagree Essay

Read and analyse the proposition and the question carefully – don't rush through this stage.

Vulturine guineafowl running, Samburu National Reserve, Kenya

A About the task

1 Read the following information about the task.

The Agree/Disagree task tests your ability to write an essay in response to a question that asks to what extent you agree or disagree with an opinion.

On the question paper you see a task which presents a *proposition* (a statement that expresses an opinion about a topic) and a question about the proposition: *To what extent do you agree or disagree?* There are also basic instructions on how to write your response. The propositions are quite general and do not require you to have any special knowledge about the topic.

Here are the basic rules for writing Agree/Disagree Essays:

- Read and analyse the proposition and the question carefully – don't rush through this stage.
- Decide whether you agree or disagree with the proposition.
- Write a brief, well-organised introduction, at least two main paragraphs, and a short conclusion.
- Be sure to state your opinion clearly in the introduction and conclusion.
- Provide support for or against the proposition by giving details and examples.
- Write in paragraphs: do not use notes or bullet points.
- Use an academic register or style.
- Write at least 250 words.
- Complete the task in about 40 minutes.

There is no correct answer. You can agree, disagree or partially agree.

2 Work in pairs. Look at the writing task below and answer the questions.

> *It is much easier to learn in a small class than in a larger one.*
> *To what extent do you agree or disagree?*

1 What part of this task is the proposition?
2 If you agree with the proposition, think of some reasons why you agree.
3 If you disagree with the proposition, think of some reasons why you disagree.
4 Is it necessary to fully agree or disagree with the proposition?
5 How long should your essay be?
6 How much time do you have to write your essay?

B Sample question

3 **Read the task and answer the question. Use the rules about the task from Section A to help you. Then compare your answer with the sample answer on page 339. Which aspects of the task did you find difficult?**

IELTS PRACTICE TASK

Write about the following topic.

You should spend about 40 minutes on this task.

> *Children all over the world should learn to speak a single, universal language fluently in addition to their native language.*
>
> *To what extent do you agree or disagree?*

Give reasons for your answer and include any relevant examples from your own knowledge and experience.

Write at least 250 words.

C Tips and tactics

4 **Work in pairs. Read the tips and tactics and discuss these questions.**

    a **Which tips and tactics do you think are the most useful?**
    b **Did you use any of these tips and tactics when you answered the sample questions in Section B?**
    c **Which tips will you use in the future?**

1 Spend a few minutes reading and thinking about the task. Make sure you understand the proposition and the question. Underline key words.

2 You don't have a lot of time, but you should make a brief plan. Write several reasons why you might agree with the proposition and several reasons why you might disagree. Is it easier to think of reasons to agree or to disagree? This can help you decide which position to take.

3 Your essay should include an introduction, two main paragraphs and a conclusion.

4 Your introduction can be brief. You should restate the proposition in your own words, and provide a little background on the topic. For example, you can explain why this topic is an important one, or why it has become more important in recent times. Then state your own opinion: do you agree, disagree or partially agree?

5 Begin each main paragraph with a topic sentence (a sentence that states the main idea of the paragraph). This sentence can be quite simple, for example, *There are several important reasons to agree with this idea*. All of the sentences in the paragraph should support the topic sentence.

6 In each of the main paragraphs, you should use linking words and phrases to move smoothly from one reason to another.

7 The second main paragraph should follow on from the first using a linking word or phrase, for example, *Furthermore, there are additional reasons to favour this idea*.

8 You should support the reasons that you give in your main paragraphs with specific details and examples.

9 The final paragraph can be brief. You should summarise the main points and restate your own position. You shouldn't introduce new information or reasons in the conclusion.

10 The final paragraph should also begin with a word or phrase to signal that it is a conclusion.

11 Your paragraphs should be clearly separated. For example, you can leave a blank space between them or indent the first line of each new paragraph.

12 Keep track of the time. You have about 40 minutes to do Task 2.

13 Make sure your handwriting is clear and legible enough for the examiners to read.

14 As you write your essay, keep in mind the criteria that the examiners use to mark your essay. (For marking criteria, see About the Academic Writing Test, page 180.)

D Skills-building exercises

EXPRESSING AGREEMENT AND DISAGREEMENT

AGREEMENT

There are a number of strong arguments to support the idea that *people share too much of their private lives on social networks.*

I agree that *it's better to raise children in a small town.*

I agree with the idea that *childhood is the happiest time of life.*

It's true that *there is too much violence in movies.*

I share the view that *children learn more outside of school than in school.*

I support the idea that *violent sports such as boxing should be banned.*

DISAGREEMENT

There are some important reasons to disagree with the idea that *teenagers shouldn't be allowed to drive a car.*

I disagree with the idea that *teachers should be paid according to their students' academic results.*

I don't agree that *traffic in the city centre should be restricted during certain times of the day.*

I disagree with the proposal that *all high-school students should study music.*

It's not true that *pure scientific research has no practical benefits.*

I don't share the view that *it's more important to learn how to use a computer keyboard than to learn how to write.*

I don't accept the idea that *electronic books will completely replace conventional books.*

PARTIAL AGREEMENT

While there are reasons to support the idea that *students need time off, I still believe that the amount of class time should be increased.*

It may be true that *poverty can never be completely eradicated. However, I think that governments should work harder to reduce the amount of poverty.*

I partially agree with the idea that *text books are too expensive, but …*

I don't completely agree that *it's better to travel in groups than alone.*

*I think **it's only partly true that** violence in video games leads to violence in real life.*

I partly agree with the proposal that *nurses should be paid as well as doctors …*

*Certainly, many people feel that games are only fun if you win, **but it's not that simple.***

Q **FOCUS**

Writing reasons why you agree or disagree with a proposition

5 **Read this proposition and write two sentences agreeing with it and two sentences disagreeing with it. Use expressions from the language box above. Remember to rewrite the proposition in your own words.**

> ***Face-to-face meetings with people are much more effective than meetings held on the telephone or via the Internet.***
>
> ***To what extent do you agree or disagree?***

There are some important reasons to agree with the idea that face-to-face meetings work better than telephone or Internet meetings.

I disagree with the concept that person-to-person meetings are more useful than electronic meetings.

6 Read this proposition. Write two sentences strongly agreeing with it and two sentences strongly disagreeing with it.

> *People learn more from failure than they do from success.*
> *To what extent do you agree or disagree?*

7 Read this proposition. Write three sentences partially agreeing with it.

> *The money used to fund space research would be better used to solve the many problems we face on Earth.*
> *To what extent do you agree or disagree?*

Q **FOCUS**

Writing an introduction

8 Work in pairs. Look at the proposition and read the sample introduction. Then answer the questions.

1 Which sentence in the introduction provides background information (1, 2 or 3)?
2 Which sentence is a restatement of the proposition?
3 Which sentence is the writer's opinion?

> *The best way to reduce emissions from vehicles is to impose a higher tax on vehicles which use a lot of fuel and a lower tax on those that don't.*
> *To what extent do you agree or disagree?*

Sample introduction
(1) *One solution to the problem of air pollution caused by cars and trucks is to increase the tax on those vehicles that use a lot of petrol and to decrease the tax on more economical cars.* (2) *Of course, it is important to find a way to solve this problem, because emissions from petrol-powered engines are a major source of air pollution and global warming.* (3) *However, I do not think this solution is fair for many people, and therefore I strongly disagree with it.*

9 Read these three propositions. Then write an introduction for each proposition. You should agree with one, disagree with one and partially agree with another.

> *The most important reason for a young person to attend a university is to increase the amount of money that he or she will earn in the future.*
> *To what extent do you agree or disagree?*

> *The use of cell phones while driving should be strictly forbidden.*
> *To what extent do you agree or disagree?*

> *It is better to run your own business than to work for someone else.*
> *To what extent do you agree or disagree?*

Q **FOCUS**

Editing your answer (punctuation and capitalisation)

10 Work in pairs. Read the question and the essay below. Then try to find as many errors in capitalisation and punctuation as possible.

> *Instead of being held in a different city each time, the Olympic Games should be held at a permanent site.*
> *To what extent do you agree or disagree?*

Currently the olympics are held in different locations. This system has been in place since the modern games began. However i agree with the idea that its preferable to always hold the games in the same city.

There are certainly some advantages to having the games in different sites around the World. First of all the Olympics are a chance for the host country to be in the spotlight and to show off it's culture and technology. For example people everywhere were impressed by the opening and closing ceremonies of the 2008 Olympics in beijing china. Moreover hosting the games has financial benefits. Hotel owners taxi drivers waiters and all sorts of people benefit because so many visitors come to see the games.

nevertheless; I think it would be a good idea to have the games in a permanent location. It's very expensive to build stadiums and other facilities for athletes and fans. For example, the london games of 2012 cost over $40 billion to stage. Furthermore, most of the sports facilities built in cities that have hosted the games in the past are not very useful after the games are over. A recent article in time magazine said 'that many of these facilities are empty or have been torn down.'

For these reasons I think it is a good idea to move the Olympics to a permanent location. If the Olympics were always held in one place the same facilities could be used over and over. I suggest that the games that are played in Summer be held in athens greece; because the ancient games were first played there, and the first modern games were also held there. Since Switzerland is a neutral country I recommend that the games that are played in Winter be held there. Having permanent homes for the Olympics is the most economical efficient way to stage this important event

11 How many punctuation mistakes did you find? And capitalisation errors?

▶▶ For more information, see Basic Rules for Punctuation and Capitalisation, pages 329–330.

Q FOCUS

Planning, writing and checking your essay

12 **Look at the topic and answer the questions. (4–5 minutes)**

> *Success in life is more a matter of luck than of ability.*
> *To what extent do you agree or disagree?*

1 If you agree with the proposition, what is your position? What will you try to show in your response? If you disagree with the proposition, what is your position?
2 Think of two or three reasons to agree with the proposition.
3 Think of two or three reasons to disagree with the proposition.
4 Do you have any personal background – knowledge or experience – that makes you support or oppose this proposition?

13 **Write your introduction.**

1 Restate the proposition in your own words.
2 Write one or two sentences of background information about the proposition.
3 Write one or two sentences indicating that you agree/disagree/partially agree with the proposition.

14 **Write the main paragraphs.**

1 Write a paragraph with one or two reasons why you agree (or disagree) with the proposition.
2 Write another paragraph with one or two reasons why you disagree (or agree) with the proposition.

15 **Write your conclusion. Write a brief paragraph summarising your main points and restating your opinion.**

16 **Check your work. (4–5 minutes)**

1 Look for mistakes in spelling, capitalisation, punctuation, and grammar.
2 Make sure that you have clearly divided your response into paragraphs, and that your handwriting is clear enough for an examiner to read.

17 **Work in pairs. After you have finished, look at the model answer on the DVD-ROM. Compare your answers with the model answer and think about the marking criteria. (See page 180 for marking criteria.)**

IELTS PRACTICE TASK

Write about the following topic.

You should spend about 40 minutes on this task.

> *Language teachers should concentrate on giving positive feedback to students when they do good work, rather than on criticising bad work.*
> *To what extent do you agree or disagree?*

Give reasons for your answer and include any relevant examples from your own knowledge and experience.

Write at least 250 words.

Which statement best describes how you feel about Task 2 Agree/Disagree Essays?

☐ I feel confident about writing Task 2 Agree/Disagree Essays.
☐ I did OK, but I still need to do more work on Task 2 Agree/Disagree Essays.
☐ I need more practice with writing Task 2 Agree/Disagree Essays. I need to focus on …

▶▶ **For further practice, see the DVD-ROM.**

TASK 2 A Discussion/Opinion Essay

Decide which position you will take.

A About the task

1 **Read the following information about the task.**

The Discussion/Opinion Essay task tests your ability to discuss opposing opinions and to give your own opinion.

On the question paper, you see a task which presents two different opinions about the same topic and a question asking you to discuss both points of view and to explain what you think about this topic. These essay questions often follow this pattern: *Some people think … Other people think …*

Here are the basic rules for writing Discussion/Opinion Essays:

- Read and analyse the opinions and the question carefully.
- Decide whether you agree or disagree with Opinion A or B.
- Write a brief, well-organised introduction, at least two main paragraphs and a short conclusion.
- Include examples to support your reasons.
- Write in paragraphs. Do not use notes or bullet points.
- Use an academic register or style.
- Write at least 250 words.
- Complete the task in about 40 minutes.

You have to explain and support Opinion A, explain and support Opinion B, and then give your own opinion.

2 **Work in pairs. Look at the writing task below and answer the questions.**

> *Some students think it is better to attend university in or near their hometown.*
> *Others think it is better to attend a university away from home.*
> *Discuss both views and give your opinion.*

1 What is the first opinion?
2 What is the second opinion?
3 When you write your essay, what three things must you include?
4 With your partner, think of some reasons to support the first opinion.
5 With your partner, think of some reasons to support the second opinion.
6 Do you have any personal experiences or background information related to these opinions?
7 What is your own opinion? Discuss with your partner.
8 In the exam, how much time do you have to write your essay?
9 How long should your essay be?

B Sample question

3 Read the task and answer the question. Use the rules about the task from Section A to help you. Then compare your answer with the sample answer on page 340. Which aspects of the task did you find difficult?

IELTS PRACTICE TASK

Write about the following topic.

You should spend about 40 minutes on this task.

> *Some people think that schools should use teaching methods that encourage students to cooperate. Other people think that schools should use teaching methods that encourage students to compete.*
>
> *Discuss both views and give your opinion.*

Give reasons for your answer and include any relevant examples from your own knowledge and experience.

Write at least 250 words.

C Tips and tactics

4 Work in pairs. Read the tips and tactics and discuss these questions.

    a Which tips and tactics do you think are the most useful?

    b Did you use any of these tips and tactics when you answered the sample question in Section B?

    c Which tips will you use in the future?

    1 Spend a few minutes reading and thinking about the task. Make sure you understand the two opinions and the question. Underline key words.

    2 You don't have a lot of time, but you should make a brief plan. Write several reasons why you might agree with the first opinion and several reasons why you might agree with the second opinion. Is it easier to think of reasons to agree with the first or second opinion? This can help you decide which position to take.

    3 Your essay should include an introduction, two main paragraphs and a conclusion.

    4 Your introduction can be brief. You should restate the two opinions in your own words, and if possible provide a little background on the issues. For example, you can explain why this issue is an important one, or why it has become more important in recent times.

    5 You don't have to state your opinion in the introduction in this type of essay. You can discuss one of the opinions in the first main paragraph, then discuss the opposing opinion in the second main paragraph, and then give your own opinion in the conclusion.

    6 Begin each main paragraph with a topic sentence (a sentence that states the main idea of the paragraph). This sentence can be quite simple. All of the sentences in that paragraph should support the topic sentence.

    7 In both paragraphs, you should use linking words and phrases to move smoothly from one reason to another and to connect the two paragraphs.

    8 You should support the reasons that you give in your main paragraphs with specific details and examples.

    9 The final paragraph can be brief. You should summarise the main points of both opinions and clearly state your own opinion.

    10 The final paragraph should also begin with a word or phrase to signal that it is a conclusion.

    11 Your paragraphs should be clearly separated, for example, you can leave a blank space between them or indent the first line of each new paragraph..

    12 Keep track of the time. You have about 40 minutes to do Task 2.

    13 Make sure your handwriting is clear and legible enough for the examiners to read.

    14 As you write your essay, keep in mind the criteria that the examiners use to mark your essay. (For marking criteria, see About the Academic Writing Test, page 180.)

D Skills-building exercises

5 Work in pairs. Look at the topic below. Then look at three introductions for the essay. Which one is best? Why? What problems do you see in the other two introductions? Discuss your answers.

> *Some people like to shop in traditional shops. Other people prefer to do their shopping online.*
>
> *Discuss both views and give your opinion.*

A

Some people find it preferable to shop in traditional stores. However, other people think it is preferable to shop online. Why? Because shopping online saves time and it is much more convenient.

B

Many people would rather shop in the traditional way. They enjoy going to shopping malls, bookstores and other places to shop. On the other hand, there are a growing number of people who like online shopping. They would rather use their computers, phones, or other devices to make their purchases.

C

There are a number of good reasons why some people like to buy things online. There are good reasons why other people would rather buy what they need in regular stores. Personally, I enjoy going out shopping with my friends.

6 Read the topic below. Then write a short introduction for this question. Use linking words to show that the two opinions are in contrast to each other.

> *Some people think that multiple choice tests are better than tests which require you to write an essay. Other people think that tests which require you to write an essay are better.*
>
> *Discuss both views and give your opinion.*

LINKING WORDS: CONTRAST AND CONCESSION

However, …	Although …
On the other hand, …	Even though …
Nevertheless, …	Whereas …
In contrast, …	Despite …
Whilst/While …	In spite of …

7 In a discussion/opinion essay, each of the two main paragraphs can discuss one of the opposing opinions from the question. Each paragraph should begin with a topic sentence that summarises the opinion. Look at the topic again and at the notes a student made to prepare their essay. How will the student start each main paragraph?

> *Some people prefer to shop in traditional stores. Other people prefer to do their shopping online.*
>
> *Discuss both views and give your opinion.*

- Introduction
- Main paragraph 1: Reasons why people favour online shopping
- Main paragraph 2: Reasons why people prefer traditional shopping
- Conclusion

8 The topic sentence of the second main paragraph should contain a linking word to link this paragraph with the first main paragraph. This type of linking word indicates concession. (You admit that information in the first paragraph is true, but you indicate that there is information that is in contrast to it.)

Work in pairs. Read the topic sentences (1–7) and answer the questions.

a Decide which sentences would make a good topic sentence for the first main paragraph. Mark those sentences A.

b Decide which sentences would make a good topic sentence for the second main paragraph. Mark those sentences B.

c If a sentence is <u>not</u> a good topic sentence, mark it X.

d Discuss your answers with a partner.

1 Although online shopping is popular, there are some advantages to shopping at traditional stores.

2 Certainly, there are some excellent reasons why people prefer online shopping.

3 A reason people prefer to buy things online is because it is convenient.

4 Increasingly, online shopping is becoming a more popular choice, for the following reasons.

5 However, not everyone likes to shop at traditional stores.

6 It is not hard to understand why more and more shoppers are buying products online.

7 Despite the convenience of online shopping, there are some reasons to prefer more traditional forms of shopping.

INTRODUCING REASONS

In the two main paragraphs, you can provide two or three reasons that support each point of view. Use sequencing words and phrases to introduce these sentences so that the paragraph flows smoothly from one reason to another.

FIRST REASON
First, … / First of all, …
One reason is that …
The first reason …
For one thing, …

OTHER REASONS
Secondly, … / Thirdly, …
A second/third reason is that …
Another reason is that …
Moreover, … / Furthermore, … / In addition, …
Equally important is the fact that …
What's more, …

FINAL REASON
Finally, …
One final reason is that …

Q FOCUS

Discussing views and giving reasons

9 Read the question about online shopping again. Then look at the two main paragraphs below. Complete the paragraphs with linking words and expressions words. In some cases, more than one word or expression can be used.

Increasingly, online shopping is becoming a popular choice, for the following reasons. **1** .... prices at online sites are generally somewhat lower than they are at traditional stores. **2** .... online shopping can be done quickly and easily. **3** .... your purchases are delivered directly to your home. **4** .... it doesn't take long at all to receive your purchases.

Despite the convenience of online shopping, there are some reasons to prefer more traditional forms of shopping. **5** .... many people enjoy shopping as a social experience. **6** .... you can examine the merchandise you might buy closely, and in the case of clothing, you can try it on. **7** .... it is usually easier to return items to a traditional store if you decide they are not right for you.

SUPPORTING YOUR REASONS

You can support your reasons by giving details and other specific information. The 'three Es' are effective ways to support your reasons: examples, explanation and experience.

EXAMPLES

For example / For instance *There are several strong reasons why students should be encouraged to work while they are attending university. One reason is that a part-time job can help prepare them for a career.* **For example/For instance***, a job in a television studio can help a student to prepare for a career in broadcasting.*

EXPLANATION

In other words *There are a number of reasons why the government should provide some support to artists. First of all, financial support gives artists creative freedom.* **In other words***, they are not forced to create art that they can easily sell.*

EXPERIENCE

In my experience / In my case *However, there are also reasons why it is preferable to study from traditional textbooks rather than electronic textbooks. For one thing, you can take notes in traditional textbooks easily.* **In my experience***, this is an important way to remember what you have read.*

Once *Once, my family had a birthday party for my grandmother at our house and it took nearly all the next day to tidy up.*

Q FOCUS

Supporting your reasons

10 **Work in pairs. Read the two main paragraphs below, which are part of an essay about the traditional/online shopping question on page 242. Then look at the sentences (A–D) and answer the questions (1–3).**

1 Are the sentences examples, explanations or experiences?
2 Add an introductory phrase (*in other words*, *for example*, *in my experience*, etc.) before each sentence.
3 Decide the best place in the paragraphs to put the four sentences. Write the letter of the sentence in that position.

A .... , they view shopping as a social experience.
B .... , Amazon.com can often deliver books or other purchases to you in a matter of days, especially if you order express shipping.
C .... I ordered an exercise machine from an online company. After I had unpacked it, I realized that it was not the one I wanted. Repacking it and shipping it back was not convenient at all.
D .... , one tool I ordered online cost half as much as it did at a local hardware store.

Increasingly, online shopping is becoming a more popular choice, for the following reasons. First of all, prices at online sites are generally somewhat lower than they are at traditional stores. Furthermore, ordering goods online is quick and easy. What's more, your purchases are delivered directly to your home. One final reason is that it doesn't take long at all to receive your purchases.

Despite the convenience of online shopping, there are some reasons to prefer more traditional forms of shopping. For one thing, many people enjoy shopping with friends. In addition, you can examine the merchandise you might buy closely, and in the case of clothing, you can try it on. Finally, it is usually easier to return items to a traditional store if you decide they are not right for you.

11 Read the exam question below about different types of test. Then look at the notes a student made before writing their essay. Using the information in the notes, write two main paragraphs. Make sure you include the following:

1 topic sentences
2 linking words
3 additional details (explanations, examples or experiences)

> *Some people think multiple choice tests are better than tests which require you to write an essay. Other people think that tests which require you to write an essay are better.*
>
> *Discuss both views and give your opinion.*

Essay tests
- allow you to express your own ideas (explain ...)
- allow students to write correct grammar (give example ...)
- don't merely test memorisation (give example ...)

Multiple choice test
- there is only one answer, so marking is fair (explain ...)
- don't depend only on writing skills, but on knowledge
- easy to mark, so students get marks faster (experience ...)

GIVING OPINIONS

EXPLAINING OPINIONS

clearly *Clearly, free higher education could benefit people, especially those who cannot otherwise afford to attend college.*

obviously *Open borders would **obviously** make it easier for tourists and business people to travel internationally.*

certainly *Smartphones can **certainly** serve an educational purpose.*

GIVING YOUR OWN OPINION

In my opinion, …
It's my opinion that …
I'm of the opinion that …
Personally, …
I'm convinced that …
As I see it, …
From my point of view, …

DISAGREEING OR PARTIALLY DISAGREEING

(Personally,) I'm not at all convinced that …
… is not always/entirely true.
I don't think that … is justifiable.
I don't share the view that …

CONCLUSIONS

In your conclusion, you should summarise the important points made in the main paragraphs. In general, you do not want to bring up specific points or new ideas. Conclusions can be introduced with linking words.

In conclusion *In conclusion, there are arguments in favour of free higher education and arguments against it.*

In summary / To summarise / To sum up … *To sum up, it's clear why some people support the idea of a 'world without passports', but it's also clear that there are reasons why some people oppose this concept.*

On the whole *On the whole, I don't agree that we should not have passports.*

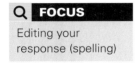

FOCUS

Writing a conclusion

12 Work in pairs. Read the sample conclusion for the online/traditional shopping question. Then answer the questions.

> In conclusion, there are advantages to both forms of shopping. Online shopping is quick and convenient, especially for busy people. Personally, however, I usually prefer the traditional form of shopping because I enjoy interacting with people when I shop.

1 What is the writer's opinion of the two types of shopping?
2 What is the purpose of the first sentence in the conclusion?
3 What is the purpose of the second sentence in the conclusion?
4 What is the purpose of the last sentence in the conclusion?
5 Do you feel that the conclusion 'completes' the essay? Why or why not?

13 Look at the box about conclusions. Then write a conclusion for the question about multiple choice and essay tests that you wrote about in Exercise 11 on page 245.

FOCUS

Editing your response (spelling)

14 Work in pairs. Read the task and the essay below. Then try to find as many errors in spelling as possible. (Note: IELTS accepts both US and British English spellings, but you need to be consistent.)

> *Some people believe that the activities of large multinational corporations mostly benefit the economies of developing countries. Other people take the opposite view and feel that these large multinationals are generally harmful.*
> *Discuss both views and give your opinion.*

There are varying opinions about the role multinational corprations (MNCs) play in developing countries. While many peopel feel that their role is primarily helpfull, many others think that MNCs damage the economys of the host countries.

It's clear that, if goverments allow MNCs to operate in their countries, there are certain dangers involved. First of all, MNCs can drive local companies out of business. Globel chains such as McDonald's, Walmart, and Coca-Cola have many more resorces that they can draw on than local companies do. For instants, they have huge bugets for advertising their products. Morover, MNCs generaly send most of their profits back to the home country, unlike local companies that keep the money within the local economy. Finally, some internasional companies 'cut corners' when it comes to enviromental issues, and they pollute the air and water of the host country.

On the other hand, it's equally obvius that MNCs can serve useful purposes. For one thing, they hire a lot of local workers. While it's true that not all of these workers have high-level positions, they still improve the employment picture in developing nations. In addition, multinationals transfer tecknology to underdeveloped nations. For example, my father was hired as an acountant by a European oil company. He used the knowlege he learned from this position to start his own bookeeping company.

In short, there are both advantages and disadvantages involved in permitting MNCs to do bussiness in developing countries. They may unfairly compete with local firms and force them into bankruptcy, and they might cause ecological damage. On the whole, however, I'm inclined to beleive that they play a mostly positive role. The presents of MNCs in a developing country is a major part of globalization. All the reserche I am familair with indicates that countries that are open to globalization are more sucesful than countries that are not.

15 How many spelling mistakes did you find? (There are 26.) Write the correct spelling of the misspelled words.

Q FOCUS

Planning, writing and checking your essay

16 Look at the topic and answer the questions. (4–5 minutes)

> *Many people believe that public facilities (e.g. zoos, museums, parks) should be free. Other people think that you should pay to use these facilities.*
> *Discuss both views and give your opinion.*

1 What are the two opposing opinions? What is the question asking?
2 Write down three or four reasons to agree with Opinion A.
3 Think of three or four reasons to agree with Opinion B.

17 Write your introduction.

1 Restate the proposition in your own words.
2 Write one or two sentences of background information about the two opinions.

18 Write the main paragraphs.

1 Write a paragraph with two or three points supporting Opinion A. When possible, add specific details (examples, explanations and experience). Use linking words.
2 Write another paragraph with two or three points supporting Opinion B. Add specific details and use linking words.

19 Write your conclusion. Write a brief paragraph summarising the important points mentioned in the two main paragraphs and clearly state your own opinion.

20 Check your work. (4–5 minutes)

1 Look for mistakes in spelling, capitalisation, punctuation and grammar.
2 Make sure that you have clearly divided your response into paragraphs, and that your handwriting is clear enough for an examiner to read.

21 Work in pairs. After you have finished, look at the model answer on the DVD-ROM. Compare your answers with the model answer and think about the marking criteria. (See page 180 for marking criteria.)

IELTS PRACTICE TASK

Write about the following topic.

You should spend about 40 minutes on this task.

> *Some jobs are based at a single work place where the hours are the same each day, while other jobs involve frequent travel and irregular working hours.*
> *Discuss the advantages of both types of job and give your own opinion about which one is best.*

Give reasons for your answer and include any relevant examples from your own knowledge or experience.

Write at least 250 words.

Which statement best describes how you feel about Task 2 Discussion/Opinion Essays?

☐ I feel confident about writing Task 2 Discussion/Opinion Essays.
☐ I did OK, but I still need to do more work on writing Task 2 Discussion/Opinion Essays.
☐ I need more practice with writing Task 2 Discussion/Opinion Essays.
     I need to focus on …

▶▶ **For further practice, see the DVD-ROM.**

TASK 2 A Problem/Solution Essay

Write about the causes of the problem and propose possible solutions.

Car overloaded with milk cans, Java Island, Indonesia

A About the task

1 Read the following information about the task.

The Problem/Solution task tests your ability to write about a problem and suggest ways to solve it.

On the question paper, you see a statement about a contemporary problem and then two questions. One question asks you to identify the cause of the problem and the other question asks you to propose solutions to the problem.

Here are the basic rules for writing Problem/Solution Essays:

- Read and analyse the problem and the questions carefully.
- Write about the causes of the problem and propose possible solutions.
- Write a brief, well-organised introduction, at least two main paragraphs and a short conclusion.
- Support your answer by giving reasons from your own knowledge or experience.
- Write in paragraphs. Do not use notes or bullet points.
- Use an academic register or style.
- Write at least 250 words.
- Complete the task in about 40 minutes.

Be sure to answer BOTH questions. You need to give the causes of the problem and you need to propose possible solutions.

2 Work in pairs. Look at the writing task below and answer the questions.

> *Every year millions of people around the world suffer from poor health as a result of air pollution.*
>
> *What do you think are the causes of this?*
>
> *What solutions can you suggest?*

1 What problem is the task asking you to discuss?
2 What does the first question ask you to do?
3 What does the second question ask you to do?
4 With your partner, think of some answers to the first and second question.
5 Do you have any personal experiences or knowledge related to this problem?

B Sample question

3 Read the task and answer the question. Use the rules about the task from Section A to help you. Then compare your answer with the sample answer on page 342. Which aspects of the task did you find difficult?

IELTS PRACTICE TASK

Write about the following topic.

You should spend about 40 minutes on this task.

> *In many parts of the world, there is not enough food for everyone.*
> *What do you think are the causes of this?*
> *What solutions can you suggest?*

Give reasons for your answer and include any relevant examples from your own knowledge and experience.

Write at least 250 words.

C Tips and tactics

4 Work in pairs. Read the tips and tactics and discuss these questions.

   a Which tips and tactics do you think are the most useful?

   b Did you use any of these tips and tactics when you answered the sample question in Section B?

   c Which tips will you use in the future?

   1 Spend a few minutes reading and thinking about the problem and the questions. Make sure you understand what the task is asking you to do. Underline key words.

   2 You don't have a lot of time, but you should make a brief plan. Think about the most important ideas you need to include, for example, the main causes and main solutions to the problem.

   3 Your essay should include an introduction, two main paragraphs and a conclusion.

   4 Your introduction can be brief. You should first restate the problem in your own words and then briefly explain why this problem is a serious one.

   5 Begin each main paragraph with a topic sentence (a sentence that states the main idea of the paragraph). In the first paragraph, the topic sentence should indicate that you are going to discuss the causes of the problem. In the second paragraph, the topic sentence should indicate that you are going to discuss the solutions to the problem.

   6 In both paragraphs, you should use linking words and phrases to signal that you are moving from one point to another.

   7 In the first paragraph, you should use vocabulary of cause and effect to explain why the problem exists.

   8 In the second paragraph, you should support the solutions you give with examples, explanations or experiences.

   9 The final paragraph can be brief. You should restate the main arguments and bring the essay to a conclusion, for example, you could indicate which solution is best.

  10 Your paragraphs should be clearly separated, for example, you can leave a blank space between them or indent the first line of each new paragraph.

  11 Keep track of the time. You have about 40 minutes to do Task 2.

  12 Make sure your handwriting is clear and legible enough for the examiners to read.

  13 As you write your response, keep in mind the criteria that the examiners use to mark your response. (For marking criteria, see About the Academic Writing Test, page 180.)

D Skills-building exercises

5 In the introduction to a Problem/Solution essay, you should restate the problem in your own words and then explain why this problem is a serious one, one that people should try to solve.

Look at the task below. Then look at three introductions for the essay. Which one is best? Why? What problems do you see in the other two introductions?

> *In many parts of the world, illiteracy rates are still high.*
> *What do you think are the causes of this?*
> *What solutions can you suggest?*

A

It's true that in many parts of the world, illiteracy rates are still high. There are a number of causes for this. There are also some solutions I will suggest.

B

Illiteracy is a global problem. The main cause of this problem is poverty. When poverty decreases, so does illiteracy. However, there are also some ways to improve this situation. Providing more educational television programs might be one solution.

C

Illiteracy is a problem in almost every country and every community. It affects the economy of a nation and causes difficulties for businesses. Most of all, the inability to read and write lowers people's quality of life.

6 Read the task below. Then write a short introduction for this question.

> *One problem faced by almost every large city is traffic congestion.*
> *What do you think are the causes of this?*
> *What solutions can you suggest?*

Q FOCUS

Writing the first
main paragraph:
describing the
possible causes of a
problem

7 Work in pairs. Look at the task below. Then read the four topic sentences to begin a paragraph about the causes of illiteracy. Two of them would be good topic sentences. What problems do you see in the other two sentences? Discuss your answers.

> *In many parts of the world, illiteracy rates are still high.*
> *What do you think are the causes of this?*
> *What solutions can you suggest?*

1 The problem of illiteracy has multiple causes.
2 One cause of illiteracy is a lack of trained teachers.
3 There are a number of ways this problem can be approached.
4 Several factors are at the root of the problem of illiteracy.

CAUSES

INTRODUCING CAUSES

One cause of … is …
The primary/main cause of … is …
Perhaps the most important cause of … is …
A second cause of … is …
… also causes/can also cause …
Another cause of … is …

Furthermore/Moreover/In addition, …
… is responsible for …
… also plays a role in …
Finally, …

UNCERTAINTY ABOUT CAUSES

If you do not know if a factor is a cause of something or not, you can indicate uncertainty about causes in a number of ways.
One possible cause is …
Perhaps … causes …
Another cause may/might be …
… may/might be responsible for …
… may/might also play a role …
… can also lead to …

8 **Look at the language box for talking about the causes of a problem. Complete the sentences with words or phrases to talk about causes. (In some cases, more than one answer may be possible.)**

1 .... illiteracy in many countries is poverty.
2 .... illiteracy is a lack of textbooks and other educational materials.
3 Geographical factors ....
4 A lack of trained teachers .... illiteracy.

9 **Look at the task about traffic congestion. Then look at the notes a student made for the first main paragraph of the essay (to talk about causes).**

1 Write a topic sentence for this paragraph.
2 Write three sentences to describe the causes for the traffic problem.
3 Use words and phrases from the language box on page 252 to introduce each cause.

> *One problem faced by almost every large city is traffic congestion.*
> *What do you think are the causes of this?*
> *What solutions can you suggest?*

Causes of traffic congestion:
• more vehicles on the road
• public transport such as buses crowded and inconvenient
• people have less time for journeys

GIVING REASONS AND EXAMPLES

These words and phrases can be used to explain why a problem exists.

CAUSE → EFFECT

therefore / consequently *Many drivers lack proper training;* ***therefore****, they don't know what to do in an emergency.*

so *Sometimes drivers use their cell phones,* ***so*** *they are too distracted to avoid dangerous situations.*

as a result *Sometimes drivers use their cell phones;* ***as a result,*** *they are too distracted to avoid dangerous situations.*

results in / accounts for *Equipment failure also plays a role. For example, a loss of brakes* ***results in*** *accidents.*

causes / leads to / gives rise to / is responsible for *Bad weather conditions in winter* ***leads to*** *an increase in the number of accidents on the roads.*

EFFECT ← CAUSE

because / since *The most important cause of traffic accidents is excessive speed.* ***Because*** *they are travelling so fast, drivers don't have time to react.*

due to / because of / owing to *Tiredness is a common cause of traffic accidents. Last year, 50 per cent of accidents were* ***due to*** *drivers not taking frequent breaks whilst driving.*

is/are caused by *Poor weather conditions, such as icy roads, may also play a role. In the winter, many accidents* ***are caused by*** *icy roads.*

10 **Complete the sentences with words or phrases from the language box above. (More than one answer may be possible.)**

1   In my country, a fairly large proportion of the population is illiterate .... they are poor.
2   Some teachers are unable to teach students to read and write .... a lack of proper training.
3   Many families barely earn enough to pay for food; .... , education is a luxury they cannot afford.
4   Illiteracy in one generation often .... illiteracy in the next generation.
5   In some cases, the problem .... by geographical factors. .... some people live in isolated communities in the mountains or the desert, their children cannot attend regular schools.

11 **Look at the task below. You are going to write a paragraph discussing the causes of stress-related illnesses in the modern world.**

1   Read the task and underline the key words.
2   Brainstorm a number of causes for this problem and then choose two or three to discuss in your essay.
3   Write a topic sentence for your paragraph.
4   Write the main paragraph, using linking words.

> *Nowadays, stress-related illnesses are becoming increasingly common.*
>
> *What do you think are the causes of this?*
>
> *What solutions can you suggest?*

Q FOCUS

Writing the second
main paragraph:
describing the
solutions to a
problem

12 Work in pairs. Look at six possible topic sentences for a paragraph describing solutions to the problem of high illiteracy rates. Three of them would be good topic sentences. What problems do you see in the other three sentences? Discuss your answers.

1 There are a number of ways the problem of illiteracy can be approached.
2 Furthermore, there are some effective ways to deal with illiteracy.
3 Although illiteracy is a persistent worldwide problem, there are a number of steps that can be taken to correct it.
4 Just as there is no single factor behind the problem of illiteracy, there is no single solution.
5 I'd like to suggest that every child receive a cheap laptop or tablet loaded with how-to-read programs.
6 Let's take a look at the reasons why illiteracy is such a big problem.

INTRODUCING AND PROPOSING SOLUTIONS

Verbs	Modal verbs	Nouns
recommend	must	recommendation
suggest	should	suggestion
propose	ought to	solution
	might	idea
	may	proposal
	could	

*I **recommend** that young drivers be required to take an additional motorway driving test before they get their driving licence.*
*My **recommendation** is that the following steps be taken.*
*I **suggest** that the government do this right away.*
*I **propose** that the government identify dangerous roads and fix the problems.*
*Manufacturers **should** build safer vehicles.*
*Laws requiring seat belts **must be enforced**.*

Remember, the question asks you to suggest solutions – not just one solution. Use linking words such as *first, another, finally* and so on, to propose alternative solutions.

▶▶ **For more information and practice of modals, see Grammar Resource Bank pages 316–319.**

13 Complete these sentences with words or phrases from the language box above. (More than one answer may be possible.)

1 One .... is for the government to spend more money on training teachers.
2 Another .... is to produce and broadcast more television shows that teach children to read and write.
3 Finally, I .... that simple reading materials be made available for free.

14 Look at the task again. Write a paragraph proposing possible solutions to the problem of stress-related illnesses.

1 Brainstorm a number of solutions to the problem and then choose two or three to discuss in your essay.
2 Write a topic sentence for your paragraph.
3 Write the second main paragraph, using linking words.

> *Nowadays, stress-related illnesses are becoming increasingly common.*
>
> *What do you think are the causes of this?*
>
> *What solutions can you suggest?*

15 Work in pairs. Read the conclusion for an essay about the illiteracy problem. Then read the explanations of the role of each sentence in the conclusion. Match the sentences in the conclusion (1–4) with the explanations (A–E). One of the explanations will not be used.

> *In many parts of the world, illiteracy rates are still high.*
> *What do you think are the causes of this?*
> *What solutions can you suggest?*

(1) There is no single cause of the problem of illiteracy, but certainly, the higher the rate of poverty, the higher the rate of illiteracy. (2) Because poverty is such a stubborn problem, illiteracy is not an easy problem to solve. (3) However, there are some practical steps that can be taken, such as improved teacher training programs, that can improve the situation. (4) Teaching people to read and write not only gives them richer lives, it benefits society as a whole.

A This sentence explains the benefits of solving the problem.
B This sentence gives an example of a solution that might be effective.
C This sentence gives the most important cause of illiteracy.
D This sentence explains what will happen if the problem is not solved.
E This sentence explains why solving the problem will be difficult.

16 Reread the task below. Write a conclusion for an essay based on this topic.

> *Nowadays, stress-related illnesses are becoming increasingly common.*
> *What do you think are the causes of this?*
> *What solutions can you suggest?*

Q **FOCUS**

Editing your
response (checking
your grammar)

17 Work in pairs. Read the task and the essay below. Then try to find as many
grammatical errors as possible. Use the table below to help you.

> *Many species of animals have become extinct in recent times.*
> *What are the causes of this?*
> *What solutions can you suggest?*

As long as humans have been in the Earth, they have exploited nature. They have cleared land for farms and cities,
hunted and trapped wild animals, and catch fish in rivers, lakes, and seas. All of these activities have put many animal
species in danger, and some have completely vanished. This has been a problem for centuries, but in the last 100 years
or so, the problem of extinct has accelerated. Dozens of species disappears every year.

There are multiple cause of this problem. One major cause is the loss of habitat. Forests have been cut down, wetlands
have been filled in, and grassy plains have been paved over. One tragic example is the rainforests of the Amazon.
Many hectares of forest land cut down daily, destroying the homes of countless species of animals. Another cause
of extinction is pollution. Farmers use fertilizers and pesticides on his land. These wash into streams and rivers and
eventually into the ocean, poisoning fish and other water creatures. Factories and cars produces air pollution, which
contributes for global warming. This endangers polar bear and many other species. Still another cause of the extinction
is hunting. In the past, animals were often hunted for food or for their skins. For example, in North America, the buffalo
almost become extinct because so many was killed by hunters. Today, rhinoceroses are hunted for their horns and
elephants are hunted for its ivory tusks, both of which is very valuable. This has led to a decline sharp in the number of
these animals in the wild.

There are certain steps that can be taken to save animals from extinction. Areas such as parks national and other types
of animal reserves need to be protected. Existing ones should be expanded and new ones should establish. Then too,
pollution and greenhouses gasses should be curbed. Finally, there needs to be more protect for endangered animals
such as rhinos, tigers and elephants. Laws against poaching should be more enforced rigorously, and people who hunt
animals illegal should be punished.

Once animals have become extinct, there is nothing that can do to help it. They are gone forever. But it is still possible to
save some of the many species of animals that share this planet by humans.

Error type	Error type
Subject/Verb agreement	Articles
Incorrect tense	Prepositions
Active/Passive problem	Word order
Pronoun agreement	Word form
Singular/Plural nouns	

18 How many grammar mistakes did you find? Correct the mistakes.

19 **Look at the task and answer the questions. (4–5 minutes)**

> *Dietary experts agree that many people have unhealthy diets.*
> *What do you think are the causes of this?*
> *What solutions can you suggest?*

1 What problem is given in the task?
2 Write down three or four causes of this problem.
3 Write down three or four ways to solve this problem.

20 **Write your introduction. Restate the problem in your own words. Then write one or two sentences of background information about the problem. Why is this a serious problem?**

21 **Write your main paragraphs.**

1 Write a paragraph with two or three causes of the problem.
2 Write another paragraph with two or three possible solutions to the problem.

22 **Write your conclusion. Write a brief paragraph summarising the important points mentioned in the two main paragraphs. Then say what might happen if this problem is not solved.**

23 **Check your work. (4–5 minutes)**

1 Look for mistakes in spelling, capitalisation, punctuation and grammar.
2 Make sure that you have clearly divided your response into paragraphs, and that your handwriting is clear enough for an examiner to read.

24 **Work in pairs. After you have finished, look at the model answer on the DVD-ROM. Compare your answers with the model answer and think about the marking criteria. (See page 180 for marking criteria.)**

IELTS PRACTICE TASK

Write about the following topic.

You should spend about 40 minutes on this task.

> *In many large cities, some people waste hours of their time every day because of traffic congestion on the roads.*
>
> *What do you think are the causes of this?*
>
> *What solutions can you suggest?*

Give reasons for your answer and include any relevant examples from your own knowledge and experience.

Write at least 250 words.

Which statement best describes how you feel about Task 2 Problem/Solution Essays?

☐ I feel confident about writing for Task 2 Problem/Solution Essays.

☐ I did OK, but I still need to do more work on Task 2 Problem/Solution Essays.

☐ I need more practice with Task 2 Problem/Solution Essays. I need to focus on …

▶▶ **For further practice, see the DVD-ROM.**

WRITING TASK 1

You should spend about 20 minutes on this task.

> *The bar chart shows the total number of tigers at all the tiger reserves in India, 1972–2002. The line graph shows the number of tigers at five individual tiger reserves in India.*
>
> *Summarise the information by selecting and reporting the main features and make comparisons where relevant.*

Write at least 150 words.

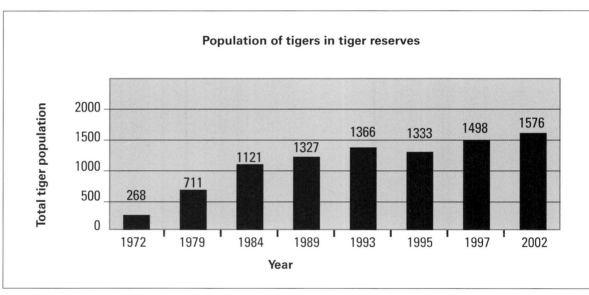

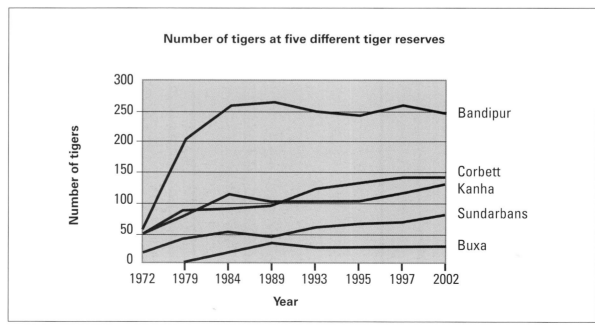

WRITING TASK 2

Write about the following topic.

You should spend about 40 minutes on this task.

> *Some people think that it is good to preserve old buildings whenever possible. Other people think that it is preferable to construct new buildings.*
>
> *Discuss both views and give your own opinion.*

Give reasons for your answer and include any relevant examples from your own knowledge or experience.

Write at least 250 words.

A The Test

Speaking	Description	Time
Part 1	Introduction and Interview	4–5 minutes
Part 2	Individual Long Turn	1–2 minutes
Part 3	Two-way Discussion	4–5 minutes

The IELTS Speaking Test is designed to test your ability to use spoken English effectively. You're given an interview time and the interview takes place in a room where you sit down at a table for a face-to-face interview with the examiner. You don't need to bring anything with you to the test, except for the identification documents required by the regulations. The test is recorded so that it can be checked later if necessary.

The Speaking test lasts for approximately 11 to 14 minutes and has three parts. Each part gives you the chance to demonstrate your English speaking skills in different ways.

Part 1 lasts for 4 to 5 minutes. The examiner asks you questions about your daily life and other everyday topics.

Part 2 lasts for 1 to 2 minutes. You speak at length about a topic that the examiner gives you.

Part 3 lasts for 4 to 5 minutes. You have a discussion with the examiner.

Part 1

At the beginning of the interview, the examiner asks for your name and checks your identity. He or she then begins Part 1 by asking you a series of questions on different topics. These questions are related to everyday subjects such as work, study, hobbies, likes and dislikes, the weather, and so on. You should give full answers, for example explaining your reasons for liking or disliking things. When you've said enough on a topic, the examiner will move on to the next question.

Part 2

In Part 2 of the test, the examiner gives you a task card. On the card, you see the topic that you're going to talk about in this part of the test. You have to talk on your own for between one and two minutes on this topic, and you have one minute to prepare before you begin. There are also some bullet points on the card. These give you some ideas about what to include in your talk. You're also given some paper and a pencil, so that you can make some notes in the preparation time. (See page 260 for an example of a task card.)

The topics for Part 2 are also familiar everyday ones, and there should be plenty to say about the topic you're given. For example, it could be a holiday you enjoyed, or something you want to buy. The examiner gives you one minute's preparation time to think about what you want to say before you start talking. Use the bullet points to help you prepare and structure your talk. When the preparation time is up, the examiner asks you to start speaking, and then lets you speak on your own for up to two minutes without interrupting you. When the time is up, the examiner stops you, asks a question to 'round off' and collects the task card and paper and pencil from you.

Part 3

In Part 3 of the test, the examiner starts a discussion with you which is related to the topic that you've spoken about in Part 2. The examiner asks for your opinion about things and encourages you to explain and justify your ideas. This part of the test lasts for about four to five minutes. At the end of this time, the examiner thanks you and tells you that the test has finished. You can then stand up and leave the room.

B Marking criteria

While you're doing the Speaking test, the examiner is listening to you and assessing your English speaking level. You're given what's called a Band Score for Speaking on a scale of 0–9. The levels range from 0 for a non-user of English to 9 for an expert user of English. It's important to remember that, as with the other modules of the IELTS test, the Speaking test isn't a test that you can pass or fail. It's a measure of your ability to communicate effectively in spoken English.

To assess your speaking ability, the examiner uses a set of criteria. The criteria are divided into four parts, which focus on different aspects of speaking. Each aspect is equally important. You are given a score of 0 to 9 for each of these four aspects, and your overall result for the speaking is calculated from these four scores.

Fluency and Coherence

Here the examiner assesses your ability to keep talking. For example, can you say more than just a word or phrase in answer to a question? The examiner also assesses your ability to express your ideas clearly and logically, so that they flow naturally when you speak at length. For example, can you link your ideas when you move from one point to the next, and can you use a range of different connecting words and phrases? The examiner also assesses whether you can do all this without long pauses or repeating yourself.

Lexical Resource

Here the examiner assesses your ability to use a wide range of vocabulary accurately and appropriately. In other words, do you know enough words to say what you mean on a range of different topics? Do you know when to use more formal words and when to use idiomatic phrases? The examiner also assesses whether you can do all this without making too many mistakes in word forms or collocations.

Grammatical Range and Accuracy

Here the examiner assesses your ability to use a range of grammatical structures flexibly and accurately. In other words, do you know which grammatical structures to use to get across the ideas you want to express? Do you know when to use simple structures and when to use more complex ones? The examiner also assesses how well you can do all this without making too many errors.

Pronunciation

Here the examiner assesses your ability to speak English clearly enough to be understood. For example, do you produce each of the sounds correctly? Do you put the stress in the right place in words and sentences? Can you use intonation to help communicate your ideas clearly? The examiner also assesses how easy it is for other people to understand your pronunciation.

For the IELTS Speaking Band Descriptors, see page 333.

C Strategies

Before the test

• It's important to familiarise yourself with the format of the Speaking test. Make sure you know exactly what you have to do in each part of the test – then you can feel confident and prepared on the day of the test. For example, you can watch the Speaking Test Videos on the DVD-ROM to see what the examiner and candidate do in each part.

• Try preparing for the Speaking test with a friend. Take it in turns to play the roles of examiner or candidate. Use the practice questions in the Speaking module to practise asking and answering questions. Try recording yourself and then listen to the recording. Focus on different aspects of your performance; for example, check your verb tenses, or the variety of vocabulary that you used, or your use of linking expressions. Ask yourself how you could improve your performance.

• When you practise answering questions in Part 1, try to get into the habit of expanding your answers. In other words, when you answer a question, try to say more than just 'Yes' or 'No'. Give a reason or an example as well.

• When you practise giving a talk in Part 2, use a stopwatch app on your phone or computer to time yourself. This helps you to get an idea of how much you need to say to keep going for about two minutes.

• When preparing for the talk in Part 2, it's a good idea to practise reading the topic, brainstorming some ideas, and noting them down on a piece of paper. Use a stopwatch to allow yourself only one minute to do this.

• Try to make the most of every opportunity to practise your speaking. For example, if you're asked to participate in a discussion in your English class, use this as a chance to practise for Part 3 of the Speaking test.

• Listen to broadcasts and podcasts in English as often as you can. Use the Internet to keep up with the latest news and current affairs in English. While you're reading or listening, think about your opinions on the issues. This can help you find something to say about a variety of different topics.

• As you listen or read about current issues, make a list of words and phrases that relate to that topic. Make a note of how the words are pronounced – a speaking dictionary can help with this. Try to review the list once a week.

• Use your study time to practise talking about a variety of different topics. Don't try to memorise talks for Part 2 – the examiner doesn't want to hear a talk that you've memorised word-for-word and the chances of your getting exactly the topic you've memorised are very low.

• Remember to practise your pronunciation. Find exercises with a recording to practise individual sounds, word stress, sentence stress and the intonation patterns of connected speech.

During the test

• The examiner gives you all the instructions during the test and guides you through the three parts. Don't worry if the examiner interrupts you at any point; it's nothing personal! The test has strict time limits for each part of the test, so the examiner may have to stop you.

• In the exam room, be friendly and polite. Sit facing the examiner and make eye contact regularly while taking part in the conversation. Be aware of your volume and speak loudly enough so that the examiner can hear you.

• Try to make the interview interesting for the examiner – remember he or she enjoys hearing what candidates have to say.

• If you make a mistake, try not to worry about it. Just keep going! It's only natural to make the occasional error. The examiner knows this and is assessing you on your overall performance during the whole test.

• In Parts 1 and 3, if the examiner asks you a tricky question, you can use a filler expression such as 'That's a very good question …' or 'Well, I've never really thought about that before, but …' to give yourself a little more time to think about your answer.

• In Part 2, when planning your talk, always use the bullet points to guide you. They are there to help you. Don't worry, however, if the examiner stops you before you've finished covering all the bullet points, because it's not necessary to cover them all.

• In Part 3, to help extend your answers, use the PREP method: make a Point, give a Reason, give an Example, and re-state your Point. Don't forget to use connecting words to link your ideas together.

• If you can't think of the perfect word to use to express your meaning, don't worry about it. Use another word instead and move smoothly on. Your ability to paraphrase (to say something in a different way) is a positive thing.

• At the end of the test, don't try to ask the examiner about how well you've done. Examiners aren't allowed to talk about this with candidates.

After the test

• It's a good idea to reflect on how you performed in the test, but don't waste time and energy worrying about any mistakes that you may have made.

PART 1

WORK/STUDY

Let's talk about what you do.
- Do you work or are you a student?
- What's your job/course?
- What does your work/course involve?
- Do you think you will stay in this job for a long time?

SEASONS

Let's talk about the seasons now.
- Tell me about the seasons in your country.
- What's your favourite season? (Why?)
- What do you like doing at different times of the year?
- What season did you enjoy most when you were a child?

READING

I'd like to talk about reading now.
- Do you like reading? (Why?)
- What kind of books did you read when you were a child?
- Is there anything you find difficult to read?
- When do you think is the best time to read? (Why?)

PART 2

Task card

Describe a photograph that is important to you.

You should say:

where and when it was taken

who took the photograph

what you can see in the photo

and explain why it is important to you.

You will have to talk about the topic for 1 to 2 minutes.
You have 1 minute to think about what you're going to say.
You can make some notes to help you if you wish.

Rounding-off questions:
- Have you shown this photograph to other people?
- Do you like taking photographs?

PART 3

Let's consider technology and photography.
- What effect has technology had on photography?
- It's common now for people to share photographs online. What are the pros and cons of this?
- What elements do you think make up a good photograph?

Let's move on now to the pursuit of photography as a profession.
- In your view, can photography be a form of art?
- Some people say that photography is a dying profession. Do you agree?
- Do you think we will still need photographers in the future?

PART 1 Introduction and Interview

Part 1 deals with familiar topics, related to everyday life, and makes you feel more relaxed.

Red Sea, Sinai Peninsula, Egypt

A About the task

1 **Read the information about Part 1. Then look at some notes a student made. Are the notes true (T) or false (F)?**

The Part 1 task tests your ability to talk about familiar topics, related to everyday life. For example, the examiner might ask you questions about your job or studies, where you live, or your hobbies. This part of the test lasts for approximately four to five minutes. As this is the first part of the Speaking test, it starts with introductions between you and the examiner, as well as an ID check. The examiner then goes on to ask you a series of questions about different topics.

Here are the basic rules for the Part 1 task:

- In this part of the test, you are showing that you can give information and opinions about everyday topics. Typical topics include home and family life, work and study, hobbies and interests, and likes and dislikes.
- Another purpose of this part is to help you settle in to the test and get over your nerves, so the questions are not meant to be too challenging.
- For each topic in the Part 1 task, the examiner asks you a number of questions covering different topics.
- When answering the examiner's questions, don't just say 'Yes' or 'No'; give your answer and also add a reason, explanation or example.

Speaking Part 1

1 The questions in Part 1 are about everyday topics.

2 This is the hardest part of the Speaking test.

3 You normally talk about one topic in Part 1.

4 This part of the test lasts for four to five minutes.

5 Don't give any extra information when answering the questions.

B Sample questions

2 ● Answer the questions. Use the rules about the task from Section A to help you. Then watch Speaking test video 1 (Part 1) and listen to a candidate answering these questions and compare your answers. Which questions did you find difficult?

IELTS PRACTICE TASK

PART 1
WORK/STUDY

- Do you work or are you a student?
- What are you studying? *or* What's your job?
- Why did you choose to study this subject? *or* Why did you choose this job?
- Have you made many friends on the course? *or* Do you plan to stay in this job for a long time?

HEALTH AND FITNESS

Let's talk about keeping fit and healthy.

- What do you do to stay healthy?
- Do you do any exercise? (What kind?)
- How active were you when you were a child?
- How important is it for children to be active?

WEATHER

Let's talk about the weather.

- What kind of weather do you like best? (Why?)
- Have you noticed any changes in the weather recently in your country?
- What do you like to do in winter?

C Tips and tactics

3 Work in pairs. Read the tips and tactics and discuss these questions.

a Which tips and tactics do you think are the most useful?
b Did you use any of these tips and tactics when you answered the sample questions in Section B?
c Which tips will you use in the future?

1 In the exam room, be friendly and polite. Make eye contact regularly while taking part in the conversation.
2 Be aware of your pronunciation. Focus on speaking clearly and carefully and take your time. Speak loudly enough so that the examiner can hear you.
3 Listen carefully to the examiner when he/she asks you a question. If you don't hear it or understand it the first time, you can ask the examiner to repeat the question; for example, you can say, 'I'm sorry, can you repeat that, please?'
4 The questions in Part 1 are supposed to be fairly easy, but if the examiner asks you a difficult question, you can use a filler expression such as 'That's a very good question …' or 'Well, I've never really thought about that before, but …' to give yourself a little more time to think about your answer.
5 Avoid giving one- or two-word answers to the questions. Try to extend your answer a little by giving a reason or an example. A full answer in this part of the test can be two or three sentences long.
6 If you can't think of the perfect word to use to express your meaning, don't worry about it. Just use another word or expression instead and move on. Your ability to paraphrase (to say something in a different way) is a positive thing. Avoid using expressions like 'How do you say …?', as they just draw attention to the vocabulary you don't know.
7 If you make a mistake, try not to worry about it: just keep going! It's natural to make the occasional mistake when speaking. The examiner knows this and will assess you on your overall performance on the whole test.

D Skills-building exercises

Q FOCUS

Talking about your home

4 Work in pairs. In Part 1 of the IELTS Speaking test, you may be asked to talk about your home. Look at the questions below. How would you answer them? Practise asking and answering the questions.

PART 1

HOME
- Do you live in a house or apartment?
- How long have you lived there?
- Is there anything you don't like about living there?
- What sort of accommodation would you like to live in?

5 🔘 35 Look at the box below. Then listen to the conversation between a candidate and an examiner and tick (✓) the expressions that you hear.

⟳ ACCOMMODATION

house	living room	bed	spacious
apartment	bedroom	sofa	cramped
townhouse	bathroom	desk	comfortable
dream home	kitchen	chair	tidy
garden	balcony	table	messy

6 How did the candidate's answers compare with your responses in Exercise 4? Choose the best option (a, b or c).

a She gave longer answers.
b She gave shorter answers.
c Our answers were about the same length.

Q FOCUS

Identifying common errors (1)

7 Work in pairs. Be careful when you answer the examiner's questions. Here are some common errors that candidates make. Discuss what is wrong with each candidate's answer.

1
Examiner: Is there anything you don't like about living there?
Candidate: No. ✗
2
Examiner: How long have you lived there?
Candidate: I have moved into this apartment about six months ago, when I have moved to this city. ✗
3
Examiner: What sort of accommodation would you like to live in?
Candidate: Well, if I would live here in this country, I would buy a house with a swimming pool. ✗

▶▶ **For more information and practice of tenses, see Grammar Resource Bank pages 303–310.**

8 Work in pairs. In Part 1 of the IELTS Speaking test, you may be asked to talk about your likes and dislikes. Look at the questions below. How would you answer them? Practise asking and answering the questions.

PART 1

CLOTHING
- Do you like going shopping for clothes?
- Is fashion important to you?
- What styles of clothes do you like wearing?
- Are there any colours that you dislike wearing?

---

9 ⬤ 36 Look at the box below. Then listen to the conversation between a candidate and an examiner and tick (✓) the expressions that you hear.

↻ **LIKES AND DISLIKES**		
LIKE	**UNDECIDED**	**DISLIKE**
I (absolutely) love …	I don't mind …	I hate …
I'm crazy about …	I have mixed feelings about …	I can't stand …
I (really) like …		I don't (really) like …
I'm really into …	I don't (really) have any strong feelings about …	I'm not (really) into …
I'm a big fan of …		I'm not a big fan of …
I'm quite keen on …	… is OK.	I'm not that keen on …

10 How did the candidate's answers compare with your responses in Exercise 8?

a She used a wider range of vocabulary and grammar.
b She used a smaller range of vocabulary and grammar.
c We used about the same range.

11 Work in pairs. Here are some common language errors that candidates make. Discuss what is wrong with each candidate's answer.

1
Examiner: Do you like going shopping for clothes?
Candidate: Yes, I like. ✗

2
Examiner: Do you like going shopping for clothes?
Candidate: Yes, I absolutely like it. ✗

3
Examiner: Do you like going shopping for clothes?
Candidate: No, I dislike it. ✗

▶▶ For more information and practice of tenses, see Grammar Resource Bank pages 303–310.

🔍 **FOCUS**

Talking about habits and routines

12 Work in pairs. In Part 1 of the IELTS Speaking test, you may be asked to talk about your habits and routines. Look at the questions below. How would you answer them? Practise asking and answering the questions.

PART 1

DAILY ROUTINES
- ■ Tell me about a typical day in your life.
- ■ What do you like to do at weekends?
- ■ . Is there anything that you would like to change about your daily routine?
- ■ How important is it for you to have time to relax?

---

13 🔘 37 Look at the box below. Then listen to the conversation between a candidate and an examiner and tick (✓) the expressions that you hear.

↻ **DAILY ROUTINES**

TYPICAL WEEKDAY ACTIVITIES	**TYPICAL WEEKEND ACTIVITIES**
get up	sleep in
get dressed	catch up with friends
have breakfast/lunch/dinner	hang out with friends
go to work/school/university/the library	go shopping
catch the bus/train	go out for lunch
	play sports

ADVERBS OF FREQUENCY

always   usually   often   regularly   sometimes   occasionally   rarely   never

ADVERB PHRASES

during the week   at weekends   when I get the chance   every so often
from time to time   hardly ever   almost never   once a week   every day

14 How did the candidate's answers compare with your responses in Exercise 12?

a   She spoke more fluently, with less hesitation.
b   She spoke less fluently, with more hesitation.
c   We spoke at about the same speed.

🔍 **FOCUS**

Identifying common errors (3)

15 Work in pairs. Here are some common language errors that candidates make. Discuss what is wrong with each candidate's answer.

1
Examiner: What do you like to do at weekends?
Candidate: Oh, I usually do my homework. I have always a lot. ✗

2
Examiner: What do you like to do at weekends?
Candidate: Oh, I have to get up early. My baby sister usually is awake early. ✗

3
Examiner: What do you like to do at weekends?
Candidate: Oh, I am sometimes surfing the Internet. ✗

▶▶ **For more information and practice of adverbs, see Grammar Resource Bank page 314.**

IELTS PRACTICE TASK

Speaking test video 2 (Part 1)

PART 1

WORK/STUDY
- Do you work, or are you a student?
- Where do you work, or what are you studying?
- Why did you choose that job or course?
- Do you think you will remain friends with the people from your course or job in the future?

FAVOURITE PLACE
Let's talk about your favourite place.
- What is the place that you most like to visit?
- Why do you like it there?
- How often do you go there?
- Is it easy to travel there?
- Is it a popular place for other people to visit?

DAILY ROUTINE
Let's talk about your daily routine.
- Tell me about a typical weekday for you.
- Do you work or study better in the morning or the afternoon?
- What would you like to change about your daily routine?
- Is there a balance between your work time and your leisure time in your daily routine?

Which statement best describes how you feel about Part 1 tasks?

☐ I feel confident about doing Part 1 tasks.

☐ I did OK, but I still need to do more work on Part 1 tasks.

☐ I need more practice with Part 1 tasks. I need to focus on …

▶▶ **For further practice, see the DVD-ROM.**

PART 2 Individual Long Turn

It's important to link the different parts of the talk together.

Golden Gate Bridge, San Francisco, California

A About the task

1 Read the information about Part 2. Then cover up the information and complete the sentences below (1–7) with what you can remember from the text.

The Part 2 task tests your ability to give a short talk on a topic that is given to you by the examiner. The examiner gives you a task card with your topic on and four points that give you ideas for what to talk about. You have one minute to plan what you want to say using the piece of paper and pencil the examiner gives you to make notes if you wish. You then talk for one to two minutes on your given topic and the examiner listens to you. The topics are familiar ones based on your personal experiences such as talking about a teacher who had a big influence on you, your favourite TV programme, a meal you enjoyed or a holiday you'd like to have. At the end of the two minutes, the examiner usually asks you a short, simple question to round off this part of the test. Your response to this question does not have to be long and detailed. In Part 2 it's important to speak without too much hesitation and to link the different parts of the talk together well.

Here are the basic rules for the Part 2 task:

- You need to speak on a personal, familiar topic for up to two minutes.
- The examiner gives you a task card. The task card helps to guide you through the talk by giving you four points to cover in your talk.
- You have one minute to prepare what you are going to say and you should use the four points on the task card to help you make notes.
- The examiner listens to you as you speak. This is your chance to show that you have good fluency (i.e you can talk at a normal speed without too many pauses and hesitations) and coherence (you can organise your talk and connect ideas together so that what you say makes sense).
- At the end of the talk, the examiner asks a short question that only requires a brief answer.

Speaking Part 2

1 The Part 2 task tests your ability to …

2 The examiner gives you …

3 You have one minute to …

4 You must talk for …

5 The topic is …

6 At the end of the two minutes the examiner …

7 In Part 2 it's important to …

B Sample questions

2 ⬤ **Answer the question. Use the rules about the task from Section A to help you. Then watch Speaking test video 1 (Part 2) and listen to a candidate answering the question and compare your answers. Which parts did you find difficult?**

IELTS PRACTICE TASK

PART 2

> **Talk about a building that you like.**
>
> You should say:
>> where the building is
>>
>> what the building looks like
>>
>> what the building is used for
>
> and explain why you like it so much.

You will have to talk about the topic for 1 to 2 minutes.

You have 1 minute to think about what you are going to say.

You can make some notes to help you if you wish.

C Tips and tactics

3 **Work in pairs. Read the tips and tactics and discuss these questions.**

 a **Which tips and tactics do you think are the most useful?**

 b **Did you use any of these tips and tactics when you answered the sample questions in Section B?**

 c **Which tips will you use in the future?**

1 Read the task card very carefully to make sure that you know what to talk about and what the four points underneath the topic instruction are.

2 Make the most of your planning time. On the paper you are given write the topic word at the top, e.g. 'a building', then write the name of the building you want to talk about, e.g. 'The Capital Gate Building', then draw a cross shape underneath so you have four boxes in which to make notes on the four points underneath.

3 Don't write sentences on the paper – you don't have time. Key words and expressions are enough to focus your ideas and give you some support as you speak.

4 Structure your talk by introducing each part of the talk and then indicating when you are moving on to the next part, e.g. 'I'm going to talk about ...', 'OK, first, the building is located in ...', 'Secondly, the appearance of the building. Well, the building looks quite strange from the outside ...', 'Now, moving on to what the building is used for ..', 'Finally, the reason I like this building so much is ...'

5 Write down some topics that you think could be used in Part 2 and try writing four points underneath the topic.

6 Practise talking about topics for two minutes so that you get a feel for how long the time lasts. Make sure you can fit a beginning, middle and end into this time.

7 Record yourself and listen to your talk. Check several criteria, e.g. timing, organisation, hesitation, use of linking words, pronunciation and range and accuracy of vocabulary and grammar.

8 As you talk, think about the marking criteria that the examiners will use to mark your response. (For marking criteria, see page 258.)

9 Ask a friend to listen to you speak and see if he or she can guess your topic and the four points you covered. Your friend could also comment on the criteria in point 7 above.

10 Don't memorise a talk to use in the test. It is impossible to predict which topic you will be asked to talk on and it is much better to sound natural.

D Skills-building exercises

Q FOCUS

Understanding
the task card and
practising the task

4 **Work in pairs. Look at the example Part 2 task card A below.**

1 Discuss what you are required to do in this part of the Speaking test.
2 Underline key words in the task.
3 Decide what grammar forms you need to use in your answer (past, present, future tenses or hypothetical language, e.g. *would*).

▶▶ **For more information and practice of tenses, see Grammar Resource Bank pages 303–310.**

Task card A

> **Talk about a holiday you have taken that you really enjoyed.**
> You should say:
>> where the holiday was
>> who was with you on the holiday
>> what you did on the holiday
> and explain why the holiday was so enjoyable.

---

5 **Now look at task card B. Discuss how it compares to task card A.**

Task card B

> **Talk about a holiday you would like to take in the future.**
> You should say:
>> where the holiday would be
>> who you would go with on the holiday
>> what you would do on the holiday
> and explain why you would like to take this holiday.

6 **Work in pairs. You are going to make notes for your talk.**

    1   Spend one minute making notes for task card A in Exercise 4.
    2   Show your notes to your partner and discuss the following questions:
       a   How are they similar or different?
       b   Did the one minute preparation time seem short?
       c   What's the best way to make use of the time?

7 **Now take turns to give your talk.**

- Time each other for two minutes.
- At the end of the talk, ask your partner one question connected to the topic.
- Tell your partner what they did well and how they could improve their answer.
- How could you improve your own answer?
- Were your notes helpful?

Q FOCUS

Brainstorming ideas and making notes

8 **Look at the following ways (A–E) in which IELTS candidates use their one minute to prepare the Part 2 task. Talk about the strengths and/or weaknesses of each approach. Which one do you think is best? Why?**

A

I went on a great holiday recently with my family. We went camping near a beach about two hours from where we live. It's a beach that's off the beaten track so there weren't hordes of tourists there.

B

C

– camping
– beach
– 2 hrs

D

– camping
– beach
– 2 hrs home
– off beaten track
– no hordes of tourists
– family, annual get-together
– swimming, cycling, picturesque villages, stunning landscape
– unwind, fun, glorious weather

E

<u>Enjoyable holiday</u>

<u>Where</u>	<u>Who</u>
– camping	– family
– beach	– annual get-together
– 2 hrs home	
<u>What</u>	<u>Why</u>
– swimming	– unwind
– cycling	– fun
– picturesque villages	– glorious weather
– stunning landscape	

9 **Prepare to talk about the topic on task card B on page 272. You have one minute to do this. Use the style of notes in E above. When you finish, look at your partner's notes and discuss what's good about the notes and how they could be improved. Use the following criteria to help you assess the notes:**

Do your partner's notes have:
- a topic title
- four key question words
- two points under each question word
- some useful vocabulary/phrases

10 Check that you have understood how to approach Part 2 of the Speaking test. With a partner, order the stages below (1–4).

a Draw a cross on a piece of paper and write a short title and the four question words.
b Check whether you have to talk about the past, present, future or a hypothetical situation.
c Read the task card and make sure you fully understand it.
d Brainstorm ideas by putting at least two points to talk about underneath each question word.

11 38 Listen to a candidate talking about one of the task cards A or B on page 272.

1 Which task card is being talked about?
2 Make notes on what the candidate says for each key point.

FOCUS

Organising your talk and useful speaking strategies

12 Work in pairs. Look at the box below. The box shows a way of organising a Part 2 answer and phrases you can use for each stage of the talk. Read the phrases aloud. Can you think of alternative phrases you could use to introduce each stage?

ORGANISING YOUR TALK

Beginning	*OK, so I'm going to talk about ...*
Where	*First of all, I'll talk about where I'd go ...*
Who	*Next, I'll mention who I'd go with ...*
What	*Thirdly, what I would do ...*
Why	*Finally, I want to say why this holiday would be so enjoyable for me ...*
End	*And so that brings me to the end of my talk.*

13 Look at the box below. It includes useful strategies for Part 2 and phrases that you can use for these strategies. With a partner, read the phrases aloud. Can you think of alternative phrases you could use for each strategy?

USEFUL SPEAKING STRATEGIES

1 Paraphrase a word or phrase to check the listener knows what you mean (clarify)	*Out of season, you know, not in the main holiday period.*
2 Paraphrase a word or phrase you don't know	*I'm not sure of the word exactly but it means ...*
3 Avoid a long hesitation	*Erm, let me see ...*
4 Refer back to something that you said earlier	*As I mentioned earlier ...*
5 Say you can't remember something	*I can't quite remember the name of the place ...*

14 38 Listen again to the candidate talking about a holiday. Tick (✓) the phrases from Exercises 12 and 13 that you hear, or write down similar phrases the candidate uses.

15 Now it's your turn. Go back to the notes you prepared in Exercise 9. Then work in pairs. Take turns with a partner to give your talk. Remember to organise what you say well and to use some useful speaking strategies from Exercise 13.

16 Work in pairs. Look at the four task cards below. Tell your partner which one you would like to talk about.

Task card C

> **Talk about a piece of equipment you own that is very useful.**
>
> You should say:
>> what the piece of equipment is
>> what you use it for
>> how often you use it
>
> and explain why it is so useful.

Task card D

> **Talk about a time in your life when you were successful at something.**
>
> You should say:
>> what you were successful at
>> when you achieved the success
>> how you managed to be successful
>
> and explain why you are proud of this success.

Task card E

> **Talk about a job you would like to do in the future.**
>
> You should say:
>> what the job would be
>> where you would work
>> what you would have to do
>
> and explain why you would like to do this job.

Task card F

> **Talk about an interesting news story that you have recently read about or heard about.**
>
> You should say:
>> what the story was about
>> who was involved in the story
>> how you found out about the story
>
> and explain why this news story was interesting for you.

17 Look at the extracts (1–4) from candidates' answers below. Which task card are they talking about?

1

A story that was in my local newspaper recently was about an elderly couple who've just celebrated their wedding anniversary; they've been married for fifty years. It struck a chord with me because I'm planning to get married in the near future. It was a human interest story about how they've stuck with each other through thick and thin. There was also an eye-catching photo of the couple with their descendants – they have a very large family now.

2

I can't get by without my coffee machine! I was recently given a brand new, state-of-the-art one by my family and I love it. I use it to make myself a really strong cup of coffee every morning. I'm an early bird and I'm usually up at the crack of dawn; I go out for a thirty-minute jog, then I come back and have my first coffee of the day. It's heaven!

3

I think I'd get a lot of job satisfaction from being self-employed. I'd love to start my own catering company from scratch and hopefully build it up into a profitable company. I'd have to find suitable premises of course, something with a decent kitchen and lots of preparation space. It would be hard work; I don't think I'd have a good work-life balance to begin with!

4

One of the things I'm proud of is when I completed a fun-run for charity. I had to run ten kilometres, which was quite an achievement for me. I wasn't exactly fit as a fiddle at that time, in fact I was a bit of a couch potato, so it was quite a challenge to train for the race and to actually complete it. I'm so glad I did it though; the experience spurred me on to exercise more regularly and get fitter.

18 An idiom is a group of words whose whole meaning is different from the individual words that make up the phrase. Look at this idiom the candidate used when talking about task card B on page 272. What does the idiom mean? Discuss with a partner.

'I've done some snorkelling in my own country a couple of times, but the marine life there is **nothing to write home about**.'

19 Find idioms in the extracts in Exercise 17 and match them with the meanings below.

1 from the very beginning even when there are problems or difficulties
2 very early in the morning
3 say or do something that makes people feel sympathy or enthusiasm
4 in good physical condition
5 a person who gets up very early

20 Work in pairs. You need to have a good range of vocabulary in order to be able to talk about the different topics that are common in the IELTS Speaking test. Task cards A and B are about holidays. Below is vocabulary connected to that topic taken from the audioscript. Can you add any more words or expressions?

21 In a notebook, make similar vocabulary notes around these four topics:

- a news story
- a piece of equipment
- a dream job
- a success

IELTS PRACTICE TASK

 Speaking test video 2 (Part 2)

PART 2

> **Talk about a meal you have had that you really enjoyed.**
>
> You should say:
>> what the meal was
>>
>> who prepared the meal
>>
>> where you ate the meal
>
> and explain why this meal was so enjoyable for you.

You will have to talk about the topic for 1 to 2 minutes.

You have 1 minute to think about what you are going to say.

You can make some notes to help you if you wish.

Which statement best describes how you feel about Part 2 tasks?

☐ I feel confident about doing Part 2 tasks.

☐ I did OK, but I still need to do more work on Part 2 tasks.

☐ I need more practice with Part 2 tasks. I need to focus on …

▶▶ **For further practice, see the DVD-ROM.**

PART 3 Two-way Discussion

You can discuss ideas in depth and at length.

Sweetwater cave system in Jackson County, Florida, USA

A About the task

1 **Read the information about Part 3. Then look at the list of statements below about the task. Are the statements true (T) or false (F)?**

The Part 3 task tests your ability to answer more general and abstract questions that are linked to the topic you were asked to talk about in Part 2 of the Speaking test. Part 3 becomes a discussion between you and the examiner and it is your chance to demonstrate that you can discuss ideas in English in depth and at length. In this part, you do not need to give personal information and examples but instead think about the question more widely. You should try to give your opinion on the topic and say why you have this opinion by giving explanations, reasons and examples.

Here are the basic rules for the Part 3 task:

- Expect to answer questions and discuss the theme of your Part 2 topic in a more general and abstract way.
- You will discuss a number of questions and speak for four to five minutes.
- In Part 3 the examiner does not have to stick to set questions; be prepared for the examiner to respond directly to what you say by asking you to give further explanation and to expand on your point.
- The questions you are asked might require you to: give an explanation, make a suggestion, say how sure you are about something, give an opinion, compare two things, make a future prediction, speculate about why something is the way it is, or agree or disagree with something.
- Your answers to the questions should be quite long and they should fully address all parts of the question.
- You should connect your ideas using linking words and phrases.
- Remember, the examiner is not asking for personal information in this part. You need to speak more generally about the topic.

SPEAKING, PART 3

1 In Part 3, you have to talk about personal topics connected to your everyday life.
2 Your answers to the questions need to be well-extended with clear organisation and linking between ideas.
3 If a Part 2 topic is about a good holiday, for example, a Part 3 question that follows it might be about the pros and cons of travelling in a large group.
4 You need to answer as many questions as you can in Part 3. This will show you have a broader range of grammar and vocabulary.
5 The examiner does not have to follow a script so carefully in Part 3. He or she will be listening to the answers carefully and might ask you to say more about an answer.

B Sample questions

2 ⬤ **Answer the questions. Use the rules about the task from Section A to help you. Then watch Speaking test video 1 (Part 3) and listen to a candidate answering the questions and compare your answers. Which questions did you find difficult?**

IELTS PRACTICE TASK

PART 3

Talking about buildings

Example questions

- Do you think it's important for the government to preserve traditional buildings, or should the money be spent on essential services such as hospitals and schools?
- Is it possible for a government to fund all of these things?
- Many people like living in modern buildings. Why do you think that is?
- What do you think homes of the future will look like?

C Tips and tactics

3 **Work in pairs. Read the tips and tactics and discuss these questions.**

    a **Which tips and tactics do you think are the most useful?**
    b **Did you use any of these tips and tactics when you answered the sample questions in Section B?**
    c **Which tips will you use in the future?**

1. Some of the Part 3 speaking questions will be quite challenging and you may need to check you understand the question. You can clarify what you think the question means by starting with, *Do you mean …? or Can I just check what you mean? Is it …?*
2. Before answering a complex question you may need a moment or two to think about what you want to say. Use phrases such as, *That's an interesting/tricky question …, Let me just think about that for a moment …*
3. Try to think of two or three key points when you answer a question and make sure you develop each point. Don't forget to signal when you are introducing the next point: *Another reason is … .*
4. Use the PREP method: make a Point, give a Reason, give an Example, and re-state your Point.
5. To give you more ideas for an answer and to help you speak for a longer time, try to consider both sides of a question.
6. Make sure you use phrases to introduce your opinion, such as *As far as I'm concerned … , Generally speaking I'd say …*
7. Another way to think of more ideas for a long answer is to think of what other groups of people in society might think. Try to consider the points of view of young people, elderly people, parents, teachers, politicians, and so on.
8. Try to give examples to make your point as clear as possible. Don't give personal examples, try to broaden the discussion. Instead of saying *There's a really old building in my street*, you could say *My city is well known for its traditional architecture.*
9. It's likely you'll be asked to compare two things, for example, traditional and modern buildings, so make sure you review comparative and superlative grammar before the test.
10. You may have to speculate about the future and make a prediction. Review phrases such as *It's likely that …, I'm fairly certain that …, I wouldn't be surprised if …*, so you can talk about this concept easily.
11. Remember, you need to link your ideas together well using apppropriate linking words and expressions.
12. As you practise, think about the marking criteria that the examiners will use to mark your response. (For marking criteria, see page 260.)

D Skills-building exercises

Q FOCUS

Identifying the right
language for Part 3

4 **Look at the Part 3 questions below (1–6). Match them with what you need to do in the answer (a–f). More than one match may be possible.**

1 Do you think young people were more polite in the past than they are now?
2 What are some of the benefits of parents teaching their children to read at home?
3 Do you think there will be less green space in cities fifty years from now?
4 Do you think it's true that writing letters is becoming a thing of the past?
5 If pollution is such a problem in big cities, why don't more people use public transport?
6 On the whole, do you think people in your country are concerned about their health?

The question requires you to:
a give reasons/explanations
b generalise
c compare
d agree and disagree
e speculate about the future
f give advantages / disadvantages

5 **Look at some answers to the questions in Exercise 4. Underline and make notes on the useful language in each answer. Look at the grammar and vocabulary. The first one has been done for you.**

1 'Definitely[1]. People had much more respect[2] for their elders[3] in the past. Let's take[4] giving up your seat on the bus as an example[4]; in the past[5] it was expected that a young person would stand up[6] for an elderly person[3], whereas now[5], youngsters[3] sit[7] playing with their phones and don't even notice[7] older people.'

1 a good word to show strong agreement with an opinion
2 a comparative structure, 'much' adds more emphasis
3 good topic vocabulary
4 useful phrase for introducing an example
5 useful phrases for introducing a comparison
6 this grammar is used for past habits
7 present simple for present habit

2 'Well, one of the biggest advantages is that the child would be in safe and familiar surroundings and if they feel relaxed they might learn more. Another positive point would be that the parent can focus all their attention on one child whereas a classroom teacher has about thirty children to help.'

3 'Well, I suppose it depends which cities we're talking about, but in general, no, I'd say that there will always be green areas in our cities and as people are becoming increasingly concerned about the environment, I think the green areas in cities will expand rather than contract.'

4 'Sadly, I think it's true that people write personal letters less often. It's very hard to compete with the convenience of a quick message sent electronically. Mail sent through the postal system is slow and, unfortunately, expensive.'

5 'Well, even though people are concerned about the environment I think there are several reasons why they don't make better use of public transport. First and foremost is the convenience. It's hard to beat the ease of going from door to door by car. On top of that, you can come and go when you like; you don't have to wait around for a bus or train that is running late.'

6 'Of course! Both young and old, men and women ... everyone is trying to exercise more and eat more healthily. There are so many diets that people follow and likewise there are crazes about the latest exercise sensation. Usually these are just fads, but it does show that on the whole people are concerned about staying in good shape.'

6 Work in groups. Look at the useful phrases for each language function. Add one more phrase to each function. Then share it with your group.

> ### ↻ PHRASES FOR ANSWERING PART 3 QUESTIONS
>
> **a Give reasons/explanations**
> one reason for this is ...
> another reason is ...
> this is (could/might be) because/due to ...
> this probably happens because ...
>
> **b Generalise**
> on the whole ...
> generally speaking ...
> many people think that ...
> in my country ...
>
> **c Compare**
> X is (far) more ...
> X is ... while on the other hand Y is ...
> there's a big difference between X and Y ...
> if we compare X and Y then ...
>
> **d Agree and disagree**
> I definitely agree that ...
> that's right ...
> to some extent that's true; however ...
> I'm not sure I agree with that because ...
>
> **e Speculate about the future**
> it's likely that ...
> I'm pretty sure that ...
> (fifty) years from now we will ...
> I don't think we will ...
>
> **f Give advantages/disadvantages**
> the good thing about X is ...
> the problem with X is ...
> another positive point about X is ...
> a further disadvantage of X is ...

7 Work in pairs. Tick (✓) two phrases from each function that you want to use in Part 3. Take a minute to remember them. Then go back to the questions in Exercise 4 and discuss them with a partner. Make sure you both use some of the phrases from the table.

8 Look at this Part 3 question. How would you answer the question? Choose from a–c.

> Do you think it's better to go on holiday by yourself or with other people?

a talk about the benefits of travelling alone
b talk about the benefits of travelling with other people
c talk about the advantages and disadvantages of travelling alone and in a group then conclude which one is better

Now spend a few minutes answering this question with a partner.

9 ◯ 39 Listen to a candidate answering the question in Exercise 8. Does she do a, b or c?

10 ◯ 39 Listen again and answer the questions.

1 How does the candidate generalise in her answer?
2 Which phrases from Exercise 6 does she use?
3 Does she use any useful vocabulary for the topic?

11 Work with a different partner. Discuss the Part 3 question in Exercise 8 again. Try to improve your answer this time.

Q **FOCUS**

Extending your
answer in Part 3

12 **Look at the Part 3 question below. Underline the key words to make sure you understand the question clearly.**

> Do the positive effects of tourism outweigh the negative impacts tourism can have?

13 **Spend one minute thinking how you would answer this question. Now look at a candidate's answer below. Do you agree or disagree with what she says?**

'Well, on the one hand, tourism can create a lot of jobs. In some areas there is high unemployment due to the decline of manufacturing industries, but if you live in an area that attracts a lot of tourists then you're likely to find some kind of employment. A second point is tourist areas generally have better transport networks, you know, better infrastructure and this benefits both tourists and local people. On the other hand, there are some negative impacts of tourism. People who live in areas that attract a high number of tourists might say traffic congestion and parking can be a big problem. Furthermore, prices in shops and restaurants can become inflated so it becomes more expensive to live in these areas. On the whole though, I'd say that the benefits outweigh the negative aspects.'

14 **How has the candidate extended her answer (i.e. given a longer answer)? Choose one or more of the following ways (a–d).**

The candidate has
a   considered both sides of the topic.
b   made at least two points about the topic and explained each point.
c   considered what other people do or might think.
d   linked ideas together.

15 **Look at the three questions and answers below. In what way/ways has the candidate extended her answers?**

1
Q: What are some of the benefits of going away on a long holiday?
A: Well, primarily it's a way to unwind and get away from it all. For workers this means getting away from the stresses of the work environment and for students it might mean being free of deadlines and exams. In addition, for everyone it's a chance to spend some quality time with family or friends and see new scenery, experience new things, you know, broaden your horizons.

2
Q: Have there been any recent changes in the kind of holiday people in your country enjoy?
A: Yes, I think the biggest change has been in the holiday destinations people are choosing. Years ago families would have had their annual holiday at a local resort, or maybe they just visited family. In contrast to this, overseas holidays have become far more accessible and it's not unusual for people to go abroad every year for a week or two.

3
Q: Do you think it's true that holidays will change in the future?
A: Mm, that's an interesting question ... well, I guess they will because travel will continue to be more affordable. What I mean by that is that budget airlines and discount accommodation will get more popular and so more people will be able to travel. Also we have so much more information now. It used to be that people had to go to a travel agent to book a holiday, now we can do it ourselves online, I guess this 'do-it-yourself' trend will just continue. On the other hand, I think the popularity of a beach holiday will never change.

16 Look at the question below. Prepare to talk about it to a partner. Use some of the strategies you have learned for using the right language and extending what you say.

> Is travel the best way to learn more about other cultures?

- give reasons/explanations
- generalise
- compare
- speculate about the future
- agree and disagree
- give advantages/disadvantages
- consider both sides of the topic
- make at least two points about the topic and explain each point
- consider what other people do or might think
- link ideas together

IELTS PRACTICE TASK

 Speaking test video 2 (Part 3)

PART 3

Example questions

Children and food

- What is the best age for a child to learn to cook? Why?
- Whose responsibility is it to teach children to eat healthily?
- Do you think children will eat more healthily in the future?

Eating habits

- Does food play an important role in your culture? In what way?
- Would you say people in your country have a healthy diet these days or did people eat more healthily in the past?
- Do you think it's important for a family to sit together to eat a meal in the evening? Why?/Why not?

Which statement best describes how you feel about Part 3 tasks?

- [ ] I feel confident about doing Part 3 tasks.
- [ ] I did OK, but I still need to do more work on Part 3 tasks.
- [ ] I need more practice with Part 3 tasks. I need to focus on …

▶▶ **For further practice, see the DVD-ROM.**

REVIEW TEST

PART 1

WHERE YOU LIVE

Let's talk about where you live.
- How long have you lived in your hometown?
- Was it a good place to grow up in? (Why?/Why not?)
- How has your hometown changed since you were a child?
- How would you improve your hometown?

THE WEATHER

Let's talk now about sunny days.
- Do you like sunny days? (Why?/Why not?)
- What do people in your country usually do on a sunny day?
- What did you do the last time there was a sunny day?
- How can you try to stay cool on a sunny day?

MUSIC

Now let's move on to talk about music.
- Do you like listening to music? (Why?/Why not?)
- What kind of music did you listen to as a child?
- Can you play a musical instrument?
- Do you think children should learn to play a musical instrument?

PART 2

Task card

Describe a book you read that you enjoyed.

You should say:

what the book was called

who the book was written by

what the book was about

and explain why you enjoyed the book so much.

You will have to talk about the topic for 1 to 2 minutes.
You have 1 minute to think about what you're going to say.
You can make some notes to help you if you wish.

Rounding-off questions:
- Have you talked about this book to other people?
- Do you think other people also enjoy this book?

PART 3

Let's consider the importance of reading.
- How important do you think it is to read books?
- Is it more important for children or adults to read books? (Why?)
- Why do you think it is that some people don't like reading books?

Let's talk now about books and technology.
- It's possible now to read books electronically. Do you think that's a positive development?
- How do you think reading an electronic book would compare to reading a paper book?
- Do you think paper books will still be in use in the future?

LISTENING

● 40 SECTION 1 *Questions 1–10*

Questions 1–6

Complete the table below.

Write **NO MORE THAN TWO WORDS AND/OR A NUMBER** *for each answer.*

SPORTS CENTRE BOOKINGS			
Sport	**Cost**	**Length of session**	**Who can book**
Squash	£10.00 per **1**	1 hour	Members only
Use of gym	£10.00	**2**	Members only
Swimming pool	£5.00	45 minutes	Members Non-members (**3** .... only)
Volleyball practice	Members free Non-members **4** £	2 hours	Members Up to **5** .... non-members per session
Basketball practice	Free	2 hours	Members Non-members: contact the **6** ....

Questions 7–10

Complete the form below.

Write **NO MORE THAN TWO WORDS AND/OR A NUMBER** *for each answer.*

PAYMENT DETAILS

Ask for membership number and **7** ....

Cash and debit card acceptable

Credit card (**8** extra .... payable)

Dress code: **9** ....

Must wear: **10** ....

---

41 **SECTION 2** *Questions 11–20*

Questions 11–16

*Choose the correct letter, **A**, **B** or **C**.*

11 The Tasca Coffee Company has been in existence for
    A 10 years.
    B 15 years.
    C 20 years.

12 The largest number of Tasca outlets are located in
    A England.
    B Scotland.
    C Wales.

13 What service do all the company's outlets offer?
    A coffee delivered to the workplace
    B rewards to loyal customers
    C live music events

14 Most outlets have successfully introduced
    A 24-hour opening.
    B free wi-fi.
    C quiet rooms.

15 All employees in the company's outlets get
    A private medical insurance.
    B a family and friends discount.
    C a share of the company's profits.

16 What do customers like best about the outlets?
    A the atmosphere
    B the level of service
    C the products on offer

Questions 17–20

*Write the correct letter, **A**, **B** or **C**, next to questions 17–20.*

    A They are available in all outlets.
    B They are usually available on request.
    C They are no longer available in any outlets.

---

17 baby changing facilities ....
18 boxes of toys   ....
19 video games   ....
20 board games   ....

● 42 **SECTION 3** *Questions 21–30*

Questions 21 and 22

*Choose **TWO** letters, **A–E**.*

According to the article the female student has read, which **TWO** facts about consumption of frozen food are true?

A The average person currently consumes 15 kilograms of frozen food per year.
B Sales of frozen foods have fallen by almost 2% in the last two years.
C Sales of frozen foods have fallen more in some regions than in others.
D Certain types of frozen food have seen increasing sales.
E Some types of frozen food are more affected by falling sales than others.

Questions 23 and 24

*Choose **TWO** letters, **A–E**.*

Which **TWO** things does the female student agree to do?

A write a questionnaire
B select consumers to interview
C enter findings on a computer
D produce graphical information
E check the original research

Questions 25–30

What does each expert think has caused changing attitudes towards frozen food?

*Choose **SIX** answers from the box and write the correct letter, **A–G**, next to questions 25–30.*

A influence of the media on cooking habits
B the amount of time devoted to cooking
C influence of advertising on eating habits
D falling household incomes
E a return to traditional values
F rising cost of frozen foods compared to other foods
G the influence of the Internet
H the quality of the frozen food on offer

25 Eric Davies   ....
26 Glenda Williams   ....
27 John Hall   ....
28 Mary Butcher   ....
29 Steve Fullet   ....
30 Anna Carey   ....

43 **SECTION 4** *Questions 31–40*

Complete the sentences below.

Write **NO MORE THAN TWO WORDS AND/OR A NUMBER** *for each answer.*

Iconic Project

31 Type of landscape where the trees are found: .... *in Chile.*

32 Reason why some trees have priority: *they're in areas affected by a* .... *project.*

33 Method used to collect the seeds: ....

34 Height of the majority of surviving Fitzroya trees: *Less than* ....

35 What the team sometimes collected as well as seeds: ....

36 The team's attitude towards targets: *a* .... *attitude.*

37 What each individual seed has in the database: *an* ....

38 How seeds will be germinated in Scotland: *in* ....

39 Important additional data collected by the research team: ....

40 Name of the broader discipline this project forms part of: ....

ACADEMIC READING

READING PASSAGE 1

*You should spend about 20 minutes on **Questions 1–13,** which are based on Reading Passage 1.*

Homes made of mud

Mud is a very traditional building material and even today, around 50 per cent of the world's population lives in traditional dwellings made of the material. Only recently, however, has 'rammed earth', as the building material is called, appeared on the curricula of modern architecture and engineering schools. Although few laypeople in the West think of it as a building material at all, mud is now being used to create some of the most advanced and sustainable homes.

Martin Rauch, an architect who is championing the use of earth for sustainable construction, explains why: 'With industrialisation and the growth of the railways from the mid-nineteenth century onwards, it became easier to transport mass-produced building materials in many parts of the world, so it wasn't necessary to build with earth anymore.' He says, 'It became a poor man's material and the image is hard to shake off.' But in the past fifteen years, interest in rammed earth construction has re-emerged alongside concerns about human and environmental health.

Rauch has used the material to build a range of structures including a cinema and his own family home in Austria. The materials he used were local, so minimal energy was needed for their production and transportation. The fact that as much as 47 per cent of anthropogenic carbon-dioxide emissions are attributable to the construction industry in a country like the UK means that such alternative methods are worth considering. What's more, the ability of earth to moderate humidity and temperature is another advantage, as it reduces the need for costly and energy-hungry central heating and air conditioning.

Not everybody accepts that the future lies in rammed earth construction, however. A central concern of sceptics is durability. The fear is that exposure to rain and moisture will cause walls to slump. However, strong foundations and an overhanging roof to protect walls seem to provide an answer. Indeed, Rauch designs for 'calculated erosion'. Every few layers, he inserts stone blocks into the surface of earth walls. These protrude as the earth erodes around them, acting as a buffer against rain running down the surface of the building.

Research conducted by the Scottish government in 2001 highlights another key issue, however. The longevity of earth buildings in the past was due, in part, to the regular maintenance regimes that were integral to traditional practice. A change of attitude would be necessary for modern earth buildings to survive equally well in a world where 'maintenance-free' products such as cement renders and masonry paints characterise the construction industry.

So how does rammed earth construction work? The construction process is not dissimilar to building a sandcastle. Earth is collected, its consistency checked, and organic matter that will decompose is removed. Next, a frame is brought in. The earth is then quite literally rammed into this, layer by layer, either manually or mechanically, using pneumatic rammers. The earth begins to harden and 'cure' straightaway and continues to do so for months or years, depending on the local climate.

This process leaves relatively little room for mechanisation. Anna Heringer, a Royal Institute of British Architects award-winner who has extensive experience with rammed earth in the developing world, views the labour-intensive nature of this form of construction as a bonus. 'We often think of sustainability in terms of high-tech solutions and it isn't possible for everyone in the world to have these. Building with earth, you can have a lot of people involved – it's about community spirit too.' And those communities have choices. Depending on the earth selected, the colour of a building can be varied, the ramming process can be designed to produce layering effects and the frame can be moulded so patterns are embossed in the walls.

Rauch is aware of the limits of the material, however. Certain parts of structures, such as the ceilings, aren't possible in earth. So he suggests using appropriate local materials, together with mud. In the western world, most earth constructions are actually stabilised rammed earth, where cement is added to the mud. 'This is the wrong way to do things,' says Rauch. 'If there is cement in the mix, then it's not real earth. We've built for 10,000 years with pure earth.' He feels that the climatic and environmental qualities of the material are lost with such contamination.

Heringer adds that when cement is mixed with earth, 'You can't recycle it. We aren't building for eternity, some day it will all return to the ground and then there's the question of environmental impact.' Having used earth in construction around the world, in the monsoons of Bangladesh and dry summers of Morocco, Heringer has proved that cement is not required with innovative, context-specific design.

Questions 1–8

Do the following statements agree with the information given in Reading Passage 1?

Next to each statement, write

TRUE	*if the statement agrees with the information*
FALSE	*if the statement contradicts the information*
NOT GIVEN	*if there is no information on this*

1   Rammed-earth construction methods are now being studied more widely.

2   Some people still regard earth as a low status building material.

3   Rammed-earth construction is actively encouraged in Austria.

4   The temperature inside earth houses can be difficult to regulate.

5   Some people think that buildings made of earth are unlikely to last very long.

6   Rauch refuses to use materials other than mud in the walls he builds.

7   Rauch accepts that buildings made of rammed earth need more maintenance.

8   Rammed-earth construction sometimes makes some use of specialised equipment.

Questions 9–13

Complete the notes below.

Choose **NO MORE THAN TWO WORDS** *from the passage for each answer.*

Views of Rauch and Heringer

Heringer: the fact that the process is **9** .... is a positive aspect –
it promotes a sense of **10** ....

Rauch: some parts of buildings, e.g. **11** .... cannot be made of earth –
local materials should be used instead

Rauch: mixing of concrete and mud is a form of **12** ....

Heringer: the presence of concrete makes mud impossible to **13** ....

READING PASSAGE 2

*You should spend about 20 minutes on **Questions 14–26**, which are based on Reading Passage 2.*

The Science of Colour

A

The body of scientific research into colour is growing, and it all points to one thing: our perception of colour really does affect our minds and our bodies. In a series of tests administered in the 1970s, it was established that red pills are more effective as stimulants than blue pills, and that blue pills appeared to be more effective in curing insomnia than orange ones. Meanwhile, green, white or blue pills, aren't as effective as red ones as painkillers. But in the experiments, the pills used were all placebos – in other words, fake pills – there was no painkiller, there was no stimulant. Meanwhile, in other experiments it was found that male prison inmates became physically weaker when they were housed in pink-painted cells and that football teams wearing red were statistically more likely to win than teams in other colours.

B

And yet, while its effects on us may be profound, colour 'doesn't really exist in the world', say Dr Beau Lotto, a neuroscientist at University College London. Blue isn't a property of denim, or skies, or oceans, but of how our eyes interpret a particular set of wavelengths of electromagnetic radiation, which we call visible light. Red isn't a property of blood or football shirts, but how our eyes interpret another, longer set of wavelengths. 'Human vision is trichromatic,' says Prof Andrew Stockman, a UCL colleague of Dr Lotto, 'like a colour television.' We have three different colour receptors, cones, in our eyes, each designed to pick up different wavelengths of light. These are red, green and blue. Most other mammals have two, meaning they can only detect green and blue wavelengths. If we had only one receptor, we'd see the world in something like black and white.

C

This is the product of billions of years of evolution. 'The whole point of colour vision is not to inspire poets, but to allow contrast detection,' says Russell Foster, professor of circadian neuroscience at the University of Oxford. 'You've got a much better chance of detecting an object against a background if you have colour vision.' The wavelength of the light around us has affected us since the dawn of life, and it still does. Foster, who researches the effect of light on sleep, says that our biological clock is profoundly affected not just by the brightness of the light we're exposed to, but also its colour. He was behind the discovery of a previously unknown cell in the optic nerve which acts as a sort of photon-counter, keeping track of how much light has hit it in the last few minutes. It is especially sensitive to blue light – specifically, the blue of a blue sky. If you're exposed to light of this colour, it will make you more alert. 'Blue light keeps us awake far more effectively than red light,' he says. 'There are apps on the market now, that change your lighting before you go to bed, to get you ready for sleep.'

D

But as Lotto says, context is everything; red can be friendly when it's associated with a ketchup bottle, less so when associated with blood. Lotto spends much of his time creating optical illusions to demonstrate how humans see and perceive colour, and the impact of context upon it. 'I can make you see blue or yellow, depending on what surrounds it,' he says. 'When I change your perception of it, what I'm changing is the meaning of the information, I'm not changing the physics of the information itself.'

E

There's even some indication that the words we use to describe colour affect our ability to see it. Benjamin Whorf, a linguistic theorist, claimed that our language limits our perception: if our language lacks a word for something, we find it harder to think about that thing. The Whorfian hypothesis has been largely discredited – after all, if we really couldn't think about things we didn't have a word for, we wouldn't need to come up with new words. Nevertheless, experiments have shown that societies such as the Tarahumara tribe in Northern Mexico, which lacks different words for 'blue' and 'green', find it harder to find the odd one out in a group of greenish-blue squares. Meanwhile, the fact that we distinguish indigo and violet as separate colours is largely down to the scientist Sir Isaac Newton, who named and split up the colours of the rainbow completely arbitrarily.

F

The cultural contexts and meaning of colours has been picked up, of course, by marketers. Purple is status, pink is femininity, and, of course, blue suggests competence while red is exciting. Using these colours in your branding or logo, apparently, will subtly instil those messages in potential customers' minds. In her paper on the subject, Zena O'Connor questions the validity of many of these highly specific claims, as the title 'Colour psychology and colour therapy: Caveat emptor' makes clear. As O'Connor says: 'The information available is often presented in an authoritative manner, exhorting the reader to believe a range of claims, such as red is physically stimulating and arousing and blue is calming and healing. However, evidence is rarely cited and, when it is, it's often in reference to findings that are outdated.' But even after the dubious claims have been weeded out, colour clearly still has a profound impact on our mental life.

Questions 14–20

Reading Passage 2 has six paragraphs, **A–F**.

Which paragraph contains the following information?

*Write the correct letter, **A–F**, in boxes 14–20 on your answer sheet.*

NB You may use any letter more than once.

14 The view that the ideas of one researcher are no longer taken very seriously.

15 An assertion that there may be no scientific basis for the distinctions drawn between certain colours.

16 A suggestion that the colour of their clothing may affect how well certain people perform.

17 A description of a recently introduced product that reflects research into the way colour affects human behaviour.

18 An explanation of the main reason why human beings developed the ability to perceive colour.

19 A description of how the perception of colour can be manipulated without people realising it.

20 An explanation of how human perception of colour contrasts with that of many other species.

Questions 21 and 22

*Choose **TWO** letters, **A–E**.*

Write the correct letters in boxes 21 and 22 on your answer sheet.

Which **TWO** of the following statements are true of the 1970s research into the colour of pills?

> **A** White pills worked best for people who needed relief from pain.
>
> **B** Blue pills worked best for people who were having problems sleeping.
>
> **C** Red pills generally failed to help any patients.
>
> **D** Pills in certain colours worked better with male patients.
>
> **E** None of the pills used contained any active ingredients.

Questions 23–26

Complete the summary below.

*Choose **ONE WORD ONLY** from the passage for each answer.*

Write your answers in boxes 23–26 on your answer sheet.

It is apparent from the **23** .... of Zena O'Connor's paper on the subject that she
has little faith in the claims made by **24** .... regarding the effect of colour on clients'
perceptions of products. She says that whilst such claims may appear **25** ....
in the way they are put forward, they often cite research which is **26** .... or are
unsupported by sufficient evidence.

READING PASSAGE 3

*You should spend about 20 minutes on **Questions 27–40**, which are based on Reading Passage 3.*

Ways of Reading

Choosing how to read books is getting harder now there's a choice of on paper, tablet, e-reader, or smartphone – and people have strong opinions on which medium is best. But is there more to the decision than expense and convenience? The answer suggested by numerous studies into the neuroscience and psychology of reading in different formats is emphatically that there is.

There's no shortage of people warning of the risks attendant on the rise of 'screen culture', as the neuroscientist Susan Greenfield calls it. She has repeatedly expressed concern that, as technology takes us into unknown territory, 'the brain may be adapting in unprecedented ways'. Though she tends to stress that these changes might be good or bad, her more negative speculations have been picked up in the media and amplified in far more strident terms.

E-reading certainly took off quickly. The Pew Research Centre reports that, as recently as 2010, hardly anyone in the USA had an e-reader or tablet. By 2014 half did, with 17 per cent reading at least one e-book in that year. But was that a cause for concern? There is some evidence that reading on screen can result in less comprehension and even affect sleep patterns. But the research here is complex and inconclusive and, in any case, it is actually doing something far more interesting than telling us which medium is superior. It's making us think more about what it means to read.

As researchers examine the differences between reading in different media, they are also having to distinguish carefully between different things we do when we read. For instance, the difference between 'deep reading', when you really get immersed in a text, and 'active learning', when you make notes in margins or put down the book to cross-reference with something else. When Anne Campbell of the Open University in Scotland compared how young people used very basic e-readers and paper books, she found that the electronic devices promoted more deep reading and less active learning. This appeared to be a direct result of design. 'They were less distracted using an e-reader,' she told me. 'They were almost being forced to focus on it because of the very lack of ability to do things like flick forward and flick back.'

Another related, widely replicated finding is that people read more slowly on screens than from paper. Sara Margolin of the State University of New York has also conducted research in this area. She says that 'slowing down may actually allow us to spend more time consolidating what we've read into a more cohesive mental representation of the text'; furthermore, 'not skipping around during reading' could be 'a good thing in that it forces the reader to process the text in order, and preserves the organisational structure the author wanted us to follow.' However, it also discourages re-reading, which is known to help with 'meta-comprehension' – readers' ability to recognise whether or not they've understood what they just read.

This example alone shows how debates over whether print beats screen are hopelessly simplistic, not least because reading on a computer, with endless distractions a click away, is very different from reading on a dedicated e-reader. Much depends on what you're reading and why. In a Taiwanese study led by Szu-Yuan Sun, the results suggested that reading linear texts in the manner of traditional paper books is better for 'literal text comprehension' but reading on computers with hyperlinks 'is beneficial to inferential text comprehension'. In other words, the joined-up environment of the web encourages people to make connections and work things out for themselves, while straightforward reading encourages them to take in and believe what's on the page in front of them. Hence the prevalence of hyperlinks and multiple windows on computers could be seen as creating either unwelcome distraction or more opportunities for active learning.

Where research has suggested that comprehension is diminished by screen reading, it is hard to know if this results from the particular piece of technology and people's ability to use it easily. 'Having a device that requires a lot of attention to operate could essentially steal working memory resources,' says Anne Mangen, from the University of Stavanger in Norway. This is a nice example of how hard it is to know whether the preferences we have for one type of reading device over another are rooted in the essentials of cognition or are simply cultural. It's equally important not to make hasty unsubstantiated claims about either form of reading. For example, Margolin says that one of the biggest problems with screen reading is that back-lit screens used by early tablets lead to eye fatigue and, if done at night, made sleeping difficult. Newer screens have overcome these problems, so earlier assumptions about the effects of screen reading on sleep need to be re-examined.

A whole other area of research concerns motivation. One of the recurrent concerns of the internet age is that teenagers are reading less. But there is some evidence that, used wisely, e-readers could encourage more reading. Campbell, for instance, found that teens read more when using e-readers than paper books. She thinks the main reason for this is that the device is small, light and portable, and you can pull it out at odd moments, such as 'when waiting for the bus to arrive'. E-readers also have the advantage that, from the outside, it's impossible to see whether someone is reading the latest teen vampire romance or a primer on differential calculus. 'You could study surreptitiously,' says Campbell, giving examples of people using their readers while getting their hair cut or even at work.

Overall, there doesn't seem to be any convincing evidence that reading on screen or paper is better per se. 'If the cognitive component is strong,' suggests Benedetto, 'the cultural one is even stronger.' For Margolin, 'the preference for reading on paper or a screen seems to be just that: a preference.' And, increasingly, younger people are opting for digital. A large National Literary Trust survey in 2013 found 52 per cent of 8 to 16-year-olds preferred reading on screen, with just 32 per cent preferring print. Mangen suggests that we need more longitudinal studies, conducted over decades, before we can figure out which effects of different reading media are due to familiarity or lack of it, and which are 'related to more innate aspects of human cognition'.

Questions 27–34

Do the following statements agree with the views/claims of the writer in Reading Passage 3?

In boxes 27–34 on your answer sheet, write

> **YES**   *if the statement agrees with the views/claims of the writer*
>
> **NO**   *if the statement contradicts the views/claims of the writer*
>
> **NOT GIVEN**   *if it is impossible to say what the writer thinks about this*

27 Convenience is the main thing that guides people's choice of whether to read on paper or on screen.

28 The media has generally exaggerated Greenfield's analysis of the risks of screen culture.

29 The Pew Research Centre's findings should not be taken too seriously.

30 Research aimed at deciding whether reading paper books is better than reading on screen has largely been a waste of time.

31 The distinction between 'deep reading' and 'active learning' is a false one.

32 Campbell found that simple e-readers were not good for developing 'deep reading' skills.

33 There is little evidence to back up Margolin's finding that people read an e-reader more slowly than a paper book.

34 An e-reader may help people to read in the way the original writer intended.

Questions 35–37

*Choose the correct letter, **A**, **B**, **C** or **D**.*

35 Szu-Yuan Sun's research established that when people read in a linear way, they

    A find it harder to concentrate on what they're reading.
    B are easily distracted by the need to look up references.
    C are more likely to be convinced by arguments they read.
    D will probably be more open to the idea of active learning.

36 What does Mangen's research suggest about electronic devices?

    A Some are better for the purposes of reading than others.
    B Some readers may be more adept at using them than others.
    C It's difficult to know why people read less effectively on them.
    D More sophisticated ones allow people to read in different ways.

37 What does Margolin's example of back-lit screens demonstrate?

    A how quickly the technology is changing
    B how unwise it can be to jump to conclusions
    C how quickly the industry responds to complaints
    D how new features can make e-readers more attractive

Questions 38–40

*Complete each sentence with the correct ending, **A–E** below.*

38 Campbell thinks that teenagers are encouraged to read using e-readers because

39 Margolin thinks that some people would rather read on e-readers because

40 Mangen thinks that some people use e-readers because

    A they may just be accustomed to the format.

    B they like the level of privacy one offers.

    C they are merely exercising a personal choice.

    D they are attracted by the content on offer.

    E they find them portable and convenient.

ACADEMIC WRITING

WRITING TASK 1

You should spend about 20 minutes on this task.

> *The graph below gives information about the origin of passengers entering Mexico on international flights, 2005–2010.*
>
> *Summarise the information by selecting and reporting the main features and make comparisons where relevant.*

Write at least 150 words.

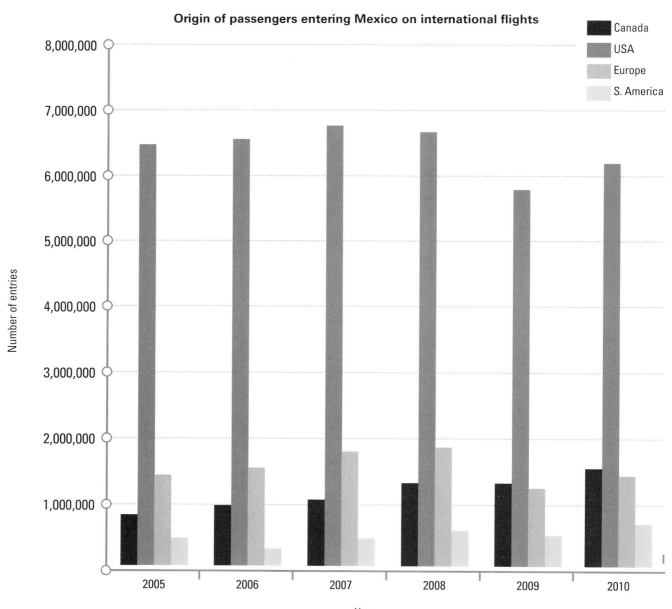

Origin of passengers entering Mexico on international flights

WRITING TASK 2

You should spend about 40 minutes on this task.

Write about the following topic:

> *Different types of environmental pollution seem to be affecting an increasing number of people in the world.*
>
> *What do you think are the causes of this problem and what solutions would you suggest?*

Give reasons for your answer and include any relevant examples from your own knowledge or experience.

Write at least 250 words.

SPEAKING

PART 1

WORK/STUDY

Let's talk about what you do.
- Do you work or are you a student?
- Where do you work/study?
- Why did you choose that job/course?
- What's the most difficult thing about your job/course?

MUSIC

Let's talk about your favourite music.
- What kind of music do you like most?
- How often do you listen to live music?
- Can you play a musical instrument?
- How important do you think it is for children to learn about music?

FOOD

Now let's talk about food.
- What kind of food do you like?
- Do you enjoy cooking?
- Did you learn to cook when you were a child?
- Which do you prefer, home-cooked meals, or restaurant meals?

PART 2

Task card

Describe a famous person (still living) that you admire.

You should say:

who this person is

why he/she is famous

what he/she is doing these days

and explain why you admire this famous person.

You will have to talk about the topic for 1 to 2 minutes.
You have 1 minute to think about what you're going to say.
You can make some notes to help you if you wish.

Rounding-off question:
- Do you other people admire this person?

PART 3

Let's talk about famous people, and fame in general.
- What do you think are some of the advantages and disadvantages of being famous?
- Why do you think companies like to use famous people to advertise their products?
- How has the Internet affected fame, and the way that people become famous?

Let's move on now to talk about leadership.
- Can you describe some of the qualities of a good leader?
- Is it possible, in your opinion, to teach leadership skills?
- Why do you think that some people become leaders, while others prefer to follow?

Contents

Units

Appendices

1 Present tenses

Present simple

Affirmative	Negative
I/You/We/They **live** here.	I/You/We/They **don't live** here. (don't = do not)
He/She/It **lives** here.	He/She/It **doesn't live** here. (doesn't = does not)

Question	Short answer
Do I/you/we/they **live** here?	Yes, I/you/we/they **do** No, I/you/we/they **don't**.
Does he/she/it **live** here?	Yes, he/she/it **does**. No, he/she/it **doesn't**.

We use the present simple:
- to talk about facts.
The Earth moves around the Sun at approximately 107,000 kilometres per hour.
- to talk about habits and routines.
I cycle to college every day.
- to talk about timetables.
The next train leaves at 14:20.

Used with: *at* + time, *every* + time period *(hour, 20 minutes)*

- to talk about states, thoughts or feelings.
He doesn't know the answer.
- to tell stories or describe the plot of a book or film.
The action in this movie takes place on a ship.

Time adverbials

We often use time adverbials with the present simple, especially when talking about habits and routines. Adverbs of frequency (*always, never, normally, occasionally, often, rarely, regularly, seldom, sometimes, usually*) generally come before the main verb but after the verb *be*. Time phrases like *every hour/morning/day/week/month/year* and *once a week/ month/year* usually come at the end of the sentence but can sometimes come at the beginning.

Present continuous

Affirmative	Negative
I**'m sleeping**. ('m = am)	I**'m not sleeping**. ('m not = am not)
You/We/They**'re sleeping**. ('re = are)	You/We/They **aren't sleeping**. (aren't = are not)
He/She/It**'s sleeping**. ('s = is)	He/She/It **isn't sleeping**. (isn't = is not)

Question	Short answer
Am I **sleeping**?	Yes, I **am**. No, I**'m not**.
Are you/we/they **sleeping**?	Yes, you/we/they **are**. No, you/we/they **aren't**.
Is he/she/it **sleeping**?	Yes, he/she/it **is**. No, he/she/it **isn't**.

We use the present continuous:
- to talk about temporary situations.
I'm living with my grandparents at the moment.

Used with: *at the moment, currently, now, this week / month*

- to talk about changes and developments.
House prices are rising again.
- to talk about an action in progress now.
We're watching TV.

Used with: *at the moment, now*

- to talk about repeated actions which are annoying.
She's always telling me what to do.

Used with: *always, constantly, forever*

Stative verbs

Stative verbs refer to states. These talk about thoughts (*believe, know, think, understand*), feelings (*love, hate, enjoy*), senses (*smell, taste, see*) and possession (*have (got), belong, own*). Stative verbs are usually used in the present simple. Some stative verbs are used in both the simple and continuous form. The verbs in the present simple refer to permanent situations, or states, while those in the continuous form refer to more temporary situations.

have   I **have** two brothers and a sister.
      I**'m having** a great time. Wish you were here.
be   We have a new boss. She**'s** very nice.
      That's enough, Jamie. You**'re being** silly.
feel   Mark **feels** we should get married in May.
      Carla can't make it. She **isn't feeling** well.
think   I really don't know. What **do** you **think**?
      You're very quiet. What **are** you **thinking** about?
smell   Can you **smell** that? I think it's smoke.
      Why **are** you **smelling** the milk? It's fresh.

Exercises

1 Complete the conversation with the present simple or present continuous form of the verbs.
A: This **1** .... (be) a photo of us in Senegal. In this one, we **2** .... (celebrate) Sean's birthday.
B: I can see you **3** .... (have) a great time. There's a guy here who **4** .... (look) exactly like Jude.
A: That's Sean.
B: Is he the one who **5** .... (swim) in the ocean?
A: No, he **6** .... (play) football over there. Oh, I **7** .... (see) the one you **8** .... (talk) about. That's Joe. Oh, yes, you're right, he **9** .... (have) some of Jude's features, although his eyes and hair **10** .... (not be) the same.

2 Look at these sentences. Correct the mistakes. If the sentence is correct, put a tick (✓).
1   I'm having a lovely time.
2   I'm believing you might be right.
3   **A**: What are you thinking?
    B: Mm? Oh, nothing important.
4   I don't understand what they are saying.
5   **A**: What are you thinking of this?
    B: I love it!
6   **A**: Do you have any hobbies?
    B: I'm enjoying listening to music.

2 Past tenses

Past simple

Affirmative	Negative
I/You/He/She/It/We/They **lived** here.	I/You/He/She/It/We/They **didn't live** here. (didn't = did not)

Question	Short answer
Did I/you/he/she/it/we/they **live** here?	Yes, I/you/he/she/it/we/they **did**. No, I/you/he/she/it/we/they **didn't**.

We use the past simple:
- to talk about completed actions and events in the past.
While at university, she played bass guitar in a band.
We went sightseeing in Rome.
There is often a clear reference to a time in the past. When there is no stated time, it is usually implied or understood.

> Used with: *yesterday, last week/month/year, two days ago*, etc.

- to list a series of events in the past in a sequence.
He had a coffee, brushed his teeth, combed his hair and left.
Sequence words can be used to show the order in which something happened.
First, he had a coffee. Then he brushed his teeth. After that, he combed his hair and finally, he left the house.

> Used with: *first, then, next, after that, finally*

Irregular verbs

Although most verbs are regular and end in -d or -ed in the past, some verbs have an irregular affirmative form.
be → was/were   do → did   go → went   write → wrote
For more irregular verbs see page 329.

used to and *would*

We often use *used to* + infinitive to talk about past habitual actions or states, or for an action that no longer occurs.

We used to go to our grandparents' house every Christmas.

Did you use to have curly hair?

When we talk about repeated actions in the past (but not past states), we use *would* + infinitive.

We would walk for hours along the beach.

Past continuous

Affirmative	Negative
I/He/She/It **was sleeping**.	I/He/She/It **wasn't sleeping**. (wasn't = was not)
You/We/They **were sleeping**.	You/We/They **weren't sleeping**. (weren't = were not)

Question	Short answer
Was I/he/she/it **sleeping**?	Yes, I/he/she/it **was**. No, I/he/she/it **wasn't**.
Were you/we/they **sleeping**?	Yes, you/we/they **were**. No, you/we/they **weren't**.

We use the past continuous:
- in contrast with the past simple, to talk about an activity in progress when something happened.
They were driving to London when they heard the news.

- to describe situations in the past.
In California, they were researching and developing a new operating system.

Exercises

1 Complete the text with the correct form of the verbs.

> (not) be   bring   come   continue   go   interrupt
> establish   invade   ~~land~~   lay   leave   start

When the Romans **1** <u>*landed*</u> in Britain in 43 AD, they **2** .... with them schools and education. When they **3** .... nearly 400 years later, education **4** .... with them. With invasions from the Saxons and other groups, there **5** .... any formal education until almost 200 years later. Then the state **6** .... a system of education known as grammar schools. This system **7** .... to develop over the next 250 years but it was **8** .... once more, this time by the Vikings. In 1066 the Normans **9** .... Britain and shortly afterwards schools **10** .... springing up all over the country. Then **11** .... the first universities, at Oxford and Cambridge. These universities **12** .... the foundations for the system which exists today.

2 Write complete sentences. Use the past simple and the past continuous in each sentence.

1 you/have lunch/when I/call?
   Were you having lunch when I called?
2 what/they/do/when you/arrive?
   ....
3 we/cancel/the game/because it/rain
   ....
4 when we/get off the plane/they/wait for us
   ....
5 she/not listen/when I/tell her/how to do it
   ....
6 you sleep/when they/take/your bike?
   ....
7 when I/say 'No'/I/not talk/to you
   ....

3 Future forms (1)

We use various forms in English to express different functions when referring to the future.

Present continuous

I'm meeting Jo at 6:00.
You/We/They aren't meeting Jo at 6:00.
Is he/she/it meeting Jo at 6.00?

For present continuous form, see page 303.
We use the present continuous to talk about future plans and arrangements.

> Often used with: a time *(at 2p.m., on 19th April)* or a place *(in the city centre, at the cinema)*

going to

Affirmative	Negative
I'm **going to** move to Germany.	I'**m not going to** move to Germany.
You/We/They'**re going to** move to Germany.	You/We/They **aren't going to** move to Germany.
He/She/It'**s going to** move to Germany.	He/She/It **isn't going to** move to Germany.

Question	Short answer
Am I **going to** move to Germany?	Yes, I **am**. No, I'**m not**
Are you/we/they **going to** move to Germany?	Yes, you/we/they **are**. No, you/we/they **aren't**.
Is he/she/it **going to** move to Germany?	Yes, he/she/it **is**. No, he/she/it **isn't**.

We use *be + going to*:
- to talk about things we have thought about and intend to do in the future.

He's going to live in Venezuela.
- to make predictions based on present evidence.

*Based on current sales, **we're going to** make a loss this year.*
We can also use *going to* to talk about future plans and arrangements, but more often use the present continuous as it is understood that the present continuous is used to denote arrangement. In a situation where A invites B out for coffee, compare the two responses:
1 *Sorry, I can't. I'm going to meet a friend.*
2 *Sorry, I can't. I'm meeting a friend.*
Both responses are acceptable, but response 2 is better because it tells us that the meeting with the friend has already been arranged (and therefore can't be broken).

will

Affirmative	Negative
I/You/He/She/It/We/They'**ll arrive** on time. ('ll = will)	I/You/He/She/It/We/They **won't arrive** on time. (won't = will not)

Question	Short answer
Will I/you/we/they/he/she/it **arrive** on time?	Yes, I/you/we/they/he/she/it **will**.

We use *will*:
- to make predictions based on experience or subjective view.

*You must meet Ewan, you'**ll love** him.*

Often used with: *think, expect, imagine, (be) sure*

- to talk about a decision made at the moment of speaking.
I'll help you. I won't forget this. I'll get him for this!
These are often requests, offers, promises or threats.
- to state facts about the future.
The government will make more cuts in the months ahead.

Often modified with: *probably* or *possibly*

Exercise

1 **Read the situations and choose the best answer (a or b).**
1 The doorbell rings.
a Don't worry, I'm going to answer it.
b Don't worry, I'll answer it.
2 You intend to answer an email.
a Don't worry, I'm going to answer the email today.
b Don't worry, I'll answer the email today.
3 A friend invites you out but you already have an arrangement with another friend.
a Sorry, I'm meeting Ruby tonight.
b Sorry, I'll meet Ruby tonight.
4 You have bought a ticket to go to Rome.
a I think I'll go to Rome.
b I'm flying to Rome next week.
5 You see a film poster and immediately decide to go.
a I'll see the film today.
b I'm going to see the film today.
6 You notice there is no bread so decide to buy some.
a I'm going to get some bread.
b I'll get some bread.
7 You are standing on a wobbly chair and don't feel safe.
a I'm going to fall off the chair.
b I'll fall off the chair.
8 You haven't completely made up your mind where to go for your next holiday.
a I'm going to Rome.
b I think I'll go to Rome.
9 You have planned to visit a friend this evening.
a I'm going to visit Jack tonight.
b I'll visit Jack tonight.

4 Future forms (2)

Present simple

We use the present simple:
- to talk about timetabled or scheduled events in the future.
The course starts next Friday.

Often used with: a time *(at 3 p.m., on Monday)*, a time period (*in/ for ten minutes, two days*)

- for a future event after certain time clauses.
I will feel more relaxed once I start the talk.

Used with: *when, as long/soon as, after, before, once, until*

be about to

Affirmative	Negative
I'm **about to** go.	I'm **not about to** go.
You/We/They'**re about to** go.	You/We/They **aren't about to** go.
He/She/It'**s about to** go.	He/She/It **isn't about to** go.

Question	Short answer
Am I **about to** go?	Yes, **I am**. No, I'**m not**.

Are you/we/they **about to** go?	Yes, you/we/they **are.** No, you/we/they **aren't.**
Is he/she/**it about** to go?	Yes, he/she/**it is.** No, he/she/it **isn't.**

We use *be about to*:
• when we want to talk about something which is going to happen very soon.
I'm about to leave now. I'll see you in an hour.

Future continuous

will/won't + be + -ing

Affirmative	Negative
I/You/He/She/It/We/They**'ll be working** in Dubai.	I/You/He/She/It/We/They **won't be working** in Dubai.

Question	Short answer
Will I/you/he/she/it/we/they **be working** in Dubai?	Yes, I/you/he/she/it/we/they **will.** No, I/you/he/she/it/we/they **won't.**

We use the future continuous:
• to talk about an activity which will be in progress at a specific point in the future.
This time next week we'll be flying to Shanghai.

Future perfect simple

will have + past participle

Affirmative	Negative
I/You/He/She/It/We/They**'ll have finished** by next week.	I/You/He/She/It/We/They **won't have finished** by next week.

Question	Short answer
Will I/you/he/she/it/we/they **have finished** by next week?	Yes, I/you/he/she/it/we/they **will.** No, I/you/he/she/it/we/they **won't.**

We use the future perfect simple:
• to talk about something that is going to be completed by a certain point in the future.
By this time next week, I'll have finished painting the house.

Future perfect continuous

will have been + -ing

Affirmative	Negative
By next Monday, I/you/he/she/it/we/they**'ll have been living** here for ten years.	By next Monday, I/you/he/she/it/we/they **won't have been living** here for ten years.

Question	Short answer
By next Monday **will** I/you/he/she/it/we/they **have been living** here for ten years?	Yes, I/you/he/she/it/we/they **will.** No, I/you/he/she/it/we/they **won't.**

We use the future perfect continuous:
• to talk about an action in progress leading up to a point in the future.
In a week's time, we'll have been working here for two years.

Exercise

1 **Complete the sentences with the verbs in brackets in the correct form.**
   1 By 2020, the student population .... (rise) by ten per cent.
   2 The number of road traffic accidents .... (decrease) significantly by 2025.
   3 The bar chart shows that this time next year, the growth rate .... (level) out but it .... (not yet reach) the desired target.
   4 The graph shows that the use of motor vehicles .... (not decrease) until there .... (be) a satisfactory alternative available.
   5 The decline .... (be) steady as long as the interest rate .... (remain) stable.
   6 As soon as deforestation .... (reach) a critical peak, nothing .... (be) able to stop the extinction of the orangutans.

5 The perfect aspect

We use the perfect aspect to describe an action or state that takes place in time leading up to a point in the past, present or future. The perfect aspect looks back from one point in time to an earlier time.
There are two different forms, the simple and the continuous. Each form has a different emphasis.
We use the simple form when we want to emphasise that the action is completed.
Have you been to Africa?
When we arrived, they had already left.
Call me at 2:00, I'll have finished it by then.

Present perfect simple

have/has + past participle

Affirmative	Negative
I/You/We/They**'ve seen** him before. ('ve = have)	I/You/We/They **haven't seen** him before. (haven't = have not)
He/She/It**'s seen** him before. ('s = has)	He/She/It **hasn't seen** him before. (hasn't = has not)

Question	Short answer
Have I/you/we/they **seen** him before?	Yes, I/you/we/they **have.** No, I/you/we/they **haven't.**
Has he/she/it **seen** him before?	Yes, he/she/it **has.** No, he/she/it **hasn't.**

The present perfect looks back from now to actions or situations in the past that are in some way connected to the present. We use the present perfect simple:
• to talk about a life experience.
***Have** you ever **climbed** a mountain?*
• to talk about recent events.
***Have** you **heard** the news about Susanna?*

- to talk about an action or situation leading up to the present time (often with *for* or *since*).
*They've **lived** here for 30 years.*

> Used with: *ever, never, just, already, recently, lately, for, since, so far, up to now, yet*

Past perfect simple

had + past participle

Affirmative	Negative
I/You/He/She/It/We/They'd **seen** him before. ('d = had)	I/You/He/She/It/We/They **hadn't seen** him before. (hadn't = had not)

Question	Short answer
Had I/you/he/she/it/we/they **seen** him before?	Yes, I/you/he/she/it/we/they **had.** No, I/you/he/she/it/we/they **hadn't.**

The past perfect looks back from a point in the past to an earlier event. We use the past perfect simple:
- to talk about something that happened before the main event.
*When we met, I knew I **had seen** him before.*
- to talk about a situation leading up to a time in the past (often with *for* or *since*).
*I knew London well. I'**d lived** there for five years.*

> Used with: *before, after, as soon as, when*

Future perfect simple

will have + past participle

Affirmative	Negative
I/You/He/She/It/We/They'll **have finished** by next week.	I/You/He/She/It/We/They **won't have finished** by next week.

Question	Short answer
Will I/you/he/she/it/we/they **have finished** by next week?	Yes, I/you/he/she/it/we/they **will.** No, I/you/he/she/it/we/they **won't.**

The future perfect looks back from a point in the future to an earlier event. We use the future perfect simple:
- to talk about something that is going to be completed by a certain point in the future.
*By this time tomorrow, I'**ll have finished** my exams.*

> Used with: *by* + a time *(by 2016), by the end of*

Note the position of an adverb that modifies a verb in the perfect simple form: *has/have/had* + adverb + past participle.
*We have **just** moved house.*
*The concrete in the path has **already** hardened.*
*The proposal on dealing with climate change had **largely** gone unchallenged.*

Exercises

1 Match the two halves of the sentences, (1–6) with (a–f).

1 By the time you pick up this message
2 The project failed
3 They have been based in Tokyo since
4 She has studied English for a year
5 We missed our flight
6 By the time we reach the summit,

a they started work there, in 2010.
b I'll have landed at JFK Airport.
c we will have climbed twelve miles.
d because the drive to the airport had been terrible.
e because it hadn't been properly managed
f as she wants to get a job in Australia.

2 Complete the text using the present, past and future perfect simple.

In 2013, the UK business community detected the start of an economic recovery. They **1** .... (wait) long enough. In 2008, the overall number of UK businesses **2** .... (decline) to a 50-year low. By 2011, morale **3** .... (reach) an all-time low. However, by the following year, there **4** .... (be) a change in fortunes. The decline **5** .... (stop). In fact, from early 2013 until now, the number of businesses **6** .... (rise) by 18,000. And it continues to rise. Although we **7** .... (see) a shift in market share, manufacturing companies **8** .... (give) way to emerging scientific businesses. One enterprise minister predicts that 'by the end of the decade, scientific and technical companies **9** .... (become) the largest sector in the UK business market.'

We use the continuous form when we want to emphasise the ongoing nature of an action, when it is not important if the action is completed.
*Have you been **crying**?*
*When we arrived, they had been **discussing** the important decisions all morning.*
*By this time tomorrow, we will have been **travelling** for seven hours.*
Note: In sentences containing stative verbs (*like, love, want, hear*) the simple form is usually used rather than the continuous form.
I've loved maths since I was nine years old.

Present perfect continuous

have/has been + *-ing*

Affirmative	Negative
I/You/We/They'**ve been waiting** for two hours.	I/You/We/They **haven't been waiting** for two hours.
He/She/It'**s been waiting** for two hours.	He/She/It **hasn't been waiting** for two hours.

Question	Short answer
Have I/you/we/they **been waiting** for two hours?	Yes, I/you/we/they **have.** No, I/you/we/they **haven't.**
Has he/she/it **been waiting** for two hours?	Yes, he/she/it **has.** No, he/she/it **hasn't.**

We use the present perfect continuous:
- to talk about recent events when the focus is on a continuous activity rather than a completed action.
*My eyes are red because I'**ve been swimming**.*
- to talk about a repeated action, or state (focusing on continuous activity rather than completed action), leading up to the present time (often with *for* or *since*).

*We'**ve been going to** the same restaurant every month for twenty years.*

> Used with: *just, recently, lately, for, since, so far*

Past perfect continuous

had been + -ing

Affirmative	Negative
I/You/He/She/It/We/They'**d been acting** for ten years before becoming famous.	I/You/He/She/It/We/They **hadn't been acting** for ten years before becoming famous.

Question	Short answer
Had I/you/he/she/it/we/they **been acting** for ten years before becoming famous?	Yes, I/you/he/she/it/we/they **had.** No, I/you/he/she/it/we/they **hadn't.**

We use the past perfect continuous:
• to talk about an action in progress, or state (focusing on continuous activity rather than completed action), leading up to a given time in the past.
*She'**d been working** on her thesis for five months before she graduated.*

> Used with: *before, after, as soon as, when, for, since, by the time*

Future perfect continuous

will have been + -ing

Affirmative	Negative
By next Monday, I/you/he/she/it/we/they'**ll have been living** here for ten years.	By next Monday, I/you/he/she/it/we/they **won't have been living** here for ten years.

Question	Short answer
By next Monday, **will** I/you/he/she/it/we/they **have been living** here for ten years?	Yes, I/you/he/she/it/we/they **will.** No, I/you/he/she/it/we/they **won't.**

We use the future perfect continuous:
• to talk about an action in progress (focusing on continuous activity rather than completed action) leading up to a given time in the future.
*At the end of this year, we'**ll have been studying** here for three years.*

> Used with: *by + a time, by the end of*

Note the position of an adverb that modifies a verb in the perfect continuous form: *has/have/had been + adverb + -ing:*
*The population has been **rapidly** declining in more rural areas.*
*The quality of service had been **generally** improving.*

Exercises

3 Complete the dialogue with the verbs in the present perfect simple and continuous. Use the continuous whenever possible.

> ask   do   ~~see~~   wait

Thelma: I don't think anyone **1** *has seen* us. We **2** .... here for over half an hour and nobody **3** .... us what we want. Ah, here's Tony. Oh, you look terrible. What **4** .... you .... ?

> catch   (not) come   (not) feel   look   take

Tony: Mrs Allen, I'm sorry no one **5** ....
your order. I **6** .... after all the tables tonight. Alfredo, our waiter, **7** .... in today. He **8** ....well. I think he **9** .... a cold.

> come   (not) forget   not give   happen   sit

Thelma: Oh, you **10** .... us, then? It's not good enough, Tony. We **11** .... here politely for the last 30 minutes and you **12** .... even .... us a menu yet.
Tony: Mrs Allen, you are one of my best customers. You **13** .... to our restaurant for over ten years and I hope you agree that this is the first time anything like this **14** ....

4 Complete the text with the present, past and future perfect. Use the continuous form where possible.
The study was set up to look at the behaviour of young adults in the UK. At the end of this year, we **1** .... (record) data over a period of 30 years. In that time we **2** .... (provide) statistics on a number of occasions for the government. Most recently, we **3** .... (collect) data on the percentage of young adults living with their parents. We **4** .... (discover) that the number of young adults living at home **5** .... (gradually/rise) over the last twenty years, although the sharpest increase was between 2002 and 2012. From 1996 to 2002 the number **6** .... (slowly/decrease) from 2.7 million to 2.2 million. However, since then it **7** .... (rise) to 3.7 million, a record high. This figure accounts for 30% of the age group. The economic downturn **8** .... (largely/contribute) to the record figures that we are seeing today. If the trend continues, the figure **9** .... (reach) 4 million by the end of the decade.

6 Conditionals (1)

Conditional sentences talk about factual or hypothetical situations and their potential consequences. There are two clauses: the *if*-clause, which states the situation, and the main clause, which presents the consequence.
We can use *if* in two positions, but a comma separates the clauses when the *if*-clause comes first:
If you freeze water, it turns to ice.
Water turns to ice if you freeze it.

Zero conditional

> *if* + present tense + present tense
> *If you heat ice, it melts.*

> Present tense + *if* + present tense
> *Ice melts if you heat it.*

We use the zero conditional to talk about situations that are generally true, e.g. for scientific truths. When we talk about predictable or repeated actions, *if* can be used interchangeably with *when*.
Lily cries if/when she watches her favourite film.

First conditional

> *if* + present tense + *will/won't* + infinitive (without *to*)
> *If I see John, I'll tell him.*

> *will/won't* + infinitive (without *to*)+ *if* + present tense
> *I'll tell John if I see him.*

We use the first conditional to talk about a future situation with a possible consequence. Both clauses refer to the future, even though the verb in the *if*-clause is in the present tense.
If you see Paul, will you ask him to call me?
If she's coming to the meeting, I'll speak to her then.
If they're going to be here tomorrow, we'll ask them to come to the exhibition with us.

In the main clause we can use *may*, *might* or *could* instead of *will* if the consequence is less certain.
If you invest your money in a high risk account, you may lose it all.
Other modals that can be used in the main clause are:
- *can* for permission.
If you finish your homework, you can come with us.
- *must/mustn't* for obligation/prohibition.
If you are at the meeting, you mustn't challenge the director.
- *should* for recommendation.
If you go to Crete, you should try to see Knossos.
If we manage the way fish are caught, there should be plenty of food for the growing number of mouths on the planet.

Second conditional

> *if* + past tense + *would/wouldn't* + infinitive
> *If I won the lottery, I'd buy a new car.*

> *would/wouldn't* + infinitive + *if* + past tense
> *I'd buy a new car if I won the lottery.*

We use the second conditional to talk about a situation with a consequence which is either improbable or impossible. The verb in the *if*-clause is in the past simple but it doesn't refer to past time. Second conditional sentences refer to the present or the future.
If I had the money, I'd visit Australia. (present: I don't have the money)
If I became rich, I'd move to California. (This is an imagined situation in the future.)
If countries with long shorelines set limits on fishing, there would be plenty of fish to go around.

We can use *was* or *were* when using *I, he, she* or *it*:
If he was/were here right now, I'd tell him to his face.

We can also use *could* or *might* instead of *would* in the main clause to talk about events that are possible but not certain.
If people used renewable energy, household bills might be cheaper.
If people didn't use so much energy, fossil fuels might not run out.

Other ways of expressing condition

unless + present tense

We use *unless* to mean *if not*:
If you don't stop talking, I'll go and work in the library.
Unless you stop talking, I'll go and work in the library.

in case + present (or past) tense

We use *in case* to talk about taking precautions against something bad happening in the future.
Take your umbrella in case it rains. (It might rain and it might not. If it does, you will have the right equipment.)
Take your umbrella if it rains. (Only take your umbrella if you see it raining before you leave the house.)
We don't usually start a sentence with *in case*.

as long as / provided that + present (or past) tense

These expressions mean *if* or *on condition that* and are often used more formally.
We will work with the same manufacturer as long as it maintains its market position.
He will not go to prison provided that he stays out of trouble.

Inversion in conditionals

In more formal speech or writing, we can put the auxiliary verb before a subject instead of using *if*.
Had the link been established, they would have published the paper.
Were he here right now, I'd tell him to his face.

We can also use *should* instead of *if*.
Should you have any questions, please don't hesitate to contact me. (=If you have any questions, please don't hesitate to contact me.)

Exercise

1   Complete the second sentence so that it means exactly the same as the first.
    1   If she doesn't work harder, she won't pass the test.
        Unless ....
    2   I'd challenge him if I was a younger man.
        Were ....
    3   You can't hope to complete your research project on time unless you have already started it.
        If you haven't ....
    4   I recommend sushi if you ever try Japanese food.
        Should ....
    5   You may use my photos if you credit me by name.
        Provided ....
    6   I advise you to eat less meat.
        If I ....
    7   I'd consider any job if it involved travel.
        As ....

7 Conditionals (2)

Third conditional

> *if* + past perfect + *would have* + past participle
> *If I had seen him, I would have spoken to him.*

> *would have* + past participle + *if* + past perfect
> *I would have spoken to him if I had seen him.*

We use the third conditional to talk about hypothetical (unreal) situations or events in the past and to speculate about things that did not happen.
If we had studied harder, we would have passed the exam. (We didn't study hard and so we didn't pass the exam.)
We use *could* or *might* instead of *would* to say that the consequence or outcome was less sure.
If we had studied harder, we might have passed. (=We didn't study hard and even if we had, it's not certain that we would have passed.)

Mixed conditionals

Mixed conditionals are a combination of second and third conditionals.

> *if* + past simple + *would have* + past participle
> *If the policy worked, exam results would have been better.*
>
> *if* + past perfect + *would* + infinitive (without *to*)
> *If he hadn't taken the money, he wouldn't be in trouble now.*

We use mixed conditionals to talk about unreal situations when the *if*-clause and main clause don't refer to the same time. We can use mixed conditionals:
• to express the present consequence of a past action.
If the aeroplane hadn't been invented, we wouldn't be able to travel the world so easily.
• to explain how a present situation influenced a past action.
If she wasn't so stubborn, she would have listened to our warnings.
In situations where we use *had*, it is possible to invert the subject of the clause and *had*, and leave out *if*.
Had I realised the consequences, I wouldn't have told him.
(=If I had realised the consequences, I wouldn't have told him.)

wish

wish + past simple/continuous

We use *wish* + past simple/continuous to express regret about a present situation.
I wish I had more money.
We also use this to express regret about an action in progress in the present *(I wish it wasn't raining)*, or to express regret about a future arrangement *(I wish I wasn't helping Jo out tonight).*

wish + past perfect

We use *wish* + past perfect to express regret about an action that took place in the past.
I wish I had bought a bigger car. (But I didn't.)
We often add *never* for emphasis:
I wish I had never bought that car. (But I did.)

wish + would + infinitive

We use *wish* + *would* + infinitive as a criticism, to express that we would like someone or something to change.
I wish he wouldn't interrupt when someone else is speaking.
This is not used with stative verbs:
I wish he would have more hair.
And the same subject is not used in both clauses:
I wish I wouldn't snore.

if only

We can use *if only* in a similar way to *wish.*
if only + past perfect
If only I hadn't bought this car. (But I did.)

if only + *would* + infinitive
If only he wouldn't speak with his mouth full. (But he does.)
if only + past simple/continuous
If only I had more money. (But I don't.)
If only it wasn't raining. (But it is.)
If only I wasn't helping John out tonight. (But I am.)

should have

We use *should have* + past participle to express regret about an action that took place in the past.
I should have gone to the meeting. (But I didn't.)
I shouldn't have trusted him. (But I did.)

Exercise

1   **Read each situation. Then complete the sentences as a conditional.**
 1   They didn't go because Jana was ill.
    If Jana ....
 2   I was late for work because there was an accident.
    If there ....
 3   Ben is so insensitive. He hurt Jan's feelings.
    If Ben ....
 4   We aren't in Rome because we missed our flight.
    If we ....
 5   I went to the party. I embarrassed myself.
    I wouldn't ....
 6   We aren't rich. We didn't buy the Porsche.
    We ....
 7   They didn't speak the language so they didn't understand.
    If they ....
 8   I didn't hear him so I didn't answer his question.
    Had ....
 9   I have a lot of money so Mel wanted to be my friend.
    Mel wouldn't ....

8 Articles and other determiners

Definite article *the*

We use *the* + singular countable nouns, plural countable nouns or uncountable nouns:
• mainly with singular nouns.
• when the listener knows what we are talking about, because it has already been referred to or it is clear from context.
*There has been **a** fall in the rate of inflation. **The** fall was caused by slower increases in food prices.*
*I was in **the** car the other day* ... (We understand from the context that the speaker is talking about his/her own car.)
• with certain geographical features such as seas and oceans, rivers, mountain ranges and deserts: *The Atlantic, The Amazon, The Andes, The Sahara*
• to talk about professional groups or bodies: *the police, the press, the navy*
• with nationalities: *The British, The French*
• with groups of countries or states and groups of islands: *The Solomon Islands, The United States, The Republic of Moldova*
• with some buildings: *The Taj Mahal, The Eiffel Tower*
• with superlatives: *the best, the most prominent*
• with newspaper names: *The Times*
• with a musical instrument: *play the piano, the guitar is a versatile instrument*

Indefinite article *a/an*

We use *a/an*:
- with singular nouns: *a project, an essay*
- when we talk about something for the first time.
*There has been **a fall** in the rate of inflation. The fall was caused by slower increases in food prices.*
- with occupations: *a student, an electrician, a scientist*
- to refer to a member of a group, or class.
*Simon Jenkins was **a** columnist for the New York Times.*
- before an adjective that describes a noun.
*There was **an** enormous explosion followed by **a** long silence.*

No article

We don't use an article:
- to talk about plural nouns (people or things) in general.
Film producers borrow widely from manuals and websites.
- with certain geographical features including mountains and lakes: *Mount Fuji, Lake Como*
- before most towns, cities, countries and continents: *New York, Egypt, Asia*
- with certain familiar places *(work, home, school, university) What time do you go to school? How do you go to work? Are they at home?*
- with meals: *breakfast, lunch, dinner*
- with *play* + a game: *play tennis, play football*
- with languages: *Arabic, Italian*
- with certain time expressions, such as days of the week, months, years: *Tuesday, August, 2012*
Note that there are some exceptions: *at the weekend, in the 1990s, in the 15th century*

Other determiners

all/ every/ each

We use *all* (+ *the, of the*) to talk about three or more people or things. We use *all* with plural or uncountable nouns:
All floors have wheelchair access.
We use *every* to talk about three or more people or things. We use *every* with singular nouns:
Both lifts stop at every floor.

> Used with: *-thing, -one, -where, -body*

We use *each* (+ *of the*) to talk about two or more people or things. We use *each* with singular nouns and *each of the* with plural nouns:
The name of each candidate is listed in Part 2.
***Each of the** names is listed in Part 2.*

both/ either/ neither

We use *both* (+ *of the*) to say the same thing about two people or things. We use *both/both of the* with plural nouns.
*We'll take **both** chairs. We'll take **both of the** chairs.*
We use *either* (+ *of the*) to say that there are two possible options. We use *either* with a singular noun and *either of the* with plural nouns.
*You can take **either** chair. You can take **either of the** chairs.*
We use *neither* (+ *of the*) to say that something is not one or the other. We use *neither* with a singular noun and *neither of the* with plural nouns.
***Neither** room has chairs. **Neither of the** rooms have chairs.*

Exercises

1 **Complete the gaps in the texts with *a/ an, the* or – (no article).**

I read in my copy of **1** ....*Times* this morning that **2** .... Prime Minister of **3** ....UK and **4** .... President of **5** .... US met in **6** .... New York and signed **7** .... agreement to offer **8** .... aid to UNICEF. **9** .... aid will be used to provide **10** .... vaccines for **11** .... children all over **12** .... developing world.

There has been **13** .... traffic accident on **14** .... M4 motorway involving **15** .... car and **16** .... truck. **17** .... driver of **18** .... truck is from **19** .... Poland, and **20** .... driver of **21** .... car is **22** .... accountant from **23** .... Oxford. Both **24** .... men are currently being treated for **25** .... minor injuries at **26** .... Reading Hospital.

2 **Complete the text with the words in the box.**

> all   all the   both   both of   each   each of
> either   either of   neither   neither of

The United States, the United Kingdom, India and Japan have **1** .... felt the effects of unseasonal weather activity this year. **2** .... these countries has experienced extreme conditions and **3** .... one has been brought to a standstill by the weather. The US and Japan have suffered snowstorms, which have closed roads and airports. The US has had extreme conditions on **4** ....side of the country; drought in the west and snowstorms in the east. **5** .... the other two countries have endured country-wide flooding. **6** .... the UK nor India expected the rains to continue as long as they did and so **7** .... them were adequately prepared for the consequences. While some people have blamed **8** .... adverse conditions on global warming, others have called the infrastructure of the countries themselves into question. Who knows, it could be **9** .... them and is most likely a combination of **10** .... of them.

9 Countable and uncountable nouns

Nouns can be countable, uncountable or both. Countable nouns have a singular form and a plural form, while uncountable nouns only have a singular form.

Countable nouns

Countable nouns refer to things we can count. They:
- have a singular and a plural form: *the chair **is** small, the chairs **are** small*
- are used with *a/an* and numbers: *a book, an examiner, one girl, 1,500 residents*
- have some nouns which exist only in plural form: *clothes, glasses, goods, jeans, scissors, trousers*
- have some irregular plural forms: *children, feet, fish, mice, people, police, sheep*

Uncountable nouns

Uncountable nouns refer to things we can't count. They:
- don't have a plural form: *advice, milk, information*

(*not advices, milks, informations*)
- have a singular verb form: *This baggage is heavy.*
- aren't used with *a/an*: *an advice, a bread*
- have some nouns which exist only in plural form: *economics, gymnastics, mathematics, news, politics*
- can only be counted/measured by using countable nouns with them: *a bit of news, a bottle of water, a loaf of bread, a piece of advice, a slice of cake, a tin of soup*
- include some words that refer to a group of people, animals or things: *audience, family, flock, government, group, herd, staff, team*

Quantifiers

some and any

We use *some* and *any* with plural and uncountable nouns to talk about the number or quantity of things or people.
We use *some* in affirmative statements:
- with plural nouns: *There are some books.*
- with uncountable nouns: *There is some milk in the fridge.*
- to talk about an indefinite (not large) quantity: *We have made some progress but there is a long way to go.*
We also use *some* in limited questions, particularly offers and requests: *Would you like some tea?*
We use *any* with uncountable and plural countable nouns:
- in negative sentences: *There weren't any survivors.*
- in questions: *Is there any news about Matthew? Do you have any questions?*
We also use *any* in affirmative sentences, usually with a singular noun, to suggest unlimited choice: *Choose any number between one and ten.*

much and many/a lot of

We use *much, many* and *a lot* of to talk about quantity. *Much* is used with uncountable nouns and *many* is used with countable nouns. *A lot of* can be used for both countable and uncountable nouns. We use *much* and *many*:
- in questions: *Do we have **much** time? Do we have **many** volunteers?*
- negative statements: *We don't have **much** time. We don't have **many** volunteers.*
- in certain affirmative statements, in a formal style: ***Many** countries have signed up to the treaty. There has been **much** discussion about DNA profiling.*

few and little/a few and a little

We use *few* and *little* to mean not much/many/enough. *Few* is used with countable nouns and *little* is used with uncountable nouns:
*There were **few** supporters of the minister at the meeting.
Hurry up, there is **little** time to spare.*
We use *a few* and *a little* to mean a small quantity/amount. *A few* is used with countable nouns and *a little* is used with uncountable nouns:
*I've had **a few** replies.
Give me **a little** time to think about this.*

too little/few/much/many

We use *too little* and *too few* to mean not enough of something:
*We have **too few** resources to last us indefinitely.*
We use *too much* and *too many* to mean more than we want or need:
*I can't pay that. It's **too much** money!*

Other quantifiers

plenty of/lots of

We use these phrases to refer to a large amount of something. They can be used with both countable and uncountable nouns:
*There is **plenty of** milk.
There are **lots of** people outside the station.*

a (small) piece of/a bit of/a drop of

We use these phrases to refer to small amounts of something. They are only used with uncountable nouns:
*Could I have **a drop of** milk in my coffee, please?*

Exercises

1 Choose the correct word.
1 I'm afraid the news *is / are* bad.
2 I hope my advice *help / helps*.
3 His team *hasn't / haven't* enjoyed much success over the last year. They are in danger of relegation.
4 Am I putting on weight? My jeans *feels / feel* a bit tight.
5 Do you think politics *is / are* important?
6 So far the police *hasn't / haven't* made any comment.
7 His advice *was / were* very helpful.
8 He was a great actor and entertained *audience / audiences* all over the world.

2 Complete the sentences with the words provided.

some / any
1 There is .... information here about the tourist sites.
2 You can take .... of these samples.
3 They don't have .... more kerosene in stock.
4 I have .... concerns about the project.

much / many
5 I can't buy that. It costs too ....
6 How .... people are attending today?
7 There has been .... excitement over the opening of the new shopping mall.
8 There are far too .... unresolved questions.

few / little
9 .... American consumers bargain when buying a car.
10 I will probably spend a .... hours at my desk this weekend.
11 There is always too .... time.
12 The latest incentive from the government is likely to have .... effect on the economy.

10 Noun phrases

A noun phrase is a group of words that have a noun as the main part. A noun phrase gives extra information about the noun. Modifiers can come before or after the noun.

modifier + noun

Modifiers can be:
- adjectives (a *brilliant* idea)
- nouns (*water* tank)
- possessives (the *student's* essay)
- adverb-adjective combinations (a *universally accepted* truth)

noun + prepositional phrase

The most common prepositions are *about, for, in, of, on, to* and *with*.
*He loved to tell stories **about** India's wild animals.*
*There's a chair **in** the corner of the room.*
*Most athletes only eat food **with** a high nutritional content.*

noun + relative clauses

*A man, **who was working** in a post office, won the lottery today.*
*The woman **who is living** at the house is Sue, Finn's wife.*
*The office buildings **that were built** last year were all destroyed.*
*The house, **which** was valued at £1 million, sold for £900,000.*

noun + participle clause

A participle clause can give the same information as a relative clause in fewer words.
We use the present participle (*-ing* form) to form a participle clause when the meaning is active.
*The man **wearing** the red jacket is my cousin. (= The man who is wearing the red jacket)*
We use the past participle (*-ed* form in regular verbs) to form a participle clause when the meaning is passive.
*The office buildings **built** last year were all destroyed. (= The office buildings which were built last year)*
*The house, **valued** at £1 million, sold for £900,000. (= The house, which was valued at £1 million)*

noun + *to* + infinitive phrase

To + infinitive can be used after a noun to express purpose.
*Let me show you the way **to go**.*
*She wants the chance **to prove** she can do it.*

Exercise

1   **Join two sentences to make one, using a noun phrase.**
   1   A man won the lottery. He was working with me.
      A man .... the lottery.
   2   A parcel was sent to my tutor this morning. It contained an award.
      A parcel .... this morning.
   3   Many teachers leave the profession before retirement. The number is rising.
      The number .... rising.
   4   Food is served in UK hospitals. It isn't of a high standard.
      Food .... high standard.
   5   Bees search flowers for nectar. They also collect pollen.
      Bees .... pollen.
   6   Can you find this cat? Anyone who does will be offered a reward.
      Anyone .... reward.

11 Adjectives

We use adjectives to describe nouns. They can come:
*   before nouns
*a **rich** country, a **useful** gadget*
*   after certain verbs
*they were acting **strange**, you look **great***
*   with other adjectives
*She's got **long, brown, wavy** hair.*

Order of adjectives

Before a noun, adjectives expressing an opinion, e.g. *fantastic, interesting* come before adjectives expressing facts, e.g. *Italian, red, oval*.
We can also use nouns (paper, leather) as adjectives to give extra details about the noun (paper plane, leather jacket).
The order of adjectives is usually:
opinion / size / age / shape / colour / origin / material / type + noun
We usually use a maximum of three adjectives, as more than three can sometimes feel unnatural.

adjective + *and* + adjective

If there are two or more adjectives after a verb or noun, we usually put *and* between the last two adjectives. Compare:
It was a small, round, green purse.
The purse was small, round and green.
When there are three or more adjectives, use a comma between the other adjectives.

the + adjective

We use *the* + adjective to describe a group like: *the rich, the poor, the sick, the wise, the homeless, the young, the old*. These adjectives function like nouns.
We can describe some nationalities in this way, particularly those ending in *-ish* or *-ese*: *the British, the Japanese, the French*. Most nationality groups, however, are referred to as plural nouns: *the Italians, the Brazilians, the Australians*.

-ing/-ed adjectives

We form some adjectives from present participles (*interest**ing***) and past participles (*interest**ed***). Adjectives ending in *-ed* often describe how we feel:
I've never been so bored! You look tired.
Adjectives ending in *-ing* describe the person or thing that causes the feeling:
He is an interesting man. It was a thought-provoking play.

-ed adjectives + prepositions

We often use *-ed* adjectives with certain prepositions, especially when talking about feelings:
*   **in**: *interested in*
*   **of**: *scared of, terrified of, frightened of, ashamed of, tired of*
*   **about**: *excited about, worried about*
*   **with**: *bored with, pleased with, disappointed with*
*   **at**: *shocked at, amazed at, surprised at*
The preposition is followed by a noun or a gerund (*I'm interested **in starting** a dance class. / I'm interested **in the dance classes** you run*.).

Other adjectives + dependent prepositions

*   **on**: *dependent on, keen on*
*   **of**: *fond of, proud of, afraid of, guilty of, jealous of*
*   **about**: *angry about, furious about, passionate about*
*   **with**: *angry/happy with (someone about something)*
*   **at**: *good at, bad at, terrible at, useless at (ability)*
*   **to**: *kind to, cruel to, pleasant to, good to, opposed to*

Adjectives followed by *to* + infinitive

We can use *to* + infinitive after certain adjectives that express feelings (*happy, pleased, surprised, angry, sorry, delighted, glad, proud*), ability/willingness (*able, ready, willing, keen, eager, unable, unwilling, unlikely*), possibility (*easy, difficult, possible, hard*) and opinion (*right, wrong, good, lucky*).

Exercises

1 Choose the correct option.

1 It's important to try to *naturally act / act naturally*.
2 When he took the stand, he *appeared nervous / nervous appeared* until he started talking.
3 Our ideal candidate would show *commitment solid / solid commitment* to the job.
4 Will we get the report in by Friday? It's not *good looking / looking good* at the moment.
5 Brazil is one of the *resource-rich countries / countries resource-rich* at the top of our list.
6 Paul's absences this term may damage his exam prospects, although we *optimistic remain / remain optimistic*.
7 Finding a manufacturer for these parts is *proving more difficult / more difficult proving* than we expected.
8 That *leather old / old leather* armchair used to belong to my grandfather.

2 Complete the text with the correct adjective form (-*ing* or -*ed*) of the words in brackets.

The graph compares the **1** .... (prefer) snack choices of boys and girls at one secondary school. We weren't **2** .... (surprise) that the results showed different preferences, but we did find some of those differences **3** .... (interest). The boys find crisps and chocolate most **4** .... (appeal). This is not **5** .... (amaze), especially as the girls liked them just as much, but more **6** .... (astound) was the finding that girls eat twice as much fruit as boys. Although the boys aren't particularly **7** .... (interest) in fruit, we were **8** .... (relieve) to learn that they do eat a lot of vegetable snacks. The girls find sweets and ice cream more **9** .... (tempt) than the boys. The results show that overall girls have a sweeter tooth than the boys, while the boys overall were more **10** .... (excite) by the saltier snacks.

12 Adverbs

Adverbs give us extra information about verbs, adjectives and other adverbs. Adverbs can be single words (*recently*) or phrases (*at the end of the road*).
You can add -*ly* to many adjectives to form adverbs: *slow → slowly, quick → quickly*.
Also note the following spelling:
full → fully, beautiful → beautifully, happy → happily, energetic → energetically, remarkable → remarkably

Adverbs of manner (-*ly*)

Adverbs of manner describe *how* something is done (*badly, beautifully, enthusiastically, happily*). Adverbs of manner usually come:
• after the object: *She opened the box **slowly**.*
• after the verb if there is no object: *He ran **quickly**.*
For emphasis, the adverb can come between the subject and verb and even at the beginning of a sentence.
*She **slowly** opened the box.*
***Slowly**, she opened the box.*

Adverbs of place

Adverbs of place describe *where* something is done (*everywhere, there, nearby, outside, on the corner*). Adverbs of place usually come after the object: *He put the dog outside.*
Adverbial phrases, which include a preposition + noun phrase, usually come after the main verb and object.
*He bought a house **near the football stadium**.*

Adverbs of time

Adverbs of time describe *when* something is done (*last week, a year ago, yesterday, for three hours, yet*). Adverbs of time can come at the beginning of a sentence or at the end of a sentence, but not between subject and verb or verb and object.
***Yesterday** we got the keys to our new house.*
*We got the keys to our new house **yesterday**.*

Adverbs of frequency (-*ly* and other endings)

Adverbs of frequency describe *how often* something is done. They usually come between the subject and main verb.
*We **usually** go to the pool on Saturdays.*
Some can come at the beginning of a sentence and after the verb (and object, when there is one).
***Usually**, we go to the pool on Saturdays.*
*We go to the pool on Saturdays, **usually**.*
Adverbs that can go in all three positions include *usually, sometimes, occasionally* and *often*.
Adverbs that only come between subject and verb include *always, never* and *hardly ever*.
Adverbial phrases like *once in a while, now and then* or *from time to time* usually come at the end of a sentence.

Examples: *regularly, hardly ever, always, frequently, rarely*

Adverbs of degree (-*ly* and other endings)

Adverbs of degree make adjectives or adverbs stronger or weaker. Gradable adjectives or adverbs can be made weaker when preceded by adverbs *fairly, quite, rather, a bit, pretty* and stronger with *very, really, particularly, extremely*.

Non-gradable (also known as extreme or absolute) adjectives are preceded by *completely, absolutely, totally*. Compare these gradable adjectives with their extreme counterparts: *cold/freezing, hot/boiling, big/enormous, small/tiny, good/fantastic, bad/awful, tired/exhausted, dirty/filthy*.
The film wasn't very good.
I thought the film was absolutely fantastic!
~~The film was absolutely good.~~

Word order

When there is an auxiliary verb, the adverb comes after the auxiliary verb and before the main verb.
I <u>don't</u> usually arrive on time. / They <u>haven't</u> often visited us.
Adverbs come after the verb *be* in the present or past tense.
I'm always late.
In a sentence where adverbs of place and adverbs of time are both used, place usually comes before time.
I'll see you here at 8.00 tomorrow.

Exercises

1 Complete the text with the adverbs of the adjectives in brackets.

She **1** .... (quick) climbed the tree and
2 .... (careful) stepped onto a large branch
and then onto the roof of the house. As **3** ....
(cautious) as she could, she **4** .... (slow)
stepped through the open window, making sure she didn't
knock over the **5** .... (beautiful) carved statue
or wake anyone up. Once in the room, she heard the
sounds of a man sleeping **6** .... (noisy) and a
woman breathing **7**................................. (quiet). She knew the
house **8** .... (good) and so she
9 .... (swift) ran down the stairs, through the
hall, down the corridor and into the kitchen. She sprang
10 .... (energetic) across the room, bowed her
head and drank **11** .... (thirsty) from a bowl in
the corner. Then she curled up in her basket and
12 .... (dreamy) closed her eyes.

2 Rearrange the words to make sentences.

1 apartment / the / coast / bought / I / an / on

....

2 freezing / absolutely / it's / outside

....

3 tennis / yesterday / played / I

....

4 Fiona / ever / see / we / hardly

....

5 a house / near / bus / they / station / rent / the

....

6 call / me / Ian / usually / doesn't / at work

....

7 month / to / my / came / stay / last / mother

....

8 filthy / wasn't / it / dirty, / it / just / completely / was

....

13 Comparatives and superlatives

Comparative adjectives

We use comparative adjectives to compare people, places or
things. When we want to compare one thing or group with
another, we use *than* after the adjective.
*The carbon footprint of Kenyan flowers is nearly six times
smaller than that caused by the production of Dutch flowers.*
If the context is clear for a comparison, it is possible to leave
out the *than*-clause.
Everything is more expensive. (than it used to be)

Superlative adjectives

We use superlative adjectives to compare a person, place or
thing with all the others in the same group.
Real Madrid is the richest football club in the world.
We can modify superlative adjectives by adding *one of / some
of* + superlative + plural noun.
*Robert Redford is **one of the best actors** in Hollywood.*
*The room contains **some of the rarest species** in the world.*

Adjective	Comparative	Superlative
Regular		
long	longer	longest
big	bigger	biggest
easy	easier	easiest
expensive	more expensive	most expensive
Irregular		
good	better	best
bad	worse	worst

Spelling rules

Regular adjectives

Short adjectives ending in *-e*, add *-r / -est*:
nice → nice**r**→ nic**est**
large → large**r** → larg**est**
Short adjectives ending in a consonant, add *-er / -est*:
cheap → cheap**er** → cheap**est**
long → long**er** → long**est**
Short adjectives ending consonant-vowel-consonant, double
the final consonant + *-er / -est*:
sad → sadd**er** → sadd**est**
big → bigg**er** → bigg**est**
Adjectives ending in *-y*, replace *-y* with *-ier / -iest*:
cloudy → cloud**ier** → cloud**iest**
easy → eas**ier** → eas**iest**
Long adjectives (three syllables or more) add *more / most* +
adjective:
intelligent → **more** intelligent → **most** intelligent
expensive → **more** expensive → **most** expensive

Irregular adjectives

good → better → best
bad → worse → worst

more/ less/ fewer + than

We can compare countable nouns with *more* and *fewer* and
uncountable nouns with *more* and *less*.
*By 2013, there was less unemployment in Uruguay and
Venezuela than in the USA.*
There were fewer job opportunities in Italy than in France.

as + adjective + as

When we want to say something is the same as another, we
use *as* + adjective + *as*.
*Rome is often **as hot as** Istanbul in summer.*

not as + adjective + as

When we want to say something is not the same as another,
we use *not as* + adjective + *as*.
*Stockholm is **not as humid as** Madrid in July.*

Adverbs

We can also compare how things are done by using *more/
less* + an adverb (+ *than*).
*Events progressed **more rapidly than** anticipated.*

Making comparatives stronger and weaker

To make a comparative stronger, we add these modifiers:
a lot, much, far, even, a good deal, considerably, significantly
+ comparative (or *more/less* + adjective/adverb)
*This year's test was a **lot longer than** last year's.*

To make a comparative weaker, we add these modifiers:
a bit, a little, not much, not a lot, slightly + comparative
or *nearly, not quite, almost* + *as* + adjective/adverb.
*The process is taking **a bit longer than** we would like.*
***This model is not quite as efficient as** the CVS-460 model.*

Quantity

When we want to compare quantity, we can use (*not*) *as much/many* + noun (phrase) + *as*:
*There aren't **as many [wild tigers] as** there used to be.*
*There is **as much water on the Earth's surface as** ever.*

Exercises

1 Complete the text. Choose the correct option.

In a recent survey, it was found that there are a lot
1 *more / most / less* mobile phones today compared with
four years ago. Now, 80% of teenagers own a mobile
phone. Half (40% of teens) own a smartphone today,
compared with 23% four years ago.
2 *Less / Fewer / The least* teens own a tablet (25%),
which is comparable to the adult population. Four years
ago this figure was just 9%. Teens generally have
3 *more / less / fewer* access to the Internet at home
because the home computer is usually shared by other
family members. Mobile access is more common among
teens, with 26% accessing the Internet exclusively
from their mobile phone or tablet. Although adults tend
to spend **4** *fewer / fewest / more* time on the Internet,
because many use it for their work, only 15% access the
Internet exclusively from handheld devices. The group
that spends the **5** *more / most / less* time online using
handheld devices is those aged between 17 and 19. The
main use for this group is social networking.
The group that spends the **6** *least / more / fewest* hours
on the Internet is those aged between 13 and 16. This is
also the group that has the **7** *fewest / less / least* access
to   the Internet, as their parents tend to have greater
control over their time online.

2 Look at the table and complete the text with comparative and superlative forms. Use the words in brackets. You may need to change the words and/or add other words.

	Public spending as % of GDP	National healthcare expenditure as % of GDP	Government spending on healthcare as % of total healthcare spending
Australia	27	9	68
Finland	40	9	75
Singapore	13	4	36
Sweden	33	10	81
UK	46	10	84
US	27	18	53

We checked a number of sources and found that
1 .... (reliable) statistics were provided by
the World Bank. According to the World Bank, national
healthcare expenditure is **2** .... in Australia
.... (same) it is in Finland, and Sweden spends
3 .... (much) the UK. As a percentage of GDP,

public spending in the UK and Finland is
4 .... (far / great) Australia or the US. However,
the statistics reveal that public spending in Singapore is
5 .... (significant / generous) than the other
countries in the survey. In fact, we can see that the
government in Singapore also spends **6** ....
(considerable) than the governments of the other
countries. The government of Finland spends
7 .... (slight) than the government of Australia
but spending in the UK is **8** .... (by far / high).

14 Modals (1)

We use *can, must, should, ought to* to talk about permission, obligation and necessity. These verbs don't change form (*she can ✓* ~~she cans~~).

We can also use *be allowed to, have to* and *need to*. These verbs require the verb *be* or auxiliary verbs and therefore change form (*she isn't allowed to, he doesn't have to, she needs to*).

Permission (*can, may, be able to*)

	Present	Past
Permission	can, is/are allowed to, may	could, was/were allowed to

We use *can* to request and give permission.
• The permission may be internal, i.e. from the speaker.
***Can** I borrow your pen? Yes, you **can**.*
• Or permission may be external, i.e. from an outside source which may be an institution or law.
***Can** I use my mobile phone here? No, you **can't**.* (It is the rule of the institution.)

We use *be allowed to* to request and give permission, usually from an external source.
*'**Am I allowed to** leave my bike here?' 'Yes, you **are**.'*
A more polite way of asking for permission is to use *may*. You can only use *may* in this context with *I* or *we*.
***May** I/we leave the room, please?*

The past form of *can* is *could* and *be allowed to* is *was/were allowed to*. There is no past form of *may* for permission.

*We **could** stay up late every night when we were young.*
*I **was allowed to** wear jeans at school yesterday.*
We only use *could* to speak generally about permission in the past. When we want to talk about a specific event in the past, we use *was/were allowed to*.

To refuse permission, we use *can't* or *may not*.
***Can** I leave early? No, you **can't**.*
***May** I leave early? No, you **may not**.*

let, allow

When we want to talk about permission to do something, we can use *let* + object + infinitive (without *to*).
*Dad **lets me use** his car from time to time.*
*Do you think Anna will **let me wear** her shoes?*
When we want to make a passive sentence, we need to use *allowed to* rather than *let*.
*We **aren't allowed to use** mobile phones in lectures.* (not ✗)

Obligation and necessity (*must, have to, need to, be allowed to*)

	Present	Past
Obligation/ necessity	*must, have to, need to*	*had to, needed to*

We use *must* or *have to* to say that something is obligatory or very important.
*You **must do** your homework.* (The obligation is from the teacher.)
*We **have to be** there at a.m.* (The obligation comes from the organisers of the event, not the speaker.)

We use *need to* when we want to say that something is necessary, but not obligatory.
*You **need to wear** a hat today.* (It's necessary as it is very cold outside.)

The past form of *must* and *have to* is *had to* and the past of *need to* is *needed to*.
He had to report his findings to the committee. (*He must reported his findings to the committee.*)
*He **needed to renew** his passport and visa.*

We use *mustn't* to say it is obligatory or important not to do something.
*You **mustn't drive** without a licence.* (The obligation is not from the speaker). (*You don't have to drive without a licence.*)

The past form of *mustn't* is *wasn't/weren't allowed to*.
*We had to complete the test. We **weren't allowed to leave** before we had finished.*

No obligation/necessity (*don't have to, don't need to, needn't*)

	Present	Past
No obligation/ necessity	*don't have to, don't need to, needn't*	*didn't have to, didn't need to, needn't have*

We use *don't have to* or *don't need to* to say that something is not obligatory or necessary. We can also use *needn't* to mean the same as *don't need to*.
*We **don't have to/don't need to/needn't go** to work today.*

The past forms are *didn't have to*, *didn't need to* and *needn't have* + past participle. The meaning between *didn't need to* and *needn't have* (+ past participle) is different.

*We **didn't have to go/didn't need go** to work today.* (It wasn't necessary, so we didn't go.)

*We **needn't have gone** to work today.* (We went but it turned out not to have been necessary.)

Exercises

1 Choose the correct option. Sometimes more than one option is possible.
1 Do they *need / have* to knock all the houses down to build the new sports centre?
2 I'll be here all week, so he *hasn't to / doesn't need to* call me, he can just come in.
3 You *needn't / need* to be here by 1p.m. tomorrow.
4 He was unsure about the quality of the laptop. He *didn't need / needn't* have worried, it was fine.
5 You *don't need / needn't* shout. I can hear you perfectly well.

6 She *doesn't need to / needn't* be nervous, they do all the safety checks before they let her jump.
7 I *didn't need / needn't* to drive there. I could have walked.

2 Look at the sentences. Correct the mistakes, if necessary. Tick (✓) the correct sentences.
1 May Sam and Leo attend the meeting too?
....
2 They have left their car in the staff car park. Are they allowed to do that?
....
3 I mustn't to be late for work again.
....
4 Shh! This is a library. You don't have to talk in here.
....
5 He needn't has done his homework. The teacher was away.
....
6 Do you think your tutor will let you hand in your assignment late?
....
7 Do we must complete this exercise today?
....
8 You don't have to have experience to apply for the job, but it'll help.
....

15 Modals (2)

We use *can (can't)* and *will (won't)* to make requests and *could (couldn't)* and *would (wouldn't)* for more polite requests.
We use *let's, could* and *shall* in suggestions and *will* and *shall* in offers.
To express an opinion or give advice we use *should, could, ought to* and *had ('d) better*.
None of these verbs changes form in the third person and we use the verbs as auxiliaries in questions.
He could go to another shop. ✓
(*He coulds try another shop.* ✗)
Will you help me? ✓
(*Do you will help me?* ✗)

Making requests (*can, will, could, would*)

We use *can* and *will* to make requests.
***Can** you open the window, please?*
***Will** you give me a lift tomorrow?*

We use *could* and *would* to make the request sound more polite.
***Could** you open the window, please?*
***Would** you give me a lift tomorrow?*

Suggestions and offers (*let's, shall, could, will*)

We use *let's* + infinitive (without *to*) and *shall* + *I/we* + infinitive (without *to*) and *could* + infinitive to make suggestions.
We usually use *let's* and *could* in affirmative sentences and *shall I/we* in questions. In expressions with *let's* and *shall*, the speaker is included in the suggestion. With *could*, the speaker is only included in sentences with *we*.
***Let's do** something this afternoon.* (I want us to do something.)

Shall we go to the pool? (I want us to go to the pool).
We **could try** that new Thai restaurant on South Street.
(I want us to try the new restaurant.)
You **could try** that new Thai restaurant on South Street.
(I recommend you try the new restaurant – without me.)

We use *will* and *shall* to make offers. We usually use *will* in affirmative sentences and *shall I/we* in questions.
I'**ll carry** your bags.
Shall we go?

Advice and opinion (*should, ought to, 'd better*)

When we want to recommend, advise or express an opinion, we use *should* and *ought to*.
You **should** do more exercise.
You **ought to** join my gym.

When we want to say we think something is not a good idea, we use *shouldn't*.
He **shouldn't eat** so much.
When we want to ask for advice, we use *should*.
Should I buy this shirt?
The past form is *should(n't) have* + past participle.
The government **shouldn't have increased** spending.
When we want to give advice in a specific situation, we use *had ('d) better (not)* + verb (without *to*).
I'**d better** go. I'm already late.
You'**d better not leave** your bag unattended.
Had we better stop there?

Exercises

1 Complete the text with the words in the box.

> should   ought   better   could

The company's output **1** .... double if they reduced the workforce by 20 per cent and invested in robot technology. The finance director **2** .... to take the initiative at the next AGM and the operations manager had **3** .... listen if she wants to keep her job.
I believe the company **4** .... start the process of streamlining the production line. This **5** .... be the perfect time to do this – it has worked for other similar companies. However, I think we **6** .... to research all the options, and we'd **7** .... not rush things. Instead, we **8** .... wait until we have the best strategy available.

2 Look at the sentences and correct the mistakes.

1 Could you mind not talking so loudly?

2 Let email the company and tell them about their mistake.

3 Do you will give me a lift?

4 He shouldn't has reduced the number of people working on his team.

5 Would you mind if you didn't talk during the presentation, please?

6 Is that the time? We would better finish the seminar.

7 Shall you pick me up after work?

16 Modals (3)

We use the modal verbs *can, could, may, might, must* and *should* to talk about certainty, speculation and deduction. These verbs don't change form.
He **may get** a different result next time. (He **mays get** a different result next time. **X**)
This group of modal verbs can be used to talk about the past, e.g. *can't* + *have* + past participle.
They **can't have arrived** already. It's too early.

Speculation (*may, might, could*)

Present and future	
may, might, could	it is possible that something is true
may not, might not	it is possible that something is not true

Past	
may have, might have, could have	it is possible that something is true
may not have, might not have	it is possible that something is not true

We use *may, might* and *could* + infinitive (without *to*) to speculate about the present and future when we think it is possible that something is true.
Cargo containers **may provide** a useful resource.
The workers in Papua New Guinea **might earn** £5 a day.
Don't make a noise. They **could be** asleep.

We use *may not* and *might not* + infinitive (without *to*) to speculate about the present and future, when we think it is possible that something is <u>not</u> true. We don't use *could not*.
They **might not come.** (=We expected them to come but it's possible they won't).
I may not go into work today. (=I would normally go into work but today it's possible I won't.)

We use *may have, might have* and *could have* + past participle to speculate about the past when we think it is possible that something was true.
His flight **may have been** delayed.
He **could have missed** the flight.

We use *may not have* and *might not have* + past participle to speculate about the past when we think it is possible that something is not true. We don't use *could not have*.
She **might not have heard** us. (We expected her to hear us but it's possible she didn't.)
They **might not have received** our message. (We sent a message but it's possible they didn't get it.)

Deduction (*must, can't, couldn't*)

Present and future	
must	we are certain that something is true
can't, couldn't	we are certain that something is not true

Past	
must have	we are certain that something is true
can't have, couldn't have	it is possible that something is not true

We use *must* + infinitive (without *to*) to deduce something in the present or future when we are sure that something is true.
*Look at her music collection. She **must love** jazz.*
*I'm sure the weight of the pedals **must be** an issue if you need to cycle fast.*

We use *can't/couldn't* + infinitive (without *to*) to deduce something in the present or future when we are sure that something is <u>not</u> true.
*I've rung the bell three times. They **can't be** in.*
*You **couldn't be** tired already – you've only just got up!*

We use *must have* + past participle (without *to*) to deduce something in the past when we are sure that something is true.
*They walked 30 miles in one day. They **must have been** exhausted.*

We use *can't/couldn't have* + past participle (without *to*) to deduce something in the past when we are sure that something is <u>not</u> true.
*He didn't send us a card. He **can't have received** ours.*
*They **couldn't have thought** much of her if they didn't call.*

Assumption (*should/shouldn't*)

Present and future	
should, shouldn't	we think something is probably true

Past	
should have, shouldn't have	we think something is probably true

We use *should/shouldn't* to make assumptions about what is probably true in the present or future.
*We **should arrive** there at about five o'clock.*
*It **shouldn't take** too long.*
We use *should/shouldn't have* + past participle (without *to*) to make assumptions about what is probably true in the past.
*They **should have arrived** by now.*
*It **shouldn't have taken** such a long time.*

Exercises

1 Read the report and then choose the correct option (a–d) to complete the text.

The court heard that Max Warneford had not been honest about his business practices. The prosecuting lawyer said that, although there is no way of knowing, this **1** .... going on for years. He added that, as Warneford had kept separate accounts, he **2** .... known that he was breaking the law. He concluded by saying that Warneford **3** .... helped his accountant, as he claimed, because his accountant had no knowledge of these accounts. Indeed, his accountant is one of his accusers. Sources say that without the testimony of so many of Warneford's victims, the case **4** .... come to court. The trial **5** .... continue for several weeks and there is a chance, if found guilty, that Warneford **6** .... face a long prison sentence.

1 a could be   b could not be
   c could have been d could not have been
2 a must   b must not
   c must have   d must not have
3 a can b can't   c can have   d can't have
4 a might   b might not
   c might have   d might not have
5 a could   b couldn't
   c could have   d couldn't have
6 a may b may not c may have   d may not have

2 Rewrite the sentences so they have the same meaning as the first sentence. Use the words in brackets.

1 I don't think it's possible that they spoke to the film director. (can't)
   They ....
2 My guess is that you were exhausted when you got back. (must)
   You ....
3 It's possible Sue didn't get my email. (might)
   Sue ....
4 I think those aren't the final results because the initial figures were incorrect. (can't)
   Those ....
5 Look at the map. I'm sure we are here. (must)
   Look at the map. We ....
6 The birds have similar markings, so maybe they are from the control group (could)
   The birds have similar markings, so they ....
7 It's possible that the bag will be too expensive for me to afford. (might)
   I ....
8 It's possible that there are people who depend on their phones too much. (may)
   There ....

17 Passives (1)

The passive voice is often used in academic and formal writing. The object of an active verb is the subject of a passive verb.

Active

subject	active verb	object
The central bank	increased the lending rate	to 12%.

Passive

subject	passive verb	agent
The lending rate was increased	*to 12% by*	the central bank.

- The subject of an active sentence becomes the agent of a passive sentence. We use *by* to introduce the agent.
- *by* + agent can often be omitted.
- The passive form is not used with intransitive verbs (*arrive, disappear, go, sit, die, wait*) because they have no direct object.
They disappeared. (not ~~They were disappeared~~.)

Forms of the passive

We form the passive with *be* + past participle (+ *by* + agent).

present and past simple	The system ***is/was used*** by large corporations.
present and past continuous	The system ***is/ was being used*** by large corporations.
present and past perfect simple	The system ***has/ had been used*** by large corporations.

modal verbs	The system **will/ should// must be used** by large corporations. The system **would/ couldn't/ can't have been used** by large corporations.
going to	The system **is/ was going to be used** by large corporations.
used to	The system **used to be used by** large corporations

Uses of the passive

We use the passive (often omitting *by* + agent):
* in formal writing.
*Your attention in this matter **would be** much **appreciated** (by us).*
* when we describe a process.
*The chassis **is coated** with a primer (by a machine).*
* when we want to present an opinion anonymously.
*It is said that Grimaldi's painting style **was influenced** by Marotti.*

We usually omit *by* + agent when the agent:
* is unknown.
The vase was made around 400 years ago (by someone).
* has already been mentioned or is obvious.
MBS Bank stated that, over the next two years, 300 members of their workforce would be laid off (by MBS Bank).
* is not important.
Our flight has been delayed (by someone or something).

We usually include *by* + agent when the agent:
* contains important information, despite not being the primary focus of the sentence.
Over twenty people were injured by a hurricane in Cuba.
The bank was robbed by a man in his thirties.
* is the name of a writer, artist, inventor or person of note.
'Crime and Punishment' was written by Fyodor Dostoevsky.

Verbs with two objects

When a verb is followed by two objects in an active sentence, there are two possible ways of making a passive sentence.

subject	active verb	indirect object	direct object
We	sent	our customers	a refund.

subject	passive verb	object	
Our customers	were sent	a refund.	

subject	passive verb	preposition	object
A refund	was sent	to	our customers.

The following verbs are commonly used with two objects.

Used with the preposition *to*: ask, give, lend, owe, pay, promise, sell, send, show, teach, tell, write

Used with the preposition *for*: build, buy, draw, fix, paint

Used with the prepositions *to* or *for*: bring, leave

for

When a passive sentence doesn't have an agent, we can add extra information with *for* + noun phrase after the verb, which describes its purpose.

*The land is wanted **for** development.*
*The books will be saved **for** the grandchildren of the writer.*

Exercises

1 Complete the description of a food manufacturing process with the passive form of the verbs in the box.

add coat compress cool cut load mix
pack pour roast wrap

The oats, nuts and rice **1** .... at a temperature of 160°c and then they **2** .... together with syrup in a large drum. Then the mixture **3** .... out onto a conveyor. Chocolate chips **4** .... and then the mixture **5** .... by large rollers to a standard thickness. The compressed mixture **6** .... into strips and then again into bars. Next, the bars **7** .... in chocolate and then they **8** ....with cold air. The individual bars **9** .... in plastic and then they **10** .... into cardboard boxes. The packed boxes **11** .... onto delivery vehicles.

2 Complete the sentences using the passive form. Include the agent only when necessary.

1 They taught us the Chinese alphabet.
   We ....
2 The bank lent the company £100,000.
   £100,000 ....
3 Unforeseen weather conditions had delayed the flight.
   The flight ....
4 The marketing manager presented us with an interesting proposal.
   We ....
5 We assure our clients a first-class service.
   Our ....
6 Anyone attending the university can use the library.
   The library ....
7 The investigation revealed a series of errors.
   A series of errors ....
8 We will assign specific jobs in the next few weeks.
   Specific jobs ....

18 Passives (2)

We form the passive infinitive with infinitive + *to be* + past participle.
*We aim **to be seen** as a progressive company.*
*GPS technology could allow snowfall **to be measured** across a wider range of landscapes.*

Used with:
verbs of thinking and feeling: *appear, choose, decide, expect, forget, hate, hope, intend, learn, like, need, plan, prefer, prepare, pretend, seem, wish*

verbs of saying: *agree, demand, offer, promise, refuse*

other verbs: *afford, aim, arrange, attempt, deserve, disregard, fail, help, manage, measure, tend, try, see, want*

We form the passive *-ing* form with *being* + past participle.
*I remember **being told** not to try getting into Cambridge.*
*He enjoyed **being tested** by the university students.*

Used after: *verbs of liking and disliking: can't stand, detest, don't mind, dislike, enjoy, hate, fancy, like, love*

verbs of saying and thinking: admit, consider, deny, imagine, mention, remember, suggest, tell

other verbs: avoid, begin, finish, keep, miss, practice, risk, start, stop, test

Reporting structures

We use passive reporting structures with certain reporting verbs.

- *it + be + past participle of reporting verb + that*

It is hoped that *more evidence may come to light.*
It is believed that *people sleep less well when there is a full moon.*

Used with: *agree, announce, argue, believe, claim, decide, disclose, expect, feel, hope, know, predict, recognise, report, say, suggest, think, understand*

- *subject + be + past participle of reporting verb + to + infinitive*

Apicius **is believed to be** *the world's oldest cookbook.*
Fifty dolphins **are known to frequent** *the saltwater coastal lakes of the rural Gippsland region.*
The Chess Turk **was revealed to be** *an elaborate and clever hoax.*

Used with: *ask, consider, believe, estimate, expect, feel, intend, know, mean, report, reveal, say, see, suppose, think, understand*

- *subject + be + past participle of reporting verb + to have + past participle*

St Mercurius **was believed to have killed** *the emperor Julian.*
This episode **is thought to have taken** *place in 1976.*

Used with: *consider, believe, estimate, know, mean, report, say, suppose, think, understand*

The speaker in passive reporting structures is usually unknown or unimportant.

have/get something done

We use *have/get + object + past participle* when someone does something for us (and we often pay them money for it).
I am **having my car serviced** *tomorrow.*
They **got their house remortgaged** *by the bank.*

have to do/need to do

We use *have to/need to + be + past participle* to talk about necessity.
Roses, for example, **have to be shipped** *by air rather than sea.*
The tyre **needs to be** *changed.*

Exercises

1 Choose the correct option.
1 I don't have a car. I hope *to be / being* driven to the party.
2 They can't stand *to be / being* watched when they play.
3 Mark had a new broadband network *installed / being installed* last week.
4 We are having the TV *deliver / delivered* next Saturday.
5 My car has to *service / be serviced* soon.
6 The recycled glass needs to be *transported / transporting* to the factory.

2 Complete the second sentence so that it expresses the meaning of the first in the passive form. Re-use the verbs in <u>bold</u>. Change the form as necessary. Don't include the agent.
1 We **expect** this year's conference to be **cancelled**.
It ....
2 People **knew** that the president **enjoyed** boxing.
The president ....
3 People **believe** that Brunel **built** this bridge.
This bridge ....
4 Some people **argued** that a strike would **harm** the company.
It ....
5 We **think** 3,000 people **took part** in the study.
3,000 people ....
6 We **estimate** 15,000 people are **attending** the festival.
15,000 ....
7 We **know** the battle **took** place in 1793.
The battle ....

19 Relative clauses (1)

We use relative clauses to give extra information about the noun, or noun phrase, in the main part of the sentence. Relative clauses can be defining or non-defining.

Relative pronouns

Relative pronouns (*who, which, that, where, when, why, whose*) link the relative clause to the main clause.
A relative pronoun can be the subject or the object of a relative clause.

Subject
There's the man who took my phone.
The man took my phone.

Object
There's the woman who I met yesterday.
I met the woman yesterday.

When the relative pronoun is the subject of the clause, it always follows the noun it refers to.
- We use *who* for people: *Martin Cooper is the man* **who** *invented the mobile phone.*
- *Muybridge was an Englishman* **who** *went to the USA at the age of twenty in search of fame and fortune.*
- We use *which* for things: *It's a vehicle* **which** *not many of us could afford.*
- We use *that* for people or things: *He's the boy* **that** *I told you about. It's something* **that** *joins one pipe to another.*
That is more commonly used in spoken and more informal written English. *That* is not used in non-defining relative clauses.
- We use *where* for places: *I don't live there now but it's the place* **where** *I was born.*
- We use *when* for a time: *She lived in the Middle Ages, a time* **when** *invasion and resettlement was commonplace.*
- We use *why* for a reason: *There are a number of reasons* **why** *they chose to leave their native country.*
- We use *whose* for possession: *This is Cathy,* **whose** *sister went to my school.*
Included in the team is a geomorphologist, **whose** *task is to examine how the coastal landscape has changed over time.*

Defining relative clauses

We use defining relative clauses to give essential information about the noun in the main clause. If a defining relative clause is left out, the meaning of the entire sentence is often unclear. Commas are not used before a defining relative clause.

It's a place where we spent our summer holidays. ✓
It's a place, where we spent our summer holidays. ✗

When the relative pronoun (*who, which* or *that*) is the subject of the clause, we must always include it in the sentence. However, when the relative pronoun is the object of the clause, it is possible to leave it out.
There's the man who took my phone.
There's the woman (who) I spoke to.

We don't use other pronouns to refer to the noun in the relative clause when the relative pronoun is the object.
There's the woman. I spoke to her.
There's the woman who I spoke to ~~her~~.

Non-defining relative clauses

We use non-defining relative clauses to give extra information about the noun, or noun phrase, in the main part of the sentence.
The dock workers, who load and unload the ships, are all government employees. (Essential: The dock workers are government employees. Extra: They load and unload the ships.)

A non-defining relative clause is separated from the main clause with commas.
J.M.W. Turner, who was a landscape painter, died in 1851.

Non-defining relative clauses are more commonly used in formal and written forms of English.
*The Brough Superior was designed by a man called George Brough, **who** was one of the early pioneers of motorcycle construction.*

We don't use *that* to replace *which* or *who*.
*The girl's name was Steffi Graf, **who** went on to win 22 Grand Slams.* (The girl's name was Steffi Graf, **that** went on to win 22 Grand Slams.)

We can't omit the relative pronoun in a non-defining relative clause.
*He travelled to Alaska, **which** had just become US territory.*
(He travelled to Alaska, had just become US territory.)

Exercise

1 **Write a single sentence with a relative clause. Choose from the words in the box. Don't forget to include commas where necessary.**

who	which	when	where	whose	why

1 The coffee beans are put into sacks. The sacks are easier to transport.

2 He's the man. His sister married my brother.

3 The Rafflesia is a plant. It produces the largest flower in the world.

4 The animals tend to live in the east of the region. There is more vegetation there.

5 These are the tools. They date back 15,000 years.

6 He grew up in the 1970s. Life was much simpler then.

7 He's an artist. He discovered the hidden painting.

8 There are three reasons. I left my job.

9 They use this device in areas. The weather can change rapidly there.

10 That's the gadget. He invented it in 1999.

11 The technique was developed in 1890. Much less was known about this type of engineering then.

12 I was talking to the biology professor. He also participated in the earlier study.

20 Relative clauses (2)

Reduced relative clauses

We can sometimes shorten a relative clause by using a participle clause instead. We omit the relative pronoun and use a present or past participle.
We use the present participle (*-ing* form) when the verb in the relative clause is in the active.
*People **living** in this area use traditional agricultural methods.* (People **who live** in this area use traditional agricultural methods.)
*She is the one **wearing** the red jacket.* (She is the one **who is wearing** the red jacket.)

We use the past participle (*-ed* form in regular verbs) when the verb in the relative clause is in the passive.
*The soldier, **stationed** in a remote area known as the Wessel Islands, was named Maurie Isenberg.* (The soldier, **who was stationed** in a remote area known as the Wessel Islands, was named Maurie Isenberg.)
*The table, **made** in Italy, was worth $5 million.* (The table, **which had been made** in Italy, was worth $5 million.)

We can't use a reduced relative clause if the relative pronoun is the object of the relative clause.
The painting, which I have been working on for a year, will be in my next exhibition.
~~The painting working on for a year will be in my next exhibition.~~ ✗

We often used reduced relative clauses in announcements and reports.
Researchers working off the coast of Africa discovered the remains of the shipwreck.

who/whom

We sometimes use *whom* instead of *who* when it is the object of a relative clause. The relative pronouns *who* or *that* are more common in less formal situations.
*He was a colleague **whom** she had never met.*
*He was a colleague **who/that** she had never met.*

It is also possible to omit the relative pronoun as it is the object of the clause.
He was a colleague she had never met.

Prepositions in relative clauses

The relative pronouns *which* and *whom* can function as the object of a preposition. When we put the preposition before the relative pronoun, the sentence sounds more formal. (It is more usual to find the preposition at the end of the relative clause.)

*this world **in which** we are living* / *this world **which** we are living **in***

*a subject **about which** I am passionate* / *a subject **which** I am passionate **about***

*a friend **with whom** I am pleased* / *a friend **whom** I am pleased **with***

*an issue **to which** you are opposed* / *an issue **which** you are opposed **to***

We don't follow a preposition with *when, where* or *why*. When we want to talk about a time, place or reason, we use preposition + *which*.

Place

*It was a wonderful place **in which** we lived for 30 years.* ✓
*It was a wonderful place **in where** we lived for 30 years.* ✗

Time

*We talked about his time at university, **about which** much has been said.* ✓
*We talked about his time at university, **about when** much has been said.* ✗

Reason

*It was a foolish thing to do, **for which** I have no excuse.* ✓
*It was a foolish thing to do, **for why** I have no excuse.* ✗

Exercises

1 **Complete the sentences using a reduced relative clause from the information in brackets.**
   1 Students *wanting to register* should speak to an advisor first. (the ones who want to register)
   2 This pen, ... , is very special. (my father gave it to me),
   3 This is an announcement for passengers .... to Manchester. (the ones who want to travel)
   4 Anyone .... to get in touch can text me. (who needs)
   5 The necklace, ... , is valued at £10 million. (Queen Victoria wore it at her wedding)
   6 I lost the book .... the addresses of my friends. (that contained)
   7 The tree .... was over 500 years old. (the wind blew it down in the storm)
   8 The painting, ... , has been on display at the Louvre since 1797. (someone stole it in 1911 and someone else recovered it two years later)

2 **Rewrite the sentences in a more formal manner. Include a preposition in a relative clause.**
   1 Shakespeare married Anne Hathaway, who not much is known about.
      ....
   2 It was the stretch of sea that the children loved to swim in.
      ....
   3 Is this the book you are referring to?
      ....
   4 Who did he live with during his time at Cambridge?
      ....

21 Connectors/linkers

conjunction	*and, or, but, because, so, although*
preposition	*in spite of, despite, due to, because of*
adverb/adverbial	*however, nevertheless, also, moreover, therefore, furthermore*

We can connect two ideas using a conjunction, a preposition or an adverb/adverbial.

Conjunctions join two clauses. Some conjunctions are not usually found at the beginning of a written sentence.
*Magnetic resonance imaging scans can accurately measure body fat, **but** are very expensive.*
Prepositions usually come before a noun, pronoun or verb + *-ing*.
***Despite** the public protests, in late 2011 Seracini and his team were given permission to continue their work.*

Adverbs or adverbial phrases usually come at the beginning of a sentence; some can come in a number of positions.
***Furthermore**, O'Hara and Smith concluded it would be difficult to change the curriculum altogether.*
***Also**, it is apparent that standards vary.* / *It is **also** apparent that standards vary.*

Connectors can be used to contrast ideas, to introduce additional information, to give reasons, to present results and to express purpose.

Contrast

despite / in spite of (+ noun, pronoun, verb + *-ing*)

We use *despite* or *in spite of* at the beginning of a sentence or in the middle. When they are used at the beginning of the sentence, the clause is followed by a comma. In the middle of a sentence no comma is required.
***Despite** the bad weather conditions, the team completed the race.*
*Sales increased **in spite of** the higher prices.*
The phrase *the fact that* can be added to either *despite* or *in spite of*.
*She was civil to him **despite the fact that she didn't like him**.*

although / even though / though / while / whereas / but

We usually use *but* to contrast opposing ideas within one sentence.
*That story is still being written **but** some of the lessons of the past are being ignored.*

We use *although, even though* and *though* to contrast opposing ideas at the beginning of a sentence or in the middle. A comma usually divides the two clauses.
***Although** the research project isn't complete, it is possible to identify some preliminary findings.*
*This was one of the few tools available to combat infections and treat wounds, **although** in many cases the treatment was ineffective.*

We can also use *though* at the end of a sentence.
*We didn't know any of the others and didn't really like action films. We still went, **though**.*

> *however / nevertheless / even so / yet /*
> *on the other hand / on the contrary / in contrast*

These adverbs and adverbials link contrasting ideas in two sentences. They are often used at the beginning of a sentence, although many can appear in different parts of a sentence, usually separated by commas.

Mason lived and worked on the outskirts of Barcelona for seven years. **However**, *he doesn't speak a word of Spanish.*

In natural systems, nothing is wasted. Human manufacturers, **on the other hand**, *use large inputs of non-renewable energy.*

We use *while/whilst* and *whereas* to contrast opposing ideas at the beginning of a sentence or in the middle.
In the game of squash, a beginner's ball would have a blue dot, an advanced player's yellow, **whilst** *an intermediate player would use a ball with a red dot on it.*

Addition

> *and / also / as well as / furthermore / moreover*

We use these words and phrases to give further information, usually to support a point of view. We use them before subject + verb.
A living wage is not being paid to a large part of the population. **Moreover**, *as the cost of living soars, the problem is destined to get worse.*

Exercise

1 Choose the correct option.
1 Ben has not made good progress this term. *In contrast, / Nevertheless,* he is expected to pass his final exams.
2 *Although / In spite of* the network no longer airs the show, the series is available online.
3 Unlike its competitors, the supermarket chain has not shown a downturn this year. *On the contrary, / However,* it has shown a significant profit.
4 The show closed after twelve performances *whereas / despite* receiving positive reviews from Broadway's toughest critics.
5 I know I promised I would call you from Paris *but / whereas* I'm afraid I won't get the chance.
6 *While / Nevertheless* the new technology has enormous potential, it is still a new technique that requires further research.
7 *On the contrary / In contrast* to the morning, which will be wet and windy, the afternoon is going to be fine and sunny.
8 These animals can often be difficult to tell apart *however / in spite of* apparent differences in size and colour.

Giving reasons

because/as/since	+ subject + verb
because of/on account of/ owing to/due to	+ noun/pronoun/verb + *-ing*
owing to the fact that/due to the fact that	+ subject + verb

We use these expressions to introduce a reason for something.
She went to Los Angeles **because** *she wanted to work in the film industry.*
Any attempt to tweak the law won't happen until 2021 at the earliest, **since** *it doesn't even take effect until 2020.*
These areas may have disappeared **owing to** *a rise in sea levels over time.*
This variety became virtually extinct **due to** *the rapid spread of a fungal infection.*
Some have questioned the validity of the letter **due to the fact that** *it is not written on House of Commons stationery.*

Result

so/therefore/consequently/ thus/as a result of	+ subject + verb
as a result of/as a consequence of	+ noun/pronoun/verb + *-ing*

We use these words and phrases to introduce a result of something.
The computer system crashed. **Consequently** *the engineer had to reboot the system.*
He is only seventeen and **therefore** *not eligible to vote.*
He lost his job **as a result of** *downsizing but continued to work for the company on a freelance basis.*

While all the expressions can be used at the beginning of a sentence or in the middle of a sentence, *so* is more commonly used in the middle of a written sentence.
Ideas are always built upon other ideas, so it's important to find a solid starting point.

Purpose

to/in order (not) to/so as (not) to	+ infinitive (without *to*)
in order that/so that	+ subject + infinitive (usually a modal)

We use these words and phrases to express purpose.
She bought her clothes from a secondhand shop and wore neutral colours **so as not to** *stand out in a crowd.*
They have slashed their prices **in order to** *recover some of the market share they have lost in the last two years.*
He set up a webcam **so that** *the world at large could witness the event.*

Exercises

2 Complete the sentences with the words in the box.

> as a result   consequently   furthermore
> owing to

1 .... of poor planning, what should have been a great conference turned out to be a flop.
2 She knew they wouldn't come. .... , she didn't prepare any food.
3 Doctors believe some bacteria are more resistant nowadays .... the misuse of antibiotics.
4 Rubbish strewn around in the streets looks and smells unpleasant. .... , there are health issues concerning rats and other vermin.

therefore	in order to	since	so that

5 .... most biofuels cost more to produce than fossil fuels, the cost on motorists is set to rise.
6 This dress is lighter than my jeans, and .... more comfortable in this heat.
7 .... speed up the registration process, please complete the personal details online.
8 We collected our coats .... we could leave.

3 Complete the second sentence so that it means the same as the first. Use the word in brackets but don't change the form of the word.

1 The failure in the system was attributed to human error. (result)
The failure in the system happened .... human error.
2 The air traffic controllers went on strike so I missed my meeting in Stockholm. (consequence)
.... the air traffic controllers' strike, I missed my meeting in Stockholm.
3 She spoke Spanish fluently as her mother was Mexican. (owing)
Her spoken Spanish was flawless .... her mother was Mexican.
4 He implicated his best friend in the crime so that he wouldn't be suspected himself. (order)
He implicated his best friend in the crime .... suspected himself.
5 The tutor has given us an extension, enabling us to meet our deadline. (so)
The tutor has given us an extension .... our deadline.

22 Reported speech

Tense change

When we report what someone has said, we use reported speech. To make it clear that we are reporting, we often move the tense of the verb backwards in time.

Direct speech	Reported speech
Present simple I**'m** busy.	Past simple He said he **was** busy.
Present continuous We**'re waiting.**	Past continuous They said they **were waiting.**
Past simple She **left** earlier on.	Past perfect simple He said she **had left** earlier on
Past perfect simple We **had arrived** before our friends.	Past perfect simple He said that they **had arrived** before their friends.
Past continuous I **was staying** with friends. →	Past perfect continuous She said she **had been staying** with friends.
Present perfect simple I**'ve been** here twice.	Past perfect simple She said she **had been** there twice.
Present perfect continuous I've **been playing** tennis. be going to. I'm **going to** see her tomorrow.	Past perfect continuous He said he**'d been playing** tennis. was/were going to. She said she **was going to** see her the following day.

will They **will** win the cup this year.	would He said they **would** win the cup that year.
can We **can** go to college together.	could She said they **could** go to college together.
may The claims **may** relate to 6% of students.	might They said the claims **might** relate to 6% of students.
must You **must** do your homework.	had to. She said we **had to** do our homework.

Time and place change

We also need to make changes to other words when referring to time or place.

yesterday → *the day before/the previous day*
last night → *the evening before/the previous evening*
today → *that day*
now → *then*
tomorrow → *the day after/the following day*
next week → *the week after/the following week*
here → *there*
this → *that*

No change

We can choose not to change the verb:
• if the reported statement refers to something which is still in progress, or true.
*I **have** a house in Brighton* → *She said she **had** a house in Brighton* / *She said she **has** a house in Brighton.*
• if the original statement uses a verb form which is already moved back as far as it will go, for example: the past perfect and modal verbs *would, could, should* and *might*.
*They **hadn't thought** of that.* → *He said they **hadn't thought** of that.*

Reporting verbs

The most common three verbs used when reporting are *say, tell* and *think*. However, other verbs give more specific information about how the original statement was made.

verb + *that*
*He later **admitted that** he'd made up the original figures.*

> Used with: *admit, agree, announce, argue, believe, claim, complain, deny, explain, insist, promise, propose, reply, request, say, state, suggest, think*

verb + *someone* + *that*
*They **informed him that** his proposal had been accepted.*

> Used with: *advise, assure, persuade, remind, tell, warn*

verb + *to* + infinitive
*The company **had threatened to pull** out of the deal.*

> Used with: *agree, ask, claim, offer, promise, propose, refuse, threaten*

verb + *someone* + *to* + infinitive
*Chloe's professor **reminded her to submit** her article to the journal.*

> Used with: *advise, ask, convince, encourage, invite, persuade, remind, tell, urge, warn*

verb + *someone* + noun
*They **promised him a research position.***

> Used with: *offer, promise, refuse*

verb + *-ing* / noun
*The chairman **suggested finishing** the meeting early.*

> Used with: *admit, deny, mention, propose, recommend, suggest*

verb + preposition + *-ing* / noun
*They **apologised for releasing** the upgrade before it had been properly tested.*

> Used with: *argue about, complain about, apologise for, insist on*

verb + *someone* + preposition + *-ing* / noun
*He **thanked his family for being** patient with him while he wrote the book.*

> Used with: *accuse of, advise about, remind about, warn about, advise on, congratulate on, blame for, thank for*

Reporting questions

When reporting questions, we change the verb in the same way as we do for statements. However, there is no question mark and we use statement word order.
When is the deadline? → *She asked me when the deadline was.* (~~She asked me when was the deadline?~~ ✗)
Question words (*what, who, why, where, when, how*) remain in the same form.

When reporting questions which require a *yes/no* answer, we use *if/whether* and we don't use the auxiliary *do/does/did*.
Does the moon affect human behaviour? → *He asked if the moon affected human behaviour.* (~~He asked did the moon affect human behaviour.~~ ✗)

Exercises

1   Underline the correct option.
1   Mr Grant *reminded / congratulated* me about the awards ceremony the following month.
2   They *assured / agreed* us that the meeting would go ahead as planned.
3   We *refused / denied* taking anything without first paying for it.
4   She *blamed / accused* the restaurant of overcharging.
5   They *proposed / persuaded* us to accept their offer.
6   The principal *promised / recommended* to include a special note of thanks to the organisers of the marathon in her end of term speech.
7   They *argued / insisted* on staying in the cheapest hotel in town.
8   Ben *told / announced* that he intended to stand as a candidate in the college elections.

2   Complete the second sentence as a report of the first.
1   I will see them tomorrow.
    She told us ....
2   You have to make your minds up here and now.
    He said that ....
3   Can we deal with this issue next week?
    She asked ....
4   Simon asked me this question yesterday.
    I said that Simon ....

5   Why can't we go to Sue's today?
    He asked us ....
6   Are you going to be late tonight?
    She asked me ....
7   They have lived here for twenty years.
    He told us ....

23 Verb patterns

Sometimes one verb form follows another in a sentence. When this happens, the second verb can take various forms depending on the first verb. We call these verb patterns.

Verb + infinitive or *-ing*

Verb + infinitive	
verb + *to* + infinitive	*They **chose to go** to Canada for their research project.*
verb + object + *to* + infinitive	*I'd **advise you to arrive** early.*
verb + object + infinitive (without *to*)	*They **watched the chicks hatch**.*

Verb + *-ing*	
verb + *-ing*	*I **enjoy listening** to current affairs programmes.*
verb + object + *-ing*	*He **kept the project going** in spite of the difficulties.*

Verb + *to* + infinitive

*They **decided to wait** and see the results before making their decision.*
Verbs with this pattern include: *agree, aim, appear, arrange, ask, attempt, be able, be likely, choose, claim, dare, decide, deserve, expect, fail, help, hope, intend, invite, learn, manage, need, offer, plan, prefer, prepare, promise, refuse, seem, tend, try, want*

Verb + object + *to* + infinitive

Some verbs are followed by an object + *to* + infinitive.
*Laura's teacher **expected her to fail** her exam, but she came top of her class.*
These include: *advise, allow, ask, choose, dare, encourage, expect, force, get, help, intend, invite, need, persuade, prefer, prepare, remind, teach, tell, want, warn*
The underlined verbs can be used with or without an object.
Used with: *feel, hear, help, let, make, see, watch*

Verb + object + infinitive (without *to*)

The most common taught verbs in this category are *make* and *let*. The verb *help* can be used with or without *to*.
*She **helped him** (to) **understand** Newton's Laws of Motion.*
Used with: *feel, hear, help, let, make, see, watch*

Verb + *-ing*

Some verbs are followed by *-ing*.
*She **considered abandoning** her career at the hospital.*
avoid, can't help, consider, deny, dislike, enjoy, fancy, finish, imagine, include, involve, keep, like, love, mention, (don't) mind, miss, postpone, practise, recommend, remember, report, resist, risk, (can't) stand, stop, suggest

Verb + *-ing* or *to* + infinitive

Some verbs can be followed by *-ing* or *to* + infinitive with little or no change in meaning.
*The particles started **to accelerate/accelerating**.*
These include: *attempt, begin, bother, can't bear, continue, hate, like, love, need, prefer, start*

Verb + object + *-ing*

Some verbs are followed by an object + *-ing*.
*I **saw her walking** into the shop.*
These include: *dislike, hate, imagine, involve, keep, like, love, mind, remember, risk, see, stop*
All these verbs can be used with or without an object
Some verbs can be used with both forms, but the meaning changes.

continue/go on

*He **went on working** long after everyone else had gone home.* (= continue an action)
*After working as a TV reporter, she **went on to become** a politician.* (one action is followed by another)

forget

*I'll never **forget meeting** you.* (= it happened and I won't forget it)
*I **forgot to call** you.* (= it didn't happen because I forgot)

remember

*I **remember meeting** him.* (= it happened and I remember the event)
*I didn't **remember to write** to him.* (= it didn't happen because I didn't remember to do it)

stop

*I **stopped speaking** to Joe.* (= one action happened)
*I **stopped to speak** to Joe.* (= two actions happened. The first stops so that the second can start.)

try

***Try holding** your breath for two minutes.* (= used to give a suggestion)
*Could you **try to keep** quiet for the next few minutes?* (= attempt to do something potentially difficult)

Verb + preposition + *-ing*

Certain verbs are followed by certain prepositions. Some can be followed by more than one preposition, depending on the meaning. When a verb follows a preposition it takes the *-ing* form.
about: *Many undergraduates these days **worry** less **about** their final exams than their job prospects beyond university.*
Used with: *complain, hear, know, learn, talk, think, warn, wonder, worry, write*
between: *It is easy to **differentiate between** an atom and an element.*
Used with: *choose, decide, differentiate, distinguish, divide*
for: *They spent years **searching for** the answer.*
Used with: *aim, apologise, apply, ask, care, forgive, hope, long, prepare, search, wait, watch, wish*
from: *A good password will **protect** you **from** computer viruses.*
Used with: *borrow, learn, prevent, protect, recover, save, suffer*
in: *She is a lawyer who **specialises in** corporate mergers.*
Used with: *believe, specialise, succeed*
of: *She did not **approve of** the use of water cannons.*
Used with: *approve, assure, convince, die, smell*

on: *Evans agreed to **concentrate on** his own studies*
Used with: *agree, base, concentrate, count, depend, insist, rely*
to: *Guest speakers will be expected to **respond to** questions they have not seen or prepared for.*
Used with: *apologise (to someone for something), explain, introduce, present, refer, respond, speak, talk, write*
with: *Volunteers will be **provided with** sacks to collect the litter and debris.*
Used with: *agree, be, deal, play, provide, stay*

Exercises

1 Choose the correct option.

Harvey decided **1** *applying / to apply* to the University of Southern California to study business. His parents warned him not **2** *abandoning / to abandon* his research but he was determined. It was harder than he thought.
He didn't mind **3** *working / to work* long hours, but he didn't understand business. He considered **4** *leaving / to leave* more than once. He let his teachers **5** *thinking / think* he was keeping up, but he wasn't. Eventually, it was his friend Westcott, who helped him **6** *getting / get* through that first semester. After that he stopped **7** *worrying / to worry* and started **8** *enjoying / to enjoy* his studies. Two months after graduating, he was invited **9** *starting / to start* up a new department at a hospital in London.

2 Complete the sentences with the words in the box in the correct form.

announce	conduct	eat	fix	get	live	pass
play						

1 Do you expect .... your exam?
2 Kieran promised .... my computer.
3 Do you enjoy .... computer games?
4 I love this place but I can't imagine .... here.
5 You should avoid .... food high in refined sugar if you want to lose weight.
6 She would prefer .... the findings at the conference.
7 The partners are considering .... together to discuss marketing strategies.
8 I intend .... a series of experiments to prove this theory.

24 Prepositions

Most prepositions have more than one meaning, depending on the context. In this unit we look at prepositions of time (***at** midday*) and place (***at** the supermarket*).

Prepositions of time

We use *in, on* and *at* to describe different times.

at (precise time, holiday periods)	*at six o'clock, at noon, at the weekend, at sunrise, at lunchtime, at the moment, at New Year*
in (periods of time, future 'from now')	*in the evening, in the summer, in December, in 2012, in the 1990s, in five minutes, in an hour, in two years*

on (days (and parts of days), dates)	on Wednesday, on New Year's Day, on my birthday, on Monday morning, on Sunday evening, on May 15th, 6th August 1945, on 1st April 2014

We use *in* to talk about periods of time (days, weeks, months, years, centuries) and we also use it to talk about the point at the end of a period of time.

I'll be there in twenty minutes. (I will arrive at the end of a twenty-minute period.)

We don't use a preposition of time with the words *yesterday, today, tomorrow* or the phrases *last, this, next.*

Other commonly used prepositions and prepositional phrases of time include:

for	We usually stay with Michel **for** at least a month every year.
since	They've lived in Berlin **since** the 1990s.
during/in	We visited my grandmother **during/in** the summer vacation.
by	Can we finish this **by** Tuesday?
until	We have **until** 8 p.m. to get this finished.
in time	I thought I was going to be late, but the traffic cleared and I got there just **in time**.
on time	Unlike my rail travel experiences in Germany and Japan, the trains here never seem to run **on time**.

Prepositions of place

We use *in, on* and *at* to describe different places:

at (next to something, located at a point)	at the table, at my desk, at the bus stop, at the corner, at home, at the end of the pier, at work, at the door
in (enclosed spaces, cities, countries, continents)	in the bank, in the garden, in a car, in Madrid, in South Korea, in America, in his suitcase, in my pocket
on (attached to/ touching something)	on the table, on the TV, on the coast, on an island, on the phone, on a train, on a bus, on the menu

We use *at* to describe a general visit, whereas *in* puts a greater emphasis on the 'enclosed' element.

Compare: *I am in the bank* (I am within the walls of the bank building) with *I am at the bank* (I'm visiting the bank, probably for a transactional purpose).

Other commonly used prepositions and prepositional phrases of place include:

opposite	The gift shop is **opposite** the entrance.
in front of	There is a statue **in front** of the library.
behind	The car park is **behind** the sports centre.
near	The airport is **near** the business park.
next to	The bank is **next to** the hotel.
between	There is a water fountain **between** the sports hall and the gym.

above	The instructions are **above** the graph.
below	Look at the diagram **below**.
under	Instead of cleaning properly, he simply sweeps the dirt **under** the carpet.
on top of	The advertising board is **on top of** the telecom building.

Exercises

1 **Choose the correct preposition of time to complete the sentence.**

1 They made the announcement *on / the* Tuesday.
2 Shall we meet *at / for* lunchtime?
3 The agreement was signed *in / on* May 2014.
4 We thought we would miss dinner, but we managed to get back *in / on* time.
5 This project has been running *for / since* a long time.
6 Are you able to finish this *by / until* the end of the day?
7 The baby is due *in / on* July.
8 They have *by / until* the end of the month to vacate the property.

2 **Complete the sentences with the words from the box. Sometimes more than one answer is possible.**

above	at	between	in	in front of
next to	on	opposite		

1 The cafeteria is .... the box office and the main auditorium.
2 You'll see the admissions office directly .... reception.
3 High .... the clouds, we could see the white vapour trail from the jet against the blue sky.
4 Mr Bartlett is not in his office at the moment. He will be back .... his desk this afternoon.
5 The twins were born .... Russia and moved to the United States when they were two.
6 The statue was .... the main entrance so you saw it when you left the building.
7 The office used to be on the first floor, but now it's .... the second floor.
8 The bathroom is at the end of the corridor, ... the fire exit.

Common Irregular Verbs

infinitive	past simple	past participle
be	was/were	been
become	became	become
begin	began	begun
break	broke	broken
bring	brought	brought
build	built	built
buy	bought	bought
choose	chose	chosen
come	came	come
cost	cost	cost
do	did	done
draw	drew	drawn
drink	drank	drunk
drive	drove	driven
eat	ate	eaten
feel	felt	felt
find	found	found
forget	forgot	forgotten
get	got	got
give	gave	given
go	went	gone/been
have	had	had
hear	heard	heard
hold	held	held
keep	kept	kept
know	knew	known
learn	learnt	learnt
leave	left	left
let	let	let
lose	lost	lost
make	made	made
mean	meant	meant
meet	met	met
pay	paid	paid
put	put	put
rise	rose	risen
run	ran	run
say	said	said
see	saw	seen
sell	sold	sold
send	sent	sent
sit	sat	sat
sleep	slept	slept
speak	spoke	spoken
spend	spent	spent
stand	stood	stood
take	took	taken
teach	taught	taught
tell	told	told
think	thought	thought
wear	wore	worn
win	won	won
write	wrote	written

Basic Rules for Punctuation

End punctuation

In academic writing, most sentences will end with a full stop.
I agree with the idea that advertisements for cigarettes should be banned.

Questions end with a question mark.
What are some ways to reduce air pollution?

Exclamation marks (!) are seldom used in academic writing.

Commas

Often, the use of a comma (,) is optional – you can use one or not. However, there are some cases when you should definitely use commas.

1. **Before introductory phrases**
   ***In 1945**, Indonesia became an independent nation.*
   ***In my opinion**, there are several reasons to disagree with this concept.*
   ***Generally**, there is more than one solution to any problem.*

2. **Between nouns or phrases in a list**
   The researcher gathered information from books, journal articles, television shows and websites.
   The final comma (before the word *and*) is usually not used in British English. In US English, it is usually used.

3. **When there are two or more adjectives describing a noun. There is never a comma after the final adjective.**
   an expensive, powerful car ...
   some thin, high clouds ...

4. **Use a comma to separate place names when one place is part of another.**
   Sydney, New South Wales, Australia
   Denver, Colorado, USA

5. **A comma follows a subordinate clause if the subordinate clause comes first in the sentence. If the main clause comes first, no comma is needed.**
   Although I agree that there is too much violence on television, I don't think the government should censor shows.
   I don't think the government should censor shows although I agree that there is too much violence on television.
   When energy prices rise, people buy more economical cars.
   People buy more economical cars when energy prices rise.

6. **After connecting words such as *therefore, furthermore* and *however*.**
   I don't like the idea of putting animals in a zoo; however, I agree that zoos serve some useful functions.
   Police officers and firefighters have dangerous jobs. Therefore, it is only fair that they receive decent wages.

Inverted commas (quotation marks or speech marks)

Inverted commas (' ') or (" ") are used around direct quotes (but not around indirect quotes).

John Lennon said, 'Life is what happens while you are busy making other plans.'

Oscar Wilde once wrote that he was not young enough to know everything.

Notice that a comma is used before a direct quote (but not an indirect quote).

Colons (:)

Colons are used before a list.

Ms. Vasquez imports tropical fruit: pineapples, mangos, and guavas.

Apostrophes

Apostrophes (') are used in place of omitted letters in contractions.

*I **can't** agree with this argument.*

***There's** one critical reason why I disagree with this idea.*

Apostrophes are also used to show possession. For singular nouns, the possessive form is *'s*.

*The **boy's** bicycle ... (one boy)*

*The **city's** problems ... (one city)*

For plural nouns that end in *s*, the possessive form is *s'*.

*The **boys'** bicycles ... (more than one boy)*

*The **cities'** problems ... (more than one city)*

For plural nouns that don't end in *s*, the possessive form is *'s*.

***women's** rights, **children's** imaginations*

Do NOT use an apostrophe to make nouns plural.

I am sure that most experts agree ... (NOT I am sure that most ~~expert's~~ agree ...)

Note that an apostrophe is used for the contraction *it's (it is)* but not for the possessive pronoun *its*.

***It's** important to look at both sides of this issue.*

*My city has a serious traffic problem. **Its** streets are jammed with cars.*

Basic Rules for Capitalisation

1 Capitalise the first word of a sentence.

   ***T**oday, people have less and less privacy.*

   ***G**lobalisation has had a profound effect on many cultures.*

2 Capitalise the first word of a direct quote but not of an indirect quote.

   *The critic Edward R. Murrow once said, '**T**elevision is a vast wasteland.'*

   *U.S. President Franklin D. Roosevelt said that **w**e have nothing to fear but fear itself.*

3 Capitalise the pronoun *I*.

   *While many people think old buildings should be torn down and replaced with new ones, **I** think most old buildings should be preserved.*

4 Capitalise names and titles if the title comes before the name. Do not capitalise the title if it is given as a description of a person. Do not capitalise a person's profession if it comes before the name.

   *I admire **P**resident **J**ohn **F**. **K**ennedy for several reasons.*

   ***N**elson **M**andela, who was president of South Africa ...*

   *The **a**stronomer **J**ohannes **K**epler is most famous for ...*

5 Capitalise the names of months, days of the week, and of holidays, but not of seasons.

   ***N**ew **Y**ear's **D**ay comes in **w**inter in the United States but in **s**ummer in Australia.*

   *My father will be 50 years old on the first **F**riday in **J**uly.*

6 Capitalise place names: the names of continents, countries, oceans and seas, states and provinces, cities, rivers, buildings, etc. (but not the word *the*).

   Africa   **S**outh **A**merica   **P**aris   **B**angkok   **N**ew **Z**ealand
   Kenya   **C**alifornia   **Q**uebec   the **T**hames **R**iver
   the **N**ile   the **P**acific **O**cean   the **M**editerranean **S**ea
   Petronas **T**owers   the **W**hite **H**ouse

7 Capitalise the names of wars, historical periods and special events.

   World **W**ar I   the **T**rojan **W**ar
   the **R**enaissance   the **M**iddle **A**ges   the **O**lympics

8 Capitalise all of the letters in initials and acronyms (but not the word *the*).

   the **UK**   **NYC**   **NATO**   the **EU**   **NASA**   the **UN**

9 Capitalise the names of newspapers and magazines.

   The London Times   Time Magazine   Paris Match

Band	Task achievement	Coherence and cohesion	Lexical resource	Grammatical range and accuracy
9	• fully satisfies all the requirements of the task • clearly presents a fully developed response	• uses cohesion in such a way that it attracts no attention • skilfully manages paragraphing	• uses a wide range of vocabulary with very natural and sophisticated control of lexical features; rare minor errors occur only as 'slips'	• uses a wide range of structures with full flexibility and accuracy; rare minor errors occur only as 'slips'
8	• covers all requirements of the task sufficiently • presents, highlights and illustrates key features/ bullet points clearly and appropriately	• sequences information and ideas logically • manages all aspects of cohesion well • uses paragraphing sufficiently and appropriately	• uses a wide range of vocabulary fluently and flexibly to convey precise meanings • skilfully uses uncommon lexical items but there may be occasional inaccuracies in word choice and collocation • produces rare errors in spelling and/or word formation	• uses a wide range of structures • the majority of sentences are error-free • makes only very occasional errors or inappropriacies
7	• covers the requirements of the task • (A) presents a clear overview of main trends, differences or stages • (GT) presents a clear purpose, with the tone consistent and appropriate • clearly presents and highlights key features/bullet points but could be more fully extended	• logically organises information and ideas; there is clear progression throughout • uses a range of cohesive devices appropriately although there may be some under-/over-use	• uses a sufficient range of vocabulary to allow some flexibility and precision • uses less common lexical items with some awareness of style and collocation • may produce occasional errors in word choice, spelling and/or word formation	• uses a variety of complex structures • produces frequent error-free sentences • has good control of grammar and punctuation but may make a few errors
6	• addresses the requirements of the task • (A) presents an overview with information appropriately selected • (GT) presents a purpose that is generally clear; there may be inconsistencies in tone • presents and adequately highlights key features/bullet points but details may be irrelevant, inappropriate or inaccurate	• arranges information and ideas coherently and there is a clear overall progression • uses cohesive devices effectively, but cohesion within and/or between sentences may be faulty or mechanical • may not always use referencing clearly or appropriately	• uses an adequate range of vocabulary for the task • attempts to use less common vocabulary but with some inaccuracy • makes some errors in spelling and/or word formation, but they do not impede communication	• uses a mix of simple and complex sentence forms • makes some errors in grammar and punctuation but they rarely reduce communication
5	• generally addresses the task; the format may be inappropriate in places • (A) recounts detail mechanically with no clear overview; there may be no data to support the description • (GT) may present a purpose for the letter that is unclear at times; the tone may be variable and sometimes inappropriate • presents, but inadequately covers, key features/ bullet points; there may be a tendency to focus on details	• presents information with some organisation but there may be a lack of overall progression • makes inadequate, inaccurate or over-use of cohesive devices • may be repetitive because of lack of referencing and substitution	• uses a limited range of vocabulary, but this is minimally adequate for the task • may make noticeable errors in spelling and/or word formation that may cause some difficulty for the reader	• uses only a limited range of structures • attempts complex sentences but these tend to be less accurate than simple sentences • may make frequent grammatical errors and punctuation may be faulty; errors can cause some difficulty for the reader
4	• attempts to address the task but does not cover all key features/bullet points; the format may be inappropriate • (GT) fails to clearly explain the purpose of the letter; the tone may be inappropriate • may confuse key features/bullet points with detail; parts may be unclear, irrelevant, repetitive or inaccurate	• presents information and ideas but these are not arranged coherently and there is no clear progression in the response • uses some basic cohesive devices but these may be inaccurate or repetitive	• uses only basic vocabulary which may be used repetitively or which may be inappropriate for the task • has limited control of word formation and/or spelling; errors may cause strain for the reader	• uses only a very limited range of structures with only rare use of subordinate clauses • some structures are accurate but errors predominate, and punctuation is often faulty
3	• fails to address the task, which may have been completely misunderstood • presents limited ideas which may be largely irrelevant/repetitive	• does not organise ideas logically • may use a very limited range of cohesive devices, and those used may not indicate a logical relationship between ideas	• uses only a very limited range of words and expressions with very limited control of word formation and/or spelling • errors may severely distort the message	• attempts sentence forms but errors in grammar and punctuation predominate and distort the meaning
2	• answer is barely related to the task	• has very little control of organisational features	• uses an extremely limited range of vocabulary; essentially no control of word formation and/or spelling	• cannot use sentence forms except in memorised phrases
1	• answer is completely unrelated to the task	• fails to communicate any message	• can only use a few isolated words	• cannot use sentence forms at all
0	• does not attend • does not attempt the task in any way • writes a totally memorised response			

(A) Academic | (GT) General Training

WRITING TASK 2: Band Descriptors

Band	Task response	Coherence and cohesion	Lexical resource	Grammatical range and accuracy
9	• fully addresses all parts of the task • presents a fully developed position in answer to the question with relevant, fully extended and well supported ideas	• uses cohesion in such a way that it attracts no attention • skilfully manages paragraphing	• uses a wide range of vocabulary with very natural and sophisticated control of lexical features; rare minor errors occur only as 'slips'	• uses a wide range of structures with full flexibility and accuracy; rare minor errors occur only as 'slips'
8	• sufficiently addresses all parts of the task • presents a well-developed response to the question with relevant, extended and supported ideas	• sequences information and ideas logically • manages all aspects of cohesion well • uses paragraphing sufficiently and appropriately	• uses a wide range of vocabulary fluently and flexibly to convey precise meanings • skilfully uses uncommon lexical items but there may be occasional inaccuracies in word choice and collocation • produces rare errors in spelling and/or word formation	• uses a wide range of structures • the majority of sentences are error-free • makes only very occasional errors or inappropriacies
7	• addresses all parts of the task • presents a clear position throughout the response • presents, extends and supports main ideas, but there may be a tendency to over-generalise and/or supporting ideas may lack focus	• logically organises information and ideas; there is clear progression throughout the response • uses a range of cohesive devices appropriately although there may be some under-/over-use • presents a clear central topic within each paragraph	• uses a sufficient range of vocabulary to allow some flexibility and precision • uses less common lexical items with some awareness of style and collocation • may produce occasional errors in word choice, spelling and/or word formation	• uses a variety of complex structures • produces frequent error-free sentences • has good control of grammar and punctuation but may make a few errors
6	• addresses all parts of the task although some parts may be more fully covered than others • presents a relevant position although the conclusions may become unclear or repetitive • presents relevant main ideas but some may be inadequately developed/unclear	• arranges information and ideas coherently and there is a clear overall progression • uses cohesive devices effectively, but cohesion within and/or between sentences may be faulty or mechanical • may not always use referencing clearly or appropriately • uses paragraphing, but not always logically	• uses an adequate range of vocabulary for the task • attempts to use less common vocabulary but with some inaccuracy • makes some errors in spelling and/or word formation, but they do not impede communication	• uses a mix of simple and complex sentence forms • makes some errors in grammar and punctuation but they rarely reduce communication
5	• addresses the task only partially; the format may be inappropriate in places • expresses a position but the development is not always clear and there may be no conclusions drawn • presents some main ideas but these are limited and not sufficiently developed; there may be irrelevant detail	• presents information with some organisation but there may be a lack of overall progression • makes inadequate, inaccurate or over-use of cohesive devices • may be repetitive because of lack of referencing and substitution • may not write in paragraphs, or paragraphing may be inadequate	• uses a limited range of vocabulary, but this is minimally adequate for the task • may make noticeable errors in spelling and/or word formation that may cause some difficulty for the reader	• uses only a limited range of structures • attempts complex sentences but these tend to be less accurate than simple sentences • may make frequent grammatical errors and punctuation may be faulty; errors can cause some difficulty for the reader
4	• responds to the task only in a minimal way or the answer is tangential; the format may be inappropriate • presents a position but this is unclear • presents some main ideas but these are difficult to identify and may be repetitive, irrelevant or not well supported	• presents information and ideas but these are not arranged coherently and there is no clear progression in the response • uses some basic cohesive devices but these may be inaccurate or repetitive • may not write in paragraphs or their use may be confusing	• uses only basic vocabulary which may be used repetitively or which may be inappropriate for the task • has limited control of word formation and/or spelling; errors may cause strain for the reader	• uses only a very limited range of structures with only rare use of subordinate clauses • some structures are accurate but errors predominate, and punctuation is often faulty
3	• does not adequately address any part of the task • does not express a clear position • presents few ideas, which are largely undeveloped or irrelevant	• does not organise ideas logically • may use a very limited range of cohesive devices, and those used may not indicate a logical relationship between ideas	• uses only a very limited range of words and expressions with very limited control of word formation and/or spelling • errors may severely distort the message	• attempts sentence forms but errors in grammar and punctuation predominate and distort the meaning
2	• barely responds to the task • does not express a position • may attempt to present one or two ideas but there is no development	• has very little control of organisational features	• uses an extremely limited range of vocabulary; essentially no control of word formation and/or spelling	• cannot use sentence forms except in memorised phrases
1	• answer is completely unrelated to the task	• fails to communicate any message	• can only use a few isolated words	• cannot use sentence forms at all
0	• does not attend • does not attempt the task in any way • writes a totally memorised response			

SPEAKING: Band Descriptors

Band	Fluency and coherence	Lexical resource	Grammatical range and accuracy	Pronunciation
9	• speaks fluently with only rare repetition or self-correction; any hesitation is content-related rather than to find words or grammar • speaks coherently with fully appropriate cohesive features • develops topics fully and appropriately	• uses vocabulary with full flexibility and precision in all topics • uses idiomatic language naturally and accurately	• uses a full range of structures naturally and appropriately • produces consistently accurate structures apart from 'slips' characteristic of native speaker speech	• uses a full range of pronunciation features with precision and subtlety • sustains flexible use of features throughout • is effortless to understand
8	• speaks fluently with only occasional repetition or self-correction; hesitation is usually content-related and only rarely to search for language • develops topics coherently and appropriately	• uses a wide vocabulary resource readily and flexibly to convey precise meaning • uses less common and idiomatic vocabulary skilfully, with occasional inaccuracies • uses paraphrase effectively as required	• uses a wide range of structures flexibly • produces a majority of error-free sentences with only very occasional inappropriacies or basic/non-systematic errors	• uses a wide range of pronunciation features • sustains flexible use of features, with only occasional lapses • is easy to understand throughout; L1 accent has minimal effect on intelligibility
7	• speaks at length without noticeable effort or loss of coherence • may demonstrate language-related hesitation at times, or some repetition and/or self-correction • uses a range of connectives and discourse markers with some flexibility	• uses vocabulary resource flexibly to discuss a variety of topics • uses some less common and idiomatic vocabulary and shows some awareness of style and collocation, with some inappropriate choices • uses paraphrase effectively	• uses a range of complex structures with some flexibility • frequently produces error-free sentences, though some grammatical mistakes persist	• shows all the positive features of Band 6 and some, but not all, of the positive features of Band 8
6	• is willing to speak at length, though may lose coherence at times due to occasional repetition, self-correction or hesitation • uses a range of connectives and discourse markers but not always appropriately	• has a wide enough vocabulary to discuss topics at length and make meaning clear in spite of inappropriacies • generally paraphrases successfully	• uses a mix of simple and complex structures, but with limited flexibility • may make frequent mistakes with complex structures though these rarely cause comprehension problems	• uses a range of pronunciation features with mixed control • shows some effective use of features but this is not sustained • can generally be understood throughout, though mispronunciation of individual words or sounds reduces clarity at times
5	• usually maintains flow of speech but uses repetition, self-correction and/or slow speech to keep going • may over-use certain connectives and discourse markers • produces simple speech fluently, but more complex communication causes fluency problems	• manages to talk about familiar and unfamiliar topics but uses vocabulary with limited flexibility • attempts to use paraphrase but with mixed success	• produces basic sentence forms with reasonable accuracy • uses a limited range of more complex structures, but these usually contain errors and may cause some comprehension problems	• shows all the positive features of Band 4 and some, but not all, of the positive features of Band 6
4	• cannot respond without noticeable pauses and may speak slowly, with frequent repetition and self-correction • links basic sentences but with repetitious use of simple connectives and some breakdowns in coherence	• is able to talk about familiar topics but can only convey basic meaning on unfamiliar topics and makes frequent errors in word choice • rarely attempts paraphrase	• produces basic sentence forms and some correct simple sentences but subordinate structures are rare • errors are frequent and may lead to misunderstanding	• uses a limited range of pronunciation features • attempts to control features but lapses are frequent • mispronunciations are frequent and cause some difficulty for the listener
3	• speaks with long pauses • has limited ability to link simple sentences • gives only simple responses and is frequently unable to convey basic message	• uses simple vocabulary to convey personal information • has insufficient vocabulary for less familiar topics	• attempts basic sentence forms but with limited success, or relies on apparently memorised utterances • makes numerous errors except in memorised expressions	• shows some of the features of Band 2 and some, but not all, of the positive features of Band 4
2	• pauses lengthily before most words • little communication possible	• only produces isolated words or memorised utterances	• cannot produce basic sentence forms	• speech is often unintelligible
1	• no communication possible • no rateable language			
0	• does not attend			

333

SAMPLE WRITING ANSWERS

Task 1 Line Graphs

B IELTS PRACTICE TASK (page 185)

The information illustrated in the graph indicates how the use of technology for watching TV changed in recent years in one city in the United States. Essentially, use of the internet rose dramatically, satellite rose slightly, wereas broadcast and cable both fell.

In 2004 cable and broadcast were the principal methods for watching TV in this city between about 70 and 100,000 households. The internet however was little utilised. In next ten years great changes occurred. Use of broadcast fell from being the most widespread way of watching TV to the least common, with very few households watching broadcast TV in 2014. Use of cable had been popular with over 80,000 households, but only 60,000 households used it by 2014.

Satellite viewing showed a gradual rise in the number of households using it from approximately 70,000 to 110,000. Use of the internet rose significantly from almost nill to virtually 200,000 households using it in 2014.

Band Score: 8

Task Achievement: 8 There is a clear overview and all the main features are covered accurately and sufficiently. There is scope for more development, as it is only just long enough at 157 words.

Coherence and Cohesion: 8 Information is arranged clearly and logically. Paragraphs are used appropriately, and ideas and information are linked. There is some repetition that could have been avoided.

Lexical Resource: 8 There is a good range of vocabulary, used flexibly, with some less common words and phrases, but there could be more variety in choice of words to describe rises and falls. There are two spelling mistakes.

Grammatical Range and Accuracy: 8 A wide range of structures are used, and most sentences are accurate. There are a few minor punctuation errors and inconsistencies.

D IELTS PRACTICE TASK (page 193)

Sample answer 1

the graph below show how teenager children aged 12–19 in America communicate each other every day use text message call on cell phone talk face to face or email to each person is november 2006 between September 2009

the first things we can see clearly in the graph is that text message most popular communicate method only 28% of all tenagers in november 2006 it is climb slightly become 52% of all teenager september 2009 then we can sees clearly in the graph is call on cell phone is almost same is 34% of all teenager november 2006 to 38% of all teenager september 2009 then we can see clearly the graph is talk face to face is go up and down dramatically is 31% of all teenager november 2006 to 38% all teenager november 2007 is 29% of all teenager feburary 2008 is 32% all tenager 2009 then we cans see clearly the graph is last is email is plunge immediately is 14% of all tennager november 2006 is 9 % all teenager september 2009

in summary we can see clearly in the graph in that text message is most popular for teenagir communicate november 2006 up to septebmer 2009

Band Score: 5.5

Task Achievement: 6 The writer addresses the requirements of the task by presenting an overview with information appropriately selected.

Coherence and Cohesion: 5 Information is presented with some organisation although some cohesive devices are over-used. The answer is repetitive because of a lack of referencing and substitution.

Lexical Resource: 5 The writer uses a limited range of vocabulary, which is minimally adequate for the task. Noticeable errors in spelling and word formation cause some difficulty for the reader.

Grammatical Range and Accuracy: 5 Only a limited range of structures is used. Frequent grammatical and punctuation errors cause some difficulty for the reader.

Sample answer 2

The graph presents data concerning communication by teenagers in the USA between November 2006 and September 2009. The most striking feature is the sharp rise in text messaging, while other methods of communication for teenagers kept a fairly similar level with minor fluctaution.

The level of text messaging by teenagers approached 30% in November 2006 and rose steadily to just under 40% but then in February 2008 it climbed rapidly to become a common means of communication for over half of US teenagers. Using a cell phone to make calls, on the other hand, remained fairly flat with a negligible rise from approximately 35 to 38%. In the same area of the graph figures for talking face-to-face fluctauted between 30 and 39%, while email remains more of a minority method for teenagers, fairly level at around 15% but then there has been a drop to below 10% by September 2009.

Band Score: 8

Task Achievement: 8 The information shown in the graph is covered sufficiently with key features described and supported with figures. It could be more fully developed, as the description is just 150 words long.

Coherence and Cohesion: 8 Information is arranged clearly and logically in paragraphs and information is clearly linked. There is repetition of 'while' and 'but then' and the word 'teenagers' is used five times.

Lexical Resource: 8 There is a wide range of vocabulary, which is used flexibly, but there are three spelling mistakes.

Grammatical Range and Accuracy: 8 Tenses are used accurately, and subordinate clauses are common. A range of structures is used, but there is one error with article use, and some tense inconsistencies in the final sentence.

Task 1 Bar Charts

B IELTS PRACTICE TASK (page 195)

The bar chart shows how the commuting patterns of employed people in a New Zealand city changed between 1996 to 2006. Nine forms of commuting are shown. However one of these is non-commuting . i.e. working at home. The use of company vehicles the bus and bicycles all show increases from 1996 to 2006 whereas commuting via private vehicle walking or working at home all decreased. However it is noteable that in both years commuting by private car or truck showed overwelming greater popularity than the other methods.

In 1996 over half number of employed people used private cars or trucks to get to work. However this had fallen to around 36% by 2006 a drop of around 14%. Use of company vehicles and walking were choosen by about 7–10% of commuters in the first year in the chart and working at home was equal with this. In contrast use of the company car or other vehicle has risen to well over 10% in 2006 but walking,jogging and home working have fallen to around 7 and 5% respectively. The use of the public bus or bicycle both showed marked rise from around 5 to over 10% in the two years. Use of trains and motorbikes were very minor in popularity as any other forms of commuting were.

Band Score: 8

Task Achievement: 9 The task requirements are fully satisfied and the writing is clearly presented and fully developed.

Coherence and Cohesion: 8 Information is arranged clearly and logically. Paragraphs are used appropriately, and ideas and information are linked. There is some repetition of connectors.

Lexical Resource: 8 There is a good range of vocabulary, used flexibly, with some less common words and phrases, but there are occasional spelling mistakes.

Grammatical Range and Accuracy: 7 A range of complex structures are used, and sentences are frequently accurate. There are a few grammar and punctuation errors, and punctuation could be clearer.

D IELTS PRACTICE TASK (page 201)

Sample answer 1

Graph gives information about visitors came to five cities in 2013 to uk. Overal most purpose of visits is holiday and also business coming many visitors to five cities. London and Edinburgh and Liverpool are most common for holiday. Manchester and Birmingham are most common for business. First London has fifety percentage holiday purpose for visitors. Other visitors come for purpose business, visiting freinds or relatives. They come about 20%. Edinburgh not so different. Big number of visitors nearly 70% come for holiday and under 20% other visitors. Manchester has more visitors for business – over 30. Holiday visits is 10% less – 22%. Many people go to Manchester for visiting friends or relatives 25%. Miscellanous is small number. Birmingham is big business city. 50 visitors are coming here. Less half this are holiday and visiting friends of relatives. Liverpool coming holiday visits lot of holiday visits 35%. But Liverpool is coming many visiting freinds or relative. nearly 30%. Business is under 20. Miscellaneous is same as business.

Band Score: 5.5

Task Achievement: 6 Information is selected appropriately and an overview is presented. There is some irrelevant or inaccurate information.

Coherence and Cohesion: 5 There is some evidence of organisation, but more use could be made of cohesive devices to link information.

Lexical Resource: 5 Vocabulary is minimally adequate, but there are several spelling mistakes.

Grammatical Range and Accuracy: 5 The range of structures is limited, and complex sentences are inaccurate. There are some simple accurate sentences, but some errors in grammar and punctuation cause difficulty for the reader.

Sample answer 2

The bar graph shows visits to five UK cities in 2013, and the visitors' purposes are shown as percentages. The main point that is noticeable is that of the five cities three are more popular as holiday destinations, London, Edinburhg, and Liverpol, while Manchester and Birmingham visitors are more for business.

Edinburh has over three times as many visitors for holidays as any other purposes. It's not popular for busines, a sixth of the number of holiday visitors. London, on other hand, has 50% of its visitors coming for holidays, and around 20% for business and visiting people. Manchester has quite an even spread of visitors across the four categories, but business visitors are a third higher in number than for holiday, roughly 34% and 22% respectivly. Birmingham, meanwhile is staggeringly more popular for business half of its visitors, which is more than twice the number than any other purpose. About a third of Liverpool's visitors come for holiday, and nearly half of this number are coming for business, about 18%, but nearly 30% are coming to visit friends and relatives. It's interesting that visiting friends are similar in all four categories.

Band Score: 8

Task Achievement: 8 The task requirements are satisfied and the writing is appropriately presented and well developed.

Coherence and Cohesion: 8 Information is arranged clearly and logically. Paragraphs are used appropriately, and ideas and information are linked.

Lexical Resource: 8 There is a variety of vocabulary, including some less common words and phrases, and a few minor spelling mistakes.

Grammatical Range and Accuracy: 8 A range of complex structures are used, and sentences are frequently accurate. There are occasional grammar and punctuation errors.

Task 1 Tables

B IELTS PRACTICE TASK (page 203)

From the table it can be seen that in 2012 London has six airports in total which vary greatly in distance from Central London and levels of passenger activity. The most striking feature of the data is that Heathrow was by far the most active of the six airports with over half of the total passengers moving through it, while it was second closest airport to the centre. In terms of change since 2011 it is Southend reveals biggest increase in activty though it was still much the smallest airport with regard to passenger numbers, and the furthest, along with Stansted from the centre of the city.

To look in more detail at the figures, Gatwick was the second most active, with around a quarterof all passengers, up slightly from 2011, and the second furthest away from London. Stansted is next, with under a fith of passengers, and slightley reduced numbers since the previous year, while London City have just 7% of passengers, showing a slightly rise, but is easily the most central of the six airports.

Band Score: 8

Task Achievement: 8 The task requirements are sufficiently covered and features are appropriately selected and presented.

Coherence and Cohesion: 9 Cohesion is skilfully managed, and repetition is avoided. Paragraphing is appropriate.

Lexical Resource: 8 There is a good range of vocabulary, used flexibly, with some less common words and phrases, but there are occasional spelling mistakes.

Grammatical Range and Accuracy: 8 A range of complex structures are used, and sentences are frequently accurate. There are occasional grammar errors or slips.

D IELTS PRACTICE TASK (page 207)

Sample answer 1

The table gives data about top languages spoken at home by students in 2008 and 2014. Spanish is in 2008 the first most common language. Numbers are 15,110 and 28,816. Korean figures are second common 3,029 and third common 2,735. Vietnamese is third common 2,557, and fourth common in 2014 1,467. Chinese is 1,875 and bigger 4,670. Arabic is small, fifth frequenty 430 and grows a lot 1,302, Russian is 414 and 1,656, and Hindi is 375 and 430. Tagalog is 138 and 512, and Polish is 110 and 82. Nepalese is 95 and 439. So Nepalese is smallest of languages spoken at home, but in 2014 it's Polish. So there are many languages spoken in students' homes, and its surprisingly variety, and many changes seen. But it's the biggest it's Spanish and then Korean, and then Vietnamese in 2008 and then in 2014 it's the biggest Spanish, much biggest, and Chinese it's second biggest.

Band Score: 5.5

Task Achievement: 5 Generally addresses the task, but there is no clear overview and details are presented mechanically. Key features are not adequately highlighted.

Coherence and Cohesion: 5 There is some evidence of organisation, but more use could be made of cohesive devices to link information.

Lexical Resource: 6 Vocabulary is adequate, but there are some errors.

Grammatical Range and Accuracy: 6 There is a mix of simple and complex sentence forms, with some errors but they do not impede communication.

Sample answer 2

From the table we can see that in this US school district Spanish is considerably the most spoken language apart from English in the home, in the both years, 2008 and 2014, with numbers doubling. The other notable changes are for Chinese and Arabic, with Chinese numbers tripling and Arabic numbers qadruple. The least common of the given languages is Nepalese in 2008, but Polish in 2014.

To describe the data in a few more detail, ten langues are shown and numbers vary in 2008 from 95 students (Nepalese) speaking a non English langage at home to over 15,000 (Spanish). The numbers range from in hundreds to low thousands, but none reach to more than a fifth of the Spanish total. In 2014 however, Spanish speakers have reached almost 29,000 while Chinese numbers are now a seventh of that (4,670), and the lowest figure is 82, a slight drop in Polish speakers. However, Nepalese numbers have increased

considerably to 439. Again no others languages come near to Spanish although, with the difference being aproximatley 23,000.

Band Score: 8

Task Achievement: 8 The task requirements are sufficiently covered and features are generally well selected and presented.

Coherence and Cohesion: 8 Information is logically organised, and cohesion is generally well managed.

Lexical Resource: 8 There is a good range of vocabulary, used flexibly, but with some occasional slips.

Grammatical Range and Accuracy: 8 A wide range of complex structures are used, and sentences are accurate. There are occasional minor grammar errors.

Task 1 Pie Charts and Multiple Charts

B IELTS PRACTICE TASK (page 209)

The pie chart and bar chart relate to the scores students achieved in a test for admission to a university in Asia compared to how many hours they had studied.

Nineteen per cent of students worked for between 101 and 125 hours. They performed best with an average test score of about 81 correct answers out of 100. Only 11% worked harder than this, doing 126 hours of work or more. However they actually got a lower score of about 79 right answers. The largest number of students, 47%, completed between 51 and 100 hours of preparation for the test. They got about 72 of the answers right normaly. Those who worked for 26 to 50 hours (15% of students) received 59 of answers correct. People who worked fewer than 25 hours could answer only 30 questions correctly.

Overall it is clear that students who did more preparation for the exam got a higher score.

Band Score: 8

Task Achievement: 8 The writer has covered all the requirements of the task sufficiently well and presents the key features clearly and appropriately.

Coherence and Cohesion: 7 There is a clear progression of information and ideas throughout the answer. Use of a wider range of cohesive devices would result in longer, more complex sentences.

Lexical Resource: 7 The writer uses a sufficient range of vocabulary to allow some flexibility and precision, although there are occasional errors in word choice and spelling.

Grammatical Range and Accuracy: 7 The majority of sentences are error free and the writer makes only occasional minor errors. On the whole, a wide range of structures have been used.

D IELTS PRACTICE TASK (page 217)

Sample answer 1

The visuals give information about the number of space craft lunched by various national governments between 1957 and 2007 and why each mission is take off. We can see that the biggest space craft is Russian the number is 53% and 3484. We can see that next biggest space craft American that is 27% and 1760. Other one very small. We can see that commersial only 8% European 4% Japanese and Chinese 1.7% Indian and Canadian 0.4% and were owned by other govermant 1.9%. Were amater is 1.3%. For what purpose space craft were lunched is many thing. Were communications satellites (civilian and military) the biggest numbers it is 27.6%. Approximately the same number is 27% that one is military reconnaissance 'spy' satellite. Delivered military services (navigation meteo etc.) and just smaller is military research and development. All of others about 5%, part of piloted (manned) programs, civiliun, studied Earth and space environment, observed Earth for civilian.

Band Score: 5.5

Task Achievement: 5 The writer generally addresses the task though the format is inappropriate in places because some details are mechanically recounted.

Coherence and Cohesion: 5 Information is presented with some organisation but the writer makes inadequate use of cohesive devices. The answer is repetitive because of a lack of referencing and substitution.

Lexical Resource: 4 Only basic vocabulary is apparent and language is used repetitively. There are some noticeable errors in spelling.

Grammatical Range and Accuracy: 5 The writer uses only a limited range of structures. There are frequent grammatical errors and the punctuation is often faulty, which can cause some difficulty for the reader.

Sample answer 2

The pie chart and table show which countries organised space missions and the reasons for them in the period from 1957 to 2007. Overall, it is clear that most space craft were either Russian or American and were for communication or spying.

Fifty-three percent of all space craft were launched from Russia, 3,484 missions in total, which was absolutely the highest figure. In contrast, America is responsible for aproximately half so many (27% or 1760 missions). European nations launched just 4% of the total while Japan, China, India and Canada each sent less than 2% of space ships into orbit. However, non-governmental bodies such as corporations and students account for nearly 10% of all space craft.

Over this 50 year period, most space missions were either done for communications or surveillance – both were 27% of the total. All of the other reasons were 8% or under: some were military space craft and a relatively small number were for science and exploration.

Band Score: 8

Task Achievement: 9 The writer fully satisfies all the requirements of the task and clearly presents a fully developed response.

Coherence and Cohesion: 8 Information and ideas are logically sequenced throughout the answer. All aspects of cohesion are managed well and paragraphing is appropriate.

Lexical Resource: 8 A wide range of vocabulary is used fluently and flexibly to convey precise meanings. The writer skilfully uses some uncommon lexical items, although there are rare inaccuracies in word choice and spelling.

Grammatical Range and Accuracy: 8 The writer uses a wide range of structures confidently and the majority of sentences are error-free.

Task 1 Diagrams

B IELTS PRACTICE TASK (page 219)

The diagram shows how electrical power is generated by the power of the wind.

The first part of the process is to find a suitable situation to build a wind generator, such as on top of a hill in a windy place. The wind then makes the blades of the generator turn around and this makes the generator produce electricity. The electricity will travel next to one of two different places. Some of it is stored in bateries so that we can still have electricity when there are days with no wind. The other part goes into a transformer where it is changed from basic electricity into a usefull form (700 volts to 38,000). After this it is transported across the country in high tension lines so that it will reach the people who will consume the power, such as our homes, factories, schools and transport systems such as electric trains.

Overall, it appears that generating electricity this alternative way is a relatively simple process.

Band Score: 8

Task Achievement: 8 The writer covers all the requirements of the task clearly and illustrates the key features.

Coherence and Cohesion: 8 The writer sequences all the information and ideas logically and manages all aspects of cohesion well. The use of paragraphs is sufficient and appropriate.

Lexical Resource: 7 The writer uses a sufficient range of vocabulary to allow some flexibility and precision. There are occasional spelling errors.

Grammatical Range and Accuracy: 8 The writer uses a wide variety of structures and the majority of sentences are error-free.

D IELTS PRACTICE TASK (page 225)

Sample answer 1

The diagram tells how to change a tyre. First running over broken glass or some dangerous and second car pulling off the road. Always find safe place to pull over. So we can clearly see picture 3 car pull over from road. Have you put your hazard light? Next, get your spare tyre, jack and wrench get it ready you will need this thing. Next get off hub cap and next get off wheel nut but don't remove wheel nut at this time just lose them. Next lift up car is 15 cm above ground and now you are ready to take out the nut. After take off weel and put another weel. Next don't tighten all the way. Then put car down. Next tight each one half way and then move to wheel nut opposite the one that has been tight and tighten halfway. Continue until it is all tight. Then is finish but don't leave anything side of road before drive down road or you will be sorry.

Band Score: 5

Task Achievement: 5 The writer generally addresses the task although the format is inappropriate in places. Detail is recounted mechanically with no clear overview.

Coherence and Cohesion: 5 Information is presented with some organisation although some cohesive devices are over-used. The answer is repetitive because of a lack of referencing and substitution.

Lexical Resource: 5 The writer uses a limited range of vocabulary, which is minimally adequate for the task. Noticeable errors in spelling and word formation cause some difficulty for the reader.

Grammatical Range and Accuracy: 5 Only a limited range of structures is used. Frequent grammatical and punctuation errors cause some difficulty for the reader.

Sample answer 2

The diagram shows how a car's tyre can be changed.

If your car experiences a puncture while driving, drive off the road in a safe place and take appropriate actions for warning other drivers. It is important for having the things you need already in the car such as a spare tyre, jack and wrench. Now, take off the hub cab and loosen the wheel nuts but dont remove them yet. Use the jack for raise the car until it is 15 cm above the ground. When this has been done, the wheel nuts can now being removed and the old tyre taken off. After this, the spare tyre is putting on and the wheel nuts is putting on loosely. Following this, put the car back on the ground and tighten the wheel nuts completely – do each one opposite the last one. Remember to put everything back in the car before driving on your journey.

Most people should be able to change the wheel of their car if this process if followed carefully.

Band Score: 8

Task Achievement: 8 The writer covers all requirements of the task sufficiently and presents the key features clearly and appropriately.

Coherence and Cohesion: 8 The writer sequences all the information and ideas logically. The use of paragraphs is sufficient and appropriate. Overall, cohesion is well-managed.

Lexical Resource: 8 The writer uses a wide range of vocabulary fluently and flexibly to convey precise meaning, although there are occasional inaccuracies in word choice and collocation.

Grammatical Range and Accuracy: 7 A variety of complex structures is used. The writer has good control of grammar and punctuation, but makes a few errors.

Task 1 Maps and Plans

B IELTS PRACTICE TASK (page 227)

The two plans show some changes that were made to the City Library over the ten year period starting in 2004. Overall, the basic shape of the library is the same but there have been significant alterations to the internal layout.

Probably the most noticeable modification has been to the addition of a large computer and media room in the south-east corner of the building. To make way for this, the gift store and art gallery have been moved across to the south-west corner, there they have been combined into a new café. This opens onto a new outdoor performance area, which has been constructed in the courtyard.

The main entrance to the Library and the reception desk are unchanged, but the old Reference Room included the Academic Journals at the later date. The whole of the northern wing of the building still contains the General Collection, although visitors to the library may now borrow from a large selection of movies and computer games.

Band Score: 8

Task Achievement: 9 The writer fully satisfies all the requirements of the task and clearly presents a fully developed response.

Coherence and Cohesion: 8 The writer sequences all the information and ideas logically and manages all aspects of cohesion well. The use of paragraphs is sufficient and appropriate.

Lexical Resource: 8 The writer skilfully uses less common lexical items but there are occasional inaccuracies in word choice and collocation.

Grammatical Range and Accuracy: 8 The writer uses a wide variety of structures and the majority of sentences are error-free. There are only very occasional errors and inappropriacies.

D IELTS PRACTICE TASK (page 233)

Sample answer 1

The two map show Tidlen Airport and land around it at first in 1985 and second in 2015.

Tilden airport is much bigger now many change is show in map now biggest one is now have new runaway. International terminal bigger have make new building now and new bus and light rail station light railway now to city of Tliden 5 miles this is important thing. Remember also new business and innovation park is replace Johnson famr now gone and housing estate and beyond side trees is gone another important things. Airport support services bigger now, but notice surprise that car park a little smaller. Also now have new hotel conference centre it is because factory shut up. Have new runway now so many more plane tideln airpot. More passenger more bus more train more car park bigger. More hotel more business innovation parks.

In conclusion, new runway tiden airport and surrounding area many new thing.

Band Score: 5.5

Task Achievement: 6 The writer addresses the requirements of the task by presenting an overview with information appropriately selected.

Coherence and Cohesion: 5 Information is presented with some organisation but at times there is a lack of progression. The text is repetitive, partly because of a lack of referencing and substitution.

Lexical Resource: 5 A limited range of vocabulary is used, which is minimally adequate for the task. There are noticeable errors in spelling and word formation that cause some difficulty for the reader.

Grammatical Range and Accuracy: 5 Only a limited range of structures is used. There are frequent grammatical and punctuation errors that cause some difficulty for the reader.

Sample answer 2

The two maps show developments at and around Tilden Airport in the thirty year period from 1985.

Probably the most important change has been building the new runway at the airport. Additionally, the international terminal has become three times bigger during this time, while the domestic terminal has not expanded at all. The car park is only slightly larger because public transport seems to have become more popular between 1985 and 2005, with the addition of a bus and light rail station at the airport.

In the area around the airport itself there have also been significant developments. On the land that was Johnson's farm in 1985 later stands a business and innovation park and a housing estate has been built in the north-east corner. In the same way, on the south side of the road, the factories have been replaced by a large building for airport support services as well as a hotel and conference centre.

In summary, there has been significant development at Tilden airport.

Band Score: 8.5

Task Achievement: 9 The writer satisfies all the requirements of the task and clearly presents a fully developed response.

Coherence and Cohesion: 8 Information and ideas are logically sequenced throughout the text and all aspects of cohesion are well-managed. Paragraphing is sufficient and appropriate.

Lexical Resource: 8 The writer uses a wide range of vocabulary fluently and flexibly to convey precise meanings.

Grammatical Range and Accuracy: 9 A wide range of structures is used with full flexibility and accuracy. Rare minor errors occur only as 'slips'.

Task 2 An Agree/Disagree Essay

B IELTS PRACTICE TASK (page 235)

Globalisation is increasing all of the time so there are many good reasons why young people need to speak a second language so that we can all communicate together and understand other people. However, there may also be some problems with this idea that we should consider them.

These days many children will end up doing a job which means they have contact with people all around the world, maybe on the telephone or the internet. Whichever one it is they need to speak a universal language so they can do business together and understand other people's thinking and culture. As a result, the world will have a greater prosperity and perhaps we can achieve global peace as well. In addition, there is scientific evidence that learning a second language is good for the brain's development. Finally, in my school in China, everybody learned English and most of them enjoy it and want to learn so this is a positive activity.

However, it is not a good way to force children to learn one language. Secondly, there are many different languages in the world and this is the variety of human life. The best 'universal language' in my region, Asia, may not be the best one in a different region of the world, so we need to be flexible.

In conclusion, it is inevitable that English has become the 'universal language'. Children get many benefits from learning a second language at school, but maybe they should be able to choose which language they learn, and this might depend what culture they come from.

Band Score: 8

Task Response: 8 The writer sufficiently addresses all parts of the task and presents a well-developed response to the question with relevant, supported ideas.

Coherence and Cohesion: 8 Information and ideas are logically sequenced throughout the answer. Paragraphs are used appropriately throughout.

Lexical Resource: 7 The writer uses a sufficient range of vocabulary to allow some flexibility and precision. Less common lexical items are used with some awareness of collocation. There are occasional errors in word choice and formation.

Grammatical Range and Accuracy: 7 A variety of complex structures have been used. The candidate generally has good control of grammar and punctuation but makes a few errors.

D IELTS PRACTICE TASK (page 239)

Sample answer 1

Some people say that language teacher should concentrate on giving positive feedbacks to student when they do good work rather than on criticising bad work but other people say this bad things. Positive feedbacks give student encourage and make them have a nice day. When you positive feedbacks, you want to study more learn fast. Criticise is easy but does it really make student good. But other peoples say, cannot have easy life every day, have to critic sometime. So it complicate subjects and many different opinion we must discuss it.

The advantage is that when he tell student your work is very good, you learn English the best way and very good. Every student want to hear his work is better than other student. In my school in my own country, every boy and girl want teacher tell is good. Then next day they work more hard and next day more hard is best way but if teacher you work is no good you lazy boy they no like English and they want stay home or study math. Make encourage is most important things and give positive feedbacks most important things.

The disadvantage that in your life is sometimes you criticising how can you improve your English when you never criticising. Have to know bad point as well as good point or is no way a good way to learn. When your english bad teacher have to tell your english bad or you say same bad things again and again. Knowing your mistake is that teacher tell you watch your mouth then you can improve your english is good way.

For conclude is advantage and disadvantage and every teacher must decide hiself if he do positive feedbacks or criticising your english because you can have both but must choose best way for student.

Band Score: 4.5

Task Response: 4 The writer responds to the task in a minimal way by presenting a position that is unclear. Some main ideas have been presented but they are difficult to identify, repetitive and not well supported.

Coherence and Cohesion: 5 Information is presented with some organisation but there is a lack of overall progression and the paragraphing is inadequate. The text is repetitive because of a lack of referencing and substitution.

Lexical Resource: 4 The writer uses only basic vocabulary, which is repetitive and sometimes inappropriate for the task. Errors sometimes cause strain for the reader.

Grammatical Range and Accuracy: 5 The writer uses only a limited range of structures and makes frequent grammatical errors, which can cause some difficulty for the reader.

Sample answer 2

In my home country of Brazil, teaching fashions have changed over the decades and today many language teachers stress rewarding good work with positive feedback more than criticising mistakes. However, giving language students criticism may still be important, but it should be done in a constructive way.

On the one hand, receiving praise for good work helps encourage students, which has essential because learning a language is often challenging for students. This is not just a benefit for individuals but it will also motivate the whole class to work harder and participate more. As we know, this is very important for language learning in particular because student must communicate and if they are not talking they cannot learn. For example, in my college there was a better relationship in some classes and all of the students learnt more with that teacher.

On the other hand, language students will keep on making the same mistakes if they are not told about it. Some of these mistakes are basic grammar and the students can correct them if they recognise that they have this error, for example, they don't use a past tense to talk about a past action. In addition, most of us will be criticised sometimes when we leave school and get our jobs so students should be prepared for this.

In conclusion, teachers should find the balance between positive feedback and constructive criticism. Also some students may react better to one or the other and teachers must think about each individual.

Band Score: 8

Task Response: 9 The writer fully addresses all parts of the task and presents a fully developed position with relevant and well supported ideas.

Coherence and Cohesion: 8 Ideas and information are sequenced logically throughout and all aspects of cohesion are well managed. Paragraphing is appropriate throughout.

Lexical Resource: 8 The writer uses a wide range of vocabulary fluently and flexibly to convey precise meanings. Some uncommon lexical items are used skilfully although there are occasional inaccuracies in word choice and collocation.

Grammatical Range and Accuracy: 8 A wide range of structures is used and the majority of sentences are error-free.

Task 2 A Discussion/Opinion Essay

B IELTS PRACTICE TASK (page 241)

Education is a very big idea and there are some different ways to understand what it means. Children at schools can be taught to work together in groups and therefore achieve a result that we can call cooperation. Or they work against each other so there is only one winner and many losers, which is competition. There are strengths and weaknesses with both ideas.

Cooperation teaches children values that are important in society, like working together and helping other people. They must negotiate and have to understand other person's point of view. What is more, some children like this way the best and do not like competition. Finally, when they get a job they will have to work in a team, for example like my father in a big corporation his job is all about team work.

However, competition can also have many advantages. One of them is many people like to compete other people and need pressure to achieve a good result. For example, in sport there always have competition so it is natural and also a good value for society. Secondly, in the work force there is always sometimes competition because people compete each other to get a job and then they compete each other for promotions, so schools should teach them how to do this too.

In conclusion we can see that both cooperation and competition are important in our life at school and after. The important thing is for schools to teach children that both have a place, but at different times and in different ways.

Band Score: 8

Task Response: 9 The writer fully addresses all parts of the task and presents a fully developed position in answer to the question with relevant and well supported ideas.

Coherence and Cohesion: 8 Information and ideas are logically sequenced throughout the answer. Paragraphs are used appropriately throughout and the writer manages all aspects of cohesion well.

Lexical Resource: 7 The writer uses a sufficient range of vocabulary to allow some flexibility. Less common lexical items are used with some awareness of collocation. There are occasional errors in word choice.

Grammatical Range and Accuracy: 8 A wide range of structures is used and the majority of sentences are error free, although the writer makes occasional errors and inappropriacies.

D IELTS PRACTICE TASK (page 247)

Sample answer 1

These day many employee travel frequently their job work irregular hour all day sometime all night you get a lot of money your job but every day is work hard all day sometime all night you have feel stres you cannot realax yourself. other jobs are single work place hour same each day you have a good job same money alway is good your stres can be save but you do one thing one place every days so you boring and you want find differant ways you some special sometime you want variety days but never have this true many people my country always same so you have to get use

The advantage some job is that close to home no train no bus no car to work you just nex door so you can work quikly and be your every day work this is good for you have more money you can have good pay can be good your family and good your future irregular hour mean you feel tire all day you can have no comfortable your life But advantage that travel often see world alway new place new experience you can know different culture and learn different knowledges not possible past like my grandfather never go place in airplan now you can go tomorrow you want you go is new things and it is very interest your life

You have job earn much money you can employee travel many place and work iregular hours have many advantage your life you can single work place this is same time start each day same time finish you know your life and you know how happen next every days and for me this most important things.

Band Score: 4.5

Task Response: 5 The writer addresses the task only partially and the format is inappropriate in places. The development of ideas is not always clear and no clear conclusion is drawn.

Coherence and Cohesion: 4 The writer presents information and ideas but these are not arranged coherently and there is no clear progression in the response. The use of paragraphs is confusing.

Lexical Resource: 5 The writer uses a limited range of vocabulary, which is minimally adequate for the task. There are noticeable errors in spelling and word formation that cause some difficulty for the reader.

Grammatical Range and Accuracy: 4 The writer makes frequent grammatical errors and the punctuation is faulty. The errors cause some difficulty for the reader.

Sample answer 2

It is common today for some workers to attend meetings in many different countries at all hours of the day. However, others will just go to the same office each day and always work a similar routine. So there are two distinct styles of work and some individuals will prefer each one.

If you travel a lot you will see many places, experiences and cultures, which is an exciting way to lead your life and an opportunity that many people cannot have. What is more, if you are working irregular hours in new places, you never know what is happening next, your day is not predictable, and this will help motivate some people. Finally, it is good for your professional developement to see how your business is in other cities and countries.

On the other hand, there are advantages to having a regular routine at work. Employees with young families may prefer to this style of working life because they can spend more time with their children and watch them grow up. Secondly, some of my friends and family members get jet lag so do not like travelling. Finally, some people are more productive in a familiar environment and would not work well always travelling.

In conclusion, it is up to each individual to decide what style of work is most suitable for them. In my own self situation, I would like to travel while I am young, but work in a more fixed environment later when I have a family.

Band Score: 8

Task Response: 8 The writer addresses all parts of the task and presents a well-developed response to the question with relevant and supported ideas.

Coherence and Cohesion: 8 Ideas and information are sequenced logically and paragraphing is used appropriately. The writer manages all aspects of cohesion well.

Lexical Resource: 8 The writer uses a wide range of vocabulary fluently and flexibly to convey precise meanings, although there are occasional inaccuracies in word choice and collocation.

Grammatical Range and Accuracy: 8 A wide range of structures is used and the majority of sentences are error-free, although there are very occasional errors and inappropriacies.

Task 2 A Problem/Solution Essay

B IELTS PRACTICE TASK (page 249)

While people in developed nations have sufficient food, there are many others in developing countries who do not eat enough. The reasons for this situation and the ways to solve it are complicated, but it is too important we cannot ignore it.

There are many causes of starvation and it depends on which region we think about. The most general problem is that world population is growing all the time to a huge number. Then, in some parts of the world there are wars and conflict that stop food coming to the people who need it. In other places there are political problems or corruption which means food distribution is affected. Lastly, in some countries such as my own home, Brazil, there are severe weather events like floods and droughts which means the harvest is bad and people cannot have enough to eat that year.

The solutions to the problem are difficult but we can see some possibilities. In China, for example, they have the one-child policy, to limit population and this could copied in other nations. In addition, scientists are finding new ways to grow crops better and more productive so we can hope for a good outcome. Lastly, the United Nations must find a way to stop all war and corruption so food supplies can reach people who are desperately starving.

In conclusion, there is no 'quick fix' for this issue as the because there are many causes. The most important thins is for everybody around the world to have a desire to solve the problem and then we can make a progress.

Band Score: 8

Task Response: 9 The writer fully addresses all parts of the task and presents a fully developed position in answer to the question with relevant and well supported ideas.

Coherence and Cohesion: 8 Information and ideas are logically sequenced throughout the answer. Paragraphs are used appropriately throughout and the writer manages all aspects of cohesion well.

Lexical Resource: 8 The writer uses a wide range of vocabulary fluently and flexibly to convey precise meanings, although there may be occasional inaccuracies in word choice and collocation.

Grammatical Range and Accuracy: 8 A wide range of structures is used and the majority of sentences are error free, although the writer makes occasional errors and inappropriacies.

D IELTS PRACTICE TASK (page 257)

Sample answer 1

In many large city some people waste hours of their times every day because of trafic congeston on the road. What you think are the cause this problems what solution can you suggest. Trafic congeston serious problem many city because too many car. Every day is big trafic queu take many hour for short travel to school works shops business everything. You cannot get there quick may be long time to go little place. Pollution very very bad many people sicks feels tired and exhasting all day pollutions very very bad and get worse all time. Goverment has to be build many train and bus and other thing like subways and invest new technology so not so many thousand of car on road and no pollutions.

Disadvantage of trafics congeston people wast hours of their times every day because of trafic congeston. Commuter must wait trafic jams only go to work. School childrens drive hour only go to school close to home. Business loos the money because trucks can not be drive and people like manager can not drive quick to other company. Pollutions is very bad problems so worker is sick and time be waste pollutons so bad people depress and stress is very terrible feelings.

Advantage of public transport is that no congestons and everyone goes more quick and better. Goverment should be building many train and bus. Have few car on road, only important one like bus, taxi, amblance and one like this. Invest new technology is best way traffic congeston.

Concluson goverment should be build many train and bus invest new technology is best way traffic congeston. No pollutions you cans have a nice day.

Band Score: 5

Task Response: 5 The writer addresses the task only partially and the format is inappropriate in places. Some main ideas are expressed but these are limited and there is irrelevant detail.

Coherence and Cohesion: 5 Information is presented with some organisation but there is a lack of overall progression. The text is repetitive because of a lack of referencing and substitution.

Lexical Resource: 5 The writer uses a limited range of vocabulary, which is minimally adequate for the task. There are noticeable errors in spelling and word formation that cause some difficulty for the reader.

Grammatical Range and Accuracy: 5 Only a limited range of structures is used. Frequent errors in grammar cause some difficulty for the reader.

Sample answer 2

The problem of congested traffic affects many cities around the world today. City streets are sometimes full with traffic jams from early in the morning to the middle of night which means that everyone waste a lot of time every day. This is a difficult issue and the solutions are not easy answers.

One of the causes is urbanisation has happened, so many cities in the world have become much bigger population. For example, in my home country China my grandparents moved from the countryside life to the city to make more money. It is a good thing that people get more money now, but it means more cars and more traffic congestion. Also, cars cost little money now in China than in the past so easy to buy for many people. Finally, many roads have been built but they are immediately full of cars so they just mean more cars are built.

The solution to traffic congestion can be done for example, in some cities in China and around the world, the government say only few cars can travel into the city centre. This is a good way, but it must have an alternative like public transport. So governments must spend more money in building public transport systems instead of people use their private cars. Another solution is to have a high tax on gasoline to discourage private cars but a subsidise on public transport to encourage people do this way.

In conclusion, traffic congestion is getting worse every year because of urbanisation. The answer is our governments improve the public transport systems and make it cost little money so we have an actual alternative to cars.

Band Score: 7.5

Task Response: 9 The writer fully addresses all parts of the task and presents a fully developed position in answer to the question with relevant and well supported ideas.

Coherence and Cohesion: 8 Information and ideas are logically sequenced throughout the answer. Paragraphs are used appropriately throughout and the writer manages all aspects of cohesion well.

Lexical Resource: 7 The writer uses a sufficient range of vocabulary to allow some flexibility and precision. Less common lexical items are used with some awareness of style and collocation.

Grammatical Range and Accuracy: 6 A mix of simple and complex sentence forms is used. Some errors in grammar are made but they rarely reduce communication.

SPEAKING TEST VIDEO 1 WORKSHEET

PART 1

1 **Look at the example Part 1 topics. Then write down three or four questions about each topic that an examiner might ask.**

Part 1 Questions	
1 Studies	
2 Health	
3 Exercise	
4 The weather	

2 **Watch Part 1 of the Speaking test interview. Tick (✓) any questions the examiner uses that are the same as the ones you wrote in Exercise 1.**

✓ **TIP**

Remember you need to use a range of vocabulary with some idiomatic language if possible, e.g. *once in a blue moon.* Try to extend your vocabulary when you answer the questions.

3 **Work in pairs. Read the statements (1–9) about the candidate, based on what he said in Part 1. Then answer the questions.**

a   Which two statements are false?
b   Check that you understand the meaning of the words in bold. Can you find a phrase with the same meaning in the script on page 348? NB There aren't phrases for the two false answers. Can you think of one?

1   He **was keen** to study engineering.
2   He **gets on well with** the people on his course and they often hang out together.
3   He's **a fitness fanatic**.
4   He's a **regular** at the gym.
5   He **has fond memories** of his childhood.
6   He thinks exercise **is crucial** for children.
7   It rains **once in a blue moon** in his country.
8   He's **sceptical about** climate change.
9   He **makes the most of** the winter weather.

4 **Work with a different partner. Ask and answer some of the questions you wrote in Exercise 1.**

PART 2

5 **Work in pairs. Look at the example Part 2 topic. Think about how you would answer it. Brainstorm some ideas for each of the four points.**

> **Talk about a building you like.**
> You should say:
>   where the building is
>   what the building looks like
>   what the building is used for
> and explain why you like this building.

6 Look at the following vocabulary. Make sure you understand the meaning of the words.

architect

cutting-edge design

functional

landmark

skyscraper

frame

foundations

curves

7 Watch the candidate completing the task. As you listen, number the words in Exercise 6 in the order you hear them. Which word is not mentioned?

8 Did the candidate answer all parts of the question? Watch again and complete the phrases the candidate uses to move from one section of the task to the other.

1   OK, I'm going to .... quite well.

2   It's in my .... , Abu Dhabi, ...
     the Capital Gate Building.

3   It's really unusual in its .... The first thing you notice is ....

4   OK, moving on to ....

5   Finally, the reason why I ....
     ....

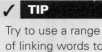

TIP

Try to use a range of linking words to improve your band score.

9 Look at the sentences (a–c). What is the problem with them? How would you fix them?

a   OK, I'm going to tell you about a building that I know quite well, and I really like it, actually. Actually, it's in my hometown, Abu Dhabi, and the name of this building is the Capital Gate Building.

b   This one is leaning because this was the architect's design. Actually, it's very strange.

c   So, if you visit my city, I'd recommend that you see this building. That's all, actually.

TIP

The task in Part 2 requires candidates to use a mixture of tenses.

10 Work in pairs. Look at the video script on page 348 and find an example of each of the following.

a   Present continuous

b   Present simple – affirmative and negative statements

c   Present perfect

d   A conditional sentence

✓ TIP

Try this to help build your confidence and ability: practise first by yourself quietly, then reflect on your performance; then practise again with a partner and reflect on your performance. Finally, practise with a different partner and reflect on your performance.

11 Now practise talking about the Part 2 topic in Exercise 5. Remember these points:

• Choose a building that you will have a lot to say about.

• Use phrases to introduce each section of your talk clearly.

• Use descriptive language to say what the building looks like.

• Use a range of tenses.

PART 3

12 ● **Look at the Part 3 question and the notes, which are based on how the candidate answered the question. Then watch the candidate answering this question.**

Do you think it's important for the government to preserve traditional buildings, or should the money be spent on essential services such as hospitals and schools?

1 The government should maintain traditional buildings
- Our heritage – connect us to the past, better than looking at photos
- A tourist attraction – many people want them preserved

2 But, also need health and education services: children and sick people are a priority too

13 ● **Watch the candidate answering two more Part 3 questions. Make similar notes around each question based on what the candidate says.**

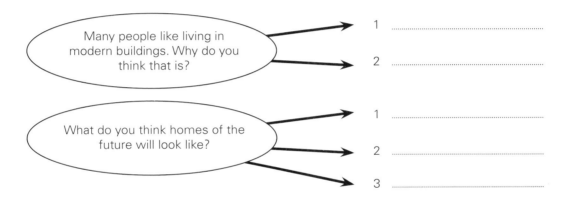

Many people like living in modern buildings. Why do you think that is?

1 ....

2 ....

What do you think homes of the future will look like?

1 ....

2 ....

3 ....

14 **Look at some phrases the candidate uses. Match the phrases (a–h) with the reasons why he uses them (1–7). More than one phrase might match a reason.**

a   That's a tricky question to answer … which one is more important …? Well, …
b   Personally … so I can imagine that many people …
c   But, on the other hand, …
d   Can I just check what you mean by 'fund', is that 'pay for'?
e   Ah, what's the word, you know, fixing them up all the time …
f   And another reason, of course, is that …
g   I think most people these days are …
h   Homes in the future … that's a good question, let me see …

1   to make sure you understand the question before you start to answer it
2   to introduce your second or third reason in your answer
3   to give yourself extra thinking time
4   to paraphrase the meaning of a word you can't remember
5   to offer a contrasting idea
6   to say what you think as well as what other groups in society might think
7   to generalise by talking about other people

15 **Work in pairs. Ask and answer the questions in Exercise 13. Remember to try and give two or three reasons for your answer and use some of the phrases in Exercise 14 to help you.**

SPEAKING TEST VIDEO 2 WORKSHEET

1 🔘 **Watch Speaking test video 2 and complete the following summary. Write one or two words for each answer.**

Lena is a student from **1** .... She is doing a Master's degree in **2** .... Studies. She never eats **3** .... and during the week, she has **4** .... for breakfast. A place that she enjoys visiting is her local **5** .... She remembers having a wonderful **6** .... in Greece. She is concerned about the amount of **7** .... that people eat these days. She thinks it is important for families to **8** .... together, if possible.

PART 1

2 **Look at the example Part 1 topics. Write three or four questions about each topic that an examiner might ask in Part 1.**

Part 1 topics

1   Work or study

2   Favourite place

3   Daily routine

3 🔘 **Watch Part 1 of the Speaking test video. Tick (✓) any questions the examiner uses that are the same as the ones you wrote in Exercise 1.**

4 **Look at the questions about your daily routine. Can you remember the order the examiner asked them in? Number the questions in the correct order. Then watch the video and check your answers.**

a   .... What would you like to change about your daily routine?

b   .... Tell me about a typical weekday for you.

c   .... Is there a balance between your work time and your leisure time in your daily routine?

d   .... Do you work or study better in the morning or the afternoon?

5 **Work in pairs.**

1   Write your answers to the questions in Exercise 4.
2   Practise asking and answering the questions with your partner.

6 🔘 **Watch Part 1 again. What does Lena say when she needs a little more time to answer the examiner's questions?**

7 **Look at the phrases that you can use to give yourself some extra time to think about your answer to the examiner's question. Unscramble the phrases and write the words in the correct order. Use the capital letters and punctuation to help you.**

1   let uh, now see Hmm, me   ....

2   an that's interesting Oh, question   ....

3   it's Well, to hard but say, ...

4   I you Well, know, guess   ....

> ✓ **TIP**
>
> One simple way to give yourself a little extra time is to repeat part of the examiner's question, but be careful not to do this too often.

PART 2

8 Watch Part 2 of the Speaking test video. Take notes while you listen.

A favourite meal	
What?	Ingredients?
Where?	Why?

9 Think about the structure of Lena's talk. How did she begin? How did she signal that she was moving on to a new point? Tick (✓) the expressions that she used.

a A meal that I really enjoyed was …
b I'm going to talk about …
c First of all, I want to start by saying …
d Moving on now …
e My next point is …

10 Now look at Lena's topic. Think about how you would give a talk on this topic. Make some notes about what you want to say.

> **IELTS PRACTICE TASK**
>
> Talk about a meal you have had that you really enjoyed.
> You should say:
>   what the meal was
>   who prepared the meal
>   where you ate the meal
> and explain why this meal was so enjoyable for you.

✓ TIP

Notice how the candidate uses a range of tenses to describe past events.

11 Your Part 2 topic may require you to talk about the past, present or the future. In this topic, you are being asked to remember a meal that you had in the past. Look at this extract from Lena's talk and underline the past tenses that she used.

I can tell you about the restaurant. I remember it was very small and we sat outside in a lovely courtyard. There were plants and flowers all around and a nice cool breeze blowing. Anyway, I decided that the safest option for me to order was a salad. I wasn't really expecting very much, but when I took my first mouthful, I was in heaven! Like, everything just tasted so fresh and full of flavour. The tomatoes were so sweet and juicy, the cucumbers crisp, and the cheese creamy. When the waiter came to take our plates he said that the secret was in the ingredients. All the vegetables had been grown in the family's garden.

12 Work in pairs. Try to talk about this topic for two minutes. Time each other and give feedback to each other using the following checklist.

Did your partner …
• address all the points on the topic card?
• talk for at least one minute?
• a range of linking words?
• use past tenses appropriately?
• speak clearly and confidently?
• make eye contact with you while speaking?

PART 3

13 **Watch Part 3 of the Speaking test video and listen to the examiner's questions. Match the question (1–5) with the language function (a–e) that it focuses on.**

Questions

1 Does food play an important role in your culture?
2 Would you say people in your country have a healthy diet these days or did people eat more healthily in the past?
3 Do you think it's important for a family to sit together to eat a meal in the evening?
4 Do you think children will eat more healthily in the future?
5 What's the best age for a child to learn to cook? Why?

Functions

a speculate
b generalise
c explain
d evaluate
e compare

✓ **TIP**

Look at the candidate's answer to Question 2 below. Notice how she makes her point over several sentences. She expands her answer by giving <u>reasons</u> and <u>examples</u>. Notice, too, how she begins with an introductory sentence and finishes with a concluding sentence. This makes her answer easy to follow.

Examiner: Would you say people in your country have a healthy diet these days or did people eat more healthily in the past?

Candidate: That's a difficult question. I think both diets could be healthy. You see, <u>traditionally in Germany people ate quite plain food</u>, <u>like potatoes, meat and bread.</u> <u>But they ate vegetables too</u>, so, in my view, I think the diet was quite healthy. And now, <u>our society is so multicultural</u>, especially in the cities, that <u>we have many other cuisines to choose from</u>, <u>such as Indian or Turkish</u>, so we can have a varied, healthy diet. So yes, I think both the traditional and the modern German diet could be healthy, just the people need to make the right choice.

---

14 **Work in pairs. Ask and answer the questions in Exercise 13. Remember to try and expand your answer by giving reasons and examples.**

SPEAKING TEST VIDEO SCRIPTS

Speaking Test Video 1

E = Examiner, C = Candidate,

PART 1 (pages 265 and 343)

E: Hello. Please take a seat. This is the Speaking test for the International English Language Testing System, held on the 25th of March at the Kent Institute. The candidate is Faris Ahmadi, candidate number 012458 and the examiner is Jane Smith, number 555687.

E: Good afternoon.

C: Hello.

E: My name's Jane Smith. What's your name?

C: My name's Faris Ahmadi. You can call me Faris.

E: Can I see your identification please, Faris.

C: Sure, here you are.

E: Thank you. That's fine. Thank you.

C: Thanks.

E: Now, in Part 1 of the test, I'm going to ask you some questions about yourself. First, do you work or are you a student?

C: I'm a student.

E: What are you studying?

C: I'm studying engineering.

E: Why did you choose to study this subject?

C: I don't really know. My parents thought it would be a good thing for me to study. And I did well at mathematics at high school, so I thought it might be interesting. It's OK, I guess.

E: Have you made many friends on the course?

C: Yes, yes, I have. There are some great guys on my course. Sometimes we get together and study after class, drink coffee, chat, that kind of thing.

E: Let's talk about keeping fit and healthy now. What do you do to stay healthy?

C: Well, I try to watch my diet. I try to eat healthy foods, you know, fruit, vegetables. But I really love meat, too. I think my diet is pretty good.

E: Do you do any exercise?

C: Yeah, sure, from time to time.

E: What kind?

C: Well, I try to go to the gym once or twice a week, and I like going for walks in the evening, when it's a bit cooler.

E: How active were you when you were a child?

C: Oh, very active, yes. I was always playing with my brothers, fighting, wrestling, playing games, you know.

E: How important is it for children to be active?

C: Oh, very important. Nowadays, kids just play video games all day. They don't get enough exercise, in my opinion. They're just couch potatoes!

E: Now let's talk about the weather. What kind of weather do you like best?

C: Rainy weather, definitely.

E: Why?

C: Oh, because it rarely rains in my region, so when it does, everyone is really happy. And it cools down the temperature too.

E: Have you noticed any changes in the weather recently in your country?

C: Any changes …? Like climate change? Oh well, I guess it's changed a little. People say it's hotter than it used to be, but I'm not really sure if that's true.

E: What do you like to do in winter?

C: Well, the winter in my country is quite short. It's nice to get outside and go for a walk. You can in winter, because it's not so hot. I sometimes go horse-riding too. I belong to a club and I go there a bit at weekends. That's really fun.

E: Thank you. That brings us to the end of Part 1.

PART 2 (pages 271 and 344)

E: Now, Faris, I'm going to give you a topic, and I'd like you to talk about it for one to two minutes. Before you begin, you have one minute to think about what you want to say. You can make some notes, if you wish. Do you understand?

C: Yes.

E: OK. You can make some notes on this paper. Here is your topic. I'd like you to talk about a building that you like.

C: Thank you.

E: All right. Now remember you have one to two minutes for this, so don't worry if I interrupt you. I'll tell you when the time is up. You can begin now.

C: OK, I'm going to tell you about a building I know quite well, and I really like it, actually. Actually, it's in my hometown, Abu Dhabi, and the name of this building is the Capital Gate Building. It's quite a new building, only a few years old, but already it has become an important landmark because it's really unusual in its appearance. The first thing you notice is that it leans over to one side. It's like the building in Italy, the Leaning Tower of Pisa, only that building is leaning because it's too old. This one is leaning because it was the architect's design. Actually, it's very strange. Um, it's a skyscraper, it's very modern-looking – really cutting-edge design, you know. It doesn't really have any sharp corners – it has a lot of curves. And it is all glass on the outside. OK, moving on to what it's used for. Well, there is a hotel inside and maybe some apartments too, and I think there are some offices as well, but I'm not exactly sure. Finally, the reason why I like it is, well, I guess it's because it's unique, it's special. Also, I'm interested in architecture, especially modern architecture, and I'm quite fascinated by how the building stays up, I mean, it doesn't fall down. I think it's because the building has a steel frame and I heard it also has very deep foundations. So, if you visit my city, I'd recommend that you see this building. That's all, actually.

E: Thank you. Do other people like this building?

C: Yes, everyone likes it. It's a real landmark of the city now.

E: Thank you. Can I have the task card and the paper and pencil, please?

C: Yes, sure. Here you go.

E: Thank you.

PART 3 (pages 279 and 345)

E: So we've been talking about a building you like and I'd like to discuss with you one or two more general questions related to this. First of all, let's consider traditional and modern buildings. Do you think it's important for the government to preserve traditional buildings, or should the money be spent on essential services such as hospitals and schools?

C: That's a tricky question to answer … which one is more important …? Well, I'd have to say both. First of all, of course the government should try to maintain traditional buildings. They are our heritage, and they connect us to a past in a way that looking at a photo in a book cannot. Personally, I don't enjoy looking around old buildings such as castles, but I know in some countries tourists flock to these type of buildings, so I can imagine that many people in those countries want to see them preserved. But, on the other hand, we shouldn't be spending so much money on them that we have poor health and education service. Educating our children and treating sick people has to be a priority too.

E: And is it possible for a government to fund all of these things?

C: Can I just check what you mean by 'fund', is that 'pay for'?

E: Yes, pay for. Can a government pay for all of these things?

C: I suppose it depends on the country. My country is fairly wealthy so yes, I think it can afford public services and money for preservation. But in poorer countries I can imagine that the majority of the people there would want better schools and good hospitals.

E: Many people like living in modern buildings. Why do you think that is?

C: Well, I think I'm one of them! Um, living in a modern home is much easier on the whole I think. You don't have to worry about … ah, what's the word, you know, fixing them up all the time – oh, renovating, that's it. You don't have to renovate new homes – they are in perfect condition. And this probably saves a lot of money. I imagine repairing and maintaining a home is very costly. And another reason, of course, is that modern homes have all the mod cons, you know, modern conveniences, and I think most people these days are looking for ways to save time.

E: What do you think homes of the future will look like?

C: Homes in the future … that's a good question, let me see … if you mean, ten or twenty years from now, I don't think they will be that different to what we have now. But perhaps 50 years from now I think it's likely that we'll see some changes. I think cities will get denser than they are now, I mean, there'll be more people living in the same area. To cope with this, I think homes will get smaller and perhaps taller in order to fit more people in. In the major cities in my country this has already happened, but 50 years from now, I think most cities and towns will be the same ... very dense.

E: Well, thank you very much, that's the end of the Speaking test.

C: Thank you.

Speaking Test Video 2

PART 1 (pages 269 and 346)

E: Hello.

C: Hello.

E: Please take a seat.

E: This is the Speaking test for the International English Language Testing System, held on the 25th of March at the Kent Institute. The candidate is Lena Richter, candidate number 012459 and the examiner is Jane Smith, number 555687.

E: Good afternoon. My name's Jane Smith.

C: Good afternoon.

E: Can you tell me your full name, please?

C: Yes, it's Lena Richter.

E: Thank you. And what shall I call you?

C: Please call me Lena.

E: Where are you from?

C: I'm from Germany.

E: Can I see your identification please, Lena?

C: Sure, here's my passport.

E: Thank you. In this first part of the test, I'm going to ask you some questions about yourself. Now, do you work, or are you a student?

C: I'm a student.

E: What are you studying?

C: I'm doing a Master's degree in Museum Studies.

E: Why did you choose that course?

C: I'd like to work in a museum or art gallery one day, and I hope that this course will help me find a job in that sector.

E: Do you think you will remain friends with the people from your course in the future?

C: Yes, I probably will. It's a very small course and we spend a lot of time together doing group assignments and studying.

E: OK, now let's talk about your favourite place. What is the place that you most like to visit?

C: Hmm, uh, let me see now … Well, I really like going to the local library.

E: Why do you like it there?

C: I suppose because it's quiet, and it has a nice selection of newspapers and magazines. And the range of books is really good too. And there's a café next door.

E: How often do you go there?

C: Probably about once a week.

E: Is it easy to travel there?

C: Yes, it is. I can catch a bus from my place to the shopping centre where it's located.

E: Is it a popular place for other people to visit?

C: Yes, it is. A lot of children go there, and it's very popular with students and elderly people.

E: Now, let's talk about your daily routine. Tell me about a typical weekday for you.

C: My daily routine … Well, I'm a student, so my classes start at 8:00, and that means so during the week, I usually get up about 6:30, have a quick shower, get dressed, catch a bus to university. I'm always running late, so I don't have time for a proper breakfast. I just grab a coffee. Um, I have classes all day, and get home at about 5 p.m. And after dinner, I usually try to do some study.

E: Do you work or study better in the morning or the afternoon?

C: The afternoon, definitely. I'm not really a morning person. It takes a while for me to wake up properly!

E: What would you like to change about your daily routine?

C: Change? Um, I suppose I should try to make more time for a proper breakfast in the morning, because by mid-morning I get really hungry.

E: Is there a balance between your work time and your leisure time in your daily routine?

C: Do you mean, like, is it equal? Um yeah, I suppose so. I've been studying a lot recently, because of the IELTS exam, but I have a week's holiday coming up, and I'm really looking forward to that. I'd like to do some more exercise, because I think it's important to take some time out from study every day.

E: Thank you. That brings us to the end of Part 1.

PART 2 (pages 277 and 347)

E: Now, I'm going to give you a topic and I'd like you to talk about it for one to two minutes. Before you talk, you'll have one minute to think about what you're going to say – you can make some notes if you wish. Do you understand? Here is some paper and a pencil for making notes and here is your topic. I'd like you to talk about a meal you have had that you really enjoyed.
All right? Remember you have one to two minutes for this, so don't worry if I stop you. I'll tell you when the time is up. Can you start speaking now, please?

C: Sure. I'm going to talk about a lovely meal that I had while I was on holiday in Greece. I'm a vegetarian, so it is sometimes hard for me to find something to eat when I travel. This meal was very simple, but it was delicious. It was a Greek salad, made of lettuces, cucumber, tomatoes, olives, and cheese. And it just had a very simple – um – sauce, I mean, dressing, poured over it made from olive oil and lemon juice. My next point is who prepared the meal. Well, I don't really know, but I can tell you about the restaurant. I remember it was very small and we sat outside in a lovely courtyard. There were plants and flowers all around and a nice cool breeze blowing. Anyway, I decided that the safest option for me to order was a salad. I wasn't really expecting very much, but when I took my first mouthful, I was in heaven! Like, everything just tasted so fresh and full of flavour. The tomatoes were so sweet and juicy, the cucumbers crisp, and the cheese creamy. When the waiter came to take our plates, he said that the secret was in the ingredients. All the vegetables had been grown in the family's garden. So that's why I will always remember that meal.

E: Thank you. Have you told other people about this meal?

C: Yes, yes, I have.

E: Thank you. Can I have the task card and the paper and pencil back, please? Thank you.

PART 3 (pages 283 and 348)

E: So we've been talking about a meal that you enjoyed and I'd like to discuss with you one or two more general questions related to this. First of all, let's consider children and food. What's the best age for a child to learn to cook?

C: Oh, I don't know, let me see … maybe about eight or nine?

E: Why?

C: Because I think it might be dangerous if the child is very young, you know, using a knife or cooking things on a stove, you know, that sort of thing.

E: Whose responsibility is it, in your view, to teach children to eat healthily?

C: Oh, the parents, definitely. It all starts with them. Parents must teach their children to eat well. They shouldn't give them junk food all the time; otherwise children can get addicted to it.

E: Do you think children will eat more healthily in the future?

C: Well, sadly, I don't think they will. Fast food is so common nowadays. And people are so busy, so it's an easy option for families. I think there will be more health problems in our society in the future caused by poor diets.

E: Moving on now to talk about eating habits, does food play an important role in your culture?

C: Yes, I think it does. When we have family get-togethers, there's always a lot of food. And we have a big meal when we celebrate religious holidays – I guess that's the same in most countries. Food usually is connected to big cultural or religious festivals.

E: Would you say people in your country have a healthy diet these days or did people eat more healthily in the past?

C: That's a difficult question. I think both diets could be healthy. You see, traditionally in Germany, people ate quite plain food, like potatoes, meat and bread. But they ate vegetables too, so in my view, I think the diet was quite healthy. And now, our society is so multicultural, especially in the cities, that we have many other cuisines to choose from, such as Indian or Turkish, so we can have a varied, healthy diet. So yes, I think both the traditional and the modern German diet could be healthy, just the people need to make the right choice.

E: Do you think it's important for a family to sit together to eat a meal in the evening?

C: Yes, ideally, if it's possible. My family lives in another town, so I can't have a meal with them very often.

E: Thank you. That is the end of the Speaking test.

C: Thank you.

The Complete Guide To IELTS
Bruce Rogers and Nick Kenny

Publisher: Gavin McLean

Publishing Consultant: Karen Spiller

Development Editor: Jess Rackham

Strategic Marketing Manager: Charlotte Ellis

Senior Content Project Manager: Nick Ventullo

Cover design: Keith Shaw

Original text design: Keith Shaw

Compositor: Oliver Hutton

National Geographic Liaison: Wesley Della Volla

Audio and DVD-ROM: Tom, Dick and Debbie Ltd

Contributing writers:

Lexical consultant (Vocabulary): Averil Coxhead

Helen Stephenson: Video lessons

Kate Fuscoe: Vocabulary lessons

Sophie Walker: Speaking module, Speaking
(DVD-ROM)

Megan Yucel: Speaking module, Speaking
(DVD-ROM)

Pete Maggs: Grammar Resource Bank

Amanda French: Vocabulary lessons (Common IELTS
topics), Listening, Reading and Writing (DVD-ROM)

Miles Hordern: Sample writing answers, Vocabulary
lessons (Common IELTS topics), Listening, Reading
and Writing (DVD-ROM)

Carole Allsop: Sample Writing answers, General
Training Writing test (DVD-ROM)

Margaret Matthews: General Training Reading test
(DVD-ROM)

© 2016 National Geographic Learning, a part of Cengage Learning

ISBN: 978-1-285-83780-2

National Geographic Learning
Cheriton House, North Way, Andover, Hampshire, SP10 5BE
United Kingdom

Cengage Learning is a leading provider of customised learning solutions with office locations around the globe, including Singapore, the United Kingdom, Australia, Mexico, Brazil and Japan. Locate our local office at **international.cengage.com/region**

Cengage Learning products are represented in Canada by Nelson Education Ltd.

Visit National Geographic Learning online at **ngl.cengage.com**
Visit our corporate website at **www.cengage.com**

CREDITS

Although every effort has been made to contact copyright holders before publication, this has not always been possible. If contacted, the publisher will undertake to rectify any errors or omissions at the earliest opportunity.

The publishers would like to thank the following teachers and consultants who commented on the course: John Anderson, British Council, MENA; Raúl Billini, ELT Teacher, Dominican Republic; Daniel Blackman, University of Sharjah, ELC, UAE; Tim Chantler, ELT Professional, Hong Kong; Russell Evans, British Council, Thailand; David Foster, British Study Centres, London, UK; Julia Hedges, Envision Language & Training Center, Dubai, UAE; Jake Heinrich, ELT Professional, Australia; Andy Howitt, ELT Teacher, UK; ILA, Vietnam; Ashley Irving, ACE, Cambodia; Maria Puro, English Language Teaching Centre, University of Sheffield, UK; Alison Ramage Patterson, ELT Writer, Spain.

Nick Kenny would like to thank Jess Rackham and Karen Spiller for the fantastic support received during the writing and editing of the book. He would also would like to thank Dr Alexander Leguia for his valuable feedback on some of the lessons.

Photos

The publisher would like to thank the following sources for permission to reproduce their copyright protected photographs.
12 © Frans Lanting/National Geographic Creative; 14 © Rex Features Ltd/Geoff Moore; 16 © Diane Cook and Len Jenshall/Getty Images; 18 © Jim Richardson/National Geographic Creative; 19 © Brent Winebrenner/Getty Images Ltd; 24 © Jim Richardson/National Geographic Creative; 26 © Rex Features Ltd/Geoff Moore; 27 © Brent Winebrenner/Getty Images Ltd; 30 © Pete Ryan/National Geographic Creative; 34 © Tyrone Turner/National Geographic Creative; 36 © Jason Edwards/National Geographic Creative; 40 © Atlantide Phototravel/Corbis; 46 © Alasca Stoock Images/ National Geographic Creative; 48 © Patrick Clark/Getty Images; 50 © Skip Brown/National Geographic Creative; 52 © Jim Richardson/ National Geographic Creative; 54 © Peter Adams/Photolibrary/Getty Images; 56 © Michael Poliza/National Geographic Creative; 58 © Patrick Clark/Getty Images; 76 © Peter Carsten/National Geographic Creative; 79 Wikipedia commons/Public Domain; 79 (inset) © Samuel Magal, Sites & Photos Ltd./Bridgeman Images; 80 © Mary Evans Picture Library; 81 © Oceanwideimages.com; 84 © Ingram Publishing/Ingram Publishing/ Superstock; 87 © Targa/Age Fotostock/Robert Harding Picture Library; 92 © Design Pics Inc/National Geographic Creative; 95 © Science Source; 96 © Eadweard Muybridge/The Life Picture Collection/Getty Images Ltd; 98 (t) Wikipedia commons/Public Domain; 98 (b) © Mary Evans Picture Library; 100 © Jodi Cobb/National Geographic Creative; 103 © oripix/Thinkstock; 106 © Michael Melford/National Geographic Creative; 109 (t) © Gusto Images/Science Photo Library; 109 (b) © DAVID MERCADO/Reuters/Corbis; 111 © MAX ROSSI/Reuters/Corbis; 112 © Paul Colangelo/ National Geographic Creative; 115 © Robert Churchill/Thinkstock; 119 © oripix/Thinkstock; 122 © Todd Gipstein/National Geographic Creative; 123 The Perfect Protein by Andy Sharpless and Suzannah Evans. Published 2013 Rodale Books; 127 © Jeremy Woodhouse/Blend Images/Corbis; 128 © Ralph Lee Hopkins/ National Geographic Creative; 129 © The Royal Society; 131 David Oakley/Arnos Design Ltd; 134 © George F. Mobley/ National Geographic Creative; 137 © CVI Textures/Alamy; 138 © Catherine Karnow/National Geographic Creative; 140 (t) David Oakley/Arnos Design Ltd; 140 (b) The Perfect Protein by Andy Sharpless and Suzannah Evans. Published 2013 Rodale Books; 142 © John Foxx Images/Imagestate; 145 © Remi Benali/Corbis; 146 © Creatas/Jupiterimages; 148 © Krista Rossow/National Geographic Creative; 151 © University of Queensland/ BNPS; 152 © Megaloden Entertainment; 154 © Franz Lanting/National Geographic Creative; 157 © ESA and ESA/NASA/JPL-Caltech/University of Arizona; 158 © ablestock/Thinkstock; 162 © Morey Milbradt/Brand X Pictures; 165 (t) © Ecovative Design.co.uk; 165 (b) © Ecovative Design.co.uk; 166 © NatashaPhoto/Thinkstock; 167 © Richard Wareham Fotografie/Alamy; 169 © Mark Moffett/Minden Pictures/Corbis; 184 © ImageState Royalty Free/Alamy; 194 © Gianluca Colla/National Geographic Creative; 199 © Mike Kemp/In Pictures/Corbis; 202 © Stephen Alvarez/National Geographic Creative; 208 © Frans Lanting/National Geographic Creative; 218 © PhotoDisc/Getty Images; 226 © PhotoDisc/Getty Images; 234

Printed in Greece by Bakis SA.
Print Number: 01   Print Year: 2015